Inheriting Stanley Cavell

Memories, Dreams, Reflections

Edited by
David LaRocca

BLOOMSBURY ACADEMIC
NEW YORK • LONDON • OXFORD • NEW DELHI • SYDNEY

BLOOMSBURY ACADEMIC
Bloomsbury Publishing Inc
1385 Broadway, New York, NY 10018, USA
50 Bedford Square, London, WC1B 3DP, UK
29 Earlsfort Terrace, Dublin 2, Ireland

BLOOMSBURY, BLOOMSBURY ACADEMIC and the Diana logo are trademarks of
Bloomsbury Publishing Plc

First published in the United States of America 2020
This paperback edition published in 2022

Volume Editor's Part of the Work © David LaRocca, 2020
Each chapter © of Contributors

For legal purposes the Acknowledgments on pp. 321-325 constitute an extension of this copyright page

Cover image: École Militaire, Paris © 2019 David LaRocca

All rights reserved. No part of this publication may be reproduced or transmitted in any form or by any means, electronic or mechanical, including photocopying, recording, or any information storage or retrieval system, without prior permission in writing from the publishers.

Bloomsbury Publishing Inc does not have any control over, or responsibility for, any third-party websites referred to or in this book. All internet addresses given in this book were correct at the time of going to press. The author and publisher regret any inconvenience caused if addresses have changed or sites have ceased to exist, but can accept no responsibility for any such changes.

Library of Congress Cataloging-in-Publication Data
Names: LaRocca, David, 1975– editor.
Title: Inheriting Stanley Cavell : memories, dreams, reflections /
edited by David LaRocca.
Description: New York : Bloomsbury Academic, 2020. |
Includes bibliographical references and index.
Identifiers: LCCN 2019058116 | ISBN 9781501358180 (hardback) |
ISBN 9781501358203 (pdf) | ISBN 9781501358197 (epub)
Subjects: LCSH: Cavell, Stanley, 1926–2018.
Classification: LCC B945.C274 I54 2020 | DDC 191–dc23
LC record available at https://lccn.loc.gov/2019058116

ISBN: HB: 978-1-5013-5818-0
PB: 978-1-5013-7132-5
ePDF: 978-1-5013-5820-3
eBook: 978-1-5013-5819-7

Typeset by Newgen KnowledgeWorks Pvt. Ltd., Chennai, India

To find out more about our authors and books visit www.bloomsbury.com
and sign up for our newsletters.

Inheriting Stanley Cavell, beautifully edited by David LaRocca, is so much more than a gathering of reminiscences and testimonials. So many of the pieces in the volume prove gripping, and they cumulatively transformed my sense of what Cavell had accomplished. This volume makes a strong case for the revolution that Cavell's extraordinary philosophic sensibility, powerful presence as a teacher, and wide-range of concerns brought about in North American philosophy. For many of the contributors, Cavell not only revived their faith in philosophy, but showed them what it meant to be alive in their feelings and thinking. He demonstrated, not only in *The Claim of Reason* but in his astonishing exploration of films, Shakespearean tragedies, and Wittgenstein, Emerson, and Thoreau, that the road back to ordinary language criticism was open, and our best hope for restoring value to humanistic study. The collection is also impressive for its decision to include dissenting voices.

> GEORGE TOLES, Distinguished Professor of English, Theatre, Film & Media, University of Manitoba, Canada, and author of *A House Made of Light: Essays on the Art of Film* (2001)

The welcoming tone rightly identified by the editor as one genius of Stanley Cavell's exacting style has demonstrably been answered by this timely volume—and in just the right blend of reminiscence, reflection, and fresh testing. The intellectual heritage proposed, and so luminously proven, across these pages—convening a lineage of distinguished readers in their role, as always, of interlocutors—honors the balance of intimacy and reach in Cavell's influential philosophical writing: a style of thought inseparable from the searching prose that gave, that gives, it shape.

> GARRETT STEWART, James O. Freedman Professor of Letters, University of Iowa, United States, has written most recently about Cavell in *Cinemachines: An Essay on Media and Method* (2020)

David LaRocca has gathered together some of the world's foremost scholars of Stanley Cavell's work for this terrific volume of essays responding to Cavell's philosophy. Collating reprints of groundbreaking essays and original contributions, the book offers wonderful insight into the breadth and depth of Cavell's influence and features a beautifully detailed and lucid introduction by LaRocca that interweaves the various strands of Cavell's philosophy and their legacies. This is without doubt a definitive body of responses to Cavell's work: a must-read for anyone interested in Cavell's work, whatever discipline they are approaching from, and whatever their level of specialism.

> CATHERINE WHEATLEY, Reader in Film and Visual Culture, King's College London, United Kingdom, and author of *Stanley Cavell and Film: Scepticism and Self-Reliance at the Cinema* (2019)

AUTHORED, EDITED, OR COEDITED BOOKS BY DAVID LaROCCA

On Emerson

Emerson's Transcendental Etudes by Stanley Cavell

The Philosophy of Charlie Kaufman

Estimating Emerson: An Anthology of Criticism from Carlyle to Cavell

Emerson's English Traits and the Natural History of Metaphor

The Philosophy of War Films

A Power to Translate the World: New Essays on Emerson and International Culture

The Bloomsbury Anthology of Transcendental Thought: From Antiquity to the Anthropocene

The Philosophy of Documentary Film: Image, Sound, Fiction, Truth

The Thought of Stanley Cavell and Cinema: Turning Anew to the Ontology of Film a Half-Century after The World Viewed

Inheriting Stanley Cavell: Memories, Dreams, Reflections

Movies with Stanley Cavell in Mind

Metacinema: The Form and Content of Filmic Reference and Reflexivity

The Geschlecht Complex: Addressing Untranslatable Aspects of Gender, Genre, and Ontology

GUEST EDITED

*Conversations: The Journal of Cavellian Studies
No.7: Acknowledging Stanley Cavell*

Try to be one of the people on whom nothing is lost.
—HENRY JAMES

CONTENTS

Introduction: Must We Say What We Learned?
Parsing the Personal and the Philosophical   1
   DAVID LaROCCA

I STANDARD CONSIDERATIONS   49

1   Must We Mean What We Say? On the Life
and Thought of Stanley Cavell   51
   MARSHALL COHEN

2   Cavell at Film Criticism: "An Unreadiness
to Become Explicit"   61
   ANDREW KLEVAN

3   Cavell as Educator   69
   MARK GREIF

4   What Cavell Made Possible for Philosophy   95
   SUSAN NEIMAN

5   Cavell Reading Cavell   103
   WILLIAM ROTHMAN

II FEATS OF ORDINARY LANGUAGE — 111

6 Cavell's Redemptive Reading — 113
    EDWARD T. DUFFY

7 Staging Praise / Owning Words — 129
    CHARLES BERNSTEIN

8 Resisting the Literal: Cavell's Conversations with Thinking — 137
    ANN LAUTERBACH

9 Revisiting Ordinary Language Criticism — 141
    KENNETH DAUBER AND K. L. EVANS

10 Monsters and Felicities: Vernacular Transformations of the Five-Foot Shelf — 161
    LAWRENCE F. RHU

III CINEMA, MUSIC, ART, AND AESTHETICS — 179

11 The Idea that Films Could Have a Bearing on Philosophy — 181
    ROBERT B. PIPPIN

12 Words Fail Me. (Stanley Cavell's Life Out of Music) — 187
    WILLIAM DAY

13 Cavell's Ear for Things — 199
    ANDREAS TEUBER

14 How to Mean It: Some Simple Lessons — 207
    TIMOTHY GOULD

15 Stanley Cavell's Doubling — 213
    REX BUTLER

IV THE SIGNIFICANCE OF EVERYDAY LIFE   229

16 The Importance of Being Alive   231
     SANDRA LAUGIER

17 Impression, Influence, Appreciation   243
     STEVEN G. AFFELDT

18 Taking an Interest in Interest   261
     RICHARD DEMING

19 Philosophy and Autobiography   269
     TORIL MOI

20 Autophilosophy   275
     DAVID LaROCCA

Acknowledgments   321
Contributors   327
Index   335

INTRODUCTION

Must We Say What We Learned?

Parsing the Personal and the Philosophical

David LaRocca

THE QUESTION OF THE TITLE CONVEYS THE URGENCY AND ANXIETY of accounting for one's education: *Must we say what we learned?* It's one thing to practice the lessons, to go about one's business (e.g., as author, academic, or editor), and have the work stand for itself, for better or worse. It's quite another to attempt reflections on how all the experiences (including memories and dreams) that come to be known as "one's education"—an always ongoing process—might be articulated and shared. Thus, the imperative to account for oneself (for what one knows or still fails to know) is coupled with the manner of accountability. Indeed, *can* we say what we learned?

With Stanley Cavell in mind—noting that his first book contained within the very space of its title what appears to be an ethical and emotional imperative—we who have gathered after his death to think about his contributions are now positioned to ask still further questions: for one, whether the implied imperative to give an account of what has been learned, along these or other lines, is itself part of the inheritance of his work. If so, who and how to heed it? Cavell's remarks, especially in the aggregate, can seem like a special case in which form and content achieve a distinctive catalytic effect, where the writing-unto-its-own and the diversity of the subject matter he addressed in it asserts the right to be praised, solicits our acknowledgment, and also—perhaps as a condition, or proof, of its virtuosity—refuses our considered efforts to do all of those things with grace and satisfaction (thereby imbedding avoidance into the process of inheritance—as well as failure and frustration). Yet, as in a classroom of gathered students and readers, we are perpetually called upon to *say* something or to say *something*. So it is on this extracurricular occasion, whether feeling a weight or a lift from such questions, the contributors to this volume were invited to speak on these and related matters, and thereafter graciously took upon themselves the task of saying something—and not just anything—about their encounters with Stanley Cavell, sometimes as teacher or friend, as mentor or colleague, but primarily from engagements with his written works and their still-radiating intellectual impact. Call these varied and discerning metaphilosophical chapters, after Cavell, "scenes of inheritance."[1]

If Cavell has provided a model of a scholar who, despite all, spoke his "latent conviction" on many subjects that traditionally lay beyond the scope of philosophy's—especially twentieth-century Anglo-analytic academic philosophy's—purview, we can wonder what it would mean to speak of his work in our own words.[2] In effect to do justice by him, if also ourselves. When Cavell once asked himself, "Can one teach tact?" his reply came in the form of an inversion: "Think of it as learning what constitutes the right to speak."[3] Have we learned this lesson? Or must we, instead, possess requisite powers of arrogation? By way of philosophical precedent, and as we consider our responses, Cavell provides some orientation, with his italics in place:

> Wittgenstein in the *Tractatus* is concerned about *what* can be said, when silence *must* not be broken. Nietzsche opens Book II of *Human, All Too Human* by declaring: "One should speak only where one *may* not be silent." In the *Investigations*, Wittgenstein is more explicitly concerned with one's standing toward the object of one's speech. He keeps coming upon the moment at which the teacher has to recognize that the one being instructed or informed has to go on alone.[4]

Here we are. And though we form a community-in-the-rough, spread across the globe, our eyes and minds and hearts are trained on a shared object. In the following dispatches, each author writes alone, but in company with the question of whether the right to speak has been constituted (earned, granted, or taken), denied, or deferred.

"This New and Capricious Classification": Notes on Naming

While a handful of the pieces collected here first appeared in periodicals, were given as public addresses, or in one case was a classified document—all chosen for the aptness of their traits—the remainder were prompted by an invitation to the present forum.[5] Whether contributors were invited to reflect on Cavell's influence on them, on their work, and suchlike, or included through curation, the timing of the assembly and other characteristics of the occasion do not allow us to name the book a *festschrift*, for that genre of celebratory writing in the honor of a person must be presented during the honoree's lifetime; *Pursuits of Reason: Essays in Honor of Stanley Cavell* seems a fair and fitting candidate for that genre.[6] We are in need, then, of another name to characterize our proceedings—in Ralph Waldo Emerson's parlance, an anointing by which "all things find their right place."[7]

But is there such a name—a term that describes what it means not just to write "in honor" of someone (after death) but, more specifically, to (honorably and ably) inherit someone's work? Such a concept might include a sense that we are cognizant of his or her philosophical achievements even as we continue to think them over and think them through—say, in our case, a mode of acknowledgment that benefits from Cavell's knowledge. Such a term would also suggest that by reading in our appointed or chosen bibliography of texts by Cavell, improving our comprehension and appreciation of them by degrees, we also come to better understand the work of others. Replies to the question of a distinctive approach to interpretation arrive in the several forms that follow, and so the shared answer appears to be, yes, there is a way or are ways to undertake the inheritance of another's work—yet that sense of affirmation leaves open what we might wish to name that happy labor.

We could begin by a process of elimination, saying that even if it were viable to adopt *festschrift*, we should not want to. It's not for lack of our enthusiasm to celebrate Cavell's life and legacy, but rather that we should prefer to honor him best by sidestepping or transforming the casual intimacy, that is, the emotional tonality of the *festschrift* (in part colored by an awareness that the honoree might be within earshot of the offerings); indeed, we are at some pains to have created, with all due respect, an anti-*festschrift*: to find a way to support and sustain the coursing spirit of celebration without undue deference to our subject and his works.

In coming up short (finding *festschrift* and anti-*festschrift* wanting for the reasons noted), we enter the predicament—is it an invitation?—to consider if there is a name for the sort of criticism and commentary that befits Cavell's writing. For example, a mode of approach that reflects his own practice, while also admitting our state of affairs (e.g., writing after him). If we are stewards, by what means? To what end? A name seems in order. On this front, I think admiringly of Kenneth Dauber and Walter Jost's conceptually innovative remarks that introduce what they call "ordinary language criticism" (for the eponymous collection they jointly edited). There, as they contend with the tradition of ordinary language philosophy and contemporary correlates, such as grammatology, ordinary language *criticism* calls out for distinction. And they mark out its contours and configuration by means of a comparative taxonomy, one that yields a list of qualities or attributes, as they admit, where "not all of the ostensibly attractive characteristics line up under OLC, and those that do are subject to corruption."[8] Whether one is adopting or adapting a name, the process is fraught—filled as it must be with the necessary tension between the general and the particular, the universal and the individual. For a name that might serve many functions, at last, will also draw out the exceptions and contradictions. Hence the welcome thought of allowing for an *experimental* approach, rather than insisting upon a declarative statement or a definitive defense. The effort itself, aside from its potential future service, may be worth the trouble—stirring us to just the kind of thinking we hope to achieve, even if given words falter. Thus, to return anew to the scene of experimentation.

If *festschrift* is disqualified and anti-*festschrift* feels mean-spirited and out of keeping with the propulsive, positive impressions that follow, let us cast about for some helpful tertium quid. The *festschrift*'s correlate for posthumous remarks is sometimes called the *Gedenkschrift*, and that term would provide a legitimate description, in so far as our work here is commemorative in nature. Given Cavell's intellectual affection for Ralph Waldo Emerson and Martin Heidegger—including his delight in noticing puns, double entendres, and exploring the interactions between graphemes across languages, thereafter developing them into moments of philosophical acumen—we could tease out variations on *Gedenkbuch* and *Denkschrift*. Taking a cue from such generative intellectual playfulness, we may attempt to sketch something suitable for the occasion.[9]

Since we are not merely writing, as it were, a post-mortem *festschrift*, that is a *Gedenkschrift*, consider a small but significant adjustment in spelling that results in *Gedankenschrift*, a layered, composite, and hopefully usefully evocative neologism (is it one?—more on this below) alluding variously to *danke* (thank), *denke* (think), *gedenken* (commemorate), and *gedanken* (thought). Whether one reads or hears these allusions remains for us to query. At a glance, *Gedankenschrift* may present itself straightforwardly as "thought-writing," or evoke a notion that "thinking is a kind of writing" all its own; and specifically addressed to the work undertaken here, it has been suggested that *Gedankenschrift* is "a term which could easily and elegantly carry the 'burden' of the Emersonian and Heideggerian oscillations of meaning between thinking and thanking."[10] These various turns of association only serve to "deepen or, rather, widen and intensify the allusive halo of the concept."

When approaching an explication of *Gedankenschrift*, some may have in mind Heidegger's treatment of thinking and thanking (*thencan* [to think] and *thancian* [to thank]), though I have been told that German speakers may, by and large, not catch such rarefied etymological resonances.[11] However, since there *is* precedent for the word in German, the designation of "neologism" is, in fact, misplaced—better, then, to say a novel application or attempted repurposing. At present, we find a German website that uses the name as a shorthand for spontaneous writing as a kind of therapeutic practice.[12] Looking further back, though, the term was featured in some nineteenth-century theories of language (e.g., on the notion that hieroglyphics might be understood as natural, unmediated transcriptions of concepts).[13] Others may take the term as a synonym for ideography (i.e., a mysterious way of directly expressing thoughts in writing—from hieroglyphs to experiments in contemporary cognitive science), and, in this case, I am told that most any native speaker of German would understand the word this way.

Yet, for those allergic to Heideggerian puns—as a native German speaker or otherwise—the *dank* of *Gedankenschrift* may not prompt any thinking of thanks. Still, in the same context that Heidegger dwells on the frisson of think/thank, he also refers to *Andenken*, which *does* present itself as a contender (even though it resists combination with *-schrift*). And here there is some traction: though *Andenken* can invoke "souvenirs," it also calls out to "recollections"—and quite crucially, the latter with a keen allusion to "keeping something in mind" as well as the having and retaining of "gratitude." *Andenken*'s own doubleness is telling: marking out a way for honoring by remembering (in the spirt of remembrance) and, in turn, showing how remembrance can serve as a reminder (memento).[14]

With native German speakers at odds, what to do? Proceed cautiously, but with the hope that these experiments in translation and nomenclature are generative for our thinking about the kind of work on Cavell we do and hope to do. Perhaps the Heidegger-and-pun-averse can adopt *Andenken*, while the rest can make something of *Gedankenschrift*—appreciating at once its provocations, humor, *and* genuineness (a fitting Cavellian trio, no?). Elaborately, an attempted translation or definition of a *Gedankenschrift*, at least for our purposes here, might read: a commemorative publication for thinking about memories—and thoughts—while being thankful for them. Or less literally: a form that encourages us to *think our thanks*. Though "celebration" [*fest*] feels appropriately cognate to terms of the Cavellian lexicon (e.g., acknowledgment, praise, cheer, etc.), *thinking as a form of celebration* seems a more proper, more appropriate gloss on Cavell's approach to these kinds of activities. Thinking-thanking on the present occasion takes for granted that memory/commemoration ("remembering together") is the *condition* for such gratitude. As we recall, "The office of the scholar is to cheer."[15] Hence "man *thinking*" is always already man *celebrating*.[16]

The work of remembering and commemorating—of stocktaking along with criticism—has begun elsewhere in, among other places, a special issue of *Conversations: The Journal of Cavellian Studies* and in *The Thought of Stanley Cavell and Cinema: Turning Anew to the Ontology of Film a Half-Century after* The World Viewed, but the labor here is conducted in a different key.[17] In the first case, commemoration was offered in a more traditional sense (e.g., remembrances situated as memorial notes of gratitude in the immediate wake of a person's death); in the second, a critical analysis that was well underway at the time of Cavell's death, and was and is aimed at pushing forward various academic fields and intellectual investigations; and now, here, a third approach, in a variation that, hopefully, befits Cavell's own work—can we call it, at last, a *Gedankenschrift?*—perhaps understood as a mode of address that assumes the philosophical pertinence and vitality of memories, dreams, and reflections, especially at those moments when personal history and public history intersect. Those gathered to offer this kind of report would appear to illustrate, by their engagement with their own memories, dreams, and reflections—*and* Cavell's—that Cavell's essays, like Emerson's, constitute a "genre of writing that shows a finite prose text to contemplate an infinite response."[18]

In this particular mood of thinking and thanking, of remembering and recollecting at the intersection of philosophy and autobiography, a reader may notice moments, many of them, when emotion—one even wants to say, the clarifying heat of emotion—generates new realms of encounter with Cavell's writing.[19] Emerson and his ancestors might have called this *enthusiasm*, which carries with it traces of intense emotionalism (conjured by the spirit, the soul, divine blessings, etc.), and in our time, the sense of an absorbing, even controlling, mental possession or preoccupation; or perhaps *genius*—admitting resemblances between the *entheos* (a god within) and the generative qualities of an abiding presence (an inner guide or guardian).

We may wonder, alone and together, whether the human arrives equipped with an instinct to thank, to acknowledge—that there within us abides a force for registering gratitude. Is it too much to say that such a motivating desire is part of the origin of the spiritual as we know it across time and tradition? That is, a disposition from which we posit a *relationship* between the individual and the other—and thus a debt to a power (and an influence) that lies beyond us but now and again makes contact with us? I think of Cavell's account of learning from Ernest Bloch, while an undergraduate at Berkeley: "I would at the end of a class sometimes find myself having trouble breathing, and I formed the habit of walking immediately after each of its sessions into adjacent hills for an hour or so of solitude, as if I had become too consecrated to touch."[20] Bloch's effect—"of the spell of an old master on a young man"—is a blessing Cavell is grateful for (because, in part, like it would be for the rest of us, it confirms meaning and significance for and in the young man), and the object of Cavell's affection would likely appreciate the impact he had, but, all told, these sanctifications are not shareable facts in the same way that a transformative reading of a text or an idea is. We can marvel at what Bloch conjures in the young Cavell, but we have to read around this radiant moment to discover, for example, something about Bloch's pedagogy ("Sometimes he was moved by a memory to give a demonstration of what conducting essentially consisted in, asking what communication is, or what constitutes a cue"[21]). However amusing the image of Cavell roaming the hills of Berkeley in a kind of intellectual euphoria may be (like Emerson before him, "Standing on the bare ground—my head bathed by the blithe air, and uplifted into infinite space"), it is in his description of a life in the company of his teacher that makes the moment available to the rest of us—those who were not in the class, who were not consecrated.[22]

In these ways, the following twenty chapters become passionate utterances of a certain sort: where ideas mingle with emotions (and are better for that coupling), where feelings give rise to thoughts—and when all of these otherwise messy, disparate elements come in for the care and attention necessary to create compositions worthy of sharing with others and capable of holding up over the long term. Not easy. While generations ahead will have the chance to write more books about Cavell's legacy—assessing and reassessing his work's significance—it is given to us, in this rare chance, at this particular threshold, to inscribe a few notes while his living voice remains alive in us. Such is a heat worthy holding and kindling.

Repurposing the *Gedankenschrift*: A Genre for Memories, Dreams, and Reflections

One of the signal attractions of the contributions that follow is the blend of rigorous philosophical reflection and autobiographical detail; or when the pieces avoid, or do not invoke personal history, they remain, nevertheless, in touch with the personal stakes of the author's voice (both Cavell's and the writer's own). Thus, in all cases, we find a specific kind of writing, what is gathered under the notion of the *Gedankenschrift*. Moreover, to aid and amplify the sense that we are here encountering a community at work in "thinking thanks," as Gertrude Stein put it, or nearly so, the chapters have arrived from across the landscape of intellectual life (poetics, politics, film, philosophy, art and aesthetics, the study of music, religious studies, language theory, literary criticism, and more).[23] The tone is often candid and heartfelt while retaining a scholar's care; the contributors regularly cannot help but reveal something of their own stories (fascinating in their own rights) on their way to saying something about Cavell, his work, and effects that have become indelible or perpetually agitating. Since these reports arrive from a range of disciplines and frames of reference, the material should be of interest—as Cavell so often is—across a wide swath of the arts and humanities, not only in academic but also in extra-academic locales. Indeed, one may return with fear and fervor—and much satisfaction—to ponder the extent to which these dispatches draw from and contribute to "themes out of school."

As with the commemorative issue of *Conversations*, the volume marks one of the first times that these authors are writing about Cavell without Cavell as a prospective audience for their work. It's not that Cavell, when alive, would somehow sanctify or otherwise approve writing, but that—in part because of Cavell's distinctive voice *as a writer*—analysts and critics of his work would often feel themselves addressing Cavell; and in turn, having Cavell as an audience (real or imagined) could later include fielding his peerless responsiveness in speech or writing. Yet this is no longer possible as he is no longer company for our thoughts. We are, in short, on our own, which is to say, we are an evolving community unto ourselves; in this respect, we write for one another as much as for the hope of reaching beyond those who already find his remarks dazzling and worthy of dedicated attention. At this juncture, a reader can hear seasoned as well as emerging scholars coming to terms with Cavell's ingenuity, his influence, while also processing what it means to think onward solely in the company of his work (and those who gather to read and reflect upon it). We could say, in this spirit of appraisal and self-aware investigation, we are witnessing a dawning of the next era in Cavell scholarship.

Arthur Danto's claim for Cavell's superlativeness and singularity—that his "is a voice like no other in philosophy, today or ever"—alludes to the fact that since its first appearance in the 1960s, Cavell's writing has become famous (and for some infamous) for its "personal" qualities—the timbre and tone of his "voice," his roving, digressive style, and so on.[24] But more than that, these qualities are, as Cavell himself has said, part of the *philosophical* measure of the work. Now, as we read the essays here collected, it is not surprising to see that the invitation and the occasion has provided a natural and fitting space in which scholars are able to test out the boundary conditions of their personal/philosophical approaches to his work—and, more crucially, more acutely, to their own work.

The way in which the authors become caught up in Cavell's methodology, or as importantly, are put in a position to contend with it, is significant for a book such as this because that *agon* provides clear and critical evidence that the new work collected here could not be *festschrift* material, even if Cavell were here to receive it. By contrast with the *Gedenkschrift*, and our experimental yet sincere *Gedankenschrift*, the *festschrift*—as a genre of remembrance and recollection—appears to enjoy a wider latitude of emotional registers, even as it may connect to fewer people with those thoughts and feelings. Considering that the *festschrift*'s mode of commemoration is adjacent to the memorial (as if soberly anticipating it), it's not surprising that in a *festschrift* one is as likely (or perhaps more likely because it is a function of the genre) to encounter variations of the emotional encomium: the work is often distinctively personal; ingratiation may be compulsory to the form, exhibited by a kind of forced bonhomie or a portentous geniality; the remarks are not so much for us (outsiders?

a general audience? posterity?) as for an insular community (perhaps, in particular, for the ears of the honoree); and part of the importance of the saying of such things is connected to the status and stakes of the writer (this happened to me and that it happened to me is why it matters). In this respect, the *festschrift* is a testimony that becomes in time a testament—but carrying with it the distinctive risk of vanities on display, both the author's and that of his or her subject. If there is a pleasure for the gathered group to make such pronouncements, it must be hard for those beyond the perimeter of such a volume to feel that candor and criticism is forthcoming. The author is flattered; those who praise risk praising themselves for their (good) judgment.

Because of the volatility of tones and temperaments characteristic of the *festschrift*, the quality of such remarks often swings widely (and in addition to vanity, one must be prepared for the sprawling, sentimental, cliché-ridden, saccharine, embellished, defensive, and uncritical). Indeed, the genre may be defined in part by the intended (limited) scope of the remarks, namely, that they *aspire* to touch a small or smaller community of the concerned, often principally the writer's immediate circle and those who wish to praise a specific person in a specific way (yet by means of a broader use of sentimentality and hyperbole). Though the honoree is still alive to hear such remarks, the *festschrift* affords proximity to the eulogy and paean. Indeed, the *festschrift* can stoke further extreme emotions in the reader, where the disturbance can lead to something like a competition for genuineness—for getting just right the sense of one's praise or one's stock-taking. Reminiscing carries the connotation of indulging in the enjoyable (and at times painful?) recollection of past events, but this needn't be the case, of course. While admitting and emphasizing that there *is* a time and place for such expressions (obviously, when the honoree is still with us), the work collected here is conducted under the auspices of a much tighter mandate (one I have sketched above and will continue to articulate below), yet with much broader ambitions to widen the scope of an interested, even *compelled* readership.

A *Gedankenschrift* would push an anecdote to the level of an enduring lesson—in the way a private joke becomes a public one, which is to say funny because shareable. All of these chapters may be understood as replies to the question: how does a personal experience—including the experience of reading a text well—become something many of us, if not all of us, can draw from, and thereafter rely upon? Yet, with such a question at hand, and as will be evident, we guard against the (philosophical?) temptation to push the anecdote into the dimension of the generic thought experiment, stripped, as it must be, of personal details. Thus, the *Gedankenschrift* aims to occupy the space between the *festschrift* and the thought experiment; it is the zone in which the personal and the philosophical find their balance, and their mutually reinforcing power. As with autobiography that exists as philosophy, the *Gedankenschrift* would see individual preoccupations foster a degree of community concern, where such remarks achieve radiating and enduring significance. Personal history becomes a matter of and for the public record.

In this way, the *Gedankenschrift* is not just for family and friends, former students, and colleagues, that is, for "those who knew him," but *for anyone* who takes Cavell's writing and thinking seriously—or who might. Indeed, for many readers, this collection may become a captivating *introduction* to Cavell: how to read his work, how to begin one's own study of its breadth and depth. Borrowing from musical parlance, and especially associations from improvisatory jazz, each piece may be seen as "a take" on salient aspects of Cavell's texts and his reading of texts—the way he writes them and the way he writes about them. One will, in turn, notice hallmark characteristics of Cavell's work in the choices made by this crowd of talented critics: eclecticism of topic, promiscuity across time and text; experimentation with tone; the sincerity of exposure (and vice versa); and the always-listening sensibility that renders insight by close observation of how language is used to make sense of our private worlds and the one we are told we share. If these notes also partake, at times, of the reminiscence, then, they find us thinking back and thinking over (and perhaps, with some knowing candor, *over thinking*—admitting the "familiar fact that philosophers seem perpetually to be going back over something, something most sane people would feel had already been discussed to death"[25]). While each contributor writes from a deeply held conviction that Cavell's work is a matter of private importance, these particular emotional commitments are translated—made available—to any and all who should become an audience for such thoughts.

Despite the memorial nature of the book's timing—that it is written in the proximate aftermath of Cavell's death—the *Gedankenschrift* hedges against any license for anodyne expression. Instead, what we find here is a company of seasoned readers of Cavell whose writing embodies an understanding of that reading—its discipline, its expectations, its standards; this is a *critical* commemorative prose through and through. If the *festschrift* allows (invites? demands?) writing immersed in one's personal opinion and feelings, the *Gedankenschrift* cautions the prospective critic: *this is not about you, it is about the work*—what it is, what it does. Memories, however precious, however much they shaped one's life, animated one's thoughts, must be made to be more than precious. We are lucky, then, to have at hand astute thinkers—ready, willing, and able to take Cavell to task—all the while convivial and candid, gracious and generous, to be sure (again, like Cavell himself), but also brave and forthright in their desire to get at the matter, even if it may upset some standing commitments and proffered attestations. The most fitting memorial tribute for Cavell—the one that would best honor his teaching, his craft, his demeanor, his legacy—would be one that acknowledges his exemplarity by direct, sustained engagement (avoiding lighthearted intimation and maudlin gestures—much less the occasional pallor or flush of the memorial). As an illustration of the foregoing (that is to say, where the private memory becomes publicly pertinent), let me add to these attempted glosses on *Gedankenschrift* a further definition by drawing on a personal memory of my own.

When I made the by-invitation-only pitch to prospective writers, I relayed something Stanley himself had said to me as a standard for his own work (at that time he was beginning composition on what would become *Little Did I Know: Excerpts from Memory*)—namely, that when he remembered or recalled something from his personal life, it must "rise to the level of philosophical significance" in order to find its way into the public record of philosophy. As I recapitulated the scene to others, and now you, the reader, Cavell's own criterion was to be the borrowed mandate, or better aspiration, the contributors to this book might adopt. Can we write in this spirit, foregoing the pro-forma praise (e.g., of the *festschrift*) so that we might push past it to achieve some measure of the gratifying weave of the personal and the philosophical that Cavell innovated, so masterfully managed to maintain for decades, and now stands as legendary exemplar of? To my great joy (and relief, though not surprise), the contributors have fulfilled this mission with elegance and aplomb. In a significant way, the book might even be presented as a kind of companion to Cavell's own successful attempts at philosophical memoir, for example, as we find them realized in *Little Did I Know*, but also elsewhere in the warp and woof of his many celebrated books, mellifluous lectures, and influential essays.

That "elsewhere" is crucial too, since the very nature of praise, acknowledgment, and cheer lies at the heart of Cavell's broadest philosophical preoccupations—from work in J. L. Austin and Ludwig Wittgenstein, Plato and Kant, Ralph Waldo Emerson and Henry David Thoreau to the Hollywood comedies and melodramas of 1930s and 1940s, and onward to Shakespeare, the Romantic poets, music, opera, Henrik Ibsen, and Sigmund Freud. In the chapters here gathered, we can take it as sign of the contributors' allegiance to the significance of Cavell's work and its legacy that they are willing, time and again, to knowingly assess and discriminatingly reassess that work and its legacy; this is the case for strangers and strident critics, no less than for lifelong friends, former pupils, and close colleagues, including students who became colleagues. The writing feels seasoned, sober, and yet, at each pace, not without heart. These are confident writers, assured of their own skills and casts of mind. Yet they all have something to say about Cavell—his effect on them and their work, and now, the palpable sense of how he will endure in the representations of his thought captured in his writing, our patrimony. That the diverse contributors all share Cavell as a preoccupation is itself a fascinating fact, especially given the diversity and range of their disciplinary precincts and the intellectual projects they are known for.

One of the visions I had, or hopes, for the volume is that it become a curated library of rigorous philosophical engagements conducted in a personal register. This coupling accords nicely with the *essayistic* qualities of Cavell's work (as well as the writing he praised most highly by Montaigne, Emerson, Thoreau, Nietzsche, and Freud) and the *autobiographical* (as it intersects with or enacts philosophical preoccupations). Indeed, Charles Bernstein has remarked that Cavell's signal contribution is as an essayist—as a writer of rare gifts who could think in prose, and do so, seconding Danto's estimation, with an unparalleled and unique voice.[26] As in the writings of the just-mentioned exemplars (Montaigne et al.), I imagine that the diversity of styles on offer here will be an asset to readers and researchers; this is to say, as in *Estimating Emerson: An Anthology of Criticism from Carlyle to Cavell*, it was the *variety* of approaches to Emerson, often at odds, arriving as disparate dispatches, that made the volume alluring and has kept us returning to it—since it was precisely the frisson between writers (their varying approaches and competing interests) that generated a spark between the pages; in this respect, the present volume might be profitably taken up as a sibling to the earlier one—both of them studies of the heterogeneity of criticism, and the ends that such criticism might be put. In both cases, we have at hand William H. Gass's trenchant question: "Quite apart from the usefulness of having all these important essays handy, readers may also toy with this simple question: when writing about a writer's work, over the years, have critics gotten better or have they gotten worse?"[27] A simple question, maybe, soliciting a complex and ongoing response.

The sentiment of the subtitle of this introduction would strike the ancient Stoics as a fitting locution for their habits of mind and action.[28] The purpose of philosophy is to improve the conduct of one's life—or better, as Cavell describes it in *Cities of Words*, to "measur[e] the value of our lives"—and thereupon to prepare for one's death (an always immediate potentiality of being human, as Heidegger exhaustively noted) by reminding us of its nearness, the pronounced pressure (if felt) that it puts on the present moment.[29] Likewise, one's daily life—filled as it is with remembrances and regrets, anticipation and anxiety, joys and satisfactions, banalities and disappointments—should inform the kinds of philosophical questions one asks, and, to be sure, also the sorts of replies one gives. In the modern era, Pierre Hadot has helped us appreciate what he calls "spiritual exercises" (*exercises spiritualle*) as the basis of the Stoic daily practice, yet this phrase may not bewitch a contemporary audience if only for the peculiar juxtaposition of these two words, which arrive, as they do, loaded with distinctly different associations.[30] Moreover, there is a challenge in thinking how such "exercises" might be part of, or inform, the procedural and methodological contours of contemporary philosophical practice—both in and out of the academy. Perhaps, then, in what follows, we can consider the ways in which Cavell provides a model for achieving the braid of the personal and the philosophical. With Cavell, the personal is almost always already the philosophical. When a student once asked busy Professor Cavell, "When do you have time to write?" he responded laconically—and with a smile: "I'm writing right now."[31]

From here we can further translate Cavell's understanding of the personal as the autobiographical—indeed, what Cavell, in a knowing echo of Hadot and the Stoics before him, calls "autobiographical exercises." An autobiographical exercise is nothing else but a "pitch of philosophy": an expression of the everyday offered in a certain key, with a distinctive phrasing, which then makes itself accountable to general philosophical preoccupations. The labor of the exercise is precisely in articulating how one's life becomes an object for philosophical investigation—and in turn, how such an inquiry folds back upon one's conduct of life, or the measuring of one's existence. Hence the allusions of a subtitle that says we are "parsing" the personal and the philosophical, for the work involves analyzing each line, each sentence, each thought in terms of its grammatical constituents, identifying along the way the parts of speech, syntactic relations and functions, inflectional forms, and more—but most of all describing or discovering (or discovering *by* describing in an illocutionary sense) the implications of such speech for the meaning our lives may have or come to possess, individually and collectively, ethically and existentially. In many respects, the conjunction (or better conjugation) of the personal and philosophical would have us regard the personal *as* the philosophical and likewise take up the philosophical *as* (always already) personal—despite having to field long-standing professional, disciplinary, we might even say ideological, protests to the contrary.

The Horse of Thought

On the first page of the foreword to *The Claim of Reason*, Cavell reminisces about J. L. Austin's visit to Harvard University in 1955, when Cavell was a graduate student in philosophy dissertating on the concept of human action.[32] Austin's arrival was auspicious for Cavell, for the material Austin presented (work now familiar in *How to Do Things with Words* and *Philosophical Papers*), "together with the procedures inspiring" these works, "procedures some of us called ordinary language philosophy—knocked me off my horse." Whether cowboy or Quixote, it's a wonderful trope, and if your name happens to be, or was made to be, *Cavell*, then so much the better. In Spanish: *caballo*. French: *cheval*. Portuguese: *cavalo*. Italian: *cavallo*. And so much the same for *cavalry* and *cavalier* and their cognates (French: *cavalerie*). How now, then, that the horse falls from his horse. Sounds like a puzzle—or a joke—fit for philosophers.

As often as Cavell has written about the season of Austin's transformative effect on his studies—as it must be, filled with the dread of abandoning hard-won research (he was far along, if at an impasse, with his first go at the dissertation) and with the particular charge afforded by a pedagogical punch—the image of Cavell falling from his horse doesn't get much traction. However we address ourselves to this first page of Cavell's most significant and extended work of world-historic philosophy, *The Claim of Reason*, it's clear that it emerges at once as a project grounded in the author's autobiography (not least for its long gestation, beginning, in part as his dissertation, but not appearing until after *Must We Mean What We Say?*, *The World Viewed*, and *The Senses of Walden*). As noted, before we even get to the infamous opening sentence, a 216-word question "heard 'round the world," we have met Cavell the philosopher as he makes his way—on horseback or on foot—to these words and the pages they fill.

In the introduction to *Emerson's Transcendental Etudes*, Cavell ponders the response or receptivity to Emerson as a philosopher (such as it is), and whether what Emerson does or achieves might be "granted [the title] thinking but not philosophy."[33] Cavell weighs the distinction: "In some sense, indeed, I think this is right," then immediately qualifies the allowance: "but it is right only if the thinking in question is seen to be a criticism of philosophy. … In the meantime, my insistence on Emerson's philosophicality is meant to account for Emerson's writing, most immediately for its tireless recurrence to descriptions of itself, or figures of itself."[34] The self-consciousness of Emerson's prose—its awareness of itself *as* prose—is noted here as a feature of philosophical significance; again, for the mainstream (analytic) philosophy of Cavell's day, and indeed, for the "continental" philosophy of Emerson's, such an attribute would have seemed mostly foreign, indeed, a characteristic more easily found and better suited to literature, and, to be sure, autobiography (from time immemorial). What Cavell is here calling the "philosophicality" of Emerson's writing might also ably pass for what others observe in the best of metafiction: a keen interest in the limning of form and content (as we see in, say, Henry James's "The Middle Years," which also includes a kindred equestrian image, "he could ride two horses at once"[35]). But then Emerson, a friend of Henry James, Sr., was well aware of the tradition of metafiction in literature, poetry, religion, and philosophy—and it would appear, aimed to emulate and transform it for his own proximate purposes.[36] One of the examples that Cavell cites as a conspicuous marker of such philosophicality is a line from "The Poet," where, as Cavell glosses it, "words are declared to be horses on which we ride, suggesting both that they obey our intentions and that they work beyond our prowess."[37] In "The Poet," Emerson wrote:

> The poet alone knows astronomy, chemistry, vegetation, and animation, for he does not stop at these facts, but employs them as signs. He knows

why the plain, or meadow of space, was strewn with these flowers we call suns, and moons, and stars; why the great deep is adorned with animals, with men, and gods; for, in every word he speaks he rides on them as the horses of thought.[38]

Cavell later in *Emerson's Transcendental Etudes*, which is to say, earlier in "Thinking of Emerson," had occasion to quote a passage in "The Poet" that appears five paragraphs after that just cited, as Emerson theorizes "the condition of true naming":

It is a secret which every intellectual man quickly learns, that, beyond the energy of his possessed and conscious intellect, he is capable of a new energy (as of an intellect doubled on itself), by abandonment to the nature of things; that, beside his privacy of power as an individual man, there is a great public power, on which he can draw.[39]

Cavell, as others, has for good reason seized on the significance of "abandonment," but, at the present moment, we can appreciate anew Emerson's parenthetical—"an intellect doubled on itself"—as a variation on the *awareness* that imparts and assures the philosophicality of his prose.[40] Not to be missed, though, is the recurrence of the horse as a figure for our consideration.

As the traveller who has lost his way, throws his reins on his horse's neck, and trusts to the instinct of the animal to find his road, so must we do with the divine animal who carries us through this world. For if in any manner we can stimulate this instinct, new passages are opened for us into nature, the mind flows into and through things hardest and highest, and the metamorphosis is possible.[41]

As it must, in the wake of the poet who sets his reins, the "intellect doubled on itself," we catch sight of the alternatives on offer, to wit: the "privacy of power" and the "great public power." We have not one but two horses, such as we encounter in 1860, when Emerson writes in "Fate," with the reinvocation of the *doubleness* that appears to inhere in our human constitution:

One key, one solution to the mysteries of human condition, one solution to the old knots of fate, freedom, and foreknowledge, exists, the propounding, namely, of the double consciousness. A man must ride alternately on the horses of his private and his public nature, as the equestrians in the circus throw themselves nimbly from horse to horse, or plant one foot on the back of one, and the other foot on the back of the other. So when a man is the victim of his fate, has sciatica in his loins, and cramp in his mind; a club-foot and a club in his wit; a sour face, and a selfish temper; a strut in his gait, and a conceit in his affection; or is ground to powder by the vice of his race; he is to rally on his relation to the Universe, which his ruin benefits. Leaving the daemon who suffers, he is to take sides with the Deity who secures universal benefit by his pain.[42]

Cavell has localized his reading of this passage in its highly charged temporal milieu, antebellum America—"taking sides with the Deity is a refusal to take sides in the human *crowing* over slavery" and as "not exactly a claim to revolution but a claim to prophecy"—and I wish to let that line of approach speak for itself in "Emerson's Constitutional Amending: Reading 'Fate.'"[43] Rather, in the strain of interest that tracks the appearance of the horse, indeed, horses ("of his private and his public nature"), I want to pick up the "Platonic image" that Emerson invokes and Cavell attests to.[44]

In the second speech Socrates gives in the *Phaedrus*, we hear about the nature of the soul, and how he wishes to "speak briefly, and in a figure" (i.e., with a bold underscoring that we have entered mythological and metaphorical territory—Plato writes literature after all), "and let the figure be composite—a pair of winged horses and a charioteer."[45] As Socrates tells it: "The human charioteer drives his [winged horses] in a pair; and one of them is noble and of noble breed, and the other is ignoble and of ignoble breed; and the driving of them of necessity gives a great deal of trouble to him." The composite figure can and has been translated into any number of psychological assessments of the human, including our moral nature (caught between good and evil, to begin with). For our purposes here, it is enough to hold onto the figure itself, or its composite nature, so we can ask, as we reflect on their meanings: who is horse and who is charioteer? Cavell, like Emerson, gives us reason to imagine some movement—and thus ambiguity or perhaps inventive fun—in our replies.

But at such a juncture, a reader may wonder: all this for an etymological pun? I should hope that the depth of references to Plato's *Phaedrus* in Emerson, and later Cavell to Emerson (and thus also to Plato), justify the pursuit of fecund resonances. But to make the endeavor somewhat more than "whim at last," I turn to the ways that Cavell's writing—its claims, demands, allowances, arrogations, and more—presents it too as a figure (or perhaps better, after Plato, a "composite figure") in company with the foregoing images and allusions, which is to say, that Cavell's name may be an accident of place and paternity (from Cavalerskii, Cavaleriiskii, or Kavelieruskii in Russia to the *Cavalier* pawnshop in Sacramento, California[46]), but there can be little doubt—or at least much wonder—at the coincidence of the terms, figures, and forms. Cavell is or was, and now his work is, I suggest, a horse of thought—and perhaps, in the light of the *Phaedrus*, also a kind of charioteer. For if the name "Cavell" bespeaks the *cavallo*, it also summons the *caballero*—thus, a horse *and* its rider. In every word and sentence Cavell wrote, he seemed to ride upon them; and we, as travelers (as charioteers of our own sort) lost and in need of orientation and propulsion onward, have time and again thrown our reins "on his horse's neck." Of this "man of the horse"—and we have said nothing of the mythological composite creature, the centaur, or for good measure that other equine hybrid, the pegasus—we can dwell with this visceral allusion, admiring the very intellectual vigor and vitality of such a figure as we find in Cavell and his thinking: an enduring, scintillating, workhorse of a mind.

From Horseback to Piggyback: A Paradox of Reliance

The following section presents a moment of meta-analysis about our inquiry in these pages and kindred ventures—their nature, methodologies, import, and promise. What is the labor of this volume and what does it reveal, for example, about the vexing, perennial issues of originality and conventionality? I begin a reply with a rejection letter, of sorts, for it is also—in a different light, or mood—an acceptance letter, or better, a confirmation letter. I invited an esteemed scholar to contribute to a collection of chapters (not this volume) and his response was full of the kind of fellow feeling and peer esteem one longs for. As he articulated his reasons for passing on the invitation to contribute, he, to my eye, had *already* contributed something crucial to those of us who have undertaken to write something about the remarkable work and legacy of Stanley Cavell. My (now anonymous) correspondent wrote:

> At this fairly late stage in my career, I am less interested than I once was in writing a piece that piggybacks on the work of another theorist, philosopher, or scholar, however much I'm indebted to them. I follow Cavell's crucial advice that I discover and attempt to articulate my own experience of a film, novel, or play, without a previously formed grid (even his) to guide me. I will draw on other thinkers as I need them, but in a catch-as-catch-can sort of way.

So the rejection is, we might say, given on Cavellian grounds. If those reasons were ratified, however, Cavell scholarship would come to an immediate and definitive end. So it is very much worth wondering why it has not—why, for example, the present book exists, why the present company of writers did, in fact, choose to write on or about Cavell. Can it be the case that they are not following Cavell's advice? Or that writing on Cavell, as on Emerson, demands an awareness—and acceptance—of paradox, in particular, a paradox of reliance?[47]

Making the decision not to write—including, on this occasion, a withdrawal from an invitation to write—conjures not just Bartleby, but more closely to Cavell, a remembrance of certain admonishments Emerson offered about imitation and taking things at secondhand; in this scene, our paradox presents itself. In the final paragraph of "Experience," Emerson remains preoccupied with questions of *realization*—what it would mean to achieve a certain kind of expression befitting one's experience: "I have not found that much was gained by manipular attempts to realize the world of thought"— while Cavell's punning observations on the human hand (manipular, handsome, unhandsome) coalesce.[48] Emerson asks bluntly: "Why not realize your world?" To which we are meant to assess whether we have not yet done so. And if not, then by what means we can marshal ourselves to the task. It is in Emerson's earlier essay, "Self-Reliance," where we read a diagnosis of our state—the reasons why we remain unrealized (as individuals, as society, as a nation, as cosmopolitan citizens): in a word, we take things at secondhand. We borrow and steal—we quote!—and we do not think for ourselves but take another's thought as our own.

How canny, then, that the earlier issue of *reliance* is so crucial to any approach to *realization*. The relationship presents itself anew in each novel context: with family, in friendship, in education, politics, and so on, and to be sure in the conduct of critical scholarship. Harold Bloom's famous formulation of "the anxiety of influence" provides some traction on the effects of trying to realize a world of thought in the grip of an admitted (or even suppressed) reliance: such stresses giving way to "misreadings" (unintentional?, unconscious?)—and I have proposed a related but distinct formulation: the anxiety of inheritance.[49] Still, the kindred phrases and their effects are familiar to readers of "Self-Reliance," and thereafter in Cavell's response to its dictates, lessons, and provocations. What would it mean nowadays in scholarship, *any* scholarship, to "speak [one's] latent conviction" and have it be "the universal sense"?[50] More than spelling the end of peer review, there is the more startling suggestion that a writer can think thoughts worthy of company with Emerson and Cavell.

Perhaps there are cases when one loves and admires a writer so much that writing "on" the subject is paralyzing; I once heard a partisan describe Cavell's effect upon some of his students as "disabling." How tragic. The greatest and dearest objects of one's intellectual affections then become what?—the subject for *others* to address—others, perhaps, who may not love the work as devotedly, but somehow feel more entitled, empowered, or otherwise legitimated in their efforts at expression? By contrast, the self-denial may suggest a case in which saying nothing protects oneself or one's work from criticism, since the absence of something is surely easier to bypass than the presence of something. The writer who writes *relies*, of course, but also opens herself to the reprimand and denigration of others; funny enough, however, plenty of exceptional scholarship is ignored anyway!

While the anonymous scholar, invoked above, decided to forego "piggybacking" on Cavell, there is something kind of wonderful about the image of piggybacking itself, calling to mind the way children ride (and rely) upon their parents—a perhaps too poignant figuration of parenting itself. And here the anonymous scholar may be showing his age: he is, at last, too old to ride upon the back of another; he is, at last, an adult. (And to be sure, it was Cavell who proclaimed how philosophy is "the education of grownups" with its attendant "anxiety of teaching"—namely, "that I myself require education."[51]) Our anonymous adult author, along with his eschewal of piggybacking, puts us in mind of Emerson's meditations on posture and representativeness: to stand upright ("tell men they are not leaning willows") and to "stand here for humanity."[52] The anonymous scholar will convey and not be conveyed. On the antagonism between the prevailing reactive or responsive approach and the option to take up the direct confessional, Emerson chooses a side: "I may also neglect this reflex standard, and absolve me to myself."[53] Is this the test to determine whether one's work is primary or secondary?

But if we think of this loving arrangement—of the mentor and his charges, of admixing of *eros* and *agon*—in the context of a scholarly life, where, say, an educator helps to convey ideas *and* students (to move them along), there is a further mental registration of such gifts: namely, that the piggybacking that one does upon another, in a conceptual way, is or can be a form of levitation, even transcendence. If one is relying upon Cavell in this book, riding upon him not after the fashion of the child on a parent's back but as one might ride upon a "horse of thought," then we could see this reliance, this dependency as possessing an odd power to liberate us, to move us onward, to ask after and reply to various "unattained but attainable" ideas and potentialities. We might be better able to "realize the world of thought" astride this galloping, capable creation. The horse itself is an emblem of the reliable and dependable, why not rely and depend upon it?

To counter my much admired anonymous interlocuter, and indeed to reframe our thinking about Emerson's counsel, I would like to defend the community of scholars here (presuming a need when there may be none) by defining their work—its principal activity—not as "piggybacking" but instead as *inheriting*. With the fitter pairing, including the more striking contrast, of piggybacking and horseback riding, these two metaphors are, admittedly, a mismatch, but perhaps that skewing is needed for shifting one's orientation to the meaning *and* significance of these new sessions of writing. Part of the reason I wish to keep the correspondent anonymous, as I did in the opening remarks for a book on Charlie Kaufman, is a desire to reveal the *sentiment* rather than a specific personality, which may distract or embarrass.[54] Our anonymous interlocuter's sentiment, again, has much to do with one's reading of an *Emersonian* sentiment: namely, what is one's relationship to precedent? In short, is an exemplar a "grid" or, as I would like to take it on special occasions, such as with Emerson and Cavell, a gird?

Though these pages possess some incisive criticism of Cavell's ideas, readings, and formulations, I think it is accurate to say that a portion of our individual (and now collective) admiration for Cavell's writing is precisely *what it makes possible*—not just for our appreciation of the works he discusses and the philosophers he deploys to discuss them but also for our own forays into the difficult labor of writing full stop, and at that, the daunting challenge of writing between or among disciplines (a practice, a temperament, a success that Cavell began exemplifying from his earliest years as a professional philosopher). As legendary screenwriter, William Goldman said: "The easiest thing to do on earth is not write." How lucky we are, then, to have found a writer in Cavell whose thought is sufficiently rich and robust, poised and penetrating, that we have—for all these years of shared life with him, and now after he has departed—found a way forward with what he has left behind. Call this our inheritance—one that is given freely, but that would make a demand on us to practice our inheritance, in effect, to learn how to inherit by offering further thoughts of our own. At the same time, and admittedly, Cavell's writing—his thought—is of a world-historical character, and so it is no easy mandate to "write!" in the company of his prose. For this reason, we "take steps," we move deliberately—sentence by sentence—and allow for a steady, incremental, and ongoing assessment. Like Cavell, we may be surprised by what lessons and benefactions await. Little did we know.

American Inheritance and Universal Provincialism

We can glean much from our reliance, if our books are well-chosen. And if we are trained to read those well-chosen books in a certain spirit (e.g., an Arnoldian one—where we focus on the author's *object* instead of, say, on how we *feel* about the author or what she has written[55]). Cavell, in this way, has been not only a curator of rare gifts—calling out specific works from distinctive creators and across mediums—but has also been a critic of rare acumen, providing us with an approach, a prevailing spirit, an irrepressible and identifiable mood (or mode) of invitation, along with a discipline of prose-writing that enables us to see those works in surprising ways (e.g., in their own right or in affiliation with another, including inventive shifts in form—coupling philosophical texts with works of film, painting and photography, theatre and theory, etc.). By showing us—illustrating such methods in exemplary fashion—Cavell has supplied the conditions for us to continue (indefinitely) to mull them over in new and generative ways and, hopefully, to sustain that practice in our encounter and instruction with the young and succeeding generations (supposing they can recognize the gravity of the project underway and a wish to participate in it). Richard Moran has written of Cavell's influence—for Moran it was first *The World Viewed*—as providing a "concept-determining effect," which entailed "discovering that intellectual voice, one for whom sophistication was not a pose, erudition not a hoard of possessions, brilliance not an avoidance of vulnerability and self-questioning but rather the means to make such vulnerabilities yield their insights."[56] Cavell helped Moran read Cavell, but also read much else, and also helped define, for a young Moran, a nascent sense of what "doing philosophy" might entail:

> Part of what I mean by the "concept-determining status" of his writing as philosophy is that whatever philosophy was, or whatever reading philosophy was, it had to, just as a reading experience, demand and reward going back over it again and again. This also meant that the writing had to bear up under any possible pressure of interrogation, of meaning, truth, relevance, seriousness, as well as the reader's demand for pleasure and delight as well as instruction. And since any writing presenting itself as philosophical or of high intellectual seriousness will also be encountered in a milieu subject to its specific forms of disappointment, even of fraudulence and fakery, for Stanley Cavell's writing to bear up under the weight of demands and promise I placed upon it, it had to be writing that could earn and keep the trust of a youth quick to disappointment (and feeling betrayed) by the representatives of intellectual life on offer that one encounters along the way. What this has meant for me is that philosophical writing that didn't place all these simultaneous demands on itself, I have forever afterwards found difficult to take seriously as philosophy.[57]

In this way, Cavell, Cavell's writing, proved to be the condition for the possibility of discovering philosophy—what it might entail, what it could do, and how one might be called to contribute to it. While many have heard in Emerson's solicitation of the *American* scholar a gesture "offensive to our pride of intellectual cosmopolitanism," indeed, "a call to nativism, or ethnocentrism," Cavell highlights the way in which Emerson was summoning philosophy as it might be on these shores, prairies, and mountains.[58] None are given to inherit a parochial thinker, but one who "asks us to consider what is native to us to do, and what is native to philosophy, to thinking."[59] In this respect, where we "find ourselves" is entangled with what we are related to in time and place; for Emerson and Thoreau in early and mid-life, this was Concord, Massachusetts, a few decades after the American Revolution and a few decades before the Civil War. In this stretch of time, writing from Walden Pond or the Sorbonne makes a difference worth dwelling on—and they did. Cavell too, in his own time and place, had his encounters, or in the case of Emerson and Thoreau's writing, his reintroductions to known but unaccounted for terrain:

> My discovery, or rediscovery for myself, of Emerson and of Thoreau seems to me a kind of hearkening to Emerson's call to American scholars. When I asked whether we may not see them as part of our inheritance as philosophers, I am suggesting that our foreignness as philosophers to these writers (and it is hard to imagine any writers more foreign to our currently established philosophical sensibility) may itself be a sign of an impoverished idea of philosophy, of a remoteness from philosophy's origins, from what is native to it, as if a certain constitution of the cosmopolitan might merely consist in a kind of universal provincialism, a worldwide shrinking of the spirit.[60]

First, the discovery. "It's important to me to say that philosophy can be discovered. Indeed what I want to say is that there is no philosophy *unless* it is discovered."[61] Hence, inheritance—as a practice of metaphilosphy—involves finding (since it concerns learning *what* one has inherited) but must also be a founding (since it demands the right to speak about, to claim authority over, even ownership of, what has been given). Think of inheritance as "learning what constitutes the right speak," discovering that power—which may include or require, at times, the arrogation of another's voice, and at other times, perhaps ideally, the potent application of one's own.[62] It remains an open question whether borrowing from and relying upon another is an illegitimate way to endeavor after the creation of one's own voice (assuming it is possible); "thinking on one's own" may be a romantic ideal, but it seems, perhaps for that reason, impracticable, even undesirable. Do we not need another to help us ratify, reject, or refine our ideas, supposing so much that they are even "ours" in the first place? Theories of friendship from Aristotle to Emerson suggest an individual's potentiality resides in relation to another. Indeed, the discovery of philosophy itself—in whatever form it takes: tract, film, work of art—appears predicated on recognizing how something that lies beyond us (a person, a teacher, a text) may call to something that abides within us.

The subject of inheritance is familiar in literal and figurative senses—from matters of descent in ancient Greek tragedy to Shakespearean court intrigue to *Mr. Deed's Goes to Town* (1936, dir. Frank Capra)—and it is a thematically rich domain for exploration, and one that Cavell was attentive to from his earliest work (such as on *King Lear* in *Must We Mean What Say?*) in the late 1960s. While Capra's classic film explicitly follows the plot of an inheritance—and the difficulties involved therein—it is worth noting how Cavell is especially receptive to the way Thoreau is invoked (and inexactly quoted) in the midst of a conversation between Longfellow Deeds (Gary Cooper) and Babe Bennett (Jean Arthur).[63] Even as Deeds contends with the fact that he has been brought to court to articulate—or, as the case may be, fall mute in—his claim to an inheritance (much as Adam and Amanda Bonner's marriage was brought to court in *Adam's Rib*[64]), Cavell recognizes his role as interpreter of American cinema *and* American philosophy—*his* inheritances. Yet, despite the vigor and clarity of Cavell's double register of inheritance (one no doubt predicated as a kind of marriage, as if one were made or meant for the other, and he for the task of uniting them), these practices were not immediately forthcoming for Cavell, did not present themselves as ready-made for his adoption.[65] Contrariwise, the four principle vectors of his intellectual labors—(1) Austin, Wittgenstein, and ordinary language philosophy; (2) "the general theory of value," including aesthetics (music, painting, photography, theatre, opera, and cinema) and ethics; (3) Shakespeare (including tragedy and skepticism), and (4) Anglo-European romantic and American transcendentalist thought (where the nation's philosophical labors may be found or implicated in the "metaphysical riot of its greatest literature"[66])—revealed their heritable and inheritable potential over time.[67] Cavell, like so many of us, had to learn not only *how* to inherit, but first *what* to inherit—and in particular, what was worth the dedication of one's precious days and nights.

We have a clinic on the discovery of philosophy in Cavell's own relationship to the work of Emerson, as he asks himself why it took him the better part of two decades "to demand explicitly my inheritance of him?"[68] If early on Cavell neglected Emerson, was this a function of Cavell's indifference (deafness?); some deficiency in Cavell's instruction by others, his teachers; or Emerson's failed instruction of Cavell (that is, where he, Emerson, could not be heard by his audience)? Perhaps in some measure all of these, but collectively these features only make Cavell's *discovery* that much more salient. "To allow the other the freedom for her or his own discoveries is then the mark of a good teacher."[69] Sometimes we must be our own teachers ("This thinking would go to show the significance of self-education; that in reality there is no other; for, all other is nought without this," wrote Emerson;[70] or as Nietzsche said of his hero, Emerson, upon whom he modeled his experiments in essaying philosophy: "he could say of himself," in the words of Lope de Vega, "*yo me sucedo a mis mismo*" [*I am my own successor*][71]). At other times we can take heart from moments of instruction that provide nourishment enough for a lifetime of discoveries; in this alternate scenario, we are Cavell's successors. Let *Inheriting Stanley Cavell*, then, be among the expressions of and evidence for Cavell's legitimate claims to achieving this rare double status. His intuitions became, in turn, our tuitions.[72] And our time with his work suggests we have yet something to say—as if his preoccupation with belatedness also carried with it a necessary latency.

Why inheriting? Because an inheritance is something you receive (or are denied), while inheriting is something you *do*. And though Cavell has given us much, handed down a fine estate to all, it is set upon us, in our experience of reading him, to actively find our way with words—his and our own. With Simone Weil and Wittgenstein, for instance, it was their executors who (after their deaths) made the canon of what counts; the editors selected and arranged the *Nachlass*. Cavell is different, since, in life, for over half a century he oversaw the publication of his core texts. Yet the critical inheritance of that work remains an ongoing project, and the perpetual question of this process is: *can* we say what we learned? And, if we can, *must* we say it? Ability (virtuosity, even) and a moral imperative—linked as they are in Cavell's writing—become our own questions, the bequests afforded by his oeuvre.

When Cavell speaks in the early 1980s about "my work to claim *Walden* as part of my inheritance" (referring, of course, to his *The Senses of Walden*), and asks later in the same decade, "why especially is it Emerson and Thoreau that I am so insistent on inheriting?" we have caught him in acts of assessing his intellectual patrimony; and in these cases, as in so many others, it is the mood or mode of these reported perceptions that we should note—that they need to be made with insistence (and perhaps incessance).[73] Emerson and Thoreau prompt us to ask not just "What is philosophy for?" but *when* is philosophy?—and can we recognize it when we see it being practiced or placed before us? As Cavell says: "I am taking precisely that condition [of Emerson and Thoreau's repression by the culture they helped found] to signify their pertinence to the present."[74] In Emerson and Thoreau's case, as in Freudian psychoanalysis (of which Cavell was a dear and dedicated student), repression is a telling sign—something to follow after not something to ignore. Hence the suitability of their thought to contemporary life precisely *because* it is, or was, neglected by the very kinds of thinkers (philosophers) who should have appreciated their bearing and relevance sooner.

If we telescope time for a moment, we have to wonder how Cavell's own work figures in this narrative of inheritance. So, as Cavell did more than any American philosopher to recover, resituate, and restore the vitality of Emerson and Thoreau for serious (i.e., legitimate, sanctioned) philosophical criticism (if only because Cavell embodied these attributes in his work), then we are, by extension from his enterprise, poised to appreciate how the present series of studies figures in the practice of "inheriting by interpreting."[75] We have far from exhausted our interpretive labors of inheritance for Emerson and Thoreau, and with Cavell, we may be in a nascent state. How expressive, insistent, and expansive *we* must be in our claims remains a matter to be revealed.

While the mood of Cavell's remark above—invoking "a kind of universal provincialism, a worldwide shrinking of the spirit"—arrives as a lament for a loss, or a concern about a diminishment, I think a "universal provincialism" can be habilitated to serve as a positive marker for the ambitions of an evolving inheritance of American philosophy beyond its continental borders.[76] In such a case, the modifier "American" becomes a sign of a certain kind of *approach* to inheritance, namely, when the world is (considered) small enough to take up Emerson and his compatriots as sentinels for a global philosophy, hence of a cosmopolitanism of mind envisioned as early as the Stoics and evaded or defeated ever since.[77] Cavell, for one, imagines a specific vision of what the inheritance of Emerson and Thoreau might look like: "In my fantasy [I] nominate them as reticent, belated founders of some eventual international philosophical culture that will include both America (both hemispheres) and Israel," an anointing predicated on "their devotion to philosophy reaching beyond Christendom, beyond the West; and their problematic of the discovery of America (which for them has not happened)."[78] In our "quest for home," we have not yet arrived.[79]

Cavell's recurrent reference to an "American inheritance" of *anything*—Emerson, Thoreau, Kant, English poetry, ancient Greek thought, cinema, pick what you like—may be understood as a reading of "American" as a synonym for *immigrant*, where we are oriented to reading and writing with a certain perpetual postponement of arrival (despite what may seem like obvious and permanent settlement on this land).[80] In this way, as Cavell puts it, we treat "the human as immigrant" and thought as oriented to a perpetual, permanent frontier.[81] As such, immigrancy (of the self, of society, of intellectual inquiry) becomes a cognate term for Emersonian (moral) perfectionism, for example, as we find it articulated by Cavell.[82] We inheritors, then, adopt the unsettled status of the immigrant as an inherent part of our outlook, call it a spiritual or autobiographical exercise; on this front, Cavell notes parenthetically: "(I guess there is no end to my wish to democratize the exclusive.)"[83] To underscore the notion of an *American* inheritance, then, is not a bid for a nationalist program, but, quite the opposite, for a kind of opened-ended meditation on and negotiation for the meaning of the terms and conditions that make (human) citizenship possible. The American is the forever immigrant—attesting to the potentialities of the human community—and therefore regards inheriting as an active and ongoing routine practiced by a person and the *polis*.

Something of Cavell's fate as an inheritable feature of our culture has been a common point of interest these last many decades—even from early on in his career, and especially in the wake of the publication of *The Claim of Reason* in 1979. The question of how to read Cavell is not something we are broaching (for the first time) after his death, then; indeed, it might be noted instead as a hallmark question of or for his particular species of philosophical method. Marshall Cohen commences the proceedings here with a two-stroke offering: first a cogent and condensed interpretation of Cavell's biography, then, something of a diagnosis of Cavell's work in the context of professional academic philosophy. Especially as the piece evolves—and certainly as it crescendos—we brace for the implications of

Cohen's claims. "Admirable as some of [the] secondary literature [on Cavell] is, however, Cavell's philosophical work will be fruitful and multiply only when philosophers engage it critically, find it useful, and perhaps develop it further. For the most part, this has not yet happened."[84] (Is this a true assessment? Is it fair? Can only philosophers bear the fruit of philosophical labors? Is there not abundant evidence that they have already done so by virtue of Cavell's contributions?) In some measure, the work of this collection involves a series of metaphilosophical meditations on these questions and their prompting by the final conjectures and implications of Cohen's remarks—for example, indications of the extent to which Cavell has mattered to philosophy (academic and otherwise) and how his contributions to, say, literature or literary thinking (at once the literary voice of, for, and in philosophy and the nature of writing sentences that achieve something perhaps unfamiliar to [professional] philosophical prose and argument) should be attested to—including by those who inhabit intellectual life beyond the boundaries of philosophy. The contestations of Cohen's conclusions make his piece, written shortly after Cavell's death, function as an invitation to the *life* Cavell lived—its perspicuous points of philosophical interest—and to the *thought* that emerged in the course of it.[85] That tender plait is, in Cohen's astute reading, a rather robust helix, and one that the rest of us spend time reflecting on.

Such concerns and questions will likely strike the reader differently depending on her familiarity with the history of what scholars like to call the "reception" of an author's work. Thus far I have spoken in the direction of the book's title, that is, with an ear for the present progressive act of "inheriting" Cavell's bequest. But, as Cohen tells us, there would seem to be reason to wonder (and worry) about the interactivity and thus complexity of Cavell's reception, for example, when we are called upon to adjudicate whether Cavell himself "refused," by turns (and turns of phrase) a willing and robust inheritance and incorporation, say, by the profession of which he called himself a member. Thus, reception and refusal seem cognate phenomena, as we hear it articulated by George Steiner, in his memoir, *Errata*:

> As the close comes nearer, I know that my crowded solitude, that the absence of any school or movement originating in my work, and that the sum of its imperfections are, in considerable measure, of my own doing. The appropriation, the exploitation of my writings and teachings by others, the blatant non-acknowledgment by those who have found its public visibility and variousness offensive may, by ironic paradox, be its true reward. But the sadness, the *tristitia*, that numbing Latin word, is there.[86]

In this passage, Steiner, to be sure, does not ventriloquize for Cavell. Yet Steiner's characterization of the inheritance of one's work, or not, by others resonates deeply; as Cavell made acknowledgment a master term of his thought, so Steiner counters (and ruefully complements) with the prospect of nonacknowledgment. What is worse, after all, to have one's writing expropriated or forgotten? Can genius summon its proper and best acolytes? The questions are asked plaintively.

In the space of the "not yet happened" (Cohen alludes to), we are now left to consider variations on a predicament: is Cohen's proposed lacuna a result of neglect or refusal or insufficient attention? In short, could *disinheritance* also be part of Cavell's intellectual legacy? The echo of Cavell's own articulated case for Emerson and Thoreau's "repression" by the intellectual culture they helped found may resound an ironic note.[87] Posterity and the long arc of time will supply ready answers to such queries; for now we seem to be merely caught up in them, trying as we can to articulate ways in which the impediments to inheritance (internal to the work *and* externally imposed on it) are evaluated in company with its enticements.

Indeed, given Cavell's discussion of Emerson and Thoreau's repression (as noted, a significant term of art in psychoanalysis) in the culture *they* helped found, why not listen for the same concern about the reception of Cavell's own work (including the remarks on Emerson and Thoreau, which, by and large, did not find an audience in dominant strains of philosophical debate and pedagogy), thereby adding irony to insight? If Cavell, in short, has made it hard for some to *begin* reading him (hence, an axiomatic or analytic definition of neglect), then we rightly marvel at those who refuse to stop reading him—as if obsessively admitting interest in the ongoing activity of reception, reading, accounting, and inheritance in a Cavellian mold or mood. Hence, Stephen Mulhall's adroit rendition of Cavell's work as defined, in part, by a "refusal to begin"—and yet, showing that the very issue of beginning becomes something to be discussed at extended, at times, comical length—leaving us to wonder how "the avoidance" of Cavell by others is *also* a theme endogenous to his work.[88] Michael Fischer has written eloquently about this feature of Cavell's writing, and how it interacts with its readers, in *Stanley Cavell and Literary Skepticism*. In his introduction to *Stanley Cavell*, "Between Acknowledgment and Avoidance," Richard Eldridge navigates the Scylla and Charybdis of his title. And more recently in her *Stanley Cavell and Film*, Catherine Wheatley offers a cogent program of the various resistances and confusions that have attended the reception of Cavell's work. By adducing some of the conspicuous hows, whats, and whys at issue, she surveys the landscape of avoidance, dismissal, denied recognition, and other forms of misconstrual and neglect.[89]

As a working case in point, though, let us consider for a moment Garrett Stewart's astute appraisal of Cavell's reception not by philosophers but by literary theorists—pausing only to appreciate the way Cavell's writing, rare among philosophical attestations, has demanded deserving response from multiple, divergent disciplines—from film studies to poetics, American studies to political theory; aesthetics, anthropology, music, literary criticism, religion, and still more—a range of interest and engagement attested to in the varied contributions to this volume. That said, after Cohen and Steiner, the diversity of Cavell's accomplishments is no guarantee of fitting interpretations or extended accolades—indeed, the breadth (i.e., the refusal of disciplinary "specialization") may itself be a criterion for dismissal.[90]

> First, what increasingly strikes a reader looking to assess the gauntlet thrown down by Cavell's work to reigning literary-critical models is that the complaints against him are best, and most often, phrased by his champions. This strikes me as close to unprecedented in the ordinary channels of academic discourse. It is as if the nuance, capaciousness, and candor of Cavell's thinking holds the seeds of dissent within the toils of their own subtlety, so that only his most devoted close readers can judge the pressure of counterargument from within the weight of original formulation. You have to be tuned in to begin with to imagine where the static might occur. Sympathetic readers of Cavell, that is, best pledge their allegiance by imagining an objection as if it were their own, so that even debate waits within testimonial as its true measure.[91]

To which Stewart masterfully concludes with a rhetorical question for the ages: "And is not this (we may come to think with a little more evidence) no less than the very proof of the Cavellian method: a reading so intense as to internalize the shadow of its own alternatives?"[92] Depending on where you stand (e.g., in philosophy, by way of literary studies, if such positions still make any sense) will inform your reply to the question (even in its rhetorical formulations), and lead to a judgment along the spectrum from assured failure to quintessential success. Reports arrive from all directions about the "difficulty" of reading Cavell, and thereafter writing about his work. No doubt, some of those persons who are daunted nevertheless manage to write; it may not always approach or equal, much less exceed, Cavell's standard, but there is plenty of admirable work to suggest it can be done with decency, tact, and ample discrimination.

While Cavell himself was said to have admired the "industry" that grew up around Jacques Derrida's prodigious writing (namely, the radiating circles of acolytes and their abundant interpretive productions), a reader might share his wonder that Derrida's work managed to hold and sustain so many for so long. Why not the same profusion (and quality?) for Cavell's work? Time will tell, of course. Yet, if we are speaking about writers who may be accused of resisting their readers or interpreters, Cavell, surely, cannot be named among the most off-putting. Indeed, one may be tempted to turn the issue inside out: that it is precisely the *welcome* Cavell affords to his reader, no matter her prior education, that may consume her—prevent or stall her initiative to respond, or even, as noted, "disable" it. Cavell's formulation of philosophy as always and necessarily the "education of grownups" makes his work permanently on offer, poised with an open invitation to readers to begin anywhere and endlessly defer the completion of such heady, gratifying explorations.[93]

As is so evident, many readers do find a way to speak of their experience with Cavell's work; as one such indication, the chapters in this collection may be understood to present what Cavell called, and we may call after him, "scenes of inheritance."[94] Still, the very fact of their being put on offer, within the present framing, immediately propels us into the further question of how that reading is conducted and what it reveals. Drawing Cavell's words out of their midrashic context in *A Pitch of Philosophy*, I wish to highlight, in our context, his phrasing about legitimacy.[95] In trying to understand why Isaac is "choosing the wielder of force over the possessor of words," Cavell responds: "This hurts me. Is it that I can hardly bear the idea that the right to an inheritance is not given by reasons? Yet it is precisely when reasons are exhausted that authority is inclined to say, [in Wittgenstein's statement] 'This is simply what I do,' namely, wait for the inheritance to be taken, overtaking the giving, treasonously."[96] We, in this volume, are not in Jacob's troubled straits, and yet, like Jacob, we are situated as those in a position to inherit from a formidable (intellectual) father.[97] If the shaping of emotion for public purposes is achieved in the *Gedankenschrift*, it may go without saying that asserting the right to an inheritance (such as this work assumes) will by necessity, and perhaps by habit, be "given by reasons." If those reasons prove, say, to be whim at last, then we too will be forced to say, "This is simply what I do." Would that be a painful outcome? To hedge that risk, we offer reasons. Whether they be reasons *enough* remains.

Apt Conjunction

In a piece entitled "On Makavejev on Bergman," that is on the Serbian filmmaker, Dušan Makavejev (and his film, *Sweet Movie*) and the Swedish filmmaker, Ingmar Bergman, Cavell writes parenthetically, indeed with *double* parentheses:

> (Since in the working of this film and in the mode of thinking it exemplifies, apt conjunction is everything, allowing the mutual excavation of concepts, I shall quote from the early pages of C. G. Jung's autobiography, *Memories, Dreams, Reflections*, without comment (as if one might use a quotation within the body of a text, that is, after the text has begun, as what you may call an internal epigraph)).[98]

Taking a cue from this layered and intriguing remark, we can say with assurance that in Cavell's writing "and in the mode of thinking it exemplifies

... apt conjunction is everything." One of those conjunctions is the invocation of an autobiographical text (this one by Jung), another is that the book was written (or more accurately dictated) by one of the two or three most significant psychologists of the twentieth century. Yet, it is the title of that work—*Memories, Dreams, Reflections*—that stands as a third conjunction, namely, since it is the subtitle of the present volume. I should wish one further favor of emulation or imitation in stating all of this "without comment," for it was not my (conscious? unconscious?) intention to echo Jung's book in the selection of the three words meant to provide a gloss on the notion of "inheriting Stanley Cavell." Yet, admittedly, my familiarity with Cavell's chapter on Makavejev and Bergman might have planted a memory of a capacious and compelling title; what shall we call this "unconscious appropriation," "subconscious citation"? If viable, such mental acts certainly trouble our sense of having an "original relation"; they also lend a new degree of complexity to the citationality of interpretation, where such use carries with it unintended connotations as well as cultivates new debts.[99] I would prefer to spell out, if briefly, what I had in mind (consciously, so far as I can tell) in the selection—and ordering—of these terms.

Already familiar with the content of the volume, an intimacy an editor naturally develops, I cast about for a few names, terms, or concepts that might account for this kind of work, especially to convey something recognizable or attractive to the eye and sensibilities of the prospective reader (whether familiar or not with Cavell). In many cases, that is to say, in most of the pieces collected here, the author is engaged in some state of remembrance and commemoration (i.e., remembering together). Yet owing to the mandate of the *Gedankenschrift*, and the vision for what it might entail, the word remembrance seemed to carry too much memorial, even liturgical, weight—as if it might betoken another prayer for the Faithful Departed. Hence I arrived at a neighboring term—"memories"—which, to my ear, sounded like a category bent on invoking some notion of the past without connoting the registration of one specific feeling or another. Moreover, it emphasized a temporal orientation, namely, that in having memories (possessing them, recalling them), we are perpetually "looking back" to some past, shared or solitary; and that in our retrospective mood ("Our age is retrospective. It builds the sepulchres of the fathers."), the past is, in fact, at our back.[100] Neuroscience now tells us that memories are no longer fixed or finished, that we can delete, modify, or invent as the case may be; I call this plasticity—this "evanescence and lubricity"—of our mental platform a further promising invitation to "experiment" as "endless seeker[s]," to think and rethink our relationship to the past we have shared with Cavell's work, and thus, how we have arrived at this particular present (an always onward moment).[101]

In the subtitle of *Little Did I Know*, Cavell speaks of his offerings there as "excerpts from memory." The syntagma is a startling one since it connotes that memories are, as it were, already written; following the logic of an excerpt, it is as if Cavell is (merely?) undertaking some kind of a retrieval (of the fragmentary, associative, and rarely serial content of some cognitive realm), and in this way he would be an editor of his experience, a curator who is selecting these portions into a compendium—"commonplacing."[102] Is he, somehow, taking dictation from himself? Memories (like dreams, and perhaps too like our memories of movies) seem to require *a translation into language*; I am thinking here of Cavell's reflections on what it would mean to quote a movie.[103] In the case of remembering a film, the work of describing what one saw and heard is harder than one might expect (hence the need for a community, which may be numbered and named a friend); but what to say about a private memory—a phenomenon that, like a dream (wakeful or while sleeping) and unlike a movie, is not available for the inspection and analysis of others? Indeed, following William Rothman, we should concur that "memories are private," not shareable in the way we think they might be, say, when we tell others about them.[104] Hence the importance of a claim like "this is how I remember it happening." Yet each time we remember, we seem poised to remember differently—to emphasize or diminish, indeed, to add or subtract without cause. In this respect, what else is a memory retold but a vision or version of a dream ("awakening, as from a dream, as from a film"[105])—a picture of a world that is no longer present to us and yet may still feel intensely real? And turned the other way, do we notice when dreams become memories, whether those dreams are understood as nighttime or daytime creations, or derived from some other mode of conjuring and fabulation—including thinking things into existence? These questions encourage us to parallel investigations such as Freud's *The Interpretation of Dreams* with (our own) interpretation of memories.[106]

Cavell's own interest in Freud—wide-ranging and beginning as early as his days of "spiritual crisis" (when Cavell was allowing a life in music to cede to a life in something else—call it philosophy, or call it something else: Freud did)[107]—stimulates questions about the kind of work we expect of philosophy, or the kinds of experiences that interest its practitioners. Among the many ordinary, everyday, common, low, and near events of a given day, dreams predominate (again, whether they arise inadvertently in the night or are coaxed into being while awake). The layered signification of dreams seems in ready evidence for any reader of Freud, as Cavell was beginning to be "for some time fairly exclusively" in the late 1940s:[108]

> I looked forward to each of my sessions of reading Freud's text as to falling into a kind of trance of absorption and a security of being known, accepted back into the human race. And my participation in Freud's sense of his discoveries as an intellectual and spiritual adventure of fateful importance to Western culture—I wouldn't have known how to begin distinguishing it from what I imagined the work of philosophy to be,

something about leading the soul to the light—led me to allow the idea of becoming a psychoanalyst to take hold of my imagination.[109]

An alternate life, as they say, and yet, how much of that imagination *did* find its way into Cavell's consequential, utterly unique enterprises of thought? For one instance to satisfy a reply, consider that when he came to formalize his written account of the lectures he gave at Harvard on moral perfectionism, that is, in *Cities of Words*, the chapter devoted to Freud offers an interpretation of Freud's "Delusions and Dreams in Jensen's *Gradiva*."[110] More than a half-century after those first encounters with Freud's texts, Cavell remained captivated by the way a conversation between psychoanalysis and philosophy is productively agitating.[111] Indeed, as Cavell felt himself having fallen into a trance, so we recall in Freud the sense of "standing under a spell" [*stünden im Bann*] where "the spell is precisely that of what we may call everyday life." Even so, it will be through what Cavell, echoing Freud, anoints the "magic of words" that we have any hope of articulating these moments of sentience.[112]

Perhaps we can say that such collected descriptions—of memories, movies, and dreams, and the reflections we append to them—inform or simply constitute who we think we are (because they reveal what we think about, the objects of our attention and affection). Moreover, we can underscore that while memories and dreams (must) remain private, as a function of how they are constituted and contained/retained, it is to our reflections (in part, on them)—in words, magical or otherwise—that we become accountable to ourselves and to one another. Folk advice tells us to take care with our dreams else a skeptic or scold may scatter our force, yet how else do we emerge from (possible) delusion—from misremembering, from dreaming, from speaking beyond sense—unless we summon ourselves to public expression, even if only with one other person? In Emerson, Thoreau, and Cavell, this figure is a friend; sometimes, if lucky, that person is a parent, teacher, or spouse.

"Reflections" is not just a euphemism for "thoughts" (still less for the cinematic allegory it summons) but also serves as a trope for the kind of encounter we have with what has *already* been seen or sensed. We *re*-flect. We see again and perhaps anew. We may even recall something of an earlier condition or cast of mind (as one catches a glimpse of one's present state in a mirror, allowing the face-to-face to prompt a recognition of one's aging, hence of time's passage, etc.). Here, reflections portend reflexiveness—that capacity to be aware of awareness, to acknowledge and "process" memories and dreams in some mysterious present (itself the logical site of future memories).

As "misreading" has been invoked for its intellectual productivity (rather than its alarm or offense), so we can appreciate how misremembering (including the misquotation of one's own texts, or the texts of others) can highlight uncanny resemblances, pushing us back on our seemingly settled assurances and commitments. We find a case in *Emerson's Transcendental Etudes* where Emerson's "secret melancholy" becomes "silent melancholy," thus inviting us to spell out the significance of this proximate but distinct pairing.[113] Or when Cavell writes in the epigraph to *Contesting Tears* that "to my way of thinking the creation of film was as if meant for philosophy" and soon after, in an interview glosses himself, but with a variation: "Film, I have said in the epigraph to my most recent book on melodrama, is made for philosophy."[114] If "meant" and "made" are the same in a colloquial sense, what about a *philosophical* one? Both words carry a valence of intention, while the first calls to mind a *destiny* and the second connotes *creation*.[115] Admittedly, at first blush, such alternate versions or moments of alteration can give the scholar-critic a shock (did *I* misremember? did *I* misquote?); but on second thought, wouldn't my variations *also* be subject to the same generosity of conceptual interest? For in these cases, we are invited to a munificent semantic field in which to consider the nuances of specific words—and how they are transformed by precise quotation, meaningful misquotation, or fecund paraphrase. How, in fact, are silence and secrecy related? What is the difference, if any, between something been "meant" and "made"? I suppose, in a certain mood, such lines of investigation draw upon the very core preoccupations of ordinary language philosophy, and so it should not be a surprise that "mis"-anything transforms from scandal to worthy fodder for philosophizing.

Several of the pieces, including my own, would appear to speak of a future, that is, a time when conditions will be different—or met with a different range of responses, hopefully for the better. To postulate a future circumstance that is discernable in the mind but unrealized in the world seems the very purview of dreams. One of the dreams we may have is conscious life itself—"Dream delivers us to dream and there is no end to illusion," wrote Emerson, hence we are ushered into an existence in the shape of "a bubble and a skepticism."[116] "Life itself is ... a sleep within a sleep."[117] Emerson follows Prospero who wrote, "We are such stuff / As dreams are made on, and our little life / Is rounded with a sleep."[118] A formidable response to such existential attributes is ever in order ("Sir, I am vex'd"), and we know that Cavell has been one of our finest interlocutors on the "threat of skepticism" and the encouragement to "live one's skepticism."[119] Time and again, we contend with the reality of dreams (or their surreal role in our lives), or by relation, the reliability or durability or recalling of memories: while I still very much seem to be myself if I cannot recall a dream, *am* I myself if I cannot remember elements of personal history from waking life?[120]

Remembering conversations with Cavell can now seem like a dream, even as it appears we, individually and collectively, continue to converse with him despite his death. Dreams, then, appear to be something like the interstitial space *between* memories and reflections. Often this in-between is called sleeping—and under the cover of darkness and with a quieted consciousness, our minds come alive with possibilities, visions, constitutions, and reconstitutions of reality. When we awaken the dreams are no more—not real—and yet, we may speak of them, write them down, attest to their (possible) significance. It is a cliché (because true) that listening to the dreams of others may leave us cold (i.e., aside from a certain strain of capable psychoanalyst), and yet, there is to follow, as far as I can tell, no satisfactory rendition of what a given author may draw from unconscious life. Consider how the specter of the dream—as a space of potentiality, of an indefinitely deferred perfectability, of futurity, even the perpetual not-yet of utopia (or its proxy, the "good city")—seemed fitting for a conversation about Cavell's take on human experience.[121] We find reason to remember a distinction Emerson drew, in which Cavell hears echoes of Kant: "I know the world I converse with in the city and in the farms, is not the world I *think*."[122] While Hamlet wonders "in this sleep of death what dreams may come," we-the-living remain confronted with our own thoughts—wondering how many of them are (mere) dreams and were never more than that.

A quick scan of associations—dreamlike in their very conjuring here—suggests further valences of significance for dreams. Even in the early decades of the twenty-first century, and despite all, we invoke with regularity the notion of the "American Dream," and as one potent and proximate example of the resonance, one of the contributors to this collection named a monograph *Stanley Cavell's American Dream*.[123] And as Lawrence Rhu tethered Cavell's American Dream to Hollywood movies (and Shakespeare), we can call to mind the notion that Hollywood has been for so long referred to as a "dream factory." When James Conant writes of "Cavell and the Concept of America," we learn that Conant's inquiry is related to the "dream of America"—the dream, drama, or even *trauma* of the American dream and the American ideal.[124] Part of that story or myth involves the shocking shift from inheritance by right of birth to the conditionality of merit—that our inheritance, such as it may be, is not given to us but made by us. Hence, we spend lifetimes discerning the difference between gifts and burdens.

Speaking of the burden of dreams, when Cavell contends, early in *The World Viewed*, that cinema offers its audience "a fair semblance of ecstasy," we may naturally turn to Werner Herzog and his dreams (borrowed from the "great ecstasy" of the woodcarver Steiner, among others); movies are as if dreams, but they also inform our dreams, become our memories, and give shape to our reflections.[125] "I believe that cinema is rooted in dreams and common desires," Herzog tell us. "I also think that cinema can use artificiality, fiction, and imagination to reveal a whole new reality that lies behind it all."[126] Whether in the movie theater or out-of-doors on terra firma, the "dream of humans" is, at last, a moral perfectionist's project and projection.[127] A "dream," in this sense, is a vision of possibility, teeming with both latency and manifestness. Consequently, we must contend with the "burden of dreams" and also with "forgotten dreams."

Indeed, Cavell's writing on film may have about it the character of writing on dreams. Why? Because Cavell is, as others have noted, not so much a close reader of film (as found in analytical philosophy of film,[128] or in the rigorous shot analysis tradition exemplified by Victor Perkins and his students[129]); rather, time and again, he takes the first line of *The World Viewed* to heart: "Memories of movies are strand over strand with memories of my life."[130] In this way, what Cavell remembers (of movies) becomes part of the atmosphere of his personal thoughts and the philosophical expressions that follow after them. For this reason, Cavell can be said to write film criticism about his *dream* of movies—not always adhering strictly to the specifics of what was seen, said, but also to the way the film lives for him, on his terms. Of course, he is careful to quote lines as they are spoken, is fastidious with plot sequencing (as exemplified by his engrossing summary notes in *Cities of Words*), but he can go beyond the films—way beyond them—to find expression for the "ponderable affinities" that obtain, or might, as *Cities of Words* shows late in his career, and *The World Viewed*, *Pursuits of Happiness*, and *Contesting Tears* exhibit earlier.[131] How else can Cary Grant and Katharine Hepburn remind him of Plato, Nietzsche, and Kant; Ibsen and Milton; Emerson and Thoreau? How else can Hollywood talkies of the 1930s and 1940s become an exemplification of Emersonian transcendental philosophy and, in turn, constitute America's contribution to global thinking about moral perfectionism? Such rhetorical questions are further illustrations—that is, evidence—of the way film was as if meant or made for philosophy, and vice versa.[132]

For their prevalence, we have accumulated without much effort several senses of dreams: night (dreams), day (dreams), movie watching and film criticism, autobiographical prose in a philosophical vein, anticipations of what may come (the American Dream, dreams of the future, imagined utopias and good cities), yet we may pause to ask how daydreams are related to what we call thoughts, how experience itself is related to a kind of hallucination—no doubt an old, old question from the skepticism of antiquity, the legacy of which is invoked just above in Emerson's phrasing ("life is a bubble," "dream delivers us to dream," and "there is no end to illusion"). Hence the ever-ready fright of asking, "Did I experience it or did I dream it?" Meanwhile, memories themselves—the residues or synaptic pathways that we feel sure are possible only because of experience—appear suddenly perspectival, fallible, and malleable. "Dream," then, is a proxy for the problematic of skepticism and self, of conceptualization and consciousness, as we find it in Cavell's work from early to late. What we have, all we have, all we are, all we know is consciousness and it is comprised of memory, anticipation (dreams), and thoughts (reflections). Everything we can be said to *know* happens in consciousness—memories, dreams, and reflections. As such, this trinity must share space with what we still call emotion and judgment, a pair that has been perennially uncoupled by philosophers, but which, in our present age, seems gratifyingly reunited, remarried even.

And for the rest of the remarks—when they did not call upon memories (of the past) or conjure dreams (of the future)—they struck me as variations on philosophical criticism. These are sometimes called "remarks" (in Wittgenstein), but I was attracted to, and then pleased by, the understated allusion—and double entendre—in a word featured in the subtitle of Cavell's *The World Viewed*, namely, reflections. And reflections being something one offers (or in the case of film, encounters) in the present—during the "running time" of the moment we call the movie—the final portion of the trinity seemed fulfilled.

Hence: memories, dreams, reflections. Past, future, and present.

And I hasten to add "without comment," that Jung and his autobiography is nowhere to be found in the pages that follow; rather, they brought us to Cavell's savvy double parenthetical above, which enabled this traveler to "throw his reins on his horse's neck," and be pulled along in some profitable direction.

As such apt conjunctions are wont to do, they spur further thoughts, some of them pertinent to the labors underway in this collection: memories, dreams, and reflections are all cognitive experiences—though activating consciousness in variegated ways (e.g., as it would seem some are passively presented to consciousness while others are called forth—conjured, created, critically constituted). Likewise, they are different but related phenomena in Cavell's work. For instance, when our prior experience of a film's projection demands from us, after the fact, to remember it, we seem to represent moving images and sounds to the mind—call them dreams. In an "Autobiography of Companions," the opening chapter of *The World Viewed*, Cavell says: "The importance of memory goes beyond its housing of knowledge. It arises also in the *way* movies are remembered or misremembered. That will be a live topic in what follows, before my way of studying films has been mostly through remembering them, like dreams. ... My business is to think out the causes of my consciousness of films as it stands."[133] In the first paragraphs of the second chapter of *The World Viewed*, Cavell continues:

> That it is reality that we have to deal with, or some mode of depicting it, finds surprising confirmation in the way movies are remembered, and misremembered. It is tempting to suppose that movies are hard to remember the way dreams are, and that is not a bad analogy. As with dreams, you do sometimes *find* yourself remembering moments in a film, and a procedure in *trying* to remember is to find your way back to a characteristic mood the thing has left you with. But, unlike dreams, other people can help you remember, indeed are often indispensable to the enterprise of remembering. Movies are hard to remember, the way

the actual events of yesterday are. And yet, again like dreams, *certain moments from films viewed decades ago will nag as vividly as moments of childhood. It is as if you had to remember what happened before you slept. Which suggests that film awakens as much as it enfolds you.*[134]

And yet, movies are *not* dreams, as Cavell notes in the chapter "End of Myths": "Here is an obvious reason not to be quick about equating films with dreams. Most dreams are boring narratives (like most tales of neurotic or physical symptoms), their skimpy surface out of all proportion with their riddle interest and their effect on the dreamer. To speak of film adventures or glamours or comedies as dreams is a dream of dreams: it doesn't capture the wish behind the dream, but merely the wish to have interesting dreams."[135] When Cavell returned, later in the same decade, to offer us more of *The World Viewed*, he wrote: "The moral of film's image of skepticism is not that reality is a dream and not that reality confines our dreams. In screening reality, film screens its givenness from us; it holds reality from us, it holds reality before us, i.e., withholds reality before us. ... To know how far reality is open to our dreams would be to know how far reality is confined by our dreams of it."[136]

Is it too much to remember that the volume in which Cavell's remarks appeared—quoted above from "On Makavejev on Bergman"—was entitled *Film and Dreams*?[137] So even as Cavell concludes "More of the World Viewed" by saying it is "wrong to think of movies in terms of dreams and hallucinations,"[138] he writes at the outset of *The World Viewed*, in the first edition, as noted above, and recapitulated here for renewed effect: "Memories of movies are strand over strand with memories of my life."[139] While the movies themselves are not dreams, they may figure in my own and yours; our knowledge of movies serving as a marker for self-knowledge, knowledge of others, and knowledge of the world that movie-knowledge is said to address and respond to. In this way, Cavell's description of the double helical relationship between movies and memories—that is, of their ineluctably and mutually reinforcing entwined existence—provides another instance when the personal is philosophical. Memories, like dreams, and the reflections we have on both, must be issued from a given place and time in the life of the mind and the experience it inhabits.

Movie watching—and the thoughts we have after such viewing—provides for our consideration an illustrative scene of such intimacies. Cavell has written compellingly, for instance, about a culture (presumably still our own) in which the rewatching of films is not habitual (perhaps save for *cinéastes*)—"(who says all films are meant for one viewing?)" he writes parenthetically. And while movies themselves do not change, we viewers do seem to change from one screening to the next (suggesting that, once again, our consciousness of film is, in great measure, susceptible to what we can see and hear, cognitively process on a given occasion, and thereafter remember).[140] After Cavell says: "I do not deny that movies, of the kind represented by the comedies and melodramas we are considering, are made to be interesting and satisfying on one viewing (drawing tears, laughter, thrills) and without serious thought," he says, again parenthetically: "(This raises the, for me, fascinating question of why a piece of music is appreciated so essentially in its endless repetition and familiarity, whereas with films, even in the era of videos, DVDs, and classical movie television channels, it is still common to hear that a reason not to see a film is that one has already seen it.)"[141] Perhaps easier access to digital content has made this pretension less widespread; or perhaps reviewing a film does not yet carry with it the demand to address its philosophical offerings.

Where would memories and dreams fall in the cleaving between the once-and-done and the pleasures of "endless repetition and familiarity"? How sad that one of our most prominent experiences of memories presented in endless repetition and familiarity appears linked to trauma—as in the expression of post-traumatic stress? Here memories are not akin to dreams but nightmares. And we are customarily told, especially when faced with our role in such pathologies, that we "tell ourselves stories," or are implicated in a movie-like scenario in which a memory was, in fact, a form of "replaying a movie." Where or what, in fact, accounts for our pleasure in some forms of repetition and familiarity and our pain in other forms? And what can be said for a person's degree of (conscious) control in the reception of a piece of music, or a film, or a novel? How regularly meaning is said to be "projected" (like a movie?) onto a memory or a dream. Emerson insists on a subjective explanation for our favor with a given work—"'Tis the good reader that makes the good book."[142] But could not our relation to the work intimate how the good book makes the reader? And likewise, while the film remains the same, it teaches us once again on each viewing (even as we come to it perennially from a different footing and therefore with a changed perspective).

After an attempted analysis of some ways that memories, dreams, and reflections figure in this collection—chasing, as I have, after some of their permutations and associations—it can seem, at last, that they are not three but one—variations on a shared theme: to remember (re-member; to put back together again, reconstitute); to dream (as if to conjure a reality or consider a vision); and to reflect (re-flect; see anew or think in a new light because something has been "bent back," returned). Thus, in the present case—as a sort of invitation to consider these three phenomena—remembering Cavell means dreaming him up (from our memories) and reflecting on both, which thereafter draws us into further memories and not a few more dreams.

However a reader approaches the terms (as a trinity or a unity), she may recognize their presence in the following memoranda from memories. Among other subjects, an abiding concern or set of questions may include: what it means to dream with Cavell as we continue to think with his work (while being thankful for it)? In remembering (looking back) and dreaming (looking ahead) do we inhabit a dialectic—a kind of backward and forward to what was or might have been, and to what might be? As we turn to the roster of reflections here gathered, let us consider the dreams contributors have had about the way Cavell's contributions figure in philosophy, film, literature, fine art, music, and other discourses. Now, after his death, what are our dreams for Cavell's patrimony? And do those dreams clarify what we should do with his work—what we must say about it and what we have learned from it?

On the question of whose task this is to do—who might be an audience for Cavell's work in the time to come, how a practice of reading Cavell's writing might create such an audience—we could do little better than invoke Cavell's own sense that we will discover those "who are alive" to the value of such projects and practices as Cavell has proposed to our attention "and who are prepared—it is heartening to see—to accept the labors as well as the pleasures of their inheritance."[143] (We may ourselves be such people, or aspire to be.) In this tandem state—bound by an obligation to do right by what has been bequeathed and animated by an attempt to enjoy the expression of discovery—we may conclude by hearkening to Stanley Cavell's own dream: "So I must hope that it has been amply obvious that I have not thought of my readings as being complete in being exhaustive, but rather as being whole in being autonomous, in achieving sufficient directedness, sufficient integrity and extent, to arrive at conclusions, but ones which are provisional, so that others are prompted to continue them."[144] Here, as elsewhere, we take up the invitation to our inheritance.

Notes

1. Stanley Cavell, *A Pitch of Philosophy: Autobiographical Exercises* (Cambridge: Harvard University Press, 1994), 36; and *Contesting Tears: The Hollywood Melodrama of the Unknown Woman* (Chicago: University of Chicago Press, 1996), 222.

2. Ralph Waldo Emerson, "Self-Reliance," *The Complete Works of Ralph Waldo Emerson*, Concord Edition, ed. Edward Waldo Emerson (Boston: Houghton, Mifflin, 1903–4), vol. II, 1841, 45.

3. "'What Becomes of Thinking on Film?' (Stanley Cavell in conversation with Andrew Klevan)," *Film as Philosophy: Essays in Cinema after Wittgenstein and Cavell*, ed. Rupert Read and Jerry Goodenough (New York: Palgrave Macmillan, 2005), 191.

4. Ibid.

5. For example, Marshall Cohen's piece first appeared in the *Los Angeles Review of Books*, Mark Greif's work was published in *n+1*, and Timothy Gould's dispatch was featured in the newsletter of the *American Society for Aesthetics*; initial versions of Steven Affeldt's, Sandra Laugier's, and Toril Moi's remarks

were given at a Harvard event a few months after Cavell's death, while Andrew Klevan's were presented at the Sorbonne a couple seasons later; and Charles Bernstein's notes began as an anonymous referee's report—now declassified—on what would become Cavell's *Philosophy the Day after Tomorrow*.

6 Ted Cohen, Paul Guyer, and Hilary Putnam, ed., *Pursuits of Reason: Essays in Honor of Stanley Cavell* (Lubbock: Texas Tech University Press, 1993). The section title is drawn from Emerson's journal: "Swifter than light the World converts itself into that thing you name & all things find their right place under this new & capricious classification." Ralph Waldo Emerson, *Journals and Miscellaneous Notebooks*, VIII (1841), ed. William H. Gilman and J. E. Parsons (Cambridge: Belknap Press of Harvard University Press, 1970), 23. See also my *Emerson's English Traits and the Nature History of Metaphor* (New York: Bloomsbury, 2013), §22, 328.

7 Emerson, *Journals and Miscellaneous Notebooks*, VIII, 23.

8 Kenneth Dauber and Walter Jost, "Introduction: The Varieties of Ordinary Language Criticism," *Ordinary Language Criticism: Literary Thinking after Cavell after Wittgenstein*, ed. Kenneth Dauber and Walter Jost (Evanston: Northwestern University Press, 2003), xvi.

9 Thanks are gratefully offered to Hent de Vries for a discussion on these topics.

10 The quotations in this sentence and the one to follow are drawn from a correspondence concerning the concept with Herwig Friedl.

11 Martin Heidegger, *What Is Called Thinking? [Was Heisst Denken?]*, trans. J. Glenn Gray (New York: Perennial, 1976).

12 See www.gedankenschrift.at.

13 See Johann Michael Schmid's *Grundsätze für eine allgemeine Sprachlehre: zugleich als Erklärung und Rechtfertigung seines Gedankenverzeichnisses* (Dilingen: Leonard Brönner, 1807), 1, 5, 117, 120. I am grateful to Kizer Walker for his invaluable input on remarks and references in this paragraph.

14 I express thanks to Peter Gilgen, who generously workshopped conceptual contenders with me and relayed astute comments with both admonitions and options.

15 Ralph Waldo Emerson, "The American Scholar," *Complete Works*, vol. I, 1837, 100.

16 Ibid., 84, 89, 91, 100. Italics added.

17 See the open-access, commemorative issue of *Conversations: The Journal of Cavellian Studies*, no. 7 (June 19, 2019): *Acknowledging Stanley Cavell*, ed. David LaRocca; and David LaRocca, ed., *The Thought of Stanley Cavell and Cinema: Turning Anew to the Ontology of Film a Half-Century after* The World Viewed (New York: Bloomsbury, 2020).

18 Stanley Cavell, *Emerson's Transcendental Etudes*, ed. David Justin Hodge (Stanford: Stanford University Press, 2003), 4.

19 For more on thinking and thanking, see my "Acknowledgments: Thinking of and Thanking Stanley Cavell," *Conversations*, no. 7 (2019): *Acknowledging Stanley Cavell*.

20 Cavell, *A Pitch of Philosophy*, 49.

21 Ibid., 48.

22 Emerson, *Nature, Complete Works*, vol. I, 1836, 10.

23 Stein writes: "No one thinks thanks." Gertrude Stein, *A Novel of Thank You* (Champaign: Dalkey Archive Press, 1994), 235. See also *Conversations*, no. 7 (2019): *Acknowledging Stanley Cavell* for additional voices on the reception of Cavell's work, including still more disciplinary vantage points.

24 Arthur C. Danto, "Philosophy and/as Film and/as if Philosophy," *October*, vol. 23, Winter 1982, 13–14.

25 Stanley Cavell, *Cities of Words: Pedagogical Letters on a Register of the Moral Life* (Cambridge: Belknap Press of Harvard University Press, 2004), 15.

26 From memorial remarks offered by Charles Bernstein in Emerson Hall at Harvard University, "Celebrating the Life and Work of Stanley Cavell," November 10, 2018.

27 William H. Gass's question was posed in response to the manuscript of *Estimating Emerson: An Anthology of Criticism from Carlyle to Cavell*, ed. David LaRocca (New York: Bloomsbury, 2013).

28 See my "Changing the Subject: The Auto/biographical as the Philosophical in Wittgenstein," *Epoché: A Journal for the History of Philosophy*, vol. 12, no. 1, Fall 2007; "Reading Cavell Reading," *Stanley Cavell, Literature, and Film: The Idea of America*, ed. Andrew Taylor and Áine Kelly (New York: Routledge Interdisciplinary Perspectives on Literature, 2012); "Note to Self: Learning to Write Autobiographical Remarks from Wittgenstein," *Wittgenstein Reading*, ed. Sascha Bru, Wolfgang Huemer, and Daniel Steuer (Berlin: De Gruyter, 2013); and "Achilles' Tears: Cavell, the *Iliad*, and Possibilities for the Human," *Stanley Cavell on Aesthetic Understanding*, ed. Garry L. Hagberg (New York: Palgrave Macmillan, 2018).

29 Cavell, *Cities of Words*, 8.

30 See, for example, Pierre Hadot, *Philosophy as a Way of Life: Spiritual Exercises from Socrates to Foucault*, ed. Arnold I. Davidson, trans. Michael Chase (Oxford: Blackwell, 1995). See also my "Changing the Subject" and "Note to Self."

31 From memorial remarks offered by Steven Affeldt in Emerson Hall at Harvard University, "Celebrating the Life and Work of Stanley Cavell," November 10, 2018.

32 Stanley Cavell, *The Claim of Reason: Wittgenstein, Skepticism, Morality, and Tragedy* (New York: Oxford University Press, 1979/1999), xv.

33 Cavell, *Emerson's Transcendental Etudes*, 2.

34 Ibid.

35 Henry James, "The Middle Years," *Henry James: Complete Stories 1892–1898*, ed. David Bromwich (New York: Library of America, 1996), 349.
36 See, for example, my "Translating Carlyle: Ruminating on the Models of Metafiction at the Emergence of an Emersonian Vernacular," *Religions*, ed. Kenneth S. Sacks and Daniel Koch, vol. 8, no. 8, 2017.
37 Cavell, *Emerson's Transcendental Etudes*, 3.
38 Ralph Waldo Emerson, "The Poet," *Complete Works*, vol. III, 1844, 21.
39 Ibid., 26.
40 Cavell, *Emerson's Transcendental Etudes*, 18. See also Sharon Cameron, "The Way of Life by Abandonment: Emerson's Impersonal," *Critical Inquiry*, vol. 25, 1998; Branka Arsić, *On Leaving: A Reading in Emerson* (Cambridge: Harvard University Press, 2010), 8–9, 92–4; and *American Impersonal: Essays with Sharon Cameron*, ed. Branka Arsić (New York: Bloomsbury, 2014), 11–13.
41 Emerson, "The Poet," vol. III, 27.
42 Ralph Waldo Emerson, "Fate," *Complete Works*, vol. VI, 1844, 47.
43 Cavell, *Emerson's Transcendental Etudes*, 198; italics in original. See also chapter 10, 192–214.
44 Cavell, *Emerson's Transcendental Etudes*, 198.
45 Plato, "Phaedrus," *The Dialogues of Plato*, trans. Benjamin Jowett, vol. I, 3rd ed. (New York: Random House, [1871] 1892), 245c–9d.
46 In *A Pitch of Philosophy*, Cavell asks of the spelling of his family surname—"Cavalerskii or Cavaleriiskii?," 28; in *Little Did I Know: Excerpts from Memory* (Stanford: Stanford University Press, 2010), he offers an alternate spelling and does not question it: "Kavelieruskii," 200. See also remarks on naming and Cavell (and his name) in my *Emerson's English Traits and the Nature History of Metaphor* (New York: Bloomsbury, 2013), esp. chapter 16, "Titles Manifold."
47 On this point, see my "Not Following Emerson: Intelligibility and Identity in the Authorship of Literature, Science, and Philosophy," *The Midwest Quarterly*, vol. 54, no. 2, Winter 2013, 115–35.
48 Ralph Waldo Emerson, "Experience," *Complete Works*, vol. III, 1844, 85; Cavell, *Emerson's Transcendental Etudes*, 136, 221, 245.
49 Prior to the development of *Emerson's Transcendental Etudes*, I devoted a third of my doctoral dissertation, *The Fate of Embodiment* (2000), advised in part by Cavell, to the topic of inheritance; "the anxiety of inheritance" is the title of a chapter in that work. In the wake of *Emerson's Transcendental Etudes*, I addressed certains habits and tendencies of Cavell's interpretative practice in "Reading Cavell Reading." In a monograph entitled *Emerson's English Traits and the Nature History of Metaphor* (2013), I explored the adjacencies and imbrications of literal and figurative inheritance—the biological and the intellectual, the gene and the meme, and so on; hence, "traits" finds its proximity to variations on conception and conceptualization.

These investigations of inheritance and Cavell's art of interpretation are, in turn, placed in relation to reading Emerson, as in: "Not Following Emerson: Intelligibility and Identity in the Authorship of Literature, Science, and Philosophy," *The Midwest Quarterly*, vol. 54, no. 2, Winter 2013; and Melville, as in: "The European Authorization of American Literature and Philosophy: After Cavell, Reading *Bartleby* with Deleuze, Then Rancière," *Melville among the Philosophers*, ed. Corey McCall and Tom Nurmi with an afterword by Cornel West (Lanham: Lexington Books, 2017). For another approach to the notion of reading (and misreading), see also Joseph Urbas, "How Close a Reader of Emerson Is Stanley Cavell?" *Journal of Speculative Philosophy*, vol. 31, no. 4, 2017, 557–74.

50 Emerson, "Self-Reliance," 45.
51 Cavell, *The Claim of Reason*, 125.
52 Ibid., 76, 60.
53 Ibid., 74.
54 See my "Introduction: Charlie Kaufman and Philosophy's Questions," *The Philosophy of Charlie Kaufman*, ed. David LaRocca (Lexington: University Press of Kentucky, 2011; with a new preface by the editor, 2019), 1.
55 See K. L. Evans, "Emerson; or, the Critic—The Arnoldian Ideal," *A Power to Translate the World: New Essays on Emerson and International Culture*, ed. David LaRocca and Ricardo Miguel-Alfonso (Hanover: Dartmouth College Press, 2015), 185–201.
56 Richard Moran, "Cavell as a Way into Philosophy," *Conversations*, no. 7, 2019, *Acknowledging Stanley Cavell*, 14.
57 Moran, "Cavell as a Way into Philosophy," 16–17.
58 Cavell, *Emerson's Transcendental Etudes*, 24.
59 Ibid.
60 Ibid., 24–5.
61 Cavell and Klevan, "What Becomes of Thinking on Film?," 190; italics in original.
62 Ibid., 191.
63 See Cavell, *Cities of Words*, 193, 195, 198, 203–4.
64 For more on *Adam's Rib*, see, of course, Cavell's "The Courting of Marriage," *Pursuits of Happiness: The Hollywood Comedy of Remarriage* (Cambridge: Harvard University Press, 1981), 189–228 and chapter 10, *Cities of Words*, 190–207. See also my "On the Aesthetics of Amateur Filmmaking in Narrative Cinema: Negotiating Home Movies after *Adam's Rib*," *The Thought of Stanley Cavell and Cinema*, 245–90.
65 For more on Cavell's coupling of film and philosophy, see my introduction to *The Thought of Stanley Cavell and Cinema*, 1–20.
66 Stanley Cavell, *The Senses of Walden: An Expanded Edition* (San Francisco: North Point Press, 1981), 33, 123.

67 For more on literary and philosophical tropes of descent, heritability, and evolution as they interact with nineteenth-century natural science, see my *Emerson's English Traits and the Natural History of Metaphor*. See also n. 49.
68 Cavell, *Emerson's Transcendental Etudes*, 26.
69 Cavell and Klevan, "What Becomes of Thinking on Film?," 191.
70 Ralph Waldo Emerson, *The Journals and Miscellaneous Notebooks of Ralph Waldo Emerson*, ed. Alfred R. Ferguson (Cambridge: Belknap Press of Harvard University Press, 1964), vol. IV, 50; see also John Lysaker, *Emerson and Self-Culture* (Bloomington: Indiana University Press, 2008), 6, 41, 159, 175.
71 Friedrich Nietzsche, "Raids of an Untimely Man," *Estimating Emerson*, 284; italics in original. See also my "Emerson Recomposed: Nietzsche's Uses of His American 'Soul-Brother,'" *Nietzsche and the Philosophers*, ed. Mark T. Conard (New York: Routledge, 2017); and "Una traduzione transatlantica: Fato e libertà in Emerson e nel giovane Nietzsche" ["Transatlantic Translation: Young Nietzsche Writing Toward Emerson"], *Nietzsche e l'America*, ed. and trans., Sergio Franzese, Nietzsceana Saggi 2 (Edizioni ETS, 2005).
72 See William Rothman, *Tuitions and Intuitions: Essays at the Intersection of Film Criticism and Philosophy* (Albany: State University of New York Press, 2019).
73 Stanley Cavell, "A Reply to John Hollander," *Themes Out of School: Effects and Causes* (San Francisco: North Point Press, 1984), 143. Cavell, *Emerson's Transcendental Etudes*, 114.
74 Ibid.
75 Ibid.
76 For more on this line of thought, see David LaRocca and Ricardo Miguel-Alfonso, ed., *A Power to Translate the World: New Essays on Emerson and International Culture* (Hanover: Dartmouth College Press, 2015), part of Donald E. Pease's *Re-Mapping the Transnational: A Dartmouth Series in American Studies*. See also, Donald E. Pease, "Re-Mapping the Transnational Turn," *Re-Framing the Transnational Turn in American Studies*, ed. Winfried Fluck, Donald E. Pease, and John Carlos Rowe (Hanover: Dartmouth College Press, 2011).
77 The very notion (proposal) of cosmopolitanism remains in flux—from K. Anthony Appiah's *Cosmopolitanism: Ethics in a World of Strangers* (New York: W. W. Norton, 2006) to Rosi Braidotti, Patrick Hanafin, and Bolette Blaagaard, ed., *After Cosmopolitanism* (New York: Routledge, 2013). In the context of reading Emerson on the national, international, transnational, and cosmopolitan, see LaRocca and Miguel-Alfonso, *A Power to Translate the World*.
78 Cavell, *A Pitch of Philosophy*, 47.
79 Ibid.
80 Richard Fleming and Michael Payne, ed., *The Senses of Stanley Cavell* (Lewisburg: Bucknell University Press, 1989), 65; Stanley Cavell, *Pursuits of*

Happiness: The Hollywood Comedy of Remarriage (Cambridge: Harvard University Press, 1981), 12.

81 Cavell, *A Pitch of Philosophy*, 144.
82 Cavell, *Cities of Words*, and earlier in Stanley Cavell, "Stella's Taste: Reading *Stella Dallas*," *Contesting Tears*, 212–13. See also Richard Eldridge, "Cavell and Hölderlin on Human Immigrancy," *The Persistence of Romanticism: Essays in Philosophy and Literature* (Cambridge: Cambridge University Press, 2001), 229–46.
83 Cavell, *A Pitch of Philosophy*, 144.
84 See in this volume, Marshall Cohen, chapter 1, 58.
85 Cohen's piece originally appeared in the *Los Angeles Review of Books* as "Must We Mean What We Say? On the Life and Thought of Stanley Cavell," April 27, 2018. See in this volume, chapter 1.
86 George Steiner, *Errata: An Examined Life* (New Haven: Yale University Press, 1998), 172–3.
87 Cavell, *Emerson's Transcendental Etudes*, 45, 60–1, 66, 114, 171, 192, 194, 210, 222.
88 Stephen Mulhall, "On Refusing to Begin," *Contending with Stanley Cavell*, ed. Russell B. Goodman (New York: Oxford University Press, 2005), 22–36. As an example of Cavell's own interest in beginning, noting the humor when he says, "Of course … I begin with afterthoughts," see also Stanley Cavell, "Notes and Afterthoughts on the Opening of Wittgenstein's *Investigations*," *The Cambridge Companion to Wittgenstein*, ed. Hans Sluga and David G. Stern (Cambridge: Cambridge University Press, 1996), chapter 8.
89 Michael Fischer, *Stanley Cavell and Literary Skepticism* (Chicago: University of Chicago Press); Richard Eldridge, "Between Acknowledgment and Avoidance," *Stanley Cavell* (Cambridge: Cambridge University Press, 2003), 1–14; and Catherine Wheatley, *Stanley Cavell and Film: Skepticism and Self-Reliance at the Cinema* (New York: Bloomsbury, 2019), see esp. "The Avoidance of Cavell" (11–17) and "Cavell and Film Studies" (17–23).
90 See again, Steiner, *Errata*, 172.
91 Garrett Stewart, "The Avoidance of Stanley Cavell," *Contending with Stanley Cavell*, 141.
92 Ibid.
93 Cavell, *The Claim of Reason*, 125. See my "'You Must Change Your Life': *The Americans* (Concepts and Cults of) Authenticity, and EST," *The Americans and Philosophy*, ed. Robert Arp and Kevin Guilfoy (Chicago: Open Court, 2018); "The Education of Grown-Ups: An Aesthetics of Reading Cavell," *Journal of Aesthetic Education*, vol. 47, no. 2, Summer 2013; "Were We Educated for This? Paideia, Agonism, and the Liberal Arts," *Girls and Philosophy: This Book Isn't a Metaphor for Anything*, ed. Richard Greene and Rachel Robison-Greene (Chicago: Open Court, 2014); and "A Desperate Education: Reading Thoreau's *Walden* in Douglas Sirk's *All That Heaven Allows*," *Film and Philosophy*, vol. 8, 2004. And see also *Stanley*

Cavell and the Education of Grownups, ed. Naoko Saito and Paul Standish (New York: Fordham University Press, 2012).

94 Cavell, *A Pitch of Philosophy*, 36; and *Contesting Tears*, 222.
95 Ibid., 37.
96 Ibid., 37–8.
97 See James Conant, "The Triumph of the Gift over the Curse in Stanley Cavell's *Little Did I Know*," MLN, vol. 126, 2012, 1004–13.
98 Cavell, "On Makavejev on Bergman," *Themes Out of School*, 121.
99 See my "On the Aesthetics of Amateur Filmmaking in Narrative Cinema," 284 n.20.
100 Emerson, *Nature*, *Complete Works*, vol. I, 3; "No facts are to me sacred; none are profane; I simply experiment, an endless seeker, with no Past at my back," Emerson, "Circles," *Complete Works*, vol. II, 1841, 318.
101 Emerson, "Experience," 49. See my "Memory Man: The Constitution of Personal Identity in *Memento* (and Some Metaphysical and Moral Implications of Choosing Not to Remember)," *The Philosophy of Christopher Nolan*, ed. Jason T. Eberl and George A. Dunn (Lanham: Lexington Books, 2017); and "Weimar Cognitive Theory: Modernist Narrativity and the Metaphysics of Frame Stories (After *Caligari* and Kracauer)," *The Fictional Minds of Modernism: Narrative Cognition from Henry James to Christopher Isherwood*, ed. Ricardo Miguel-Alfonso (New York: Bloomsbury, 2020).
102 Cavell, "A Reply to John Hollander," 144. See also my *Emerson's English Traits and the Natural History of Metaphor*.
103 See Cavell and Klevan, "What Becomes of Thinking on Film?," 169.
104 William Rothman, "Cavell on Film, Television, and Opera," *Stanley Cavell*, ed. Richard Eldridge (Cambridge: Cambridge University Press, 2003), 209.
105 Cavell, "On Makavejev on Bergman," 132.
106 Cavell, *Little Did I Know*, 132.
107 Cavell, *Cities of Words*, 15. "I was surprised to find Freud repeatedly denying that what he did was to be called philosophy, since it was nothing if not an examination of one's life."
108 Cavell, *Little Did I Know*, 231.
109 Ibid., 234. See also *Cities of Words*, 283, where "the method of analysis, which Freud was so proud to have discovered," was connected to "the world-historical discoveries of Copernicus and of Darwin."
110 Cavell, *Cities of Words*, 283.
111 Ibid., 290.
112 Ibid., 292.
113 Cavell, *Emerson's Transcendental Etudes*, 19, 39, 172, 222, 252n12. See also, Emerson, "New England Reformers," *Complete Works*, vol. III, 1844, 269. See also how the substitution of terms ("silent" for "secret") ripple

into commentary by others, as in Cohen's attribution in this volume, chapter 1, 56.

114   Stanley Cavell, "Reflections on a Life of Philosophy: An Interview with Stanley Cavell," *The Harvard Review of Philosophy*, vol. 7, 1999, 25.

115   See my "Reading Cavell Reading"; and Joseph Urbas, "How Close a Reader of Emerson Is Stanley Cavell?" *Journal of Speculative Philosophy*, vol. 31, no. 4, 2017, 557–74.

116   Emerson, "The Poet," vol. III, 33; "Experience," vol. III, 50, 65.

117   Emerson, "Experience," vol. III, 84.

118   William Shakespeare, *The Tempest*, IV.1, Folger Shakespeare Library (New York: Simon & Schuster, 1994, 2016).

119   Stanley Cavell, "Texts of Recovery (Coleridge, Wordsworth, Heidegger)," *In Quest of the Ordinary: Lines of Skepticism and Romanticism* (Chicago: University of Chicago Press, 1988), 52; Cavell, *The Claim of Reason*, 437, 447, 449.

120   See note 86 and see also William Day, "I Don't Know, Just Wait: Remembering Remarriage in *Eternal Sunshine of the Spotless Mind*," *The Philosophy of Charlie Kaufman*, ed. David LaRocca (Lexington: University Press of Kentucky, 2011), 132–54.

121   For Cavell's remarks on utopia and the utopian in *Cities of Words*, see 17–18, 207, 413, 447.

122   Emerson, "Experience," vol. III, 65.

123   See Lawrence F. Rhu, *Stanley Cavell's American Dream: Shakespeare, Philosophy, and Hollywood Movies* (New York: Fordham University Press, 2006).

124   James Conant, "Cavell and the Concept of America," *Contending with Stanley Cavell*, 55–81.

125   Stanley Cavell, *The World Viewed: Reflections on the Ontology of Film* (Cambridge: Harvard University Press, 1971, enlarged edition, 1979), 5–6.

126   *To the Limit and Then Beyond It: The Ecstatic World of Filmmaker Werner Herzog* (1989), 00:03:38.

127   See my "'Profoundly Unreconciled to Nature': Ecstatic Truth and the Humanistic Sublime in Werner Herzog's War Films," *The Philosophy of War Films*, ed. David LaRocca (Lexington: University Press of Kentucky, 2014), 437–82.

128   See, for example, Noël Carroll, "Revisiting *The World Viewed*," *The Thought of Stanley Cavell and Cinema*, 41–62.

129   See in this volume, Andrew Klevan, chapter 2.

130   Cavell, *The World Viewed*, xix.

131   Cavell, *Cities of Words*, 293.

132   See my introduction "Philosophy's Claim to Film, Film's Claim to Philosophy," *The Thought of Stanley Cavell and Cinema*, 1–20.

133 Cavell, *The World Viewed*, 12; italics in original.
134 Ibid., 16–17; italics in original.
135 Ibid., 67.
136 Ibid., 189.
137 Vlada Petrić, ed., *Film and Dreams: An Approach to Bergman* (South Salem: Redgrave, 1981).
138 Cavell, *The World Viewed*, 211.
139 Ibid., xix.
140 Cavell, *Cities of Words*, 159.
141 Ibid., 272.
142 Emerson, "Success," *Complete Works*, vol. VII, 1870 (from lectures given in 1858–9), 296.
143 Cavell, *Pursuits of Happiness*, 278.
144 Ibid.

I

Standard Considerations

1

Must We Mean What We Say?

On the Life and Thought of Stanley Cavell

MARSHALL COHEN

THE BOUNTIFULLY GIFTED STANLEY CAVELL was unique among American philosophers of his generation in the range of his philosophical, cultural, and artistic interests.[1] He resisted the split between Anglophone and Continental traditions that has characterized post-Kantian philosophy, writing with distinction about epistemology and aesthetics, Emerson and Thoreau, Shakespearean tragedy and Hollywood comedy, as well as about modernism in film and music. Modernist works, he believed, divide audiences into insiders and outsiders, create unpleasant cults, and demand for their reception the shock of conversion. Such works are not easily received, as Cavell, who regarded himself as a modernist writer, painfully discovered. Many features of his writing have been found troublesome and even offensive by a significant number of readers. I believe these features are not an expression of modernist impulses but rather manifestations of personal idiosyncrasies that Cavell's autobiographical reflections, in his 2010 book, *Little Did I Know: Excerpts from Memory*, can help us to understand, if not accept.

Little Did I Know obeys a double time scheme. It comprises a series of entries presented in their order of composition from July 2, 2003, to September 1, 2004. The depicted events reporting Cavell's Emersonian journey occur in loose chronological order, interrupted by philosophical meditations, portraits of friends, and editorial comments about the original drafted entries. The formal arrangement honors the fundamental importance granted to the time and context of utterance in the work of J. L. Austin and the late Wittgenstein. The depictions allow Cavell to exploit techniques reminiscent of psychoanalysis (free association) and film (flashbacks and flash forwards, jump cuts, close-ups, and montage). And modernism's experimental departures from traditional narrative facilitate his representation of philosophy as an abstraction of autobiography.

At the age of seven, Cavell and his parents left south Atlanta, where their extended family and most of the city's Eastern European Jews lived. During the next ten years, they moved back and forth between North Atlanta and Sacramento five times. This wandering life left Cavell, an only child, isolated and friendless, and he claims never to have drawn a happy breath in those years. His mother, an exceptionally gifted professional pianist blessed with perfect pitch, said she would rather be Stanley's mother than the mother of an emperor. She was trapped in an unhappy marriage and suffered migraines, a sort of melancholy that Cavell would later study in Hollywood melodramas. Cavell believed that his father, a struggling pawnbroker, wished him not to exist. His father's shame at his precarious business would later help Cavell recognize King Lear as ashamed (and find tragedy in a loving daughter's efforts to protect him from knowing it).

Cavell refused to take sides in his parents' quarrels, suggesting that this reaction manifested itself again in his reluctance to take sides in metaphysical conflicts. Cavell compares his own labors in the pawnshop to Dickens's in the blacking factory. His only solace in his adolescent years came from playing jazz in high school bands and ultimately lead alto in an otherwise black big band. But he discovers a poetry of pawnbroking many years later when writing *The Senses of Walden* (1972), finding Thoreau's book to be explicitly about the economic dimensions of human existence. His immigrant father, lacking any "ordinary" language, is nevertheless a masterful teller of well-pointed Yiddish stories. They attune Cavell to Austin's stories and examples (such as shooting one's donkey by accident or by mistake) that reveal the subtle but significant distinctions embodied in ordinary language. At the age of six, Cavell permanently damaged his left ear in an automobile accident, and possession of an "ear"—crucial to the detection of "voice"—became a major theme of his thought.

His blissful, irreplaceable undergraduate years at Berkeley were devoted to music and theater. Writing incidental music for a production of *King Lear* revealed that he was more interested in the actions and ideas and language of the play than he was in the music in which he expressed what he could of his sense of those actions and ideas. In a music theory class with Ernest Bloch, his ability to discern and appreciate the difference between a Bach chorale played on the piano with and without a halftone altered spoke to him of a domain of culture beyond the world he knew. Cavell dates from that time the knowledge of the moral life as containing a dimension of what he came to call Emersonian perfectionism. But it was not until ten years later that he found elements of a voice in philosophy that permitted his participation in that perspective.

Although he matriculated for a year in the Juilliard extension division ostensibly continuing his composition studies, he in fact spent ten to twelve hours a day reading Freud, attending Broadway plays, frequenting 42nd Street revival houses, and devouring little magazines like *Partisan Review*. Indeed, his account of his childhood and adolescence is strongly reminiscent of the Jewish fiction *Partisan Review* was publishing in that period. He next undertook the study of philosophy at UCLA and then at Harvard, where he commenced his lifelong struggle with professional philosophy—and, until he met Austin, almost abandoned it.

When Cavell entered the Harvard graduate program in philosophy in 1951, it did not seem an obvious place for someone with his talents and inclinations to inaugurate his career. (I entered the program in the same year and make a number of appearances in Cavell's memoir.) As Cavell saw it, logical positivism constituted the avant-garde in many of the major philosophy departments, and he often considered leaving philosophy before he came into contact with Austin in 1955. Cavell reports that rarely in a life can one know intellectual gratitude of the kind he felt after attending Austin's seminar and finding in his theory of performative utterances a way beyond positivist theories of meaning. More generally, Cavell found in the ordinary language philosopher's practice of asking "what we say when" a way to use himself as a source of philosophical evidence. In doing so, he felt for the first time his pertinence to philosophy. He had begun to find his voice.

The second half of Cavell's memoir is, he says, mainly an account of an American academic life. In his case, it was a notably distinguished one: fellowships in Harvard's Society of Fellows and at the Institute for Advanced Study at Princeton, faculty appointments at Berkeley and Harvard, where he was Walter M. Cabot Professor Emeritus of Aesthetics and the General Theory of Value at the time of his death in 2018. Over the course of his career, he developed significant friendships with Terrence Malick, Michael Fried, John Harbison, Thomas Kuhn, Seymour Shifrin, Morton White, Bernard Williams, and Hilary Putnam, as well as with the two philosophers he was closest to, Rogers Albritton and Thompson Clarke. But the main topics of the second half of Cavell's book are his struggle to write and the difficulties attending the reception of his work.

In the months before Cavell came East to take up his faculty position at Harvard, Jerry Fodor and Jerrold Katz of MIT published an attack on the two articles Cavell had submitted (along with his dissertation) for consideration in his tenure candidacy. Cavell remembers them as saying that the articles were "deleterious to the future of philosophy." (What they actually said was that they were "pernicious both for an adequate understanding of ordinary language philosophy and for an adequate understanding of ordinary language.") Cavell regarded their dismissal as unmitigatedly vicious. (This incident will remind the reader of the moment in Cavell's childhood when his enraged father picked up his son's empty clarinet case and threw it into the garbage.) These essays were included in his first book, *Must We Mean What We Say?* (1969)—which, he reports, was greeted with a silence and dismay that, with fond exceptions, lasted for twenty years.

Cavell revised his dissertation irregularly over sixteen years; it was published as *The Claim of Reason* in 1979 and is regarded by those who make strong claims for Cavell as a philosopher as his masterpiece. In 1980, it was the subject of a symposium at the American Philosophical Society (at which I was present); the occasion proved a fiasco for Cavell. Barry Stroud, a distinguished epistemologist and former Berkeley colleague, offered a careful, penetrating examination and critique of Cavell's approach to skepticism and to Cavell's use of the concepts of acceptance and acknowledgment. Cavell responded abusively and unprofessionally to Stroud's highly professional, respectful paper. In reflecting on the event, Cavell concludes that his work creates infectious ill will among an imposing body of philosophers who know of it.

I believe Stroud bore Cavell no ill will and displayed none on this occasion, but there are certainly many who have been put off reading Cavell by the eccentricities of his prose and the obstacles put in the way of gaining a clear understanding of his arguments and positions. This is true even of many who acknowledge the fact that he is also capable of great eloquence and deep insight. I believe Cavell paid a great price for persuading himself, as he says in the memoir, that one can no more choose how one writes than one can choose what makes one happy. This is a preposterous claim and one that an Emersonian friend (editor, analyst, professional colleague) might have helped him abandon.

Many, especially philosophers, who aspire to impersonality in their work are offended by the insistent foregrounding of self in Cavell's writing. Some are also allergic to the craving for profundity he frequently exhibits. (Austin regarded this impulse as the mortal enemy of philosophy.) Is it helpful or simply pretentious to invoke Kant's metaphysics in explicating the barrier screen in *It Happened One Night* (1934)? Cavell's convoluted sentences frequently run sixty to eighty words in length; the main text of *The Claim of Reason* begins with a sentence 216 words long. Not surprisingly, his grammar has been found unstable and his intent often obscure. Asides, parentheses, and extended fragments constitute frequent distractions and diversions. His seventeen published volumes are repetitious and their frequent reformulations confusing. One reason for this is that Cavell would not let go of intuitions, allowing them into print before they had been satisfactorily refined, elaborated, or defended—before, as he says, the intuitions had been transformed into Emersonian tuitions. This is true even of the concepts most central to his philosophy—skepticism and the ordinary.

Cavell took skepticism to be the essential business of (modern) philosophy. In modern philosophy, skepticism is understood as a set of arguments supporting the view that we do not know (with certainty) the existence of the external world, of oneself, or of others. (In *The Claim of Reason*, Cavell perversely defines it as any view that raises the question of knowledge, whether it affirms or denies its possibility.) Richard Rorty and others consider the arguments of the epistemologist a frivolous form of academic make-work. By contrast, Cavell, like Thoreau and Emerson, found in skepticism something other than what skepticism finds in itself.

The refutation of skepticism was a major preoccupation of ordinary language philosophy, and in the years following his conversion Cavell became dissatisfied with the approach of Austin and the orthodox Wittgensteinians. The orthodox Wittgensteinian believes that one can refute skepticism by appeal to the criteria that govern the use of ordinary language. Thus, if someone's behavior satisfies the criteria for being in pain (wincing, groaning), the person exhibiting this behavior is in pain and one can know it. Cavell contends that this is a mistake and a misreading of Wittgenstein. The person may be feigning pain or exhibiting some other form of appearance. There are, at best, criteria of pain behavior, but there are no criteria for distinguishing feigning from reality. Furthermore, criteria depend on conventional agreements and it is always possible to violate conventional usage, to speak "outside the language game." The costs of employing language apart from ordinary criteria are high, however: not knowing what we are saying, having the illusion of meaning something, making claims to impossible privacies suggestive of madness. The skeptic cannot be refuted, but what the force of skepticism suggests is that, since we cannot know that the world exists, its presence to us cannot be a matter of knowing. In Cavell's view, the world is to be accepted and the presence of other minds acknowledged.

For Cavell, Shakespeare's tragedies engage the skeptical problematic. Lear knows that Cordelia loves him and Othello knows that Desdemona is chaste, but each of them brings on tragedy by attempting to disown the burden of knowledge. Lear interrogates Cordelia and Othello requires "ocular" proof; in each case, avoidance is disguised as a quest for knowledge. Tragedy is the place where we are not allowed to escape such cover. Othello's problem is his inability to forgive Desdemona for existing separate from him, for being flesh and blood. For if she is flesh and blood, then so is he, and this possibility tortures him. The source of Lear's tragedy is his inability to accept the human condition—his finitude, his separateness—to acknowledge what he already knows: that Cordelia loves him. Just as the skeptical epistemologist in his search for certainty loses the presence he craves, so the tragic hero in his quest for knowledge avoids what he already knows. What we need is not more knowledge but the willingness to forgo knowing. Cavell thereby aligns himself with Wittgenstein and Heidegger, who in their radically different ways call into question modern philosophy's obeisance to epistemology's preference for (certain) knowledge.

Cavell rejects the view that skepticism is simply a theoretical claim. Rather, it is, he thinks, a cover for an attempt to convert the human condition, our metaphysical finitude, into an intellectual difficulty. Sometimes he identifies this attempt with skepticism itself, sometimes he calls it an interpretation of skepticism; mainly, he conceives of it as a *cause* of skepticism. But while some such evasive cover may be at work in Othello's doubt about Desdemona's chastity or in Lear's of Cordelia's love, there is little reason to think that the modern epistemologist is engaged in any similar covering activity. Nor is he typically engaged in pondering the catastrophic skeptical consequences of the "New Science" to which Cavell frequently alludes. In the case of the ordinary language philosopher, his objective has not been to avoid acknowledging love or human separateness but to defeat skepticism and uncover bad arguments.

In addition to serving as a cover, Cavell believes that skepticism has as many guises as the Devil. It is this discovery that allows Cavell to bring so much of his thought, however sketchily, under the concept of skepticism. What is known to philosophy as skepticism is known to literature in Emerson and Thoreau's "silent melancholy" and "quiet desperation," in Wordsworth's perception of us as without "interest," in Poe's "perverseness." But it was most elaborately exhibited by Cavell in his analyses of the Shakespearean tragedies, in which he finds skepticism figured and allegorized. What philosophy knows as doubt, Othello's violence allegorizes as jealousy. Tragedy and skepticism have similar structures and rhythms. The precipitousness of skepticism's banishment of the world is figured in the precipitous banishments of the Lear story as it is in the extreme rapidity of progress from the completeness of Othello's love to the perfection of his doubt. But elsewhere, Cavell suggests a still closer connection: Lear's "avoidance" of Cordelia is an instance of the annihilation inherent in the skeptical problematic. And this suggests at some level of abstraction that the structures of skepticism and tragedy (and, presumably of all the other guises the Devil assumes) are identical. Tragedy, Cavell says, is an interpretation of what skepticism is itself an interpretation of. What that is, however, he does not say.

Cavell's concept of the ordinary undergoes an expansion similar to the one he located in the case of skepticism. Cavell tells us that what he has meant by the ordinary is something Emerson and Thoreau have meant in their devotion to the common, the familiar, the everyday, the low, the near. It is what Wordsworth means by the rustic and the common; it is figured in Plato's image of the cave and enacted in a dance routine of Fred Astaire's. The figuration Cavell has examined most carefully is, of course, that of marriage or the domestic. Skepticism is cloaked in literature as that which attacks the domestic. And, as skepticism is overcome by returning language to its ordinary uses, so threats to marriage are overcome by remarriage or by the restoration of the mutual, diurnal devotion of the ordinary or the everyday. A crucial moment in the development of Cavell's philosophy occurs when he intuits that Emerson and Thoreau's commitment to the ordinary underwrites the procedures of ordinary language philosophy. Cavell says that most of his colleagues would find the idea of underwriting ordinary language philosophy by transcendentalism about as promising as enlivening the passé via the extinct. I expect that the less historically minded among them would be more likely to find it about as promising as grounding the under-analyzed in the irrelevant. And they would certainly want to know more about what Cavell means by underwriting.

Cavell from the start discerned the essential elements of Emersonian perfectionism in the Hollywood films he studied. He found that these films investigate the personal relationships neglected by the dominant academic moral theories, utilitarianism, and Kantianism. The aim of moral perfectionism is not to lead one from irrationality to rationality through an appropriate distribution of satisfactions, as in Mill, or from a will corrupted by sensuous concerns to one measured and chastened by the moral law, as in Kant. The perfectionist journey is not from bad to good or from wrong to right; it involves a divided self that has lost its way moving from confusion to clarity. The aim is not to achieve the rational perfection of the Platonic sage but to progress toward an attainable next self in an attainable future society. For Emerson, the perfectionist journey takes one from unthinking conformism to self-reliance, a state in which one summons the courage to say, "I think," "I am." In doing so, he transforms himself from a ghost haunting the world to an existing human being. Emersonian morality defeats Cartesian skepticism, allowing one to find one's own voice.

In his 1981 book, *Pursuits of Happiness: The Hollywood Comedy of Remarriage*, Cavell studies a genre in which a romantic pair are not trying, as in classical comedy, to get together but to get *back* together. The women in these comedies are descendants of Ibsen's Nora: they are on a spiritual quest and in need of an education, which must be provided by the man within an atmosphere of equality. Nevertheless, the man will carry a taint of villainy, thus preparing the way for the complementary genre, the melodrama of the unknown woman. In Milton's conception, "a meet and happy conversation" is the chief and noblest end of marriage and it can be achieved only if the man relinquishes control (he must often play the fool) and the woman acknowledges her desire. The improvisatory battle of the characters in these "talkies" is an adventure in finding the truth.

The generic features of the melodrama of the unknown woman, studied in his 1996 book, *Contesting Tears*, can be derived by negation from those exhibited in the comedies of remarriage. The woman in the melodramas rejects marriage, which is destructive in the world she knows. The man is psychically frozen, and the woman alone seeks change. He cannot provide the education offered by the man in the comedies and he struggles against mutual recognition. Conversation is everywhere defeated by irony. There is no shared language, and the woman is unknown. But, like her comedic sisters, she is on a spiritual quest. Marriage is transcended (not reconsidered), and she seeks a self-reliance that will allow her to achieve her attainable but unattained self.

What philosophy calls friendship and the comedies figure as marriage is a central feature of moral perfectionism. The journey of perfectionism cannot be taken in the absence of the credible words of a friend who helps one find one's way. In the marriage comedies, the male character is the friend; in the melodramas of the unknown woman, the heroine must find and assert her own truth in the absence of a friend. The friend will need to be a provocateur, even an enemy, who contests one's present attainments. In the absence of such a friend's perhaps painful provocations, those unconscious or repressed thoughts and desires that represent one's unattained but attainable self would not be accomplished.

Emerson represents his writing as such a friend, and Thoreau considers writing an exposure to be read. Cavell, who was strongly attracted to Wittgenstein's use of philosophy as therapy and to Freudian psychoanalysis, offers an analytically oriented account of reading that considers the text as analyst and the reader as analysand. Such a reading will return one's repressed thoughts and desires to consciousness. They are the rejected thoughts that Emerson tells us will return with a certain alienated majesty. They represent our unattained but attainable self, and their return provides the perfectionist reader with the freedom to take a step toward a next attainable self.

With the change of the millennium, Cavell, a reverse Rip Van Winkle, awoke from a dream of work and found that there were a considerable number of strangers who apparently recognized him, or knew what he had been doing. I believe their numbers continue to grow. But much that has been written about him, especially by his philosophical admirers, appears to be motivated, as Cavell observes, by the sense that if his work were only explained a little more clearly, its readership would suddenly become fruitful and multiply. Admirable as some of this secondary literature is, however, Cavell's philosophical work will be fruitful and multiply only when philosophers engage it critically, find it useful, and perhaps develop it further. For the most part, this has not yet happened.

In his foreword to *The Claim of Reason*, Cavell writes that, when he says of Wittgenstein that he is "still *to be* received," he means to suggest that Wittgenstein's writing, "and of course not his alone, is essentially and always to be received, as thoughts must be that would refuse professionalization." It is the pathos of Cavell's situation that he longed for a wider professional acknowledgment that his work so often, and in my view so often unnecessarily, refuses.

Note

1 This essay first appeared in the *Los Angeles Review of Books*, April 27, 2019. Sincere thanks are extended to executive editor Boris Dralyuk for permission to reproduce the work here.

2

Cavell at Film Criticism

"An Unreadiness to Become Explicit"

ANDREW KLEVAN

This paper was originally delivered to a colloquium at the Sorbonne in Paris in June 2019 to commemorate Stanley Cavell's work one year after his passing. In it I repeat, while reorienting, some of my earlier work on Cavell so as to explore a feature of his writing, which I hadn't hitherto specifically addressed. Aside from some tidying, I have kept the paper in its original form as something written to be read out.

CLOSING HIS REVIEW OF STANLEY CAVELL'S BOOK *Contesting Tears: The Melodrama of the Unknown Woman* in the *Times Literary Supplement*, J. David Slocum wrote that the book succeeded "in extending the author's illuminating excursions into the lambent depths of film."[1] *Lambent depths*—this phrase resonated for me. My dictionary defines "lambent" as "of light or fire, glowing, gleaming, or flickering with a soft radiance, or softly over a surface." Flickering over a surface, and yet "depths"—"lambent depths"—as if it were something deep in these films that was causing the radiance. "Lambent depths" might even be suggesting a gleaming from the depths that was *not* quite reaching the surface. For this understanding, it is the depths that are lambent, not the surface. Either way, this is quite different from the glow that was so often attributed to Hollywood films of the Golden Age.

The commonly attributed glow emanated from something more like a shiny veneer, sprinkled with stardust, shrewdly created through technological and industrial trickery, playing out on that silver screen.

Lambent depths—flickering, gleaming perhaps, present, but not demonstrative, or palpable. There is a sense that, in the best films, there is more than is meeting the eye.

Stanley Cavell was one of the first writers, and has remained one of the best, for me, for capturing the sense, in relation to film, of "more than meets the eye." This is something I had thought was especially true of the best Hollywood films, but seemed also to be true of many good films (not only those from Hollywood). And furthermore, his best film criticism does not simply reveal the depths—much good criticism does that—but somehow remains faithful to the lambency, to the flickering, to the glow. At its best, his criticism doesn't turn up the light up too brightly. It's an art to illuminate and not overexpose.

I often find, when encountering work on or related to Cavell, that it is his thematics—skepticism, remarriage, the ordinary, unknownness, acknowledgment, perfectionism—that are alighted upon; or his theories about medium ontology; or his philosophy more generally and the philosophers he values. This is understandable because these things are present and important in his work. What I'm highlighting here is something else, and something more (than meets the eye).

Cavell is discussing the persistent use of double entendre in the film *Bringing Up Baby* (1938, dir. Howard Hawks). He writes:

> While an explicit discussion, anyway an open recognition, of the film's obsessive sexual references is indispensable to saying what I find the film to be about, I am ... reluctant to make it very explicit. ... It is part of the force of this work that we shall not know how far to press its references ... If it is undeniable that we are invited by these events to read them as sexual allegory, it is equally undeniable that what [Katharine] Hepburn says, as she opens the box and looks inside, is true: "It's just an old bone." Clearly George [the dog] agrees with her. The play between the literal and the allegorical determines the course of this narrative, and provides us with contradicting directions in our experience of it.[2]

"It is part of the force of this work," Cavell writes, "that we shall not know how far to press its references." For Cavell, an "explicit" articulation or transcription would be unfaithful to the suspension and latency, or embedded condition of the meanings, which distinguishes the film, and his experience of it. A straightforward translation or decoding could ride roughshod over the aesthetic experience by simplifying the precise ways meaning operates in the scheme of a work. It is this sensitivity to the aesthetic quality of the film and the aesthetic experience of it (for him) that I want to highlight. It's what can be lost in academic and critical work too quick simply to explain or expound what the art object means.

Cavell writes: "I am reluctant to make it very explicit." How does one do this in one's criticism without becoming unhelpfully vague, or evasive, or smugly knowing, or pretentious, or lazy (in simply not spending the time to work through a satisfactory articulation)?

Cavell writes: "Contradicting directions in our experience." While I was putting together this paper, I looked back over the published conversation between Cavell and myself in the book *Film as Philosophy: Essays on Cinema after Wittgenstein and Cavell*.[3] I was taken with how much of that conversation was circling round the idea of explicitness, and providing variations upon it (even though we had not designed it to do so). At one point, I give the example of writing about Joan Bennett's Alice in Fritz Lang's *The Woman in the Window* (1944). Bennett plays some sort of prostitute I say, although the film doesn't explicitly signal this. I reported to Cavell that I was originally wanting to use the word in my writing. Perhaps I needed to expose her as a prostitute to signal to the reader my candidness or my worldliness. Anyway, I ultimately decided, and after sage advice, I shouldn't use the word because the film does not use the word. Now there may be good arguments for saying that I was wrong to consider using the word "prostitute" at all because in certain contexts it is now considered an inappropriate word: in the United Kingdom, "sex worker" is the preferred parlance. In fact, Bennett is probably playing, what was once called, a "kept woman." Anyway, regardless of which name I might have applied—"prostitute," sex worker," or "kept woman"—the question was how might I imply aspects of Alice's livelihood, which would be sensitive to the film's suggestiveness, while not, at the same time, appearing to be evasive. Cavell replied that in such a case: "you're not avoiding anything. You are just wary of being false to the experience."

Later in the conversation, in the middle of a discussion about the different ways philosophy and film might meet, I expressed the danger of educational institutionalization. This week we're teaching *Mr. Deeds Goes to Town* (1936, dir. Frank Capra) and the accompanying reading is Descartes and—oh dear—some artificial and contrived things happen to the film and to Descartes. (Descartes may be able to take the hits, but I'm not sure the films always can!) This seemed nothing like the spirit of "discovery" that Cavell seemed to advocate in his work, and to be advocating in our conversation. How does one keep the spirit of discovery within a more institutionalized, curriculum-led teaching environment I asked? Cavell replied: "This again sounds like the problem of naming the prostitute. You want Descartes to be there, but if you just say 'This is Descartes' you've killed it."

Cavell writes of the couple in *It Happened One Night* (1934, dir. Frank Capra) as having "an unreadiness to become explicit."[4] He had a sixth sense for aspects of films that seemed to be ordinary and straightforward, and which he revealed to be quietly mysterious—precisely those moments he considered easily missable (and, we might add, dismissable). In *Pursuits of Happiness*, Cavell writes about "words that on one viewing pass, without notice, as unnoticeably trivial, on another resonate and declare their implication in a network of significance."[5] In *Now, Voyager* (1942, dir. Irving Rapper), Charlotte, Bette Davis, asks Dr. Jacquith, Claude Rains, if he can help her, to which he replies: "You don't need my help." This is puzzling to Cavell because "he is not refusing her plea; but if he is granting it, why isn't his answer a flat lie? She patently does need his help." Cavell takes the line to be "a peculiar compression, meaning something like, I'll help you come to see that you are not helpless." He then continues: "The writing requires a kind of Hollywood abbreviation of allegorising in narration that is hard to characterise."[6] Much art compresses, condenses, crystallizes, but often more artfully—not characteristically in such a prosaic, matter of fact way. Cavell however finds "you don't need my help" to be suggestive, and he finds it to be a much more multifaceted articulation than it may appear (on one viewing, or many).

Cavell does make meanings explicit in his criticism, of course, and he presents a meaning here: "meaning something like"—note, though, "something like"—"I'll help you come to see that you are not helpless." It would therefore be disingenuous to lead one to believe that he doesn't ever make things explicit. However, some of his strategies for making explicit may be of related interest. This is Cavell on *Vertigo* (1958, dir. Alfred Hitchcock) and fantasy from *The World Viewed*:

> I speak of "establishing a world of private fantasy" ... More specifically, [it] is *about* the power of fantasy, and in particular about its power to survive every inroad of science and civility intact, and to direct the destiny of its subject with, finally, his active cooperation ... *Vertigo* seems at first to be about a man's impotence in the face of, or faced with, the task of sustaining, his desire; perhaps, on second thought, about the precariousness of human verticality altogether. But it turns out to be about the specific power of a man's fantasy to cause him not merely to forgo reality—that consequence is as widespread as the sea—but to gear every instant of his energy toward a private alteration of reality.[7]

Cavell is concerned not simply with what *Vertigo* means but with the approach to meaning, and the journey through meanings. He seems initially to announce what the film is "about"—"the power of fantasy"—but then he goes through a process of refining. "At first" it seems to be about "a man's impotence in the face of ... his desire" or slightly differently, "a man's impotence ... faced with ... the task of sustaining ... his desire." This then leads to a "second thought" that the film might be about "the precariousness of human verticality altogether." The move to this point of general importance is stimulated by, and simultaneously allows, a tactful elaboration on the problems of *impotence*—"precarious ... verticality." Just after his "second thought," the film in fact "turns out" to be about something else: "the specific power of a man's fantasy ... to gear every instant of his energy toward a private alteration of reality." Cavell is not simply providing alternatives, he is, with "perhaps, on second thought" and "But it turns out," marking the stages of alteration and adjustment. I said he goes through a refining process, but it would be more accurate to say that he demonstrates a process. He is expressing how ideas come to him as he views, one prompting another in the mind, the train of thought. Even if we consider the prose to be a literary contrivance, there is nevertheless an attempt to recreate or evoke the viewing experience as a series of developing impressions.

Cavell's film readings depend on a profound and sustained attentiveness toward the films. We might say, using Cavellian terms, that he forms a companionship with them: he marries them and, of course, needs to remarry them. This could lead, and has led, to him being characterized as a close reading critic, but he is not in the main a close reading critic in the classic sense (although he was perfectly capable of close reading on occasions; indeed he was capable of operating within many critical modes). In the example I've provided about *Vertigo*, he tends to generalize, to tell us about meanings rather than build them out of careful analysis of the film's form. He does not validate and substantiate as close readers would. I am someone from a close reading tradition, who practices it, advocates it, teaches it, and my students will testify to their exhaustion with my repeated exhortation to show rather than tell. Show through analyzing the film's form. By contrast, when Cavell writes that he understands the film to be "about the precariousness of human verticality" it is suggestive in a way that indicates further potential for viewing; it prompts the reader to think through the instances of "verticality" in the film, to look more closely for themselves. The proposition, for Cavell, does not seem to require evidencing, or the careful illumination of instances of execution (of "verticality"), but rather, once again using a favored Cavellian term, invites conversation. How much can Cavell safely leave unsaid? He trusts his reader, and there are no assurances. Cavell's writing here, like "human verticality" is precarious. Perhaps, thrillingly so.

There is a closely related contrast that is worth remarking upon. I have been recently studying the ordinary language philosophers of the 1950s Oxford school: most prominently, Gilbert Ryle, J. L. Austin, and P. F. Strawson. It is interesting that although Austin, in particular, is an important influence on Cavell, and although impulses in ordinary language were commentated on, adapted and developed by Cavell, and although the concept of the ordinary is a profoundly motivating one for him, he is not an ordinary language philosopher in the way Ryle or Austin and Strawson were. Aside from the odd essay (particularly some early work), and aside from fleeting instances, he mostly does not proceed by way of their method. Moreover, the writing exhibits profoundly different sensibilities. Classic OLP is English, dry, unsentimental, practical, sternly exact, enumerative, to the point (and skeptical of Theory). Aside from the odd moments of crossover, Cavell's writing is American, romantic, emotional, happy to be suggestive, elaborate, expansive (and open to Theory and theoretical philosophers, e.g., Freud and Heidegger). One only has to see what Gilbert Ryle does with the concept of "feeling" in the classic collection *Aesthetics and Language*, listing the different ways we use the one word (feeling) in different contexts, unemphatically, preferring to articulate a series of distinctions rather than an argument, to see how far away Cavell is from the English OLP tradition.[8] And the English OLP tradition joins hands with the great English literary close readers, for example, William Empson (and Empson's *Seven Types of Ambiguity* is an OLP project in the Austinian mode as much as it is a work of literary criticism; just as Austin's work often reads as if it were close literary criticism as much as it does philosophy).[9] Indeed, Cavell, as we know, leans more to Emerson than to Empson. Of course, the close readers in the new critical and practical critical traditions were also interested in suggestiveness, unresolved tensions, paradoxes, symbolic containment in the language and so on, but they would meticulously unpack these things and lay them out. In film, the great inheritor of the OLP/close reading tradition would be one of Cavell's academic friends on the other side of the Atlantic, V. F. Perkins. One way of seeing the differences in the critical traditions is to compare how Cavell and Perkins tackle the same film—one that had a privileged place in the work of both—*Letter from an Unknown Woman* (1948, dir. Max Ophüls). Perkins takes one sequence, the one set in Linz, and painstakingly analyzes each movement and development in the shots, compositions, postures, gestures, and sound in their precise context. His essay, aside from a long final section of thematic elaboration, is more strictly a piece of aesthetic evaluation in that it wants to show how an apparently anomalous and uncharacteristic scene in the film, and which could possibly be seen as a lapse or at least relatively weak, is carefully synthesized with the rest of the film and is a complex achievement in itself. Cavell's essay, on the other hand, explores the film in a psychoanalytic mode, and despite drawing attention to singular, resonant details in the film, it remains largely speculative, nebulous, oblique, recalcitrant even.

So often in Cavell's work there seems to be the desire not to pin things down, but rather to keep things open. Hence a desire, a compulsion perhaps, to keep returning to the same films and moments. For example, he discusses the closing moments of *Now, Voyager* in at least six different books and essays. He doesn't return in this way necessarily to become more exact about a moment, clarifying or correcting a previous occasion, nor is it necessarily to be newly and flexibly responsive to the film, but rather to let his particular constellation of concerns and themes circulate, yet again, in relation to the film. And circulate is what Cavell's criticism often does. The risk is that this circulation will amount to merely going round and round in circles, but for Cavell the journey around, to, from, and back is as important and telling as the arrival. Cavell certainly does arrive, but somehow only to move on, not only to develop the topic, but so he has the opportunity to come back again, come back round again, to see how the same things are getting on.

This circulation, moreover, isn't simply about opening up new occasions for the film and the critic's concerns to meet. I think it reflects a belief that the critic should be present in the writing to *self-consciously* and dramatically enact, and thereby expose, the processes of response and understanding. In this regard, if not others, Cavell's method might be likened to the crusading English critic, F. R. Leavis. Cavell believed, as Leavis did, that the moment-by-moment "interior drama," which goes hand in hand with attentiveness toward the work, should be presented to the reader.[10] The extract about *Vertigo* displays this "interior drama." The "running presentation" might be regarded by some as an unnecessary and irritating record of deliberations that could be condensed or erased, and too much of an imposition of personality; for Cavell though it "constitutes," as Michael Bell has said of Leavis's work, "a clear and open-handed source of authority."[11]

If it is true to say that Cavell was acutely cognizant of his *approach*, then it is also true to say that he had no one way of approaching. It is very difficult to categorize Cavell's *modus operandi* even within customary philosophical methods or domains: sometimes aesthetic, sometimes phenomenological, sometimes moral, sometimes linguistic, sometimes analytic, sometimes continental, sometimes psychoanalytical, and sometimes many of these at once. And the same applies to critical method: sometimes ontological, sometimes cultural, sometimes evaluative, sometimes thematic, sometimes theoretical, sometimes scholarly, sometimes essayistic. And so too with regards to prose style. It is sometimes expansive, at other times clipped (some points will be dwelt upon while other crucial points will be left hanging in the air, seemingly incomplete). It is sometimes pellucid, at other times tangled. It is sometimes pointed, at other times subtle and suggestive, full of implication. It is sometimes serious, at other times witty. It is sometimes momentous, at other times lightly passing over or dispersing. It is sometimes withering or stern, at other times tactful. Throughout Cavell's work there is this push-pull: suspended between making clear and "an unreadiness to become explicit." Like the best films, perhaps? Perhaps.

Notes

1 J. David Slocum, *Times Literary Supplement* 4945, January 9, 1998, 17.
2 Stanley Cavell, *Pursuits of Happiness: The Hollywood Comedy of Remarriage* (Cambridge: Harvard University Press, 1981), 116–18.

3. Rupert Read and Jerry Goodenough eds., *Film as Philosophy: Essays in Cinema after Wittgenstein and Cavell* (Basingstoke, Hampshire: Palgrave Macmillan, 2005).
4. Stanley Cavell, "A Capra Moment," *Cavell on Film*, ed. William Rothman (Albany: State University of New York Press, 2005), 139.
5. Cavell, *Pursuits of Happiness*, 11.
6. Cavell, "The Image of the Psychoanalyst in Film," *Cavell on Film*, 299.
7. Stanley Cavell, *The World Viewed: Reflections on the Ontology of Film*, Expanded Edition (Cambridge: Harvard University Press, 1971/1979), 85.
8. Gilbert Ryle, "Feelings," *Aesthetics and Language*, ed. William Elton (Oxford: Basil Blackwell, 1970), 56–72.
9. William Empson, *Seven Types of Ambiguity* (London: Pimlico, [1930] 2004.
10. Michael Bell, *F. R. Leavis* (New York: Routledge, 1988), 74.
11. Ibid., 74–5.

3

Cavell as Educator

MARK GREIF

To poor students

Profess

WHAT CAN I PROFESS?[1] The age of new doctrines has closed. The role of a professor may be to confess to what is already known. Thus, one professes an established faith, as an adherent. But to what, or whom, could I cling? Is there any single thing, learned in school, that you can stick to for a lifetime?

The professor of philosophy stands at the junction of two worlds: the original and the rote. Emerson teased the scholar, calling him a divided philosopher. Impartial, but reduced thereby to part and halfway commitments. The scholar borrows plumage, a "parrot" of his betters. "The boy is not attracted. He says, I do not wish to be such a kind of man as my professor is."[2] Or such a bird. Thoreau put in, fatefully, in 1854: "There are nowadays professors of philosophy, but not philosophers. Yet it is admirable to profess because it was once admirable to live."[3]

At least Thoreau was a little encouraging. Professing, on his admonition, partway reclaims, at least recalls, what it formerly was to live. Life glows on one side of a chasm. And philosophy, curiously, shines from that same side, across from wherever we're stuck.

But if philosophy and life are opposite to us, it still isn't obvious what is on our side, or where we are. How do you name our entanglement in an unlived life? How could to *live*, in better, bygone times, ever have meant to *live as a philosopher*?

Nearly every great philosopher in the era of the university has said somewhere that there is no such thing as education in schools. Nearly every one of these, too, taught or lectured (Nietzsche, Heidegger, Wittgenstein,

James, Arendt), or was entangled as far as to have learned from a university, in its lecture halls and library, what philosophy would be.[4] The terminal degree the modern university grants every PhD recipient declares him or her a doctor of philosophy. As compensation, novice teachers of philosophy help themselves early to the ultimate title of their profession, and any young professional in a department of philosophy calls himself or herself, nowadays, a philosopher. Even graduate students try on the honor. To others in the university, this can seem like a presumption, unless they are putting on others' coats themselves. Only lay readers, outside the university, of Plato, Rousseau, Kierkegaard, Nietzsche, know it to be a sin and a betrayal, as the occupation of an unearned office.

Philosophy must be a practice apart, to those of us who resent the philosophy professor as no philosopher. We will keep the crown unworn if need be. By the royal road, *to be a philosopher* is something we think only genius can do. In the backyard, philosophizing is something that is done by anyone awake, without credentials, indifferent to degrees, not troubled by a neighbor's waking. The enterprise belongs to night thoughts and daydreams.

Who, in modern America, can be the doer of philosophy? Ours is supposed to be the most practical, therefore unphilosophical, of societies. Yet we are not unschooled. The advancing campuses of our schools creep over the landscape of the country like an infinitely extensible college green.

Stanley Cavell is the only university professor of philosophy I knew personally to preserve a distinction between professing and doing. He thought enough, and solemnly enough, about the condition of philosophy, to ask whether he could say he did it, and what he was doing when he didn't do it, when he couldn't.

His career started with asking what is on this side of the chasm, where we all live, most of the time—what we are doing *here*. And what, in what we do here, will lead us to any other side? What acts, or speech, will erect a bridge from here to there, or lay a plank, or throw the philosopher's "rope over an abyss"?[5] Or what will move us, shuffling our feet, until perspective reveals the distance to the other side to be only a step, if life were differently viewed?

Mood

I was seventeen when an older friend took me onto the Harvard campus to see a college lecture for the first time. The topic was the later Wittgenstein. I thought then, as I do still, that it is almost never too early for anybody to read anything. An exception for me seems to have been the earlier Wittgenstein, the *Tractatus Logico-Philosophicus*, which I had read that year. But in addition to certain bad reasons to be present at the lecture, having to do with my fog about Wittgenstein (and no lecture was going to clarify it), I had one good reason, which was that I was in some anxiety to know what college was like.

Philosophy spoke to me then because I liked the way I thought under its influence. It gave a sensual pleasure, as I lay on the broken couch in the high school music room, in fall term, after classes, and looked from the chalkboard ruled in noteless staves up to the casement where the evening chalked clouds over Boston's roofs. Then back down to *Nausea* or *The Birth of Tragedy* in my lap, thinking: "Sartre, or Nietzsche, thinks just the way I do." I still feel this as embarrassing, or unsayable. But is it only a thought of a seventeen-year-old, or permanent and universal, until one gives up on oneself, on one's own seriousness? I felt that these philosophical books helped me excavate some darkness within, pulling it up in buckets, of which college would give me the analysis.

Whoever built the philosophy building in Harvard Yard, Emerson Hall, seems to have had in mind a savings bank. My host met me on the steps, which had iced perilously on that winter morning, and led me to the stream of students pushing into the humid lobby. The hall held a list of professors' names, of movable letters in a glass case, like a marquee. The students climbed upward in a mass like sibling strangers, producing the noisy shared disregard of a family relation. Streams drained off at each landing to the tall doors of lecture rooms.

In our room, the students hung their coats on a line of wooden pegs. I kept my coat as I found my seat, fearing theft, and perspired as the crowd called over its murmuring. I thought I saw contemptuousness in the faces of the listeners. It was a mood I would later understand was common to lecture halls, but which I didn't know how to judge rightly until, a year later, Cavell had us read in Emerson about some conditions for his kind of philosophy (i.e., Emerson's, who was installed as a bronze statue downstairs):

> The nonchalance of boys who are sure of a dinner, and would disdain as much as a lord to do or say aught to conciliate one, is the healthy attitude of human nature. A boy is in the parlour what the pit is in the playhouse; independent, irresponsible, looking out from his corner on such people and facts as pass by, he tries and sentences them on their merits, in the swift, summary way of boys, as good, bad, interesting, silly, eloquent, troublesome. He cumbers himself never about consequences, about interests: he gives an independent, genuine verdict.[6]

I was, I suppose, afraid, reverent, cynical, primed for disappointment, eager for an ideal, avid and withholding. Cavell was pointed out to me, and he mounted a few steps, put down his coat, and adjusted the microphone. The philosopher looked like "a philosopher" to me: I mean like a statue already. He was then sixty-seven to my seventeen.

He opened with words to me unforgettable (by which I mean also that I hope I don't misremember them). Settling his papers, he began:

> Friends have said to me, "You must have been in a bad mood when you wrote chapter four of *The Claim of Reason*." It's certainly possible. The question is, what would it mean, philosophically, about these materials, with these perplexities, to be in a *bad mood*?

I laughed. I have a loud laugh. I supposed I had been asking myself, *What does it mean to be in such a bad mood?* for my whole life. Here was the reward, at long last, for the hell of being a child. Under the thumb of tyrants—parents and teachers, "whom an audaciously honest person has called *nos ennemis naturels*."[7] Not understanding myself, trying, for years, to discover myself in books. In college, people *wouldn't* lecture on *other* people only. They would stand up as thinkers themselves. We had moods. And any mood was a pool into which you could dive. Cavell was at last really a *philosopher*, I came to understand, a species I had never before seen in the flesh, with wisps of white hair at the back of his head, an appropriately owlish face behind glasses, immense goodwill, and mortal frailties. Those included a visible, intense self-regard, critical as well as passionate, vulnerable to odd wounds from friends or critics.

The lecture moved on and lost me. It became fifty minutes on aspects of the *Philosophical Investigations*, the later Wittgenstein, as promised in the course title, and I took no more profit from it than from the book I'd read.

We know the real target of philosophy is life. Everyone feels it who has not been irreparably debauched by learning. Graduates who took one philosophy course in college will remember that etymologically it is *philosophia*, the love of wisdom, or love of truth. In most traditions, philosophy is not only the pursuit of truth but also a discipline for managing suffering. Don't the limitation of pain and access to the truth go together, through ties obscure but sensible to all? If one sees the target, then, how to draw the bow? And from what tree's bough is the best arrow cut?

Skepticism

Skepticism, in modern philosophy, names the fear, or thought, that one cannot be certain of knowledge. The philosophical chronology of modern skepticism starts with Descartes, when in his *Meditations* he looked into the street in northern Holland and recognized that the men he saw hurrying might be clockwork men; he might be dreaming; a demon might be deceiving him. It enters Hume's attacks on causation and induction, and reaches Kant's attempted settlement and solution, letting us possess and know the categories of the understanding, but depriving us forever of access to the things behind appearances.

These fundamental challenges to certainty continue, with other philosophers' ripostes and new bases for proof, proceeding over centuries; who can say when they will determine an answer? The arguments seemed idle to me at first, like moves in games of chess played by correspondence, mailed from one generation to the next. Where was the feeling beneath them? What is the dread that lets you doubt the external world is knowable or still there?

At his arrival in philosophy in the early 1960s, Cavell became known for his investigations of modern skeptical thought and its solutions. He added to skepticism about the physical world the problem of a fundamental doubt about other minds, taken over from solutions proposed by his teacher, J. L. Austin. That problem arises at its simplest when I ask whether I can know that another person is angry, or that his or her pain feels like my pain.[8] Then, if I can know another's thoughts are like mine. At its far extension, rarely asked, whether I can know that in my neighborhood, even in the world, there exists a single other mind like my own.

I was often puzzled how skeptical thought could be so central to someone whose philosophy is so social, talkative, communal, and diurnal as Cavell was on the lecture platform. Yet I do remember, or know I thought I heard, him sounding the note of failure or fear. In terms of his own voice.

"To whom am I speaking?" He spoke to us, in the afternoon gloom of a darkening hall. The terror seemed to be that no one might have listened to these words coming back to him from the maple-paneled walls, over a forty-year career. Or that no one might care. "For whom am I speaking, by what right?" The platform, raised off the floor, couldn't be departed until the end of the hour. The wooden lectern and the table bound the circle of the world. Why don't professors let themselves leave mid-lecture, as audiences can do? Maybe there was no one here who could receive the thought as it needed to be taken. "What is that voice of philosophy?" Cavell might say. The voice spoke into a void.

I had never seen the isolation of the lecturer staged like this: the isolation that fears the step from solitude to solipsism. The school *produces* the unreality; it cages the speaking, if the teaching is rote, or unlistened to.

But the philosopher was not lecturing on others' behalf—not, at least, for the sake, or soul, of anyone else but himself and those in the room. "By what right does the philosopher say 'we?' 'We' speaks of a consent that is not common, that, by rights, is *yours*." "Can you hear me? Am I making myself ... clear?"

In laying bare the conditions of his enterprise, he repelled as many people as he enchanted. Although "the arrogation of voice," the theft of the right to speak for others, was one of Cavell's signal topics about how philosophy is pursued, it was personal arrogance, and the pursuit of his own unique interests, that others (peers in professional philosophy, principally) accused him of. The master violated philosophy's consensus on what was an "interesting problem," as well as the circumspection and terseness with which one was supposed to enunciate it. Cavell didn't like to be disliked, but he knew what was said about him. An explanation he once wrote concerning Wittgenstein:

> So some of Wittgenstein's readers are made impatient, as though the fluctuating humility and arrogance of his prose were a matter of style. … To me this fluctuation reads as a continuous effort at balance, or longing for it, as to leave a tightrope; it seems an expression of that struggle of despair and hope that I can understand as a motivation to philosophical writing.[9]

I remember in the lecture hall *thinking* reassurance at him. Knowing also that, if, by magic, this thought got through, it would vitiate the doing of his philosophy, a part of its mood, the density of it, the talking in loneliness. The philosopher puts forward true words, as best he or she can, true in the moment, and can't tell what sensitivities will twitch. When my pen moved, I wasn't heaping up facts. I was allowing a recording of inner tremors, as with a stylus on the paper of the soul.

I found things said that I felt I already knew from birth, and was newborn. Lineage in education is unusual. In philosophy, the philosopher doesn't choose who will be the offspring of his or her thought. Ordinarily, creative power is all in a parent's hands; I don't choose my father and mother. Yet the apprentice philosopher fills in his own birth certificate and signs it. He roams the halls and selects his theater of delivery. The "boy" can be surer of this parentage than of anything else, knowing what it was that changed him, or allowed him to change himself.

Garden

The first class he offered that I could enroll in was a general education course in "moral reasoning," a field of study the university required of all students. It meant, for Cavell, that he could teach a course for anyone and everyone.

It was good to be springlike, green and receptive. I brought along any friend who would listen to my advertisements for the possible experience of a lifetime. Lectures occurred two days a week. I took the class with my new girlfriend, and others we knew, or came to know, as the lecture hall brought us together. So I always sat with friends. One of the secrets of a modern American college is that before undergraduates take up "extracurriculars," or if they choose not to take up any (as I didn't), studying is itself the passion and the activity. The challenge is to be curricular—to run through the course set by civilization up to one's own time, and then exceed it.[10]

To be a first-year student is to be so coddled, patted, petted, fed, housed, to have so little expected of you, as a new arrival, to be so incipient, that it seems a misfire of spirit not to commit yourself to some single concern: even reading. I could read day and night, in bed, walking to and from lectures, or while eating dinner, without shame. The library was overgrown. Beneath one layer of fronds was another. Books that would have been precious or restricted or unheard of in my town library were fallen leaves here.

What do people ever mean by community? Lucy took the course with me. She could equally say that I took the course with her. We offered each other confirmation. "Was that incredible—what he said?" It was. None of us knew Cavell or talked to him. I thought of Cavell standing in the frigid slush waiting for the trolley in Brookline, or pulling wet galoshes off in his entrance hall, calling to his family, waiting to learn if anyone was home, while we eighteen-year-olds lived as gods, talking, reading, romancing, in our Cambridge garden, knowing good and evil thanks to him. We took the course unknown, we did the reading privately, and yet we lived together in dorms, ate together, had a Friend City produced for us by university forces we otherwise considered sinister. If we could have farmed, on the ludicrous green where tourists are invited to pump a wooden replica of the college well, we would have recaptured the whole virtue of Oneida or Brook Farm, and with more freedom. There is something better in communities whose leaders inhabit a connecting world, not far, just adjacent. Leaders who do not rule, who do not set limits to action. Who won't know you, or what you do. Who only talk, largely in colloquy with themselves—who only insist, regardless of the world's habits, that life is this worthy of inspection and concentration. Leaders like this hand over what they have to teach like the previous tenant's ring of unlabeled keys. They give their followers the courtesy of retreating, to let youth live its life with the reminders of an inspirer's pressure of experience.

To body forth a philosophy on a stage, you would think, is not to live. Unless the teacher could take his or her meals there, and read the paper. Fight with a spouse, make up, make love. But it is enough to speak of life sometimes. To put yourself in front of eyes and let yourself be taken in.

Socrates was the first to take a seminar outside. In the streets of Athens, he taught as one should. Certain kinds of things can only be said outside, free of walls. Plato removed to the Academy, after Socrates's death—the closed porch of a temple. Aristotle followed his example when founding the Lyceum. Epicurus put two worlds back together, indoor and outdoor. He took a house, pleading for the ordinary life, and in his garden made a school. The school had the name of its locale. In the Garden he taught women as well as men, something neither Aristotle, Plato, nor Socrates had ever done or conceived. Here he proposed a philosophy once again devoted to learning to live—and live in company—not just to know.

> Let no one delay the study of philosophy while young nor weary of it when old. For no one is either too young or too old for the health of the soul. He who says either that the time for philosophy has not yet come or that it has passed is like someone who says that the time for happiness has not yet come or that it has passed. Therefore, both young and old must philosophize, the latter so that although old he may stay young in good things owing to gratitude for what has occurred, the former so that although young he too may be like an old man owing to his lack of fear of what is to come.[11]

To be poised halfway through a course, after fourteen lectures with a master, knowing that there are fourteen still to go, is a rare position, as against feeling a great treatise coming to an end, seeing a great painting, watching a great movie, and knowing that event to be closed. The blessed thing is not ending. Joy is continuous, discovery daily. The term is far off, and all the training has led to motion that is effortless. There is not one world in books, and another that is ours. You cannot hold on to the fear that the age of new doctrines is over. Our time is as great as any time, greater because it's ours.

Cavell, rather than being the type of all college professors, turned out to be unique. His tutelage at that time seemed the big experience of my life, and I can't say that it wasn't, even now. I was afraid of him, personally—afraid, I mean, of damaging the relation by something personal. I went in later years to his lectures on aesthetics, attended his screenings of operas and films, tried to focus on sessions on Wittgenstein, on language and epistemology.

I have often asked between then and now what I got myself in for, not that it was Cavell's fault, not that I wouldn't have gotten in for it anyway. Nietzsche, when young, advised the initiate, in "Schopenhauer as Educator," which we read at Cavell's direction, to cultivate an *impersonal self-hatred* in order to grow, hating that within yourself which is weak and inferior.[12] It took me more years than it should have to learn that this advice wouldn't work for me; hatred became personal. (This year, fourteen years later, I saw a note of Nietzsche's set down when he was fourteen years older: "I wish men would begin by respecting themselves: everything else follows from that. To be sure, as soon as one does this one is finished for others: for this is what they forgive last: 'What? A man who respects himself?'—"[13])

At least I can say I had a teacher in my life, who laid a table. He couldn't be responsible for what I took.

Philosophize

Cavell communicated four central doctrines, I would say now, of various degrees of novelty. They were the doctrine of knowledge as acknowledging;

of perfectionism as the succession of next selves; of the world on film as our world, viewed; and of marriage between equals as remarriage.

I've often asked myself what it means for there to be completeness to a philosophical system. Kant's critical philosophy, our modern reference point for systems, became integral in three critiques, but no one but Kant himself could have predicted that the completion of his epistemology and ethics would have required an aesthetics. Cavell's sequence of writings seems particularly idiosyncratic, more irregular than most thinkers'. There is, however, I think, completeness to the system; it has to do with the ways one can surpass the boundaries of isolation and find relations to a world of other people. (Maybe this is nothing more than other interpreters say naturally, that Cavell's work is an unending investigation of reactions to skepticism, considered in its widest view. I'm just not sure that does justice to the whole, making it more like the line of an obsession, a tunnel into the earth, than an illustrated map of the whole earth's surface.)

The underlying ambition of his philosophy is to become *worldly*, with all the accents of cosmopolitanism, civilization, and maturity that the word bears. A surprising quantity of philosophy, both Anglo-American and European, wants the opposite, wishing to become simple and primordial. Cavell's ambition for the person who lives philosophically is not to give himself or herself to the world primordially, nor privately, nor metaphysically, nor alone. Cavell's worldliness implies, however, that one remembers standing on the threshold, waiting to enter or join. The isolation of the novice does not end with the overcoming of adolescence, but will recur, at intervals, wherever and whenever one is cut off, or one's words are not listened to, or one's best thoughts pass unheard.

The divisions in his philosophy correspond to three relations to the world which human life can disclose, from the standpoint of that threshold. There can be the world *with* me, which leads Cavell to the recovery of the ordinary, in the action of acknowledgment. There can be a world *beside* me, which leads to the discovery of a next self, in the action called perfectionism. Perhaps most difficult to accept, or honor, there is a world *without* me, which leads to something Cavell least names; call it, in its hopeful instances, community or eternity. Its actions are viewing and conversation, once you see that these commend thinking and listening as much as seeing and talking.

Acknowledgment

As college-level training in American philosophy became consumed with logic, logic became the origin for increasing numbers of Cavell's fellow students and colleagues in the 1950s. Math and science didn't impel Cavell to philosophy. He came to it, as he said, from "crisis." It appeared to him as a solution when, pursuing graduate study at Juilliard in New York City, he discovered that he no longer wanted to be, or would never really be, a composer of classical music, which had been the subject of his undergraduate degree at Berkeley and supplied much of his sense of self.

> The first thing I did ... was to recognize that music was no longer my life and thereupon to avoid my composition lessons. The next thing I did was to realize that I was in a state of spiritual crisis. My solution to that realization, not to say my expression of it, was to decide that I had learned nothing in college and to resolve to know and to see everything worth knowing and seeing. This led me, or released me ... to attend the theater or the opera almost every night and to see at least two films a day and to begin reading whatever it was that people called philosophy. ... While I had studied essentially no philosophy in college (except for a semester course in aesthetics, which as I recall it, required no reading), I had heard that philosophy had something to do with examining one's life.[14]

In graduate school at UCLA and then at Harvard, he became expert in Kant and logical analysis but did not see how someone with his talents and interests could make a contribution that others couldn't already offer. At that time, 1955, J. L. Austin came to Harvard for a semester from Oxford and delivered the series of lectures that would become *How to Do Things with Words* (a book of 1962, published, like all of Austin's books, only after his untimely death). On the basis of the oral teaching, Cavell determined that what Austin did, he could do. History does not record what Austin made of this decision about patrimony.

Austin's philosophy worked by diagnostic examples, from our ordinary speech, not an ideal speech formalized as logic,

> those examples apart from which ordinary language philosophy has no method, [which] required what you might call "ear" to comprehend (as in, more or less at random, setting out the difference between doing something by mistake or by accident, or between doing something willingly or voluntarily, carelessly or heedlessly, or between doing something in saying something or by saying something, or between telling a bird by its call or from its call).[15]

Taking Austin's method as his own, becoming an "ordinary language philosopher," Cavell discovered that he could give the American philosophical mainstream a superior account of something it wanted to understand. This was the new post-analytic language philosophy coming from Oxford, where Austin and Gilbert Ryle taught. Logical analysis, as it had developed into logical empiricism or logical positivism or the Anglo-American "analytic" orientation, had leaned on ideal or artificial languages to sift out the real questions of philosophy from superstition, irrationalism, and religion. It formed its first generation from Russell, Carnap, and the early Wittgenstein, and found its best publicist in the 1930s in Ayer. But a second generation (including also Quine and Sellars in the United States) identified flaws in the project of the first. Austin and Ryle specifically showed how natural language, what we all speak, contains necessary dimensions not articulable in truth-functional propositional logic. Yet ordinary language also rebuked traditional philosophical "superstitions" (e.g., mind-body dualism and external-world skepticism) in even more credible ways. The most profound revisionist, unnervingly, was believed to be Wittgenstein himself, whose last decades of work had become known only after his death in 1951. Thus just a few years after Cavell had committed to Austin, he found himself in circles where Wittgenstein's *Philosophical Investigations*, which also belonged to the enigmas and discomforts of ordinary language, even more urgently demanded an explainer and defender.

The papers with which Cavell engaged the philosophical profession through the 1960s were collected at the end of the decade in *Must We Mean What We Say?* (1969). They show why Cavell could be recognized within analytic philosophy and also why he was an odd duck. He taught the usefulness of Austin to his peers in his title essay and pleaded the "Availability of Wittgenstein's Later Philosophy" in another. But he also wrote on Kierkegaard, not a mainstay of the Harvard curriculum, and on *King Lear* and *Endgame*, which were acceptable, but preferably in the literature classrooms of Sever Hall. It could be said that Cavell satisfied philosophy's residual obligation to aesthetics, at least, a field on the distaff side of a now-scientized discipline, whose masculine hierarchy of fields rewarded epistemology and philosophy of math.

The assessment of ordinary language, which his colleagues were unprepared to make, in a sense became Cavell's Trojan horse, the gift he brought to Harvard philosophy, hiding foreign impulses inside. Another way to see the matter is that the collection of talent at the university in the 1960s was strong enough to welcome the intrusion. Cavell received lifetime tenure in 1963, at age thirty-seven. There was a moment by the end of that decade when the department had assembled in one place W. V. O. Quine, John Rawls, Hilary Putnam, Nelson Goodman, and Robert Nozick, with Michael Walzer and Judith Sklar nearby in Government. They freed him to roam the fortifications without fear, because what even Cavell's most "establishment" colleagues were doing—second- and third-generation analytic philosophy, with Quine the aging iconoclast and leader; a wholesale reorientation of political philosophy toward distributive justice, led by Rawls; ethical and political grappling with the student revolts, democracy, and the Vietnam War—was all momentous, all strange.

Cavell took up the old question of skepticism from the core of modern epistemology. How do I know with certainty that the world is as I experience or perceive it? Wittgenstein's *Philosophical Investigations*, Cavell confirmed, wielded ordinary language philosophy to confront philosophical skepticism. Yes, skepticism's inadequacy to us was thereby revealed. But, no, a proof against skepticism is not therefore attained. To the will to argue against the skeptic, Cavell's interpretation said both yes and no. Wittgenstein showed (by Cavell's lights) that the notion of a final, certain disproof of the challenge to certainty, a solution by some new move of conventional knowledge, repeats the impulse to skepticism.

Skepticism is reunderstood not as a series of experiments or challenges within reason, but broadly as the intellectualist separation of ourselves from our shared condition of being in the world—which, however it starts, issues inevitably in a refusal of that world's reality without us, and denial of our conversation with other minds within it.

Cavell insisted that the resumption of the world was not a matter of knowing it. It was rather what he called "acknowledging." As early as *Must We Mean What We Say?*, he could write:

> ... [W]e think skepticism must mean that we cannot know the world exists, and hence that perhaps there isn't one (a conclusion some profess to admire and others to fear). Whereas what skepticism suggests is that since we cannot know the world exists, its presentness to us cannot be a function of knowing.[16]

Because Cavell was a devotee of language, his basic therapeutic thought, voiced in many keys, was that the thing that saves what we have in common, and preserves your claim upon others and theirs on you, is recovering the certainty that our shared medium is words. Speech hooks you, or invites you, entices, incites. He inquired into forms of that linguistic acknowledgment, how it occurred and where it failed. And, in many scenes, on the lecture room stage and in written works (especially an unfolding series of essays on Shakespeare's plays), he dramatized it. "Our relation to the world as a whole, or to others in general, is not one of knowing, where knowing construes itself as being certain," Cavell reiterated in 1979, in *The Claim of Reason*, his midcareer summa. It was both the book that drew most from his analytic practice (as a partial rewriting of his 1961 graduate dissertation, *The Claim to Rationality*) and an expanded brief against dry knowledge, ending in a sort of experimental writing, with aphorisms and an infection of the literary—it possessed "style." Still later in his career, in a little summary:

> ... [T]he idea of thinking as reception ... [puts] forward the correct answer to skepticism. ... The answer does not consist in denying the conclusion of skepticism but in reconceiving its truth. It is true that we do not know the existence of the world with certainty; our relation to its existence is

deeper—one in which it is accepted, that is to say, received. My favorite way of putting this is to say that existence is to be acknowledged.[17]

Thus the analytic tradition, via Wittgenstein, was found to be treading a different path to the same clearing that the Continental line, as it issued in Heidegger, had sought: a therapeutic restoration of contact with a world that exists in touch with us, ordinarily, whether we admit it or think about it or not. Skepticism implied an intimacy with fear or anxiety, an unsettledness, loneliness, homelessness, which the philosopher should address but cannot get rid of. This prescription, indeed, sounded "existential." Keeping our condition open to the skeptical threat, trying to find a way to some commonness, or community, that acknowledged but did not give in to it—these were not the sorts of words with which analytic philosophy had wanted to do things. And as Cavell added terms that were ultimately intolerable to much of his collegial, Anglo-American world, he also said explicitly that he did not think philosophy was worthwhile without some recovery of the Continental. So it was said, in return, that what Cavell did was "not philosophy."

The years after 1979 Cavell perceived as his years in the wilderness. "The ordinary" in Cavell's hands spread from ordinary language to a positive philosophy. No longer just a term for a methodology, it seemed to name a sphere or view of our life. It became obligation-creating. You might think a commitment to the ordinary would spell an acknowledgment of whatever already is. Instead it became an investigation of what we hide from ourselves, what our intellectual condition divides us from, therefore what sort of condition we really are in, and how else we might be.

Cavell pursued these questions through previous civilized efforts to recover touch with the world, like the English Romantic poets' reversion to common language to regain contact with nature, set off from them by Kantian Enlightenment (fully considered in *In Quest of the Ordinary*, 1988), and the skepticisms staged by Shakespeare (collected finally in *Disowning Knowledge*, 1987). Yet the most fruitful and unexpected of his lines of thought had been opened quite a bit earlier, before he had come openly into conflict with his discipline. He had had a year off, and a contract from Viking (rather than the university presses that published almost all his other books), and found the inspiration for two nearly simultaneous, very short books: *The World Viewed* (1971) and *The Senses of Walden* (1972). In these he had asked, with little enough seemingly at stake: Where in his life did he see twinklings of the positive philosophy he cared for? And what was it that America offered philosophy, the America in which one could get usefully lost, as once he had been lost in New York City, and find oneself again?

To which Cavell had issued two unexpected and confounding answers: He saw a positive philosophy, and an American motive, in cinema, which aesthetics had not yet acknowledged was a philosophically distinctive art;

and he found them, too, in the always-unclassifiable book *Walden*, by Henry David Thoreau, crank and nature writer, which the American university did not yet conceive as a great work of philosophy.

Perfectionism

> Everyone is saying, and anyone can hear, that this is the new world; that we are the new men; that the earth is to be born again; that the past is to be cast off like a skin; that we must learn from children to see again; that every day is the first day of the world; that America is Eden. So how can a word get through whose burden is that we do not understand a word of all this? Or rather, that the way in which we understand it is insane, and we are trying again to buy and bully our way into heaven; that we have failed; that the present is a task and a discovery, not a period of America's privileged history; that we are not free, not whole, and not new, and we know this and are on a downward path of despair because of it; and that for the child to grow he requires family and familiarity, but for a grown-up to grow he requires strangeness and transformation, i.e., birth?[18]

These are Cavell's words, in *The Senses of Walden*, but not his sound. He imitates biblical prophecy, of which Thoreau was a better imitator, though it wasn't Thoreau's native tone, either. Despite the slight strain for each man, when he turned to the tenor of prophecy, the point was in part, in each case, to remind himself that coming later does not mean coming late. Prophecy persists, even with a change of key.

If the Founding Fathers had laid down the rules and hopes of America, Thoreau was a son who tried to say what it meant to live in the world they had made. Thoreau questioned what had been supposedly settled. He wanted something uncommon still from his neighbors' common language, and something better from the country's democracy. How do you make a new founding, if the country has just been founded for you—and is now inherited property? The scales Cavell heard Thoreau warming up were, first, the writer's plays on the meanings of words—his famous punning exercises. They run deftly in *Walden*, on both black and white keys, up to ultimacies and back to the mundane things, as if testing the language for its temper.

The simplest and most fundamental pun was Thoreau's opening joke on his readers who "are said to live in New England." The doubt was not about whether we have our addresses here, but whether we live, so dead do we seem in spirit. Cavell's interpretation of Thoreau's way of existing in these double entendres, in an inherited language, was that they asked what inheritance meant, generally, and whether acknowledgment must mean acquiescence. It need not mean, in Thoreau's word, *resignation*, as if one had to simply re-sign the social contract, once one grew to adulthood and learned it.

Such fated acquiescence, simply for having lived and attained majority in a country or society, is of course a core topic of the liberal doctrine of consent, as it was articulated in Locke. A standard alternative is to out-migrate, to flee to a new world. Thoreau's proposal was that one could be an emigrant even at home. ("I have traveled a good deal in Concord.") America had once been Locke's word for the untenanted places of the earth. "Thus in the beginning all the world was America."[19] If one were already here, and still found a foolish conformity, there was no hope of going anyplace else. America had to be the place of the migration as well as the place of home. Cavell summarized the Thoreau of democratic question-and-answer in this way: "His problem—at once philosophical, religious, literary, and, I will argue, political—is to get us to ask the questions, and then to show us that we do not know what we are asking, and then to show us that we have the answer."[20]

What was the fundamental American question in the generation of Thoreau? The young writer moved to Walden Pond on July 4, 1845. He built a visible Republic, with its one representative subject, himself, in Concord (in the vicinity of the Battle of Lexington and Concord), sixty years after the founding of the larger Republic. That should have been long enough for a country to have reached the age of wisdom. Or, at the very least, to have generated one wise man—an authority, a father—whose wisdom would obviate the need to find new values. Yet Thoreau said he knew no such wise men; or, anyway: "You may say the wisest thing you can, old man,— you who have lived seventy years, not without honor of a kind,—I hear an irresistible voice which invites me away from all that."[21] His own voice, of course. Once all men had been created equal, in other words, what became of their sons and daughters? To what would they be equal?

The great founding act of philosophy in the United States, of thinking in an American vein, had been made by Jefferson. He challenged fundamental right as it had been established by Locke and the English liberal tradition. Locke had proposed the unalienable rights to be those to "Life, liberty, and property." Jefferson, in the *Declaration of Independence*, transformed this trinity, overseen by Franklin and Adams. For their America, "Life, liberty, and property" would be too fixed. Right would now be to "Life, Liberty, and the pursuit of Happiness." In "the pursuit of Happiness," the problem was to pursue something that enjoyed endless evanescence and renewal. Something perishable, more like wild apples on the trees than the gold in a bank vault. Where did the pursuit lead, what had the sons chased, and were they happy? "I see young men, my townsmen, whose misfortune it is to have inherited farms, houses, barns, cattle, and farming tools; for these are more easily acquired than got rid of ... The better part of the man is soon ploughed into the soil for compost."[22] (Locke's doctrine of property had specified it as those parts of nature into which one mixes one's labor. But what a man then mixed into property might be his youth and, soon enough, his bones.) Improper property was the worst dependence, a Northern institution of slavery.

Thoreau's answer seemed, in that awkward American vernacular, a self-improvement. In law, you can improve a property. In cliché, you can improve the time. But Thoreau spoke of improving "the nick of time" rather than our idleness or our houses. If the world is to be really with us, we must run to catch it. If it sometimes seems too much with us, there must be other ways of accessing its abundance, urgent means which will help us make it new. This ecstatic need might be articulated in the modest terms of *besideness*. Cavell made much of Thoreau's pun, "With thinking we may be beside ourselves in a sane sense." Here I am, myself; but there is also another self, just beside me:

> The writer specifies my relation to the double as my being beside it. Being beside oneself is the dictionary definition of ecstasy. To suggest that one may stand there, stay there in a sane sense, is to suggest that the besideness of which ecstasy speaks is my experience of my existence, my knowledge "of myself as a human entity," my assurance of my integrity or identity. This condition—the condition of "having" a self, and knowing it—is an instance of the general relation the writer perceives as "being next to."[23]

In making the inner and emotional ("I was beside myself") outward and topographical ("what I truly wanted, all along, was right next to me"—and there is something still next to it, and next beyond that), an important modification is made to self-improvement. I may live in this world, acknowledging it. But I also know a just slightly better one beside it. Say my more urgent world is just next to the town of Concord—on the shores of Walden Pond. And next to me, in my sojourn at Walden, may be a world still better. (As to be next to the pond, in Thoreau's comic mythology of Walden as the clearest, deepest, freshest, and most perfect of all ponds, fed by an inexhaustible source, is a way to get next to the infinite waters of rebirth. To make your settlement on the banks of an element that will inspire you to be renewed again.)

Recalling an old sectarian term for the utopian Protestant project of self-improvement, a knot in the American grain, Cavell identified this pursuit as *perfectionism*. (In 1848, one year after Thoreau left Walden, Christian Perfectionists established their Oneida Community, and stayed there thirty years; Thoreau's vision proved the longer-lasting.) Perfectionism is certainly not the most attractive name for a philosophy of today. Cavell's election of the historic term, with its modern noise and interference, pushed his hearers to ask its provenance, how far back the impulse goes. It has been part of the project of philosophy, Cavell would ultimately insist (in *Cities of Words*, 2004), in Emerson, Kierkegaard, Thoreau, Nietzsche, and many others in modern times. It was part of the permanent project of philosophy in ancient times first indicated by Socrates or Epicurus. But the name should not connote the illusion of human perfectibility. It must not imply finality. In perfectionism, there is no perfect state to be attained. You do not become perfect; nor could you. Nor would you want to, were it conceivable. Perfected stasis of character would be the termination of the self, the end of hope.

Over three decades, Cavell moved from the specificity of Thoreau's pictures in *Walden* to a generalized philosophical project, making the journey by traveling with Emerson, Thoreau's neighbor and teacher. What Cavell ultimately named "moral" or "Emersonian" perfectionism is oriented to an interior dynamism. It does not displace the kind of moral philosophy that addresses lying, theft, saving lives, and letting die. It does not dispute the title of such issues to the name of ethics. It simply wants me to admit that, day to day, I have very little occasion to decide when three lives may be taken to save five, or whether it is right to steal radium for my ailing spouse. Whereas, morally, there isn't a day that goes by that doesn't involve some perfectionist reflection on what the persons and things around me would call me to do, if I were to become different, new, and better—not because of their spoken demands but by their example, positive or negative, of other forms of life than mine, and my decision whether it would be conformity or growth, death or life, to become like them.

The call to a next self may come from trees, paths, creatures, and seasons (as Thoreau tells us). It may come from an artwork or manmade representation (as Rilke tells us with his archaic torso of Apollo). The call may come from persons who don't yet exist, free spirits, imaginary future friends who inspire us to become more now than we are (as Nietzsche tells us). The call may come from past exemplars, the honored dead, those "representative men" who issue a call to revolution in the self (as Emerson tells us). Or from living friends (as the philosophical reflection on friendship since Plato and Aristotle tell us).

What matters most is that the next self isn't above the clouds, but right beside you, at the edge of vision. You might sometimes step right into who you might be, without breaking stride. The rebuke the next self issues is that it is right there: not in India, not in Africa, not in prayer. It may be nagging, but it is not inconsiderate. Its expectations are only your own, in hearing the call that is from outside; no one else has a right to expect so much of you.

Perfectionism in the American context does indeed resemble the enterprise called self-improvement. It can't entirely disclaim a family connection with *How to Stop Worrying and Start Living* or *Wherever You Go, There You Are*. Things that matter to us in philosophy will always have a range of eruptions. What matters in a book is that it is the book you need, not where in the library it may be found. Perfectionism admonishes self-improvement only as far as to say that the spirit of popular improvement has shown a susceptibility to fixity, or recipes for career success, rather than spiritual succession. Perfectionism's lead title would be *How to Succeed Yourself*.

World Viewed

How many paintings do we possess, as opposed to how many movies or photographs, that linger in the American mind as some expression of what is essential about Americans? Rothko's, I suppose, and Eakins's, Cole's, O'Keefe's, and Rockwell's. No one, though, seems to earn as much respect and commitment, both high and low, as Edward Hopper.

Hopper is our national portraitist of the act of thinking. It is possible to see his scenes as lonely. The diners and windy bright apartments can have that look, since solitude without speech may look like isolation. Yet these are places we would often be happy to be ourselves. His solitary female figures have embarked on meditation. "Nighthawks," the lonesome diner sheltering city-dwellers in a darkened street, lit with the uncanny brightness of heaven, has become a national black-velvet painting. It has been repopulated, in pastiche, with James Dean and Marilyn Monroe and Humphrey Bogart and Elvis, dream visions of our most extravagant selves.

The picture I find myself thinking of most, "New York Movie," is one of several Hopper painted of moviehouse interiors. The figure in this painting is an usherette, standing on the right, inhabiting a different light from the silver reflected on the auditorium seats by the screen on the picture's left edge. Under the yellow luminary of a sconce by the exit, marking a staircase up and out, the usherette *thinks*. She does not watch the movie. Maybe she's seen it too often. The pessimistic critic's interpretation is that she is mocked in her isolation by the aristocrats on-screen and their love affairs; she is a worried girl, servant to a missing audience of, presumably, unhappy fantasists like herself. My intuition, thinking about the painting over the years, is that she is pictured as watching the movie, metaphorically, and that it is the source of her troubled introspection. The seats seem mostly empty because she is the audience. In the picturing of her meditation, we face an allegory of the kind of thinking that gets done covertly by an American before her entertainments, which can indeed be more like introspection or worry than like thoughtless escape.

The movies, which became so major a subject of Cavell's philosophy, held a place at the center of his childhood, as his mother took him along on her part-time career as a piano accompanist to silent films in Atlanta moviehouses. In 1950s New York, when he was a young person seeking an ultimate vocation, cinema ran alongside his days as a second life. Cavell did not remember moviegoing ever to have been the pursuit of escape, precisely—though people so often termed films escapist.

It was certainly a place where citizens gathered. The cinema Cavell started with was one where there weren't timed seatings and evacuations of theaters, as for a stage play, but a continuous cycle of A-movie and B-movie, short and newsreel, into which you could wander. A world ran there all the time, alternative to and separated from this one. In the "movie palace," all social classes met. The rich went to movies and the poor went to movies. And the films concerned rich and poor. Their democratic character was obvious to Cavell when he first saw the movies of the 1930s, as a child, and anyone could know them to be a reflection on America in the Depression and New Deal. The medium had seemed suited to a nation of movement already in its silent era. From the first sound movie, in 1927, it found it could talk as rapidly as it moved.

Obstructing a philosophy of movies, however, stood something like 1,000 years of sophistication to undo, if one were to claim a relation of film to thought rather than to illusion. One can acknowledge retrospectively what Cavell was up against, in attempting to construct in the 1960s an *American philosophy of film*, after Bazin, Kracauer, Arnheim, as well as the revilers of the "culture industry"—but also after Plato. For cinema conjured a most primordial philosophical picture. Cinema could seem to literalize Plato's original allegory of illusion and ignorance of a "true world" as perhaps no other material artifact of human life ever had. The cave in the *Republic*, with a source of light projecting the enlarged silhouettes of idols upon a wall, exhibited deceptions to an enchanted and enchained humanity. This seemed like a blueprint for the movies' projected images of absent stars upon a silver screen. The enraptured, fantasizing audience handed over two bits for the privilege of "escape," to sink deeper into a prison of unconsciousness. This ogre of intellectual sorcery or enslavement sneaked into intellectuals' critique of ordinary Hollywood movies. The idols of the matinee could be added to Bacon's other idols of the mind. Nor had the Platonic critique of all representations vanished: that any manmade picture of the real signified a copy of a copy, twice removed from the Idea.

In *The World Viewed* Cavell upset these notions on every side, yet genially, calmly, as if he were not upending basic truths. What was the *medium* of film? Cavell answered evenly that its medium was the world. Photosensitive emulsion on celluloid simply did not fill the role that pigments and oil did for painting or bronze and stone for sculpture. Unmetaphysically, the thing projected in film was actually our world, the true and only one. Here was the photographic condition, as he distilled it: "A photograph does not present us with 'likenesses' of things; it presents us, we want to say, with the things themselves. But wanting to say that may well make us ontologically restless."[24] Cavell cheekily defined a moving picture, for the sort of readers who needed a definition, as "*a succession of automatic world-projections.*" An artist puts an eye to a viewfinder and frames his or her shot, to be sure. But the automaticity and dehumanized mechanics of the camera, its assemblage of light, film, and the material world, does all the representational work. And viewers took these real people, filmed through automatic mechanisms, to teach things beyond the filmmakers' intention, as if the model had taken over from the painter.

Cavell pointed out that the core of film satisfactions involves the actor not falling into the role and disappearing. The actor is kept before the mind by attention to his or her unalterable incarnate features, closely observed. When a hat is lifted above a previously shaded face, it is John Wayne's face, not the character's. The cigarette is flourished in Bette Davis's hand, not the role's. Every movie the star played in previously is carried into this one, as a dimension of who he or she is or can be here, this time. And the roles themselves are often not so much fictional persons as types. Here, the star plays a cowboy, stepping into one functional place in the nation—here a military man. Here she is an heiress, here a striver. This is not a weakness, but an intelligible feature. Unlike ordinary fiction or drama, the odd overlap is with our experience of evaluating people in a democracy. We exalt the single individual, making him representative, and simultaneously think in types, groups, and factions, the repeating positions that arise in a collectivity. Likewise, the audience taking seats in a theater, coming and going, is not unlike a rotating jury of one's peers, or a seated assembly chosen by lot. Our talk before movies, after them, and even during, to friends we've arrived with, or to the screen and everyone—for those who won't contain themselves, who even want to *enhance* the democratic feeling with their remarks (earning grateful audience laughter or angry shushing)—makes probably our most vivid and warmly beloved sphere of national chatter, politics and sports included.

In the late 1960s, Cavell had felt the danger for the first time that the movies were becoming modernist in the way that painting had, meaning that this vast audience could be divided. "Sophisticated" taste would no longer coincide with the common, shared, democratic run of movies, the best that the Hollywood studio system had created. Cavell started to encounter people in Berkeley or New York or Cambridge who wanted to talk about Bergman and Antonioni but not Cary Grant or the Marx Brothers—that is to say, he met fools of a dangerous type. Snobbery would cause the loss of a unique aesthetic forum, and, unless someone philosophized movies differently, it would be the fault of the intellectuals. "The movie seems naturally to exist in a state in which its highest and its most ordinary instances attract the same audience (anyway until recently),"[25] Cavell wrote. "My claim is that in the case of films, it is generally true that you do not really like the highest instances unless you also like the typical ones. You don't even know what the highest are instances of unless you know the typical as well."[26]

If film were truly respected for all that it can do, it would be seen that cinema could offer the audience, as a "people" and also as a million individuals, a total vision recognizable as an impulse to philosophy. The views projected by film show you above all else what the world looks like without you in it. Film may be necessary, in the methods of democracy, to gain the vantage of shared objectivity. Here, the "I" and one's own voice, and all the temporary collective passions of the audience, are not the all in all. Movies constitute an ordinary, non-supernatural way to reflect on our situation, singly, in a world of others. And also to reflect upon the mortality that is our human portion without waving our fear of it away. In the still somewhat terrifying and unexpected last words of Cavell's book:

> A world complete without me which is present to me is the world of my immortality. This is an importance of film—and a danger. It takes my life as my haunting of the world, either because I left it unloved (the Flying Dutchman) or because I left unfinished business (Hamlet). So there is reason for me to want the camera to deny the coherence of the world, its coherence as past: to deny that the world is complete without me. But there is equal reason to want it affirmed that the world is coherent without me. That is essential to what I want of immortality: nature's survival of me. It will mean that the present judgment upon me is not yet the last.[27]

Remarriage

The point on which all these paths converged was marriage. It seemed the most incongruous step imaginable. The book of 1981 that announced this unforeseen expansion and reworking of so many themes from Cavell's career possessed a title like a coffee table book: *Pursuits of Happiness: The Hollywood Comedy of Remarriage*. It constituted a work, too, of diagnostic philosophy—not quite argument, deduction, or even speculation—unlike almost anything else in philosophy, though it featured Kant and Mill and Nietzsche alongside Katharine Hepburn and Cary Grant. Cavell's curious intuition was that there existed a class of Golden Age film comedies as great as anything Hollywood had made, appreciated as such, indeed loved and shared (*The Philadelphia Story*, *It Happened One Night*, *His Girl Friday*, others)—which we also have appreciated so much because they give a rare, perhaps unique account of equal marriages that we could ratify, without allowances or reservations, for our times. If Cavell could diagnose why these films formed a set, and why they were unique in our esteem and acceptance, and also what remained painful or went unsaid in them, then he would identify much else that was right and wrong in our condition.

But why marriage, at all? It is not a subject unknown to philosophy, but it is certainly one of philosophy's most excruciating topics, on which the tradition, historically, had gone most wrong. This is because the tradition had been only male, and, more than that, misogynist. By tradition, Socrates walked the streets of Athens, schooling boys, because the alternative was his wife Xanthippe to go home to. Not until the Enlightenment learned emancipation do you see the publication of women philosophers like Wollstonecraft—who would be refused by all but political radicals—or de Staël, who was set aside as a midwife to male thought. Marriage as its own topic found its most interesting male exegetes among nineteenth-century thinkers who pathologically could not marry. One likes to think that their sensing of the inequality and stunting of women was the root of their trouble (in an era, after abolitionism, when feminism began to liberate women politically). But the men remained, themselves, hysterical, castrated, unenlightened: Kierkegaard, in *Either/Or* and *Stages on Life's Way*, obsessing over the ethical possibility or impossibility of marriage; Nietzsche, betraying his gifts with his stupid epigrams on "woman" in *Beyond Good and Evil*, his desperate loneliness, and the curdled will to power. From such acting out of contradictions, which leaves one puzzled but dirtied, to seek cleansing from recent male philosophers of marriage, like Roger Scruton, is worse, like scrubbing your eyes with soap.

Marriage accomplished some purely philosophical syntheses for Cavell. Speaking of the world *without* us, it gave a special institution for us to take views of—a test case for the fatefulness of viewing, in which my position as audience, outside, accentuates my intimacy with "the marriage," the shared creation that neither married partner can quite see. (This transpires first in our ancient views of mother and father, the most basic couple we ever stand to view; judging the pair affectionately and implacably, a child is material witness, and sitting jury, and the party most affected by any decision.) As Cavell looked for the world beside us, marriage made perfectionism social and reciprocal. It overcame the bind that kept perfectionism isolated and egocentric, in its communion of self with next self. The model of a conversation between one self and another, which called to it but was not the same, could be the conversation between men and women.

As for the post-skeptical world *with* us, marriage made a real task for acknowledgment, a most ordinary and yet most difficult one. Acknowledging the external world isn't hard for most of us, when we're not in the skeptical mood. Acknowledging other minds like ours, equally feeling and capable, is a generosity we routinely pretend. But the true acknowledgment of another mind—even just one other—in equal marriage is, our civilization knows, the most difficult, and most outwardly verifiable, act of acknowledgment we face. There is nothing harder in the world than acknowledging the other who is under your roof, who is as close to you as you are to yourself but has other wishes and another will, another past and loves; who is fundamentally different, in the smallest thing, that looms largest.

Marriage also let Cavell intersect feminism. What should an American become equal to, in our times? To equality between men and women. There had been a new birth of equality and genius in America, from 1848 (the time of Seneca Falls) to the 1920s (suffrage and the New Woman) to the present, and it was unfinished and still too unappreciated. The first women to become world-historically significant and transformative openly as philosophers, standing at the forefront of their generations—Arendt and

Beauvoir preeminent among them—were educated in Europe in the 1920s and 1930s. Among Cavell's contemporaries, maturing in Anglo-America in the 1960s and after, the explosion occurred of women philosophers as contributors to the tradition that has made our time superior, in this respect, to all previous eras. Today, to be a person educated only in English-language philosophy, one can be expected to have run into the work of Murdoch, Langer, Anscombe, Foot, Jarvis Thomson, Baier, Nussbaum, and Butler (Judith, not Joseph); then, if one has broader interests, Sontag, MacKinnon, Dworkin, Gilligan, Chodorow, Okin, Pateman, Daly, Sedgwick (Eve, not Henry), Felman, Benhabib, Fraser, Haraway, Spivak, Scarry, Moi, Ronell, and Kipnis (missing many other thinkers on this first tour d'horizon). Not all these thinkers are feminists. But second-wave American feminism is the native intellectual movement that constitutes the United States' post-1968 contribution to world thought, in the years when Cavell was partly alienated from the analytic establishment. And radical feminism is our philosophical achievement on par with European poststructuralism, but more practical, deeper, more activist, more productive of change, less hermetic. It took 200 years, but feminism in America developed with an intensity and genius unmatched by any other country. By 1976, we completed a new 1776.

Thinking has not taken place enough from the male side about how philosophy changes when it ceases to be divided in half—as if equality only needed to be thought through by the equalizers. There are too few feminist books by men. Taking up remarriage comedy meant Cavell's finding in himself (via the world on-screen) a certain maleness that had held a character of immaturity, exclusion. You can feel a radical change in tone from his books of 1971–2, which are male in expectation and a kind of ordinary blindness, to the altered books of the early 1980s forward. The "we" in *The World Viewed* still looks from the point of view of men at women, without a reverse angle or speculation on how views will be different through other, including female, eyes. ("A woman in a movie is dressed (as she is, when she is, in reality), hence potentially undressed. ... [I]n seeing a film of a desirable woman we are looking for a reason.") That changes. The "I" can start male; the "we" should not, or not without acknowledgment of all the places it may find itself.

Cavell returned for his diagnosis to a set of films he remembered from his childhood. They belonged, starting with the earliest, *It Happened One Night* (1934), to the era that "discovered" sound, with the old plots of heiresses and high society intact. But it was the era, too, of the equality-minded women who entered the media and professions and government, evident in such masterpieces as *His Girl Friday* (1940) and *Adam's Rib* (1949) before America suffered the post–World War II backlash that Betty Friedan named a decade later in *The Feminine Mystique*. It was as if what movie sound first discovered, what it could record most extraordinarily, was the rapid and ingenious conversation and banter between men and women (also song, which Cavell saw as closely related) that defined their new equality in social mores, well past their new assurance of political equality. As the movies spanned the period through the Depression and the war, one couldn't help but notice, too, that these films had things to say about money, democracy, and a nation fragmenting or pulling together in love and justice. The right comic pair, trying to reach a marriage under conditions of equality, without falsification or tyranny, formed itself as the microcosm on which all other burdens rested.

Without asking what marriage was in advance of watching and rewatching these filmed examples, Cavell tried to say neutrally what plots, motifs, turning points, conditions, and constellations of figures reoccurred across all the masterpieces of the genre. He noticed, for one thing, that it was *remarriage* that was at stake in these films. Whether because a pair had already split or was in jeopardy of separation at the start of each film, the movies seemed uninterested in first love, purity, or the usual ideas of virgin fate—here was marriage under conditions of divorce, in a world of experience. Yet when the movies presented the ultimate success of the pair, it was necessary to conjure an allegory of wholeness based on a shared experience prior to, and surpassing, all others—as in a common childhood, sometimes real, sometimes symbolic. The proof of that experience was not a matter of sex (no children, and a certain libertine indifference to the prurience of others), but the ability of this pair to sustain a *conversation*.

That conversation was never the cooing of lovebirds or infants. Nor did it deny that the pair stood at odds even in what attached them. They must give as good as they get; the speed and fitness of their language is its quality of lovers' magic, and that they hear each other (as we do, too, getting their jokes). The survival of conversation meant having known the tyranny of each partner upon the other, and holding it in mind, while still managing to forgive. While forgiveness meant, in practice, largely continuing their conversation, regardless of what had been said or done. In part they chose to continue with each other because of love; in part because only from this other person could they get the right education. In part, because any other people, hearing them talk, just wouldn't ever understand them right.

More people I know have read *Pursuits of Happiness* than any other of Cavell's books, and rightfully so. The only comparably rich modern book I know on marriage is Phyllis Rose's *Parallel Lives* (1984), and these two books of the early 1980s, successors in an everyday spirit to more solemn utopian and critical achievements of 1970s and 1980s feminism, stand almost alone for asking, artfully and playfully, what can be *redeemed* in the institution, by sane people, equals, once marriage's tyrannies and inequities have been exposed.

But the turn in Cavell's project to inequities, and a different set of tools for critique, continued to develop. As did his need to ask by what right an American philosopher spoke, and who else was not being listened to.

Perfectionism became a ground for democracy and distributive justice in what may be his most philosophically important later book, *Conditions Handsome and Unhandsome* (1990). Cavell returned, in his late books, to seek insistently within the subject matters that had always spoken to him most powerfully for the danger (and redress) of men's ignorance of women's voices, the drama of women not being attended to even at moments of highest expression. This meant, in classical music, the exploration of opera (*A Pitch of Philosophy*, 1994). In film, the melodrama, "weepie," or "women's film" (*Contesting Tears*, 1996). In the tradition of ordinary language (to which Cavell owed his career), the recognition of a fatal refusal in Austin's theory of performatives to acknowledge unmasculine, "emotional" speech acts. These special speech acts, Cavell termed "passionate utterances," devoting one of his last, or latest, philosophical papers to date ("Performative and Passionate Utterance," in *Philosophy the Day after Tomorrow*, 2005) to an astonishing effort "to question a theory of language that pictures speech as at heart a matter of action and only incidentally as a matter of articulating and hence expressing desire."

As the author of a philosophy that forgives and acknowledges, that seizes the second chance first, that has a place for man and woman and each in the other, Cavell becomes distinct, as I understand him, from Emerson and Thoreau. Even if he claimed their authority for the perfectionism he excavated and reconstituted, he differs from them ultimately. He becomes a founder. It makes sense to speak of Cavellian perfectionism, and to know it as a major philosophy independent of all that precedes it.

Love is one thing Cavell doesn't often write about explicitly. Yet one can't help but think of him as a philosopher of the forms of love. The other central thing he doesn't often write about explicitly is music. Yet it, too, seems like a ground of whatever is particular in his philosophy. Love and music are the conditions, say, respectively, for thought and for speech. Together they mark the movement toward the world. This journey becomes the tutored recognition that one is already irresistibly inside the shared world. The transit from the outside in is actually a circulation inside something without limit or exterior. Together, however, love and music also teach the limitations of this world, made by men and women, in this world's failure to meet up to and fulfill all that men and women can be, desire, and need. "Music, like infancy, marks the permanence of the place of understanding as before what we might call meaning, as if it exists in permanent anticipation of—hence in perpetual dissatisfaction with, even disdain for—what can be said."

Notes

1   This essay first appeared in *n+1*, Fall 2011, issue 12: *Conversion Experience*. Sincere thanks are extended to the author, Mark Greif, and the journal's editor,

Mark Krotov, for permission to reproduce the work here. The bibliographical notes, below, are reproduced from the standards and formatting of the journal, and supplemented as necessary.

2   Emerson, "Beauty," *The Conduct of Life*.
3   Thoreau, "Economy," *Walden*.
4   Nietzsche was a professor at Basel, Heidegger at Freiburg, Hegel at Jena, James at Harvard, Wittgenstein at Cambridge, and Arendt at the New School. Thoreau early in life taught school with his brother, but otherwise returned to Harvard only for its library. Of the two main figures at the late edge of a pre-university moment in two peripheral countries, Emerson became a star of the American lecture circuit; Kierkegaard went to Berlin to see Schelling teach but defended his dissertation (*The Concept of Irony*) in Denmark and published independently. Both retained the marks of their nations' premodern institution of ideas, the Church.
5   Nietzsche, *Thus Spoke Zarathustra*, Prologue.
6   Emerson, "Self-Reliance," *Essays: First Series*.
7   Nietzsche, *Human, All Too Human*, II, §267.
8   Austin, "Other Minds," *Philosophical Papers*.
9   Cavell, *The Claim of Reason*, 44.
10 Cf. Kierkegaard, "Preliminary Expectoration," *Fear and Trembling*.
11 Epicurus, "Letter to Menoeceus."
12 Nietzsche, "Schopenhauer as Educator," *Untimely Meditations*.
13 Nietzsche, *The Will to Power*, §919. The note importantly clarifies: "This is something different from the blind drive to love oneself: nothing is more common, in the love of the sexes as well as of that duality which is called 'I,' than contempt for what one loves."
14 Cavell, *Cities of Words*, chapter 15.
15 Cavell, *A Pitch of Philosophy*, 21.
16 Cavell, *Must We Mean What We Say?*, 324; and *Disowning Knowledge*, 95.
17 Cavell, *Emerson's Transcendental Etudes*, 16.
18 Cavell, *The Senses of Walden: An Expanded Edition*, 59–60.
19 Locke, *Second Treatise of Government*, V, §49.
20 Cavell, *The Senses of Walden*, 47.
21 Thoreau, "Economy," *Walden*.
22 Ibid.
23 Cavell, *The Senses of Walden*, 104.
24 Cavell, *The World Viewed*, Enlarged Edition, 17.
25 Ibid., 5.
26 Ibid., 6.
27 Ibid., 160.

4

What Cavell Made Possible for Philosophy

SUSAN NEIMAN

Opening remarks for a memorial conference celebrating Stanley Cavell at the Einstein Forum in Potsdam, Germany, October 2018.

I WANT MOST OF ALL TO THANK THE PHILOSOPHERS who came, at fairly short notice, to celebrate the work of a man whose influence on philosophy was profound. Just how profound it was can only be understood if we try to remember what philosophy was like before Stanley Cavell decided to give up a career as a jazz musician. For a philosopher, that's a bit like trying to remember what the world was like before the internet—you may have been there, but much of what it felt like is hard to recover. I had the good fortune to begin studying philosophy about the time Cavell was transforming it—indeed, I probably would have given it up had he not been doing so. The effect of his work was like opening a window in a small, stuffy room. Anglo-American philosophy had rewritten the history of Western philosophy to suit its own peculiar inclinations—described by Quine, one of its greatest practitioners, as a taste for desert landscapes. Quine was also known for what he called the principle of charity: the idea that before you criticize someone's work, you should read it in the way that makes most sense to you. The idea sounds generous, and even innocuous, but its effects were not: thousands of years of metaphysics—attempts to understand the structure of G-d and the world—were reduced to epistemology, the attempt to understand the structure of knowledge. Thousands of years of attempts to understand the meaning of life were thrown overboard in the rush to determine the meaning of meaning. I don't know if anyone made the obvious reference in response to Quine's landscape preferences—"they make a desert and call it peace." I do know that, in the constant references to the principle of charity, no one questioned the problem with the concept of charity itself, namely, its very hierarchical nature, its assumption of noblesse oblige. In applying the principle of charity to the history of philosophy, Anglo-American philosophers were deigning to treat their benighted predecessors as if they were responding to the same small dry questions that had (partly) moved the Vienna Circle, which was committed to putting philosophy on what Kant had called the sure path of a science. I emphasize "partly" here because the fact that many of the Vienna Circle were politically active, and saw their work as a blow against fascism and for socialism was left out of the story. This was not because, as Jean Améry later put it, Carnap's attempts to undermine Heidegger through logical exercises neither Heidegger nor his followers took seriously were laughable. Rather, it was thought that the Vienna Circle's political commitments were private matters, because political and moral convictions had no place in a philosophy meant to be scientific.

A brief clarification for the Germans among you: science, for the Vienna Circle and its American followers, meant natural science. Those of us who learned that the German language had a word for *Geisteswissenschaften* were thrilled, for we thought it meant that Germans took philosophy, literature, and history more seriously than the British or the Americans. In the intervening years I've come to find this mistaken, and to believe that the concept *Geisteswissenschaften* actually betrays a nod to positivism, and its sanctification of the natural sciences, in a way the Renaissance concept "humanities" does not. But I mention this question to clarify the background, not to open a debate.

When I began to study philosophy in the Harvard of the 1970s, natural science was the model for serious philosophy, and we were grateful for any attempt to make space instead for culture. It is almost never logic that draws people to study philosophy, but once inside that study, any sentence that couldn't be numbered was treated with contempt. A friend spoke of visiting another department and being asked why he'd chosen the field. His answer was simple: "Like most people, I read Nietzsche and Sartre and decided to go on." The withering answer of the department chair was equally terse: "Yes, but most people grow out of that." The friend went instead to Harvard and studied with Cavell and Rawls, who did not insist we grow out of the kinds of questions that moved Nietzsche and Sartre, but insisted that those questions were, somehow, still central to philosophy. The effect was as liberating as realizing that growing up, in general, does not require resignation to a life of mediocrity and boredom. It was also frankly erotic. When another fellow student ironically captured the feeling one had after a Cavell seminar—"Say more words, Stanley"—we all knew what he meant.

I was not a typical Cavell student. I did not share his passion for Austin, I could never stand Heidegger, and I was lukewarm about Emerson and

Thoreau until I learned of the ways they defended John Brown. (In my last visit with Stanley I wanted to talk about that, but that day he was too ill to have the kind of conversation he had so enjoyed earlier.) Most of all, I do not think skepticism is the central question of modern philosophy. Long ago I talked to Stanley about my inability to take skepticism seriously. He said it was because I was a woman; a woman can never be gripped by the worry that their child might not be their own. I wasn't convinced by his response and thought it vaguely reductive; my book *Evil in Modern Thought* was a gender-neutral argument for rejecting the prominence of skepticism in modern philosophy. I sent him a copy, though I suspect he was too busy with his own work to read it. Yet despite all the ways in which I wasn't a typical Cavell student, his passing has been an occasion for me to think about the ways in which I was influenced by him—beyond the very general debt owed by anyone who yearned to see, as he put it in the introduction to *Must We Mean What We Say?*, how philosophy can support life, giving us encouragement for going on, against the grain, in the field.

Cavell made everyone around him think about language, but not in the ways known to philosophers of language: he made you want to speak better, to learn to navigate the riches words offer. Cavell was a master both of seriousness and of playfulness; indeed, he convinced me that to be deeply serious, and seriously playful, you need to be both. I'm sure my lifelong crusade against the use of scare quotes was started by the very question, "Must we mean what we say?": it's a matter of subterfuge and laziness not to do so, and scare quotes are an act of both. Surely Cavell's example was one that allowed me to write in the first person. Traditionally, many great philosophers had done so: Rousseau, Kierkegaard, Thoreau, Nietzsche, Sartre, de Beauvoir, and the still inadequately acknowledged Jean Améry. But they were long ago, and in another country; Cavell was in Emerson Hall. His daring to write autobiographically was one reason why many philosophers dismissed him. (At the time I was at Harvard, there were no courses on any of the philosophers cited above—except for one course on Nietzsche in 1982 given by Jack McNees, one of Cavell's first students.) The scientism of analytic philosophy made writing as a subject look, well, subjective. And writing in the first person can be problematic, verging on the self-indulgent, even the narcissistic. (Certain passages of Nietzsche cross that line.) But Cavell *raised* the problem of subjectivity, making writing in the first person a way of taking responsibility for one's words. Perhaps that's the reason *Little Did I Know* is one of my favorite of Cavell's books, allowing him to let his taste for that kind of responsibility flow freely. That subjectivity isn't solipsism was made clear in *The Claim of Reason*, where Cavell wrote, "The wish and search for community is the wish and search for reason." Though he never wrote about it systematically, the seeds of a different conception of reason than the one to which we were used were in Cavell's mature work all along—presumably one ground for changing the title of his dissertation, *The Claim to Rationality*, to the title the extensively revised version now bears.

But who needs systematic? Cavell's work is at its best when it focuses on the particular, and it was only recently that I realized my own insistence on particulars must have been learned from him. Principles may provide frameworks, but they never take you very far in questions of real moment: understanding evil, or realizing justice, is never helped by constructing definitions. Careful analysis of particulars always takes you further—whether you want to understand the world as it is or the world as it should be. Contrary to popular opinion, this much was clear to Kant.

As important as these principles have become to my own work, Cavell's influence wasn't confined to them. It was Stanley who wrote the first sentence of my first book: "Every time I see you I think of Dachau, baby." I had just returned from my first year in Berlin. Over lunch at the Harvard Faculty Club, he asked me, as one Atlanta Jew to another, what it was like to be a Jew in Germany. There were very few of us in 1983. "It's weird," I told him, "And intense and fascinating. You'll be sitting in a biergarten and someone will say 'Every time I see you I think of Dachau.'" Stanley looked at me from under his eyebrows and replied, "Oh, but Susan. That's *every time I see you I think of Dachau, baby.*" I sat up; I hadn't mentioned that I was having an affair with the man who had uttered that sentence. I went on to rave about Berlin, with a line I would later come to see as youthful exaggeration: there was more philosophy in any bar in Berlin than in Harvard seminars. Stanley listened for a long time, with exquisite interest. "I have just one question," he said after a time, "Do they get you?" I was dazzled, as one often was in his presence. "No they don't," I had to answer, for all my enthusiasm, "they don't get me at all. At least not the way you do." I am sure he made hundreds of people feel the same way.

Here's what Richard Rorty said about Cavell's work: "Cavell is among professors of philosophy the least defended, the gutsiest, the most vulnerable. He sticks his neck out farther than any of the rest of us." It's a true and generous statement, especially if you know that Rorty, who was far more widely read, was long considered to be Cavell's rival. Hadn't they both turned from analytic philosophy of language to ... *literature???* (As a former Cavell student, I am trying to capture the tone of obnoxious wonder that accompanied such remarks at the time.) Well, they did both attend to, and write about literature, but if they had literary models, as one philosopher put it, Rorty was American philosophy's Hemingway and Cavell was its Melville. And that has much to do with the different traditions they came from within analytic philosophy. Unlike Rorty, who after his landmark book *Philosophy and the Mirror of Nature*, declared philosophy to be finished, Cavell made it easy to go on.

His work threw most of the assumptions of analytic philosophy into question, not by challenging them from outside, or rejecting them as arid and irrelevant—the standard responses of most European philosophers at the time—but by turning analytic philosophy itself inside out. I am not, in fact, convinced by the central way in which Cavell made it easy to go on with traditional philosophy. But even if you believe, as I do, that twentieth-century philosophers were mistaken in placing skepticism at the heart of modern philosophy, Cavell's understanding of it was brilliant and explosive. He returned again and again to the problems of skepticism that have plagued modern philosophy: do we ever know anything at all? Might Descartes's nightmare come true? Could I be alone in a world made of dreams and shadows, surrounded by other human bodies who only seem to be blessed with minds like mine? These questions dominated not only twentieth-century philosophy but also twentieth-century philosophy's reading of philosophy's earlier history. With directness, depth, and humor Cavell gave flesh to the problem(s) of skepticism. In his hands the mind-body problem becomes, among other things, the question of whether you weep for the prince who has become a frog in the pond, or feed him flies on a golden plate; what it means to say Jesus is the word made flesh, and is bread at the same time; whether Othello's murder of Desdemona takes place because he thought she was faithful to him or because he thought she was true. Skepticism, for Cavell, was not an intellectual problem, something that evidence and argument could resolve, or even affect, but a question about how we stand to our own humanity, and how we respond to the humanity of others.

Other thinkers have rejected the question of skepticism: Dr. Johnson by kicking a stone to refute Berkeley, G. E. Moore by holding up his hands to demonstrate the existence of something. Cavell did nothing of the sort. Rather he shows us the strangeness of skepticism, a problem treated in the center of philosophy but which can never be resolved because it isn't a problem that is cognitive. The solution is not therapeutic, except insofar as Wittgenstein's methods have been called therapeutic, though Cavell shows that the madness that was a theoretical possibility in Descartes's *Meditations* becomes terrifyingly real in Shakespeare's tragedies. In arguing that skepticism arises from the urge to escape or restrict our humanity, either as cynics or as sages, Cavell's work showed how philosophy, and literature, can bring us back to the parts of our lives that were threatened.

Intensely influenced by Wittgenstein's *Philosophische Untersuchungen*, and by first-hand work with Oxford philosopher J. L. Austin, Cavell took ordinary language analysis in directions it had never seen. To begin with, he enriched it by bringing it to bear in places where no one had thought to take it. Cavell reveled in the ordinary in ordinary language philosophy. His discussions of real children learning real languages, of mistakes in common usage, and of fairy tales and myths are as penetrating and funny as anything twentieth-century philosophy ever offered. At a time when many people believed that Wittgenstein's philosophy and ordinary language analysis were either completely implausible or spelled the end of philosophy, Cavell showed how they could be its new beginning. As he wrote of Wittgenstein's teaching in *The Claim of Reason*, "What feels like destruction, what expresses itself here in the idea of destruction, is really a shift in what we are asked to let interest us, in the tumbling of our ideas of the great and the important, as in conversion." For in addition to making ordinary language philosophy more grounded, more genuinely common, he also used it to analyze the English language at its most sublime—foremost in an extraordinary series of essays on the tragedies of Shakespeare.

Armed with a far more powerful conception of ordinary language philosophy than anyone had imagined possible, Cavell proceeded to use it to reinvent analytic philosophy—in ways that often went misunderstood and unappreciated by the fields that were being reinvented. He was the first to show that to assume an unbridgeable gap between what used to be called analytic and continental philosophy was to be sterile and silly, and to show it from both sides: to give English-speaking philosophers a sense of the European philosophy, without trying to tame it; and to give those trained in European traditions, who viewed analytic philosophy as dry and pointless, an idea of its moral power and urgency. Cavell introduced a number of other ideas we now take for granted: for example, that to view philosophy's relationship to its history on the model of the natural sciences is just to get it wrong. We don't relate to our intellectual past as a series of great steps, and well-intentioned mistakes, to be followed or abandoned in building an edifice of knowledge. Rather, if philosophy is crucially about self-knowledge, as Cavell was the first in his generation to remind us, our history is with us all the time. (The voices of Socrates and Freud can be heard in conversation throughout Cavell's work, their apparent contemporaneity either uplifting or maddening, depending on one's mood.) The dialogue between philosophy and its past is more akin to that in the arts; the fact that philosophy and poetry have been in conflict since Plato is a place to start thinking, not to stop. Ideas like these were anything but obvious before Cavell. And anyone who thinks they only undermine the dogmas of empiricism—that is, the provincial assumptions of Anglo-American philosophy—should think about the distinction between *systematische und historische Philosophie*, which still holds most German philosophers captive.

All this might be enough to make an argument for calling Cavell the American philosopher *überhaupt*, for it's part of showing how certain steps that were crucial in moving philosophy forward internationally were first taken in America. But Cavell went several steps further, and made the idea of America a central focus of his work. To recall just how daring this was, one must recall that Europeans weren't the only people who long regarded Americans as cultural barbarians. Like any good ideology, this was a view that its subjects internalized. In the America Stanley Cavell appeared in, anyone who wanted to be an intellectual found it unwise to admit he'd ever *been* to the movies—with the possible exception of *Jules et Jim*. Cavell turned all that around. He was the first American philosopher to take on a task sometimes taken on by European philosophy, namely, reflecting on the culture in which one finds oneself. But he did it in a distinctly American way, for he didn't exactly write about culture, or even about film; he wrote about the movies. You might wonder what else one should write about if one wants to understand something essential about America—and what better task could an American philosopher set himself? But that is a question that could only be asked, once again, after Cavell, who wrote as passionately and complexly about Thoreau and Emerson as he did about Cary Grant. For much of his life, this seemed to put him exactly nowhere. People who wanted to hear about Emerson and Kant were embarrassed by references to Hollywood, and people who didn't want to hear about Emerson and Kant didn't want to think about the movies as well as to watch them. In fact, Cavell's attempt to establish a department of film studies at Harvard in the early 1980s—now hardly a revolutionary gesture—failed entirely, when the powers that were determined that literature was culture, but movies were not. Unlike some contemporary film students, Cavell's understanding of Shakespeare was as deep and subtle as his understanding of Hollywood comedy; what was revolutionary was to insist on viewing both with equal attention. Similarly, he was a deep and seriously trained student of classical music, but he insisted on adding jazz to the musical repertoire. In fact Cavell's English is as American as jazz, with some of the same meanderings and surprises that a great jazz soloist will bring to bear. Another student aptly described his classes in jazz terms: Cavell would riff on a question for a while, without actually answering it, then throw it over to someone else to riff back, in what was not exactly an answer but a form of deep play. In 1996, Cavell became the first person ever to be elected president of the American Philosophical Association by popular, write-in ballot; though he held a chair in the philosophy department at Harvard since 1963, his subjects and his style made most academic philosophers question whether he was a philosopher at all. Many of my most memorable conversations with Cavell took place over lunch at the Harvard Faculty Club. I remember one—it must have been the early 1980s—at which he spoke of the pain at being dismissed by most of the profession. "Sometimes I want to tell them: go away, call it what you like, just let me get on with my work," he told me, before a dramatic pause and a lowered voice. "But I wouldn't let them have *that word*." It didn't need saying that the word was "philosophy," and that we both felt there was something deep, almost sacred about it. For many years afterward, I wondered whether he'd been so right to insist on maintaining his claim to it. His work had more reach than that of most people whom the profession calls philosophers, and—unlike some of us who were influenced by him—he had no need to worry about being employed. Why should we bother about the opinions of people whose work we don't find interesting? But acknowledgment was a central category in his work, and today I think he was right to insist on it. Of course what he did was philosophy.

In all these ways, Cavell was clearly the most important American philosopher since Ralph Waldo Emerson, whose work he resurrected. As strange as it sounds today, though the Harvard philosophy department is housed in Emerson Hall, whose entrance has a larger-than-life bronze statue of the Concord philosopher, no twentieth-century Anglo-American philosopher had thought to examine Emerson's work; when Cavell did so, it was with help of the European Nietzsche, whose admiration for Emerson made it seem acceptable to take Emerson seriously. Cavell's resurrection of Emerson and Thoreau, as well as his reminder that the Vienna Circle that so influenced Anglo-American philosophy was actually Viennese, was part of his effort to insist on a philosophy that was specifically American—itself part of an effort to insist that culture did not come from Europe alone, there was such a thing as American culture. This insistence may be outdated; we now rightly feel compelled to look beyond both Europe and the United States when we look for culture. But amid all the critiques of Eurocentrism, it's worth remembering how recently we've come to take them for granted. When I first came to Berlin and introduced myself as a graduate student in philosophy, more than one acquaintance replied with a condescension that seemed natural: are there any philosophers in America—besides Marcuse?

I'm grateful to Cavell for providing an answer, and for a work that, I suspect, will give commentators fruitful tasks in the future: understanding, perhaps more systematically than he ever could do, how Cavell's separate works add up to a vision of, as the title of one of his last books suggest, "this new yet unapproachable America." In doing so, however, I hope they will acknowledge the ways in which Cavell's work shows something problematically American. In his fine autobiography, *Little Did I Know*, Cavell wrote: "If there are two kinds of people, those whose instincts of response to a crisis is primarily political and those whose instinct is psychological, I suppose I belong to the latter kind."

Indeed he did, and it's worth mentioning that this passage occurs in a section discussing how he nevertheless was politically engaged in supporting the creation of an Afro-American Studies department at Harvard, also considered revolutionary at the time, because a number of black students had requested it. He also volunteered to teach at Tougaloo, a black college in Jackson, Mississippi, during Freedom Summer. Still, Cavell was right to call himself a philosopher of psychological rather than political instincts—a standpoint that is itself as American as apple pie, certainly since the Civil War but perhaps implicit in America's inception. It's my hope that those who will continue this part of the work that Cavell began—creating a cultural canon that both represents and problematizes the idea of America—will attend to the distinction between the psychological and the political that is so crucial in understanding, and occasionally undermining, America itself.

5

Cavell Reading Cavell

WILLIAM ROTHMAN

Remarks given at a memorial conference, "Continuing Cavell: *Must We Mean What We Say?* at Fifty," held at Boston University, February 2019.

MUST WE MEAN WHAT WE SAY? HAS BEEN IMPORTANT IN MY LIFE since I was Stanley Cavell's student half a century ago. But once I threw my lot with the fledgling field of film studies and found my voice writing about movies I loved, I rarely felt the need to open the book. I'd already learned from it what I required for my own work. When Marian Keane and I wrote *Reading Cavell's* The World Viewed, I reread *Must We Mean What We Say?* to detail ways Cavell's little book about film continued its thinking. But that was twenty years ago. Since then, my writing has focused almost as much on Cavell as on film, but I've primarily immersed myself in his late writings. When I reread *Must We Mean What We Say?* to prepare for this paper, it was for the first time in two decades. I was overwhelmed by the sense that Cavell's later thought is all there in his early essays, but no less by the magnitude of all that separates them. What separates them is also what joins them: a body of work that movingly stands in for a human life.

In sorting through the emotions rereading *Must We Mean What We Say?* stirred up in me, it helped to have had a reliable guide: Cavell. There's no better reader of Cavell, no better guide to reading Cavell, than Cavell. For his own writing—the way he wrote, why he wrote that way, and how, given what his writing *is*, it is to be read—was one of his abiding subjects. The new preface he wrote for the 2002 edition of *Must We Mean What We Say?*, for example, is his profound response to returning, more than three decades later, to his first book. This practice of returning to his earlier writings, continuing their thinking but from a transformed perspective, is essential to Cavell's philosophical enterprise. I am thinking, for example, of his new preface, written in 1998, to the paperback edition of *The Claim of Reason*; the innumerable passages in his books and essays in which he "goes back" to earlier writings, such as his recounting, in "What Is the Scandal of Skepticism?," of his use of Descartes's Third Meditation in *The Claim of Reason*. Then there is *The Claim of Reason* itself, in which Part 4 responds to, departs from, and in that way continues the thinking in the first three parts, which he adapted from his dissertation. And *Cities of Words*, doubly a return in that he adapted it from lectures for a course called "Moral Reasoning" he first offered almost twenty years earlier, and because in it he returned to movies he'd written about in *Pursuits of Happiness* and *Contesting Tears*. But the ultimate instance of Cavell reading Cavell is *Little Did I Know*, which tells the story of his life up to *The Claim of Reason*, a story in which the philosophical and the personal are inseparable. Then again, his late turn to autobiography was anticipated in Cavell's early writing. It was already a theme in *Must We Mean What We Say?* that philosophical appeals to ordinary language have an autobiographical dimension.

Must We Mean What We Say? begins with a foreword, "An Audience for Philosophy," that exemplifies another of Cavell's ways of returning to his earlier writing. The last-written essay, it addresses the book as a whole, and articulates a perspective only completing the rest of the essays enabled him to achieve—a foreword that doubles as an afterword and asks to be read twice—as if the reader's logical next step, after reaching the book's end, is to begin it again, but from an altered perspective. "An Audience for Philosophy" does not, as Cavell's later forewords-that-are-also-afterwords will, also chronicle the occasions of the writing of the individual essays in terms that, anticipating *Little Did I Know*, reveal the mutual implication of the philosophical and the personal. But, like them, it brings its book full circle and, to invoke Ralph Waldo Emerson, draws a circle around the circles drawn by the other essays, enabling *Must We Mean What We Say?* to take a step beyond the steps its individual essays take—as if, like Emerson's essay "Experience," as Cavell was to read it, the book gives birth to itself. (No wonder it has enjoyed so many happy returns.) That he embraced this practice so early can be seen, from the perspective of his late writings, as a manifestation of the profound affinity with Emerson that he would come to recognize in stages, to borrow a term from his preface to the 2002 edition of *Must We Mean What We Say?*, where he writes:

> I understand the presence of notable, surprising anticipations to suggest something specific about the way, or space within which, I work, which I can put negatively as occurring within the knowledge that I never get things right, or let's rather say, see them through, the first time, causing

my efforts perpetually to leave things so that they can be, and ask to be, returned to. Put positively, it is the knowledge that philosophical ideas reveal their good only in stages.

When Cavell adds that it isn't clear "whether a later stage will seem to be going forward or turning around or stopping, learning to find oneself at a loss," he's not registering a concern that a new stage might be a step back. He's distinguishing three ways a philosophical idea might "reveal its good" (an odd locution marking a link, which asks to be returned to, with his essay "The Good of Film," then hot off the press). The three ways are going forward; changing direction—that is, undergoing a conversion; and—here his wording resonates equally with Wittgenstein and with Emerson—"learning to find oneself at a loss." Cavell is saying that the philosophical ideas in *Must We Mean What We Say?*, as there expressed, were at an early stage of revealing their "good." They "left things" so that they might be, and *asked* to be, returned to. Each such "return" is a new departure whose own "good" reveals itself only in stages.

In the new preface, Cavell observes that he was struck, returning to the book's earliest essay, by "a double anticipation" in a formulation that speaks of Socrates "coaxing the mind down from self-assertion—subjective assertion and private definition—and leading it back, through the community, home." The sense of the philosopher as responding to one lost will become thematic for me as my understanding of Wittgenstein's *Investigations* becomes less primitive than it was"—and, I would add, when he discovers Emerson. "The literary or allegorical mode of the formulation," Cavell adds, "is something I recognized early as a way of mine of keeping an assertion tentative, that is, as marking it as a thought to be returned to." In the new preface, he cites the wonderfully aphoristic line in "An Audience for Philosophy," "If philosophy is esoteric, that is not because a few men guard its knowledge but because most men guard themselves against it," both as a response to the call of students at the time for relevance in their studies—count me among them—and as an instance of his practice of invoking an arresting concept, like "esoteric," that "halted" him, made him learn to "find himself at a loss." The pertinence of this practice, he writes, "I felt strongly in connection with ordinary language practice (how could we become alienated from the words closest to us?—but then again, from what others?), but which I would not be able to speak about with much consequence until years later"—until Part 4 of *The Claim of Reason*, for a start.

In "The Avoidance of Love," Cavell remarks, "If philosophy can be thought of as the world of a particular culture brought to consciousness of itself, then one mode of criticism (call it philosophical criticism) can be thought of as the world of a particular work brought to consciousness of itself." The term "philosophical criticism" acknowledges a distinction between his readings of *King Lear* and Beckett's *Endgame*, which one might want to call literary criticism, and the other essays, which are evidently philosophy, while affirming that the kind of criticism his readings exemplify *is* philosophy. But in a 1989 interview, when his philosophical ideas about these matters were at a later stage of "revealing their good" to him, Cavell claims that it is *defining* of philosophy that it is "at every moment answerable to itself," indeed, that *any* place—Cavell's readings show that *Endgame* and *King Lear* are such places—"in which the human spirit allows itself to be under its own question *is* philosophy." When criticism is of a work of philosophy, when it questions a work that is under its own question, it "allows itself to be under its own question," too. Philosophical criticism is philosophy. And philosophy *cannot but be* criticism. In a work of *philosophical* criticism—that is, in any work of philosophy—it is the work itself that is "at every moment answerable to itself, that is allowed to do the questioning, that allows the questioning to happen, that is compelled to answer candidly every question it asks itself"—being so compelled what "being answerable" means. Such a work renders moot the distinction between criticism and philosophy by bringing to consciousness of itself the world of a particular work *and* the world of its culture—the language, the form of human life to which the work gives expression. In a 1999 Sorbonne colloquium organized by Sandra Laugier, Cavell remarked that the study of film cannot be a "worthwhile human enterprise" if it "isolates itself" from the kind of criticism Walter Benjamin had in mind when he argued that "what establishes a work as art is its ability to inspire and sustain criticism of a certain sort, criticism that seeks to articulate the work's idea; what cannot be so criticized is not art." Nor, I would add, is it *philosophy*.

A philosophical work seeks to articulate its *own* idea. But a philosophical idea, as Cavell will in stages come to recognize, "reveals its good" only in stages. I suppose it is the idea of this paper, which I hope has some "good" to reveal, that *Must We Mean What We Say?*, like every one of his writings, is a work of philosophical criticism. And that this can't be separated from the feature of his writing this paper has so far dwelled on, that Cavell writes so that his words can be returned to, *ask* to be returned to, enabling his philosophical ideas to "reveal their good" in stages. The "good" of his writing, for Cavell, was to bring the world of each work, the world of the entire body of his work, the world of philosophy, the world of his culture, our culture, *his* world, *our* world, to consciousness of itself.

Must We Mean What We Say?, Cavell observes in his new preface, "freed me for I suppose the most productive nine months of my life, in which I recast the salvageable and necessary material of my PhD dissertation as the opening three parts of what would become *The Claim of Reason* and completed small books on film and Thoreau. I consider those small books to form a trio with *Must We Mean What We Say?*, different paths leading from the same desire for philosophy." Finding paths from the trio's *achievement* of philosophy, however, proved problematic. In his preface to the 1998 edition of *The Claim of Reason*, Cavell notes that he felt confident enough with his work in *Must We Mean What We Say?* to announce there the imminent publication of his dissertation. The rashness of this announcement showed itself to him when he completed drafts of *The World Viewed* and *The Senses of Walden* and, as he puts it, "The conclusions so far achieved in the dissertation revision seemed to me outstripped by those pieces." Soon enough he would discern "the direction" the revision was "hauling itself toward." It "had to do with the connection of the two concluding essays of *Must We Mean What We Say?*, the reciprocation between the ideas of acknowledgment and of avoidance, for example as the thought that skepticism concerning other minds is tragedy." But how he might *arrive* at such a conclusion was "distinctly less clear."

In his preface to the 1998 edition of *The Claim of Reason*, Cavell tells us that to work his way through this blockage he began what he calls a "limited philosophical journal"—it was like a journal because, in his words, "the autonomy of each span of writing was a more important goal than smooth, or any, transitions between spans," and because "there would be no point, or no hope, in showing the work to others until the life, or place, of which it was the journal, was successfully, if temporarily, left behind, used up." Returning to this passage after so many years, I was stunned by its uncanny similarity to Cavell's description in *Little Did I Know* of the procedure he adopted to work his way through a comparable blockage when he was seeking to get his "philosophical memoir" on track. And what *Little Did I Know* tells us about the consequence of completing *The Claim of Reason* is that after his success in blazing philosophical paths between acknowledgment and avoidance, between skepticism concerning other minds and tragedy, between his "trio" and *The Claim of Reason*—his success in putting his dissertation behind him—he was never again to doubt his ability to go on within philosophy.

"Philosophy's all but unappeasable yearning for itself is bound to seem comic to those who have not felt it," Cavell's 1980 essay "North by Northwest" begins. "To those who have felt it, it may next seem frightening, and they may well hate and fear it, for the step after that is to yield to the yearning, and then you are lost."[1] To put his dissertation behind him, Cavell had to find himself lost. *The Claim of Reason* declares his existence as a philosopher. That's why *Little Did I Know* concludes with that book's publication. In turn, *Little Did I Know* brought to an end the period of Cavell's life that began where the story it tells ends—the period in which he fully yielded to his yearning for philosophy. Writing the book that tells this story is inseparable from the story it tells. Telling the story brought its meaning home. *Little Did I Know* is not only "under its own question," it also finds the answer it seeks. When the writing was completed, the life of which it was the journal was successfully left behind—for good. For Cavell, philosophy had achieved its end. In writing *Little Did I Know*, Cavell's way of "walking in the direction of the unattained but attainable self," to again invoke Emerson, was by looking back. Then again, "looking back" was also a return—I can almost hear Cavell's spirit whispering in my ear—where would his spirit be today if not here with us?—that I should add "to a place he had never been."

In *The Claim of Reason*, Emerson's name appears once, in passing, as it does in *Must We Mean What We Say?* In *The World Viewed* and, remarkably, *The Senses of Walden*, Emerson's name *never* appears. 1978, the year he completed *The Claim of Reason*, was also the year he wrote "Thinking of Emerson," following it two years later with "An Emerson Mood." Cavell's discovery of Emerson was a seismic event—as consequential as *Must We Mean What We Say?*, which began his philosophical life; *The Claim of Reason*, which declared his existence as the only kind of philosopher who could have written such a book or could have wanted to; and *Little Did I Know*, which closed the book on his life in philosophy. *Pursuits of Happiness* invoked Emerson several times, but had he written "Thinking of Emerson" and "An Emerson Moment" *before* beginning his book on the Hollywood comedy of remarriage, Emerson would have played as privileged a role as in *Cities of Words*, where Cavell returns to those films to continue thinking about them—only a little differently, this time. It wasn't until the late 1980s that the full magnitude of Emerson's importance for his own work became clear to Cavell. And with the publication in 2004 of *Cities of Words*, based on the "Moral Reasoning" course he first gave in the late 1980s, he acknowledged that Emerson had assumed a privileged place in his thinking. He declared himself to *be* an Emersonian perfectionist, the way in *Must We Mean What We Say?* he had declared himself to be a modernist. Or had he?

In "A Matter of Meaning It," Cavell embraces a distinction between the modern and the traditional, in philosophy and out. "The essential fact of (what I refer to as) the modern," he writes, "lies in the relation between the present practice of an enterprise and the history of that enterprise, in the fact that this relation has become problematic." He goes on, "The various discussions about the modern I am led to in the course of these essays are the best I can offer in explanation"—thanks to Emerson, his late writings will have a better explanation to offer—"of the way I have written, or the way I would wish to write." But nowhere does Cavell call himself a modernist. I find a clue to this in his essay "North by Northwest," which follows the line I quoted, invoking philosophy's "yearning for itself," with "From such a view of philosophy I have written about something called modernism in the arts as the condition of their each yearning for themselves, naming a time at which to survive, they took themselves, their own possibilities, as their aspiration—they assumed the condition of philosophy." *Must We Mean What We Say?* was, as it says, written from within a "modernist situation," but that doesn't make it modernist. If "yearning for itself" is philosophy's *tradition*, what could *count* as modernism within philosophy? When Cavell observes, in the foreword to *The Claim of Reason*, that Wittgenstein's *Philosophical Investigations*, "like the major modernist works of the past century at least, is logically speaking, esoteric," he isn't saying that it *is* a modernist work, only that, like such works, it seeks "to split its audience into insiders and outsiders (and split each member of it)." "A Matter of Meaning It," in characterizing *Must We Mean What We Say?* as *modern* philosophy, suggests that its writing too "seeks to split its audience." But in *The Claim of Reason* Cavell leaves it an open question whether his writing is esoteric in this sense—an instance of "leaving things so that they can be, and ask to be, returned to." And when he does return to this question in *Cities of Words*, his answer is "No."

In "A Matter of Meaning It," Cavell writes, "Innovation in philosophy has characteristically gone together with a repudiation—a specifically cast repudiation—of most of the history of the subject. But in the later Wittgenstein, the repudiation of the past has a transformed significance, as though containing the consciousness that history will not go away, except through our perfect acknowledgment of it (in particular, our acknowledgment that it is not past," adding, "'The past' does not in this context refer simply to the historical past, it refers to one's own past, to what is past, or what has passed, within oneself. One could say that in a modernist situation 'past' loses its temporal accent and means anything not present." Wittgenstein describes his later philosophy "as an effort to 'bring words *back*' to their everyday use," as though "the words we use in philosophy, in any reflection about our concerns, are *away*." Unacknowledged, history, too, is "away." To acknowledge that history is not past is to bring it back, to acknowledge its presentness, which is to acknowledge its pastness, enabling it to "go away" in the sense that we can leave it behind; we are free to move on.

When Cavell adds that later Wittgenstein seems to contain the consciousness that "one's own practice and ambition can be identified"— he says "identified," not "pursued," but for the modernist artist as for the modern philosopher, *pursuing* and *identifying* one's practice and ambition can't be separated—"only against the continuous experience of the past." Using the word "one's" rather than "his" acknowledges that this is a *general* feature of the modernist situation in which he, too, finds himself. The word "against," connoting opposition, seems to reinforce the word "repudiation," as if to underscore that in a modernist situation a work can declare what it is, what it was intended to be, solely through its repudiation of the history it rejects. That's how I used to understand "A Matter of Meaning It." But that can't be right. One of the leading philosophical ideas in *Must We Mean What We Say?*, an idea Cavell never stopped returning to, most consequentially in his discovery of his affinity with Emerson, is that history is to be *acknowledged*, not repudiated. Fortunately, there's another way of interpreting the word "against" in the formulation "one's own practice and ambition can be identified only against the continuous experience of the past." In the last chapter of *The World Viewed*, Cavell uses "against" in a way devoid of any association with repudiation. He invokes the concept of "the ground of consciousness," the "further reality film pursues," what he calls "the reality of the unsayable"—an "arresting concept," if there ever was one. In characterizing the unsayable as the ground of consciousness, Cavell means "ground" as distinguished from "figure." His point is that only against the unsayable as a background can the figures of consciousness stand out, be apparent to us, *identifiable*. Similarly, in the modernist situation the "continuous experience of the past" is the ground, the background, one's practice and ambition need to stand out, to be experienced, in the present, as figure. But then the past, too, must be experienced in the present, experienced—experienced *continuously*—as present, for in modernism, as Cavell understands it, an art cannot but assume the condition of philosophy and, as he will at a later stage put it, philosophy is answerable to itself *at every moment*.

In *Little Did I Know* Cavell tells us that after completing *The Claim of Reason* "going on" in philosophy was no longer problematic for him. If the "essential fact" about the modern is that "the relation between the present practice of an enterprise and the history of that enterprise has become problematic," he couldn't go on thinking of his work as modern, as opposed to traditional, philosophy. That distinction had become moot for him. And so, the words "modern" and "modernism" dropped out of his lexicon. And it's no coincidence that this occurred simultaneously with his discovery of Emerson. When writing *Must We Mean What We Say?*, Cavell, like Wittgenstein, found himself in a modernist situation in relation to the tradition of philosophy in which he had been trained. Reading Emerson opened Cavell's eyes to the fact that he had also inherited, without realizing it, an alternative philosophical tradition, founded in America by Emerson, embraced by Emerson's great readers Thoreau and Nietzsche, and kept alive in American culture, and in *himself*, by the films he watched in the years when going to the movies was a normal part of his week. Cavell didn't find himself in a modernist situation in relation to *that* tradition. By the late 1980s, he was ready to give a name—"Emersonian perfectionism"—to the way of thinking he had come to recognize as his own, no less than Emerson's. In finding Emerson, Cavell found himself. Then, happily, he was *really* lost.

Note

1 Stanley Cavell, "North by Northwest," *Themes Out of School: Effects and Causes* (San Francisco: North Point Press, 1984), 152.

II

Feats of Ordinary Language

6

Cavell's Redemptive Reading

Edward T. Duffy

ONLY ONCE DID I HAVE THE GOOD FORTUNE to chat with Stanley Cavell. It was at the 2008 Edinburgh conference on his place in literary criticism. The morning after the close of the conference, the two of us found ourselves together over the buffet in the hotel's almost empty lobby. On the basis of a brief encounter two days earlier in the same but much more crowded space, I presumed to strike up a conversation. On that earlier occasion he had joined a small group of people well known to him and that I was part of thanks to Richard Eldridge. I seized the day rather too strongly and blurted out my gratitude for his work, to which his response was embarrassment and some kind words the only one of which I recall is "nice." This quiet morning, I thought I had a better conversational gambit, namely that I had been so struck by the similarities between him and Seamus Heaney that I sometimes fantasized about how the two of them might be getting on with each other at Harvard. He genially let me down, saying in effect that they had missed out on each other's company. We both chuckled at this, and I left him with the recommendation or plea that he read a short poem of Heaney's, entitled "The Pitchfork." He countered with a smiling confirmation of just how much he was interested in pitch, as in *A Pitch of Philosophy: Autobiographical Exercises*, where he expresses his delight with this windfall of a word which "quite apart from taking on music and baseball and vending ... speaks, not darkly, of a determined but temporary habitation and of an unsettling motion that befit the state of philosophy as a cultural fact always somewhat at odds with philosophy on its institutional guard."[1] (Like many of Heaney's poems, "The Pitchfork" is an *ars poetica*. It begins with an unidentified "he" expressing his delight in how the "springiness, the clip and dart" of this tool came "near to an imagined perfection," but it ends with his having learned to follow the "length and sheen" of that far-darting power "past its own aim, out to an other side / Where perfection—or nearness to it—is imagined / Not in the aiming but the opening hand.")[2]

My acquaintance with written Cavell began some thirty-five years earlier. All through graduate school I had maintained an interest in Austin and Wittgenstein picked up from the very demanding requirements of Manhattan College's liberal arts program where as juniors we read the entirety of Spinoza's *Ethics* and Kant's *Critique of Pure Reason*, in addition to a good deal of Descartes, Locke, and Hume. The following year my formal education in philosophy ended with a senior presentation on John Austin's "Other Minds" and Wittgenstein's *Blue Book*, bound together in the first volume of Barrett and Aiken's *Philosophy in the Twentieth Century* (1962).[3] With that, I contracted a habit of reading these two endlessly interesting probers into what we do with words, but not without being nagged by the thought that this guilty pleasure was not especially relevant to the degree in English and Comparative Literature that I was pursuing at Columbia.

It was almost a full decade further on that as a newly minted assistant professor of English at UC, Santa Barbara, I accidentally came upon Cavell's work on Austin and Wittgenstein. At the beginning of the second quarter in January, he was scheduled to deliver a series of lectures that were to become *The Senses of Walden*. Michael O'Connell told me that Cavell had written a great essay on *King Lear*. So I went. But I was not bowled over. My education in American literature had been sorely neglected, and most of what this visiting luminary had to say about *Walden* was lost on me. In addition, even if I had been more abreast of Thoreau, the argument seemed too dense for such a large gathering and the delivery too, as it were, *read*, as if it could all be as readily processed as the evening news. But I must have heard just enough to look up the *Lear* piece, and there in the pages of *Must We Mean What We Say?* was one essay on Wittgenstein and two on Austin, both written with a fervent air of discovery. Reading them, I began more clearly to understand and more confidently treasure my ostensibly distracting interest in their work. I started reading Cavell even more persistently than Wittgenstein and Austin. Still another decade later when Cavell announced, in *In Quest of the Ordinary*, that the philosophy he practiced was "calling" for the romanticism that I daily read and taught, I knew, with a Wordsworthian feeling of "a presence not to be put by," what I most wanted to do.

The long deferred first fruits of this new focus bore as its title "Stanley Cavell's Redemptive Reading," as its subtitle "A Philosophical Labor in Progress."[4] Here I would like to dwell on what strikes me as a further step in this progress, one signaled by Cavell's declaration that the question of "the capacity and the right of praise"[5] holds together the ten essays in *Philosophy the Day after Tomorrow*. It was as if after fashioning *The Claim of Reason* so as to close on *Othello* as a modern "tragedy [that was] the working out of a scene of skepticism," Cavell felt compelled to amend the thought with how "comedy in contrast works out a festive abatement of skepticism, call it an affirmation of existence."[6] Call it also a further step or leap in the Wittgensteinian investigation of the "possibilities of phenomena," namely "the possibility of praise, of finding an object worthy of praise and of proving oneself capable of praising it."[7] Cavell was now strongly suggesting that praising or cursing the world you have been shown constitutes a pair of interlocked contraries in the conduct of a human life that is more fundamental than the knowledge or ignorance of it or even the doing of good or evil in it, "as though expressing gratitude"[8] for your birth or natality is the only alternative to the self-destructive cursing of it.

Just as Austin crisply pointed out that felicitous illocutionary speech acts were bound to certain facts, so does the Cavell of *Philosophy the Day after Tomorrow* see passionate utterances of praise as liable to certain constraints. They can misfire, and often do. One prominent instance that Cavell dwells on is "that highest false praise called idolatry"[9] so ingeniously explored in a Henry James story about the keeper of a museum designed to "celebrate the memory of one identified as 'The Supreme Author,' always capitalized (as are pronouns referring back to Him) but never named, and unmistakably tipped off to us as the deity sought by the name of Shakespeare."[10] The museum and the story are named "The Birthplace." One visitor to this Holy Place of Bardolatry proclaims that given the paucity of biographical information on the Supreme Author, "practically ... there *is* no author ... for us to deal with. There are all the immortal people—*in* the work; but there's nobody else." Another visitor pushes back against this and is about to query "But *wasn't there*—?" when the director answers her question with "There was somebody ... But They've killed Him. And dead as He is, They keep it up ... They kill Him every day."

The other misfire that Cavell concentrates on is blasphemy, when the praise is not "earned or acceptable" and so more "vain" than false.[11] In "Fred Astaire Asserts the Right to Praise," Cavell acknowledges that this damning characterization could be, and has been, applied to Astaire's opening song-and-dance routine in *The Band Wagon*, directed by Vincente Minnelli in 1953. The song's title, taken from its opening line, is "A shine on your shoes," its venue a Times Square amusement arcade where the Astaire character, a once famous song-and-dance man, makes a "comeback" and "finds his feet again" as a direct consequence of his bumping into a black shoeshine man dozing or meditating at the foot of his chair. This chance encounter sparks a solo by Astaire that extravagantly focuses on dancing feet and dancing shoes. It ends with a duet between Astaire and the shoeshine man, which Cavell praises as a "homage to the transcendent accomplishment of black dancing"[12] as if "the whole routine had as its purpose, or say its cause, their finding the will and the right to dance together."[13] But the rub, against which Cavell organizes his praise of Astaire's performance, is its liability to the charge that it is a particularly egregious example of the American entertainment machine appropriating and "dominating" the black dancing to which it is so indebted.[14]

In the present critical climate enthralled by a hermeneutics of suspicion, anyone wanting to enter this claim about this dance scene in a Hollywood movie of the early fifties can find a wealth of evidence in its opening moments, when Astaire is high up on the shoeshine chair and the black man shining his shoes is hunched over at its base. But Cavell both more lyrically and more accurately says of this "fantastic or phantasmic" scene, *first*, that Astaire is not there installed on a throne but "planted in air, his feet rhythmically shifting on golden pedestals ... dancing on air," and, *second*, that the camera zooms in on how the "wands" and cloths of this black man are putting the shine on the shoes of his white customer with such brio and flair that it begins to look like the "object is not alone to transform shoes but to transform the creature on earth who wears shows."[15] This prepares for how as the scene progresses the man initially in the subject position will eventually become the other and necessary member of the dance when Astaire "leaps to earth ... not finding a new body but finding his body anew."[16]

Cavell claims that Astaire's routine acknowledges the deplorable cultural history without which it would never have come into being. He sees this acknowledgment most clearly at play in a stretch of bewildered "frenzy" when Astaire becomes verbally stuck on a manic repetition of "shoe shine, shine on my shoe." Cavell notes that at the time "shine" was a common derogatory term for black people and that Arthur Freed, the producer of *The Band Wagon*, could not possibly have been unaware of this cultural fact. This state of play and allusion Cavell interprets as the preconditions or makings of "a masterpiece of dance," which, in the face of and as a beneficiary of historical calamity and injustice, still can find the feet and summon the spirit to enact "the origin of dancing in ecstasy" and so "recall Nietzsche's requirement of a Sacred Yes to existence."[17]

Cavell's reading of this scene is itself a masterpiece of film criticism with the openly avowed motive of seducing its reader into sharing the pleasure he takes and the value he sees in Astaire's performance. As with many of Cavell's most original essays, any summary of this one cannot do it justice, so I will just recommend it, along with William Rothman's "On Stanley Cavell's *Band Wagon*." This excellent piece spends most of its time on an earlier sequence (also explored by Cavell in *Philosophy the Day after Tomorrow*) but does touch on the arcade dance and gives a fuller account both of the history of Astaire's engagement with black dancing and of Minnelli's significant placement of other black men in the scene on which he focuses.[18] As Rothman also notes, Cavell highlights his debt of gratitude to Kant's *Critique of Judgment*, specifically to its portrayal of the universality and necessity of aesthetic judgement, namely as grounded in its demand for agreement with its response to its object as one of pleasure without a concept. Criticism accordingly becomes a work of determining, as it were after the fact, the grounds of (the concepts shaping) pleasure and value in the working of the object. In this light criticism becomes a conduct of gratitude.[19]

Conduct, I would add, becoming a human creature endowed not only with the need for praise but also "the need to praise."[20] Cavell flags the philosophical ambition of this particular instance of his film criticism when he characterizes it as a "passionate utterance" of his own that is "now placing my demand that you [my readers] agree with the pleasure I take ... [in this] routine of Fred Astaire and hear out how I ground the pleasure in this object."[21]

Although Cavell's scrupulously critical praise is here addressed to the made thing of a film, his discourse of praise constantly crosses the line between the aesthetic and the existential, as when in writing about a movie he invokes Nietzsche on the human requirement of coming out with, and thus going on with a "Sacred Yes to existence" or how comedy as a genre is an affirmation of existence. This conflating of an artistic object and the whole of where we find ourselves is an old story as exemplified by the venerable trope of the Book of Creation declaring the glory of its Creator. But Cavell's turn from humanly made things to precisely these things here before us that make a world has many precedents in the writers he most admires. It is perhaps most memorably evident in the turn Thoreau executes between the "Reading" chapter of *Walden* and its successor entitled "Sounds." In "Reading" Thoreau praises literary classics and religious scriptures to the sky and declares that they constitute a "pile" of "trophies deposited in the forum of the world [by which] we may hope to scale heaven at last." But then with the very first word of "Sounds" he surprises us:

> But while we are confined to books, though the most select and classic, and read only particular written languages, which are themselves but dialects and provincial, we are in danger of forgetting the language which all things and events speak without metaphor, which alone is copious and standard. Much is published but little printed. The rays which stream through the shutter will be no longer remembered when the shutter is wholly removed. No method nor discipline can supersede the necessity of being forever on the alert.[22]

This alertness that Thoreau is constantly urging manifests itself mostly in the prophetic disdain with which he addresses the "sound sleepers" who are "said to live in New England." But underlying and indeed motivating such disdain is the determination to see the world in a brighter light that he so robustly declares at the outset of *Walden*: "I do not propose to write an ode to dejection, but to brag as lustily as chanticleer in the morning, standing on his roost, if only to wake my neighbor up."

Accordingly, one of the earliest preludes to the discourse of praise running throughout *Philosophy the Day after Tomorrow* involves not a work of art but the philosopher's life as the provider of the conditions of his philosophical calling. One condition to which he gives particular attention is the "perfect pitch" enjoyed by his mother and other members of the Segal family. He admits that this condition "is apt to be the hardest to recognize, and the most variously or privately ratified."[23] But for this very reason, both the necessity and the value of what he understands by it are without question. "Perfect pitch," Cavell explains, is his chosen "title" for "experiences ranging from ones amounting to conversions down to small but lucid attestations that the world holds a blessing in store, that one is, in Emerson's and Nietzsche's image, taking steps, walking on, on one's own," that one has been, in slightly more normative philosophical language, favored by existence itself with "the attestation of one's autonomous powers of perception."[24] One epoch-making conversion that Cavell would claim for himself was the one occasioned by the lectures of John Austin that he attended as a graduate student at Harvard. Another earlier one, detailed in *A Pitch of Philosophy*, featured the music theory seminar of Ernest Bloch, which Cavell attended the summer of his sophomore year at Berkeley. There the teenager, who only a year earlier had been astonished to learn from the university catalogue that "*Faust* was a play before it was an opera,"[25] blissfully experienced what in retrospect he is now happy to have received as "the trauma of the birth of culture."[26]

These advents, in the one case of culture and in the other of philosophy, were "flashing dramatic events"[27] of transformation taking place at illustrious institutions of learning. But in the spirit of Cavell's devotion to the ordinary I want to explore the essentially private blessing of what as a representative "modern subject ... perpetually seeking peace, therefore endlessly homeless," he alternately expresses as his hope or despair of being at home in the world.[28] This is a constant concern of his that resonates with Heidegger on dwelling, with Thoreau on settling, with the Hollywood comedies of remarriage, and with what he defines as romanticism's quest (and inquest) of the ordinary, unpacked by him as the task of bringing back to life a world that, having somehow died at our own hands, now demands either "a new creation of our habitat" or the "creation of a new inhabitation."[29]

On the cue of Cavell's manifest concern about "dwelling, settling, houses, about call it domestication,"[30] I now turn to the third part of *Little Did I Know* as a "resettlement of the everyday,"[31] which is accomplished by literary means and thus a demonstration of his claim that it is often less helpful to proceed on W. V. Quine's assertion that philosophy is a chapter in the history of science than to admit art and particularly literary art as a continuing and necessary chapter in philosophy, a view earlier expressed in Cavell's assessment of the exemplary philosophical work of Emerson and Thoreau as a "writing [which] is, as it realizes itself daily under their hands, ... the accomplishment of inhabitation, the making of it happen, the poetry of it."[32]

The two dwellings of Cavell that I follow him in dwelling on are the house in Atlanta where he spent the first seven years of his life and his final residence in Brookline where he and his wife raised their two sons, and from which he dates the July 29 to mid-August 2003 entries that comprise Part 3 of *Little Did I Know*. The first of these two houses, the Segal family home on the south side of Atlanta, was one of "continuous interest and talk and music."[33] Expelled from this paradise at seven, young Stanley moves to an apartment on the other side of town where he is very much alone with his father's rages and his mother's prolonged silences. Within two years he descends into an unsettled life of shuttling back and forth between Atlanta and Sacramento. While the father is trying to make it in one failed venture after another, the son finds himself in an "unlikely, unlovely world."[34] He is a misfit at every one of his many new schools, about whose workings his parents are clueless. He falls into a protracted "paralysis of spirit,"[35] and the rage bottled up inside him concentrates on his father and is powerfully conveyed in one scene, where he and his mother arrive in Sacramento shortly after his father and where instead of a warm family reunion (writes the seventy-five-year-old man) "my father guided my mother into a back room and shut the door," leaving the abandoned eleven-year-old paralyzed "on the sofa, as though all of space was dangerous to move through, trying to understand the feeling that someone wished me dead" and making it clear that he harbored a complementary wish.[36]

After several pages on working in his father's Sacramento pawnshop, pages that begin with "the poetry of the pawnshop" evident in its use of words like *grace* and *redemption* and *interest*, Cavell writes of what he here welcomes as a "gesture" or prompting toward redeeming the experiences of shame and desperation "lodged" in every object of that store. Like his father, he was a teller of family stories, many of which featured the pawnshop and his father's scrupulously honest business practices. At their Bar Mitzvahs, both of his boys "publicly" took pride in this aspect of their immigrant grandfather's life and trade. Relying on their father's stories, they stressed how he took "extreme care" that those who pawned things with him would be afforded "every chance to redeem them."[37] This pride had a feedback effect on their philosopher father who here testifies that this implicit praise of their grandfather played "a direct part in *making feasible my present writing of this segment of my life, hence in finding usable perspectives upon further stretches of it*. I believe there may have been a time in my life so low that I would have been prepared to refuse instead of to cultivate this gesture of redemption precisely because of the redemption it must extend to my father's desperate life. Curing or curbing this vindictiveness, this recurring, self-destructive longing to consign one's father to hell is also something for which I owe my children an unending debt of gratitude" (emphasis added).[38]

To the extent that Part 3 of *Little Did I Know* has a plot, it is the rehabilitation or redemption of the father. For it is here that Cavell confronts the most lacerating sins of his father and makes a start toward finding that the man is nonetheless worthy of praise as when, in the last words of Part 3, the son declares the father "an admirer of serious men," as evidenced by his delighted amazement at witnessing and his skill in recounting how in 1930s Atlanta a white man, upon being introduced to a black man, "actually stood up!" and shook his hand.[39] (On the rehabilitation of Cavell's father with a particular emphasis on the accomplished storytelling handed down from father to son, see James Conant's "The Triumph of the Gift over the Curse in Stanley Cavell's *Little Did I Know*.")[40]

Cavell has written that "we do not know where the inspiration to give up revenge comes from,"[41] but I venture to suggest that the potpourri of motives from which the miracle of forgiveness wells up to the surface of this writing must include, as he himself notes, both the perils of a self-destructive cursing of one's father and the promise of a further perspective not unlike Emerson's "neutrality." By perspective I mean, at least to begin with, nothing more than the long view of his life and history that Cavell takes up in these recollections, featuring his first and his final house and spanning four generations from his maternal grandfather to his two sons, the effect of whose Bar Mitzvah remarks strikes me as an analogue in family and oral history of T. S. Eliot's remark that every new contribution to a literary tradition will, in incalculable ways, change the whole of the previously received tradition.

Cavell ends his August 12, 2003 entry with a return to the Atlanta house that over a hundred pages earlier had been celebrated as a child's garden of delights, which he catalogues, *con amore*, in one long sentence ending on how to ride in the rumble seat of his young aunt's bright yellow Buick coupé was to be "heaven bent."[42] Here he zooms in on the similarly youthful delight he took in the coal regularly delivered to the house at which the Buick would pick him up. The coal truck would pull up the driveway, align its chute with an opened basement window, and down would come a rush of coal that settled into a neat mound just a few steps from the furnace. In his next entry two days later, Cavell reminds us and himself of how his mother liked to tell the story of how when she was a young girl in this house, her father would rise very early on winter mornings and shovel coal into the furnace, taking care to leave open only the vent to the room where she and her brother would practice their music before going to school. A generation later it was a "treat" for young Stanley to help his uncles shovel coal into the furnace of this house, which with its ducts and vents communicating with every room in the house now strikes him as "a stationary, uncomplaining beast who tirelessly supported the house with its limbs and breath." At this point, he more openly shifts a half-century further on to his home in Brookline, when long before this writing he would take habitual pleasure in how his "mother's tale of a worthy father" would still "occasionally whisper to him" when he performed similarly paternal duty for his two grade-school sons simply by turning up the thermostat as a first step in a daily routine of waking them up, getting breakfast, and driving them to the school bus. About this series of mere household events, Cavell testifies that he remains "grateful for these simple manifestations of my admiration and encouragement of our two sons, manifestations while in themselves trivial labors were at the same time acts that have helped irreplaceably in the work of repairing broken arteries of my childhood."[43]

Two paragraphs later, Cavell comes back to a more specific and private "image" of the coal in the house of his first affection. Not all the coal would fall neatly into the mound. Some of "this substance of mysterious origin" would be strewn at its foot in large "isolated" blocks that the six- or seven-year old, on his own and "inadvertently," learned to split "cleanly" into two. With the blunt side of a nearby axe he would tap a block first lightly but then with "increasing force" so as "to determine the point at which, if I hit it right, it would instead of chipping or crumbling, split apart cleanly into two intact pieces ... with perhaps one or both of the halves falling over under its own newly discovered imbalance to rest on a new facet of itself." Already Cavell's writing up of this moment is pulsing with ideas of an opening up of oneself to the world and one's others in it, and the possibility of any imbalances (or losses or confusions) becoming opportunities for righting oneself on a new facet or aspect of oneself. The enormous personal and philosophical significance Cavell divines in these solitary moments, akin to Wordsworth's spots of time, becomes explicit when, from his present perspective, he concludes with the admission that "I did not yet confide to myself the knowledge that I was still at the beginning of learning how to be tapped so that the hardness in my feelings and fixations in my mind would, if I could become ready, split open as of their own desire, the better to be consumed."[44]

Cavell then recalls his blocked arteries in need of catheterization, so starkly announced in the book's opening sentence and here further associated with the "broken arteries of [his] childhood." Catheterization for blocked arteries, he suggests, can be thought of as a "reasonable continuation" of the "more ancient image" of tapping into the self that is internal not only to the traditional philosophical ideal of the examined life but also to what he elsewhere calls "the most forbearing act of thinking ... to let true need, say desire, be manifest and be obeyed; call this acknowledgement of separateness."[45] Cavell slips this eventually revealed "task" of his life into a concluding sentence whose syntactical shape places that task as equivalent to his "instinct to respond" with (I assume) now desire for this, now aversion from that. But unlike the catheterization entrusted to the professional skill of a surgeon, the task of the thinking and writing cure that Cavell has in mind must be a work of his own hands.

To those who might detect a category error in how Cavell seems to fold into one another a *task* of his life and his *instinct* to respond, I would suggest that the instinct (and the responsibility) of responsiveness seemed atrophied beyond repair during this "multi-year period of coma." For such a loss of "the track of desire itself,"[46] the remedy as a human being was to recover an interest in his life, and as a writer to manifest and realize that recovery by an engaged and even impassioned recounting of this life whose overriding motive would be to track down the buried (hence stored and preserved) treasure of those moments when he was alert to his world and his others in it, those moments of perfect pitch when he was granted "an attestation of [his] autonomous powers of perception."

The paradise lost that was the Segal house on Atlanta's south side was first described and celebrated in strict chronological order many pages earlier. The question to be asked, then, is what interest is drawing Cavell back to this "house of his first affection." The beginning of an answer lies in the fact that Cavell's path back to this house runs through the back door, near which he finds his memory speaking of a black "domestic" whom the hardly affluent Segals hired during the Great Depression. This young woman was, as Cavell recalls, a lively person and easy to talk with, and she was usually found working in the kitchen whose outside door led to the small porch in the rear. To that back door came frequent visitors wanting to see her: a hungry man who could depend on her for a meal; a numbers runner who for a coin or two would record the number she had divined from her "dream book." In addition to having dreams and recording them, she used snuff and said that she liked to fish. Such "expressions of her pleasure," writes Cavell, "alerted me, if not quite awakened me, to the fact that she had a life beyond this house, one with its own desires. Where did she live and where could she fish?"[47]

For young Stanley this was a fledgling moment of perfect pitch. It was not a conversion, nor was is it then experienced as a "blessing." But he now, with this writing, pays a debt of gratitude to it as one of those small but lucid attestations "of one's autonomous powers of perception [that] may come in recognizing the autonomy or splendid separateness of another, the sheer wonder in recognizing the reality of the presence of someone whose existence you perhaps thought you had already granted."[48] This entry is entitled "What are domestics, anyway in Atlanta before the U.S. entry into World War II?" In the world conjured up by this title, any perception of the vividly human presence of the inevitably black domestic in the Segal kitchen would be for most white folks most of the time blocked by that very designation. But as Cavell would write of Fred Astaire's "gratitude" for the existence of the shoeshine man and "for his own" as a masterful song-and-dance man able to perform a fitting "homage to the transcendent accomplishment of black dancing," so here with this real and much more common encounter between white and black. In a benign reversal of the admonishment that as you judge so shall you be judged, Cavell's youthful openness to the human reality of this "domestic so-called" now comes back to him as a ratification of his own autonomy. This and other small but lucid moments of perfect pitch helped him on his way toward the reenvisaging of his world as one holding a blessing in store for him, because for as long as he could remember he was already taking steps in this practice of seeing things for himself. He was already walking on, on his own.

From what in retrospect is seen as an inchoate gesture toward "recognizing the splendid separateness" of this young woman, Cavell moves to the place of the discovery: the liminal area of the porch and the icebox situated on it. About this object Cavell confesses that he has thought more often about it than he "can account for," and then proceeds to give a simple reason for its staying power. He "enjoyed" watching the ice being delivered, thrilled to the weekly drama of the iceman handling the huge and sharply pointed tongs into a sure grip on the large blocks of ice. But he adds that he "liked even more watching the coal delivered, which was differently dramatic."[49]

A "domestic so to speak" was the first description of this woman. The hedged word follows seamlessly from the opening story of the August 12 entry concerning young Stanley's brief but manifestly unforgettable encounter with another (in the strictest sense of the word) impressive black person in the Deep South of his birth. It was the summer of solitary "floating"[50] when he was near fourteen and spending his last lazily painless summer in Atlanta and would daily find his way to the swimming pool at the new, more posh incarnation of the Jewish Progressive Club. Unlike his father, his Uncle Mendel was still a member and had secured visitor's privileges for him. The club, for which a golf course was planned, was still under construction. As a result, the path through the woods to the main building and pool often changed without notice, so on one particular day when Stanley exited the bus he was not sure which way to go, and stood there on the sidewalk wondering whether he should fall in behind "the surprisingly large clump of white grown-ups and children" who had descended from the bus with him. As he stood there, not knowing how to go on, he heard behind him "a man's cultivated and Northern voice" asking, "Are you doubtful about the direction to the Progressive Club?" When he turned to hear where this query was coming from, he "[discovered] a youngish, trim man neither white nor black, with heavy, slightly waved, shining black hair combed straight back, dressed in a tuxedo, without a tie, the collar of his gleaming white dress shirt unbuttoned and looking as if it belonged that way." With the same kindness and terse formality, the man explained, "The paths change as the construction work progresses. You may accompany me if you wish." An "amazed" Stanley could not but take him up on the offer and "whether [the man was] oblivious to my stunned silence, or tactfully responsive to it, he observed: 'Thursday is domestics' day off'" as the explanation for all the white adults at the pool with their children. Although Stanley eventually figured out that this mystery man was "the headwaiter of the club's formal dining room" and made that his punch-line, for a while he groped for a way to place him. The best he could come up with was Cab Calloway on the silver screen. Was he then "a band leader or an entertainer, and if so why was he headed alone through what seemed a private path through the trees for the Progressive Club approaching noon as if this was part of his everyday life? And what, if anything, was his relation to those he called domestics, a term I would have bet was unknown, or unused, by any other human being within a thousand miles of where we were walking together?"[51]

Cavell the memoirist then cuts to the "two domestics, so to speak" at the house, the icebox on the porch, the coal delivery and finally the intimate delight of cutting, say articulating or breaking down, this hard and combustible material of mysterious origin into two cleanly divided and intact parts. Before concluding on his reading of this activity as a foretaste of his life's task of responsiveness, he reveals that these basement sessions of tapping and splitting large blocks of coal had collectively become one of his most private touchstones of aesthetic judgment. When he was rehearsing his high school dance band, for example, he would advise against overdoing the syncopation with "just split the notes cleanly and let them fall." And even earlier when by tapping the block he learned how to hit it right, the very "sound" of it and the sight of its happy result would "[produce] in me a primitive equivalent of the almost silent shout of appreciation with which my mother would greet a perfectly managed musical ornament or cadence"[52] as when at a Fritz Kreisler recital in San Francisco she so memorably communicated her pleasure with "an all but inaudible high cry" and gestures that "I knew well and would glory in when directed to something I had done."[53]

Periodically in *Little Did I Know* Cavell laments that the life he was shown when he lived with his parents was, with the distinguished exception of his mother's musicianship, "unleavened." At one point he equates this word with a "charmless"[54] lodging or existence, one without ornament, savor or relish. But eventually he comes to realize that even "the experiences of the pawnshop need not have been without leavening even as they were collecting,"[55] because, as he expressly indicates, they were infusing him with words like *redemption*, *interest*, and *counting*, all of them waiting for him to become alive to their larger possibilities in Thoreau and elsewhere. At the still young age of thirty, Cavell will project this sense of something infused or stored that is waiting for its more manifest expression and actualization onto a runaway male cat who, when eventually caught and locked up in a small cage, did not snarl and rage but just lay there, giving Cavell "the distinct feeling that he was already saving himself, storing his hopes, waiting."[56]

This image of a relaxed readiness occurs at the beginning of the second entry and is clearly triggered by the elaborately detailed memory coming just before it in the preceding and opening entry of Part 3. There a ten-year-old Cavell, only recently arrived in Sacramento, both produces and stars in a monodrama of storing, preserving, and waiting. For several days, his favorite after-school activity was watching the digging and construction work at a nearby service station that was being renovated and furnished with new underground gasoline tanks. A short time after the completion of the work he found himself "wandering alone" one afternoon in the familiar patch of land behind the service station when he found a large glass jar "almost buried in dirt and leaves" with its metal cap punched with holes so as, evidently, to make it a livable space for some bug or insect. Immediately he set about loading the jar up "with one of each different thing or creature" he came across: leaves, bugs, twigs, stones, a bottle cap, a candy wrapper, a stamp, a penny. Then he stuffed it with dirt and grass, "closed it tightly and contemplated it, feeling that I had accomplished something important, even solemn. Something will be discovered to grow from this, if it is well preserved, and we wait long enough." He was sufficiently impressed with the solemnity of what he was doing that he borrowed a shovel from the service station so that he could "[store his] work deep." Then as a cap to this ritual of not floating but burying a Noah's ark for each of the things and creatures of his world, he heard a "low hum as if produced by the ground, which, I explicitly said to myself, others could not hear," and which in the table of contents he calls "the hum of the world."[57]

As he does on this solemn childhood occasion, Cavell characteristically associates this sense of, call it, banked fires with the promise that what has been buried or impounded in memory can, if rightly tapped and excerpted, be made manifest with not only clarifying but also transforming effects for the human subject in which it has become lodged. What he saw in the cat twenty years later was something that he obscurely sensed in himself: that he was "already saving himself, storing his hopes, waiting." A similar confidence in what the world was holding in store for him finds more or less explicit expression when at the beginning of Part 3 he acknowledges that the writing he cares most about and would here emulate is in the business of "inviting surprises, and not ones prepared by a future but ones creating a future."[58]

Cavell eventually arrives at the grown-up philosopher's explanation that with this act "I was burying my life, perhaps to preserve it for some time in which it might be lived, or chosen."[59] But then he immediately differentiates that thought of his older self from how then and there on the alien ground of Sacramento and at that still tender age it was obscurely felt as "a message cast into time, for a future self I was to become, or unpredictably to receive, perhaps to rue or to mock or to abandon or to embrace." The last twenty or so words find their center of gravity in that "future self" that he would not in due and banal course *become* but "unpredictably receive," a glance this at Emerson's "all I know is reception," which is then followed by an emphatic series of alternative ways of receiving that life, with the climactic position reserved for "embrace"—the gestural equivalent of saying yes to your existence as distinguished from the other three, each of which is one or another way of saying no to it and going down the darkly descending way of the damned in Dante's *Inferno* drawn irresistibly toward Charon's boat while (and because) they cannot stop (in Heaney's translation) "blaspheming" or cursing "the place and date and seedbed / Of their own begetting and of their birth."[60]

To end where I began, I will indulge myself in the pleasant fantasy that if Seamus Heaney and Stanley Cavell had become friends, the poet might well have eulogized the philosopher with his translation of Rilke's "The Apple Orchard," a poem replete with their shared master tones of patience, obscure promptings, wind-fall fruitions, and the need and chance of attaining a full-throated and perhaps sacred yes to existence.[61]

> Come just after the sun has gone down, watch
> This deepening of green in the evening sward:
> Is it not as if we'd long since garnered
> And stored within ourselves a something which
>
> From feeling and from feeling recollected,
> From new hope and half-forgotten joys,
> And from an inner dark infused with these,
> Issues in thoughts as ripe as windfalls scattered
>
> Here under trees like trees in a Dürer woodcut—
> Pendent, pruned, the husbandry of years
> Gravid in them until the fruit appears—
> Ready to serve, replete with patience, rooted
>
> In the knowledge that no matter how above
> Measure or expectation, all must be
> Harvested and yielded, when a long life willingly
> Cleaves to what's willed and grows in mute resolve.

Notes

1 Stanley Cavell, *A Pitch of Philosophy: Autobiographical Exercises* (Cambridge: Harvard University Press, 1994), ix.

2 Seamus Heaney, *Seeing Things* (New York: Farrar, Straus and Giroux, 1991), 25.

3   William Barrett and Henry D. Aiken, *Philosophy in the Twentieth Century* (New York: Random House, 1962).
4   Edward Duffy, Stanley Cavell's "Redemptive Reading: A Philosophical Labour in Progress," *University of Toronto Quarterly*, vol. 65, no. 4, Fall (Toronto: University of Toronto Press, 1996).
5   Stanley Cavell, *Philosophy the Day after Tomorrow* (Cambridge: Harvard University Press, 2005), 3–4.
6   Ibid., 26.
7   Ibid., 31.
8   Ibid., 68.
9   Ibid., 37.
10 Ibid., 63.
11 Ibid., 66.
12 Ibid., 79.
13 Ibid., 76.
14 Ibid., 69.
15 Ibid., 74.
16 Ibid., 72.
17 Ibid., 78, 68.
18 William Rothman, "On Stanley Cavell's *Band Wagon*," *Film-Philosophy*, vol. 18, no. 1, December 2014, 9–34.
19 Cavell, *Philosophy the Day after Tomorrow*, 67.
20 Ibid., 52.
21 Ibid., 67.
22 Henry David Thoreau, *Walden*, 2nd ed., ed. William Rossi (New York: W. W. Norton, 1992), 75
23 Cavell, *A Pitch of Philosophy*, 47.
24 Ibid.
25 Stanley Cavell, *Little Did I Know: Excerpts from Memory* (Stanford: Stanford University Press, 2010), 205.
26 Cavell, *A Pitch of Philosophy*, 50.
27 Stanley Cavell, *Themes Out of School: Effects and Causes* (Chicago: University of Chicago Press, 1984), 190.
28 Cavell, *Little Did I Know*, 100.
29 Stanley Cavell, *In Quest of the Ordinary: Lines of Skepticism and Romanticism* (Chicago: University of Chicago Press, 1988), 53.
30 Ibid., 175.
31 Ibid., 176.
32 Stanley Cavell, *The Senses of Walden: An Expanded Edition* (San Francisco: North Point Press, 1981), 134.

33 Cavell, *Little Did I Know*, 97.
34 Ibid., 113.
35 Ibid., 112.
36 Ibid., 104–5.
37 Ibid., 115.
38 Ibid., 118.
39 Ibid., 145.
40 James Conant, "The Triumph of the Gift over the Curse in Stanley Cavell's *Little Did I Know*," *MLN*, vol. 126, no. 5, December 2011, 1004–18.
41 Cavell, *In Quest of the Ordinary*, 75.
42 Cavell, *Little Did I Know*, 16.
43 Ibid., 133.
44 Ibid., 135.
45 Stanley Cavell, *This New Yet Unapproachable America* (Albuquerque: Living Batch Press, 1989), 45.
46 Cavell, *The Senses of Walden*, 51.
47 Cavell, *A Little Did I Know*, 132.
48 Cavell, *A Pitch of Philosophy*, 47.
49 Cavell, *Little Did I Know*, 132.
50 Ibid., 123.
51 Ibid., 130.
52 Ibid., 134–5.
53 Ibid., 53.
54 Ibid., 308.
55 Ibid., 118.
56 Ibid., 101.
57 Ibid., 98–9.
58 Cavell, *Little Did I Know*, 97.
59 Ibid., 99.
60 Heaney, *Seeing Things*, 106.
61 Seamus Heaney, *District and Circle* (New York: Farrar, Straus and Giroux, 2006), 70.

7

Staging Praise / Owning Words

CHARLES BERNSTEIN

The following remarks are adapted from a 2002 reader's report for the University of Chicago Press for what became Stanley Cavell's *Philosophy the Day after Tomorrow* (Harvard University Press, 2005), which was then titled *Staging Praise / Owning Words* and included only half of the essays later featured in the published book. As far as I know, Cavell never used the earlier title. Page references here are to the Harvard edition.

STAGING PRAISE / OWNING WORDS IS A MAJOR NEW COLLECTION OF ESSAYS by Stanley Cavell and as such can be counted to be a major event for American philosophy and literary/media studies. The work can perhaps best be compared to such earlier Cavell books as *In Quest of the Ordinary*, *Conditions Handsome and Unhandsome*, and *A Pitch of Philosophy*. However, this book is something of a tour de force in the prescient combination of (on the face of it) dissimilar materials, brought together in terms of a powerful and provocative underlying theme. For the essays are drawn together closely by their organizing theme, an investigation into the concept and practice of praise, understood as a performative speech act (in J. L. Austin's sense) but also, and more crucially, something difficult, and sometimes impossible, to perform.

Cavell collects addresses from a Shakespeare congress, his presidential address to a meeting of professional philosophers, and a series of lectures in Amsterdam. The diversity of these addresses itself becomes an element of the book, allowing Cavell to consider his topic in terms both of varying addresses and permutating angles of approach. Many of the essays include some key in the location of their presentation, which works for Cavell by establishing particular and shifting addresses. The subject matter itself works in this way, moving from Fred Astaire to the new textual criticism, from Shakespeare to Henry James, and finally A. J. Ayer and J. L. Austin. An underlying concern for Emerson's (neglected) contribution to American philosophy connects this book very explicitly with Cavell's work over the past two decades. But a surprising, in some ways unexpected, turn to Walter Benjamin, who is a persistent voice in this collection, is welcome and provocative. Cavell also addresses some very pressing and topical questions in contemporary literary criticism. In fact, this book could easily be seen as Cavell's philosophy of literary criticism, with echoes of Kenneth Burke's *Philosophy of Literary Form* intended, as, in these pages, Cavell addresses, and praises, Burke.

In *Staging Praise / Owning Words*, Cavell raises several philosophical problems with the textual criticism of the new historicism (he specifically responds to Peter Sallybrass and Margreta de Grazia), which he sees as a kind of textual skepticism in the refusal (as I might reformulate it) to acknowledge the existence of Shakespeare's plays because of the impossibility of establishing definitive editions. For Cavell, this is one form of a negativism that he wishes to counteract with an Emersonian, and as it turns out Jamesian, commitment to a criticism of praise. Cavell goes on to address, in the form of a critique of Michael Rogin, a certain moralizing negativism within cultural studies (also evident in Michael North's *The Dialect of Modernism*), when he eloquently responds to charges of racism leveled against an Astaire routine. In contrast, Cavell's account of Astaire is marked by its measured (i.e., not blind) but unmistakable praise.

Reading this collection provides the pleasure of thought and reflection. I found myself pausing after many sentences to consider the new insight and the finely tuned reflection. With Cavell, it is just as much a matter of the thinking provoked (or better to say evoked) along the way than any final position that can be summarized. The work is composed not so much of arguments as *considerations*.

The subject of praise is related to Cavell's ongoing concerns with the ordinary and skepticism. The issue first emerges as a central feature of his philosophical work in his great essay on *King Lear*, "The Avoidance of Love" (in *Must We Mean What We Say?*). In some ways, this book revisits the concerns articulated in that essay (in Cavell's first published book): the enormous consequences of Lear's inability to praise, especially as played out in our contemporary philosophical and critical and scholarly environment in terms both of skepticism and a certain reflexive negativity.

I enthusiastically recommend publication. This work would have a similar audience as Chicago's previous Cavell books, though I think it should garner even greater interest from those concerned about the fate and state of contemporary literary criticism. Philosophers (those interested in aesthetic issues anyway), scholars of early modern literature, and film theorists will all find the book quite significant, not to mention readers of Henry James. And possibly, indeed probably, some number of general readers. No revisions are recommended. My commentary comes from enthusiasm and engagement not from any sense that this work requires changes; that is, I offer these comments in praise.

Chapter 1: "Something Out of the Ordinary"

The contrast is made between the *academic* and the advanced and in the next sentence the *advanced* and the *philistine* (14). While this distinction is not central to the essay, it is nonetheless a significant issue, and one that threads through the book as a whole, enough so that these terms may not be the most elucidating. "Academic" would seem to include not just the academy but also the adjudicating "middle brow" taste of mainstream media, newspaper critics, book publishers, and art dealers, presumably captured later by "philistine," although it would have to include those art boosters who would be the first to attack the philistines, or even attack as philistine "innovative" or exploratory works of art. "Advanced" is also possibly not the best word to describe the other side of this coin, since some of the work on that side would be at pains to question the assumption behind the idea of "advance." Sometimes "academic" is used to describe difficult or complex work and sometimes just the opposite. In one sense, you could simply talk of the popular and the unpopular: work that requires finding new audiences versus work that can count on an already formed audience. In any case, even a slight elucidation by Cavell on the issue of mass culture and its others would be welcome, at a time when segments of the literary academy seems to have appropriated "the low" in its abandonment of the aesthetic. Opera itself is of course a fascinating case of the "popular" being transformed into "high" culture even as its contemporary institutions resist any "advanced" work in the genre. The case of film remains quite interesting—but the point is not that Astaire is "advanced" or "low" but that these terms don't help in understanding the sublimity of his work. Later in the book, Cavell addresses this question in terms of Emerson's "possession of the public's mind," which suggests perhaps it may be an issue of public versus private, accessible versus inaccessible, or conformist versus an aversion of conformity (also from Emerson), to cite crucial motifs for Cavell. And of course Shakespeare, in Emerson's account of him, in Cavell's next essay, is also both most public and verging on the incomprehensible. Later in the book (97), Cavell uses "philistine" to mean those with a reductively negative critical method, even associating this stance with Adorno; of course, for Adorno this form of negativity is a rebuke to the philistine. And especially since Cavell does address Adorno, through Benjamin, Adorno's critique of mass culture does resonate, in advance—not only his foolish dismissal of jazz, relevant to the discussion of Astaire, but also his sharper understanding of the Disneyfication of art, a theme Cavell himself address at a later point. In the Henry James chapter (chapter 4), Cavell states his alarm at the slide from "art and technology to cartoons and jazz and slapstick comedy to mass art and mass laughter, and to Hollywood and America" (91). I would only add that in the 1920s, at least, the term "jazz" was not necessarily associated with America or with the artform with which it is now associated, but with cacophony, with frenzy, and, relevant to his reading of Astaire, frenzied dance.

In the Astaire chapter, Cavell comes back to this theme in ways that do seem to contrast mass or manufactured culture with art, or "work that bears up under critical pressures and questioning" (chapter 3, 70). Or is the contrast here rather with "entertainment": not works that entertain but work for which entertainment overrides other values. (I suppose it might also be worth noting that *The Band Wagon* has its own war of the "high" and "low" in which the high is skewered as so much posing; but, then, what's "real" are what's a turkey is another story. Then too there's the ballerina's transformation into a Broadway dancer.)

Another place this turns up is chapter 4, again in a discussion of *The Band Wagon*, where Cavell contrasts the realm of fashion and its negation, including fashionable philosophy. This is intriguing because it suggests the positive function of negation and another opposition of the reflective without its other. Cavell goes on to disparage (dispraise) entertainment in the particular sense of "flag waving ballyhoo" (84).

Since Cavell addresses the rhyme scheme of lyrics, why not Gershwins, Ira and George, in the plural, rather than "Gershwin" in the singular, meaning just George? Also, (Lorenz) Hart is mentioned but other lyricists might also be noted, for example, Oscar Hammerstein II. As significant as any of the names in this passage would be Howard Dietz and Arthur Schwartz, who together wrote "By Myself," and also choreographer Michael Kidd.

Chapter 2: "Arguments of Praise"

(retitled "The Interminable Shakespearean Text")

It's exhilarating to see Cavell take on the subject of textual criticism, and by implication new historicism, bringing in a philosophical depth that is too often lacking in these discussion. This essay will be of immense value to many people working in literary studies.

It is worth noting that there are forms of textual criticism that would be more resonant with Cavell than the particular example he chooses. I am thinking in particular of Randall McLeod or Jerome McGann. I imagine another—Cavellian—way to respond to the severe textual skepticism that troubles him would be to reject the idea that there is one perfect ur-text (which plays into the hands of skepticism by setting up criteria that cannot be met). In contrast, we can acknowledge that different versions of a work are *played out*, that is, performed. In this sense, the "work" is to be found in the performance and not in the impossible-to-fix original. Then perhaps the constellation of versions would be said to have a family resemblance one to another and it is this *constellation* that is the *source* to which we respond. Any given performance—either by a text editor or a director—would involve the creation of new instance. In such an idea of "anoriginality," no original, uncorrupted text would be required or sought, nor would a version that tried to collate all other versions be given any epistemic priority. So, for example, when Cavell speak of the issue being an argument over the "concept of revision" (47), one might alternately speak of the possibilities of versions. (Compare also the dispute over the Gabler edition of Joyce.)

Another way of putting this is that the problem is not in fixing on the impossibility of a single authoritative original or source but of the necessity of constellations of possible performances or versions, giving status (giving praise, responding to) particular *instances* not their inscrutable source, not, that is, in the Wittgensteinian sense, imagining that what lies underneath or behind has the ultimate authority. "The play's the thing."

One of the remarkable things about Cavell's work is that it will often respond to a reader's questions, if one has patience. And I do find Cavell directly addressing these points in the last pages of the essay; for example, where variation is keyed as central (53) and, a few pages later, where Austin's theory of performance is specifically invoked.

Finally, just to note that the phrase "maelstrom of significance" (49) is marvelous.

Chapter 3: "Praise as Identification"

(retitled "Fred Astaire Asserts the Right to Praise")

On "Shine on My Shoes": Given that Walter Benjamin figures in such interesting ways in this book, perhaps there is some relevance to the fact that one of his key terms is "shine" (*schein*), a word central to Cavell's reading of *The Band Wagon*. The discussion of John Cage revisits issues in one of Cavell's crucial early essays, "Music Decomposed" (and its pair, "A Matter of Meaning It"), also in echoing Michael Fried on similar concerns of the time. Here Cavell writes, "Cage displays his public as locked into a form of participation with human work in which absence (of both work and participation) is enlisted as presence" (65). This is significant because it becomes another instance of negativity as opposed to praise, or relates to it. As Cavell concludes, "It suggests that humankind would rather praise the void than to be void of praise" (65). But I think the account of Cage is rather too stern and doesn't adequately account for the many forms Cage invents and the specificity of the sounds his work articulates and to which, as listeners, we respond (not imitating the look of nature, maybe, but its conditions, to put a Cavellian cast to the argument). Cage's work concerns the structures and forms of attention; his aim is to allow for greater awareness of particulars and indeed of the ordinary (a refocusing attention on the everyday and away from the metaphysical displacement of the everyday). The void is not the object: as he notes in his early experience with the anechoic chamber at Harvard, he hears his own heartbeat. "Void" or "silence" is not possible. In this sense, Cage's work is an aesthetics of praise of the given particulars of the world. Oddly, Cavell here plays the skeptic when he focuses on the putative absences in the work.

Chapter 4: "Praise as Consent"
(retitled "Henry James Returns to America and to Shakespeare")

"Philistine gravitas" (97) brings back the issue of the philistinism evoked in chapter 1, though not bringing home the significance of the issue. Here the philistinism is the turn against the aesthetic in the name of higher value, so hardly a distinction of high and low culture, especially as the charge hovers close to Adorno. I wonder, though, if Adorno's methodological negation might be separated from the "philistine gravitas" that Cavell is right to identify as a strong wind in our cultural climate. I would want to suggest that Adorno's negativity is not naysaying but can itself be a practice of praise, also like Zarathustra's joy.

Cavell speaks of James's self-characterization as "the repatriated absentee" (100, 105): *is this repatriation something like remarriage*, in Cavell terms?

Chapter 5: "Performance and Passionate Utterance"
(retitled "Performative and Passionate Utterance")

This essay offers a detailed discussion of a central figure for Cavell, J. L. Austin. Cavell takes up the issue of "passionate utterance" (what Austin called "performative utterance") (176) as a way of averting (or refusing) moralism in the pursuit of, if not happiness, then expression (and by extension, praise). He has a contrast here that could, anyway would usefully, enter into our lexicon: that between "the responsibilities of implication; and the rights of desire" (185). This is the most strictly philosophical chapter and also the one that is least explicit about its connection to the unifying theme of the book—praise and praising—although, as Cavell announces in the volume's introduction, the philosophical status of the act of praising is something Austin's work crucially elucidates. The link to praise becomes closest to explicit when Cavell paints moralism as another form of negativity, here a kind of scolding—that is, the opposite of praise.

As far as I know, Cavell never used the title "Owning Words," but the phrase connects to his conviction that we must mean what we say, that we are implicated in meaning beyond our ostensive intentions and mercurial inventions. —If we do own our words, own up to them, it is because they own us and we are in their debt.

Owning words is also owing words.

But the debt we owe to language is paid not to words but to one another.

8

Resisting the Literal

Cavell's Conversations with Thinking

ANN LAUTERBACH

A FEW CONDITIONS, NEITHER HANDSOME NOR UNHANDSOME, to begin: I never had the lucky privilege to study with Stanley Cavell, although we met on a number of occasions at his daughter Rachel Cavell and son-in-law Norton Batkin's house in Rhinebeck, New York, where we had some convivial conversations. My reading of his work has been intermittent and is not entirely thorough, as his most powerful allure for me streams from his love of Emerson, which I share, and his evident desire to renovate our assumptions about philosophical thinking to include, or admit, the particular relation between experience and experiment, which characterizes a specifically American, Emersonian, disposition. My delight in reading Cavell has to do to a great extent with receiving his own delight in language as the key material for linking these etymological siblings, in a kind of mental conversation of animated discovery.

If I am correct in my view that we are living in a time, in times, of abject literalism, in which what might be called figurative or imaginative language has been exiled in favor of an explicitness so pervasive as to be a kind of stall or stare, as at a *wall*, then thinking about Cavell's interest in ordinary language (philosophy) becomes a compelling challenge.

That is to say, Cavell's sense of the "ordinary" cannot be equated with the literal, but rather with the specific intimacy of listening. Reading Cavell, wherever one starts or stops, stalls or stares, makes one acutely aware of single *words*. This is a shared acuity and a shared awareness between philosophy and poetry, and is one reason why reading Cavell as a poet, that is, when one is, as I am, a poet, is rewarding.

Cavell uses words with an evident attention and pleasure that I affiliate with his knowledge (and love) of music. He knows something about how cadence affects sense, how repetitions and variations inform our reception of meaning, and so influence our perception of sense, our understanding, not entirely aligned with the merely rational. Beyond these affinities, Cavell's writing has another poetic trait, a fascination with the generative and elastic qualities of individual words and phrases, which might be construed as a resistance to literalism, to reductive strategies of meaning-making, in favor of an almost infinite expansiveness. Almost, but not. He doesn't so much argue, or persuade, as ruminate and trouble. He likes to catch hold of a word and move it around and through, like a musical note, noticing how it changes its tonal color within an evolving syntax, the melodic line, of a given concern. He understands the deeply affective consolations of the recursive, the refrain. These traits I am mentioning are familiar to anyone who has read Cavell, and I iterate them here by way of affirmation of the particular pleasures availed in my own reading of him, and in thinking of his affinities with Emerson, another writer who moved along the edge of thinking as it unfurled, the way I imagine surfers move on the cresting curl of a wave. Both writers must have taken pleasure in this experience. Cavell clearly took pleasure in reading Emerson, as if he were in a kind of dance or embrace, the two figures, one verbal or textural, the other still corporeal, and yet one feels their reciprocity, their intimacy, the bond of affirmation allowing for conversation, or conversion. Indeed, Cavell is almost always saying as much as he is writing; he seems to have preferred the habitat of a voice speaking.

Cavell's writing seems to directly inscribe his thoughts; reading him, we feel as if we were on a kind of giddy ride along a track whose destination is not known, neither by horse nor rider. I have come to think that the writing I love most is writing that feels as if it is happening in "real time"—that the author is writing to find something out, to discover or uncover or even recover thought itself as it is happening. And so I am reminded of William James's claim, that "truth is what happens to an idea," where the emphasis is clearly on the process itself—process or time as the only test of true knowing. In any case, for Cavell, this *making of linguistic tracks* is not purely instinctive or associative; he is not a poet and so he must make certain explicit claims on knowledge as fact; he must, for example, cite Kant and Rawls, and he must pause over the difference between, say, a *specimen* and an *exemplar*.

Cavell's call comes, often as not, in the form of a question, maybe "a pack of questions," which suggests that he proceeds through thought by having a more or less constant interlocutor. He quotes easily, as if he were exhaling rather than reading the cited words, and his writing has a kind of breathing exigency, a method of exchange: in, out, in, out, sometimes with long, sometimes with short, abruptly inhaled air, as if life depended on it.

Sometimes the interlocutor is his own former self, an earlier rendition of an insight, revisited. No matter. There are sometimes useful animations in solipsistic frames and usually he is revising himself. Indeed, Cavell's writing proceeds by a kind of pulsing rhythm in which ideas or thoughts are offered and then emended or revised, these alterations often in the service of finding a better, more apt word or phrase for the burgeoning thought. We feel we are with him at the inception, and this gives us a sense of freshness and urgent apprehension, the opposite of witnessing the already formed, digested ideas of certain thinkers. Cavell has knowledge to impart but he's less interested in flaunting his erudition than he is in bringing it to bear on his evolving considerations, insights, and themes—testing or trying rather than asserting or concluding.

Cavell's writing moves at a rapid pace, so fast you might find yourself breathless, trying to stay in think-sync. Part of this experience has to do with his habit of interrupting himself, not to pause but to elaborate, add on, add in, so that the pace of thinking becomes ever more strenuously compounded. His love of language, the play of language, is the engine of these turns and filigrees, tendrils and parentheses. He isn't digressive, exactly, since he expects his readers or listeners to keep all the incidents or events in play simultaneously, as if one could see each twig aflame in a fire. Furthermore, all this enthusiasm seems motivated by a cheerful good will and humor—a distinct delight in the elasticity of his own agile mind as it spins its web of associations and inferences and questionings. He shares this trait with Nietzsche, I think, another of his favored interlocutors. These strategies of engagement are like invitations to join in the plenitude of linguistic possibilities, as they reach for clarities that in turn resist reduction, if conclusions can be said to be reductive. He seems not to want so much to prove as to entice, to draw us in to the drama on a mental stage where a kind of figurative opera is unfolding, with its arias and recitatives, melodies and harmonies and plots, demonstrating the urgency and wit of the unfolding composition. One could feel like a voyeur, a mere spectator, witnessing this ingenuity, and one is reminded of Cavell's love of film, where perhaps he found a form equal to his own habit of turning singularities into multiplicities.

There is, then, something essentially dialogic in Cavell's turn of mind. He seems not to need or want to stand alone, and this reluctance feels like a choice, not to be the kind of philosopher who needs to establish a system or a theory but rather to present a way of thinking as an engagement with and through others. (This reminds me of his near-contemporary John Ashbery, a poet who also found a paradigmatic multiplicity, an inclusivity, in the characteristic pronominal play of his work). Philosophical discourse, for Cavell, is a form of gathering into an arena, or commons; we are all invited to attend. We could call this—acknowledge this—as distinctly democratic, distinctly American. *E pluribus unum.*

9

Revisiting Ordinary Language Criticism

Kenneth Dauber and K. L. Evans

To the late J. L. Austin I owe, beyond what I hope is plain in my work, whatever is owed the teacher who shows one a way to do relevantly and fruitfully the thing one had almost given up hope of doing.
—STANLEY CAVELL, *Must We Mean What We Say?*

What is ordinary language criticism? The answer to this question is more surprising and less ordinary than one might expect, but then real things usually do surprise us.
—KENNETH DAUBER AND WALTER JOST, *Ordinary Language Criticism*

K. L. EVANS'S NOTE AHEAD OF HER DIALOGUE WITH KENNETH DAUBER: As part of a largely unheeded series dedicated to "Rethinking Theory," Kenneth Dauber and Walter Jost edited a volume called *Ordinary Language Criticism: Literary Thinking after Wittgenstein after Cavell* (Northwestern University Press, 2003). In his afterword, Stanley Cavell praises the sustained level of distinction in the collected essays and declares that he is heartened by the variety of interests and texts that they take up. He also notes that "it is largely the editors who undertake to sketch something of a program meant to show connected promptings among the essays" or who explain in some detail what might be made of the new name ordinary language criticism. The essays themselves, Cavell writes, including those by the editors, "tend fairly directly to settle down to a work of critical thinking at hand."

Unclear is whether Cavell is pleased, displeased, or simply disarmed by what he identifies as a certain "directness" in the collected essays, the result of their authors' notably un-hung up or unphobic capacity for getting on with the work of reading and critical reflection. He is, however, certainly absorbed by what has *enabled* or *occasioned* the knack these writers have of naming their engagements, in language unburdened by jargon or an unhealthy professionalism. Cavell's interest in this question is conceivably made evident by just how much of his afterword is given over to offering context for why the writing that prompted these essays, Cavell's own literary thinking after Wittgenstein, from *Must We Mean What We Say?* (1969) to *Little Did I Know: Excerpts from Memory* (2010), does *not* feel so unconstrained. Most contributors to the volume are writing in explicit sympathy with Cavell's work, but curiously that work is not an uncontested example of ordinary language criticism.

Why isn't it? What is ordinary language criticism, as these editors envision it? And if it is no more than a name for literary criticism that has recovered some equilibrium after the convulsions in theory of the last half-century, as the editors not unhumorously hint, why does Cavell's expressed hope that the "handsome" writing in these pages inspire more writing of like quality remain so bewilderingly unfulfilled? Why was the reception of this edited volume so abysmal—not negative but wholly and resoundingly absent? Why has ordinary language criticism become not only a label without resonance in the academy but also a critical practice noticeably short of practitioners?

With some expectation of addressing these questions I spoke with Ken Dauber in his office at the State University of New York at Buffalo, the largely unchanged site of his tireless labors as an ordinary language critic since 1970, and the backdrop to countless sustaining discussions during my years as his doctoral student. The subsequent four-hour exchange was prompted by both of us having been asked to contribute to this new volume, *Inheriting Stanley Cavell*, and revisiting the claims of *Ordinary Language Criticism* felt like a pressing issue. The topic was a new one for us, but the conversation was not so different from those we had been having with one another for the last two decades.

* * * *

Perhaps only someone who had a teacher who modeled "how to do relevantly and fruitfully the thing one had almost given up hope of doing" can have a sense of how precious those conversations are, how profoundly and irrevocably reorienting. Talking with such a teacher is like getting to understand oneself and one's world. The teacher does not correct but clarifies, or holds up to the student who says something what it is precisely she is saying. The student learns what labor with words really means. She learns why it is necessary to use a particular word here, employ a particular phrase there; she discovers that saying something one way is not the same as saying it another way. Unquestionably, this way of teaching is arduous and protracted (and costly and chancy). But the teacher who is an ordinary language critic wouldn't have it another way and doesn't know one, anyway.

Thus the ordinary language critic, stubbornly bent upon teaching us that words matter, has a manner of address strikingly unlike the other voices remonstrating at us from the marketplace of critical theory. The special difficulty of ordinary language criticism is that it would "reconnect us to our words, with which, increasingly, we have been losing connection."[1] It is for this reason that the "ordinary" in ordinary language criticism doesn't mean bog standard. As Dauber and Jost write, the term ordinary language criticism might be appropriately used by any reader to signify almost any critical practice "committed to an intimacy with the experience of texts in all of experience's provisionality and potential for unforeseen reversal." Ordinary language criticism stresses the encounter between the supple, receptive temperament of the alert reader and the written work. And yet it isn't just *any* reader who, with the ordinary language critic, invests in works rather than disciplinary knowledge;[2] who puts her questions in terms less technical than is usual in current academic discourse;[3] who steers clear of fashionable political agendas and preferred catchwords in order to take up the special difficulty of staying alert to the thoughts she is in danger of knowing too well;[4] or who grasps that her attunement to what she reads is sooner achieved by a kind of heightened attention or consideration of what she is doing than through the construction of a theoretical overview.[5] In this respect the "ordinariness" of the ordinary language critic is deceptive, since what it delimits isn't criticism with no special or distinctive features. In truth, it is quite hard to find a critic intent on achieving the aim of ordinary language criticism, which as Dauber and Jost maintain "is not to re-create the works it criticizes in the terms of a doctrine that may be serviceable to some higher position or politics, but to discover how they are *already* serviceable and, *for that reason*, in need of being shown why they require ongoing inquiry into their nature and implications."[6]

Accordingly, when Dauber and Jost propose that "we might go so far as to say that all criticism is really ordinary language criticism, that is, when criticism *is* criticism as opposed to something else (quasi-scientific theory, or ideology, or even nonsense)," they are in fact winnowing down quite significantly the critics who may be included in this category. They are not dismissing the excitement of the last several decades of literary theory so much as resisting criticism that turns theory into a means of mitigating or undoing reading altogether. Such criticism vaporizes the literary object while endlessly multiplying opportunities for redescribing it. For the editors of

Ordinary Language Criticism, "this is not merely an academic issue, though it has wide implication for the academy, in which an ersatz sophistication of too many professors has shorted the circuit between literary works and the real lives of those reading and teaching them."[7]

* * * *

With the obvious limitations of my format firmly in mind, then, I offer some glimpses of our conversation: an opening salvo on the perils of joining the "managerial class," followed by the question of why ordinary language criticism has no audience. This is a little like asking why the profession as a whole seems to have forgotten criticism's value. We then put forward for consideration two ways philosophy is not like literature or literary criticism. First, that one of philosophy's central features is its spiraling self-consciousness, without which it would have no real audience. And second, that teaching and writing philosophy—or producing philosophical criticism—is inextricable from philosophy's love of the good. By pointing to this second feature of philosophy we mean, with Cavell, that whatever teaching or practicing philosophy might be, there is something it *must* be: "the *personal* assault on intellectual complacency, the private evaluation of intellectual conscience."[8]

If rekindling some shared concerns about criticism (criticism after Wittgenstein and after Cavell) does nothing other than send a few readers back to the beautifully crafted, intensely deliberated introduction to *Ordinary Language Criticism*, the effort will be worthwhile.

KENNETH DAUBER: When academics become part of the managerial class, they begin to think like a managerial class. So, here at SUNY Buffalo we're just losing a provost to another university. Thank goodness. But the point is that what's good for his résumé to get a better job are the new programs he's created, the new initiatives. I mean, you can't move within an academic bureaucracy by saying, "I've made the physics department better, the English department better." But if you can create an initiative in *physical chemical biological English*—then you really have something to put on your *cv*. And that spills down to the kinds of rubrics that are put in place. I can't remember now—it's been years—since this department has talked about "What should our students learn?" "What do they need to learn?" We want to talk about these things. But the rubrics put in place by our managers won't allow us to. Instead, what we talk about is which courses do we have to offer to get students enrolled in the new programs of physical chemical biological English to make those programs seem to be a success so that we can get funding to hire more people who will teach those programs and who will be less and less concerned with "What should our students learn?" and "What do they need to learn?" It has totally gutted any sense of what we are doing here, either in terms of, you know, our own research, or in terms of basic education. What are we trying to tell our students? What do we want them to know? It's simply just gone by the board. And I think that is happening everywhere. Just everywhere.

That's the external part of the problem. And internally—well, you know the currents in literary thinking. So many people in the humanities have lost a certain faith in reading. They themselves read extremely well. That's what brought them into the profession—a love of reading and the desire to teach it. But it's as if reading, belief in which was once a quasi-religious faith, has become a practice in which we no longer have faith. We justify ourselves to ourselves instrumentally, as if the prime reason for teaching reading is no longer that our students might then learn how to read—to read texts, to read the world, to read themselves, which might be useful politically and sociologically, too—but to teach politics or sociology directly by means that require hardly any instruction in reading at all. How is what we do useful in utilitarian terms? That's what we ask ourselves. Well, it teaches students skills. Yes, it does that. But the core of what it is supposed to give them is just absent, and the absence leaches into our own work. At best, we read each other to discover templates, theories, stances that may be taken in reading. Okay. I want to know about different ways of reading. I want to know what stance you take. But I want to know it because it is *your* stance—that is, the stance of a plausible someone, not a stance itself institutionalized. And the disappearance of someones into their stances is even formalized, these days, in the vogue of the disappearance of the subject. I know the doings of my colleagues, but I don't know what my colleagues are doing.

K. L. EVANS: Even your friends?

DAUBER: We all have colleagues who are our friends and friends who aren't colleagues. But collegiality ought itself to be an offer of friendship, which means listening, in a collegial way, to the stance of another you might plausibly consider as one you should take up and asserting your own stance with the same expectation. And the joint work of colleagues in a department is, in friendship to our students, making those stances available to them. But what it's not is creating programs, even within departments, whose measure of success is their success in institutionalizing themselves as programs, because in that way we talk not to each other, not as colleagues, but to establish ourselves as members of rival colleges to whom we can't really talk at all.

EVANS: I know. I find that I am almost resigned to the point of thinking, okay, if I only talk to one person a year … I mean, I've scaled back so much, my expectations are so small in regard to who there is to talk to. By that I mean *work with*. And there is an obvious consequence for the profession and especially for its newest members when a standing assumption about anyone's ability to say something (and mean what they say) or see something (something worth seeing, that *can* be seen, that is not merely projection) is doubted to the point of destruction. It's as if, since none of the writers could possibly mean what they are saying or understand its implications, none of the readers can be expected to be anything but uncomprehending—or at best, bent on refuting and disqualifying what they read. This is a genuinely disheartening situation, especially for those young students who—as Cavell says somewhere—"are entering the profession and still deciding whether it can support life." And then, what about the effects of all this on, you know, the *world*? *[Laughs]*

DAUBER: I mean ... *[very long pause]*. When I was chair here, I organized a regular meeting of all the chairs of all the English departments around Buffalo.

EVANS: What did you call it?

DAUBER: We called it the OED—Organization of English Departments. And the subject of teaching composition came up, because that's what a lot of teachers did at Erie Community College ... and I remember asking about what the strategies are, what they do, what kinds of problems they encounter. In particular, however, I remember asking, "You know, we all say that everybody really can learn to write. Is that true?" And there was a kind of pause, and then several people said, "You know, not really." Maybe in some technical way, but not really.

They may have been right. It is something teachers of reading and writing can't help but worry about. And by worrying in company, I found some consolation for my own distress in teaching composition and, sometimes, teaching in general. If these experts in teaching writing doubted the possibility of their success, didn't that justify a certain fecklessness in my own teaching, since what could be done anyway? But I wasn't reading their response well, because I now find in the pause before their response an element of hope to which they held on, that it's necessary to hold onto and hold oneself to. Let's put it in the religious context of faith in reading we were talking about where, traditionally, doubts of this sort abound. People are called to various callings. God puts his finger on you—or your culture does or your training or your disposition. "You can read. You can read especially well." But reading, you must believe, is a god that anyone can see if only it is pointed out. Your greater intimacy with reading is what you have to believe you can share despite all the obstacles, the rather different trainings or dispositions of your students.

Now it used to be that the people who could read would come to English departments, and what they tried to do with students was show them what they did so that their students would begin to understand, might even, according to their own dispositions and callings, begin to do it. There was a certain faith in that kind of reading. I don't think that's the case anymore. Or let's say, yeah, people read and that's why they come into the field. But it just very quickly ... there is no longer that faith that "I know how to do something. I see it. I can read. And my job is to share some of what I can do with other people. To model it for other people, to show people that." We don't believe it. We don't do it. And I don't know what's to be done about that. And the ability, the skill ... you know, you stop reading, it diminishes. You forget what it is you are doing. You know, here and there, individually—perhaps individually for all of us—but as a *general project* of the academy ... reading isn't what we're teaching.

EVANS: ... Reading isn't what we're teaching.

* * * *

EVANS: But Kenny, it was such a pleasure to return to your introduction to the OLC book.

DAUBER: I haven't read it in all these years. I read it this morning. It's not bad!

EVANS: [*Laughs*] It's pretty good. And, maybe it's age, but I also read Cavell's afterword to the volume quite differently. I remember finding it just completely unsatisfying when I first read the book. But it's different now.

DAUBER: Ah, ah. That was my first reaction too, way back when we came out with the book. When I read it now....

EVANS: It's different, right? You come to a certain place and you go, oh, okay.

DAUBER: Yeah, "oh, okay," but as in a settlement. Because reading it now, I understand it better, and I'm satisfied that I understand. But that doesn't mean I'm exactly happy with what I understand. Cavell appreciates the contributions to the volume. Surely he appreciates, too, how they were inspired by his own work. Yet "they tend fairly directly to settle down to a work of critical thinking at hand." And this is a criticism, because they seem to Cavell too direct and too settled.

EVANS: Then we are back to the matter of reading and writing in the profession. I feel like what you lay out there, extremely clearly, for the future generations, well, it's essential. But [*long pause*] who is doing it?

DAUBER: It had no resonance whatsoever. Anywhere. No reverberations, anywhere. Maybe it was too clear. Too settled, anyway. It is what it is. What can you do with that?

EVANS: But it was transformative for my life; it was transformative for the lives of the students who I worked with ....

DAUBER: Ah, that's very nice to hear.

EVANS: But how did it not change everything? How was it not a *clarion* call for literary critics? Or—to lower my expectations a little—why is the call for ordinary language criticism so inaudible? I've lived my life according to the lessons of the introduction to *Ordinary Language Criticism*; I feel like I did, and certainly as a teacher, since you find the people who can hear it. So, here's this program, it's the right program, the things you say are so reasonable, and they are doable, and there are people who are so desperate for this change. So the question, at least partly, is, What is the obstacle? Why aren't we doing it? Why isn't there *more* criticism that isn't uncomprehending, isn't forged out of enmity, isn't just so much ideology or the stuff of political agendas? And are there ways to figure out how to better implement the kind of change in register you call for? I mean, there is so much work to do. In any event, isn't the fact that ordinary language criticism wasn't picked up at all related to what we were talking about before, with academics entering the managerial class?

DAUBER: Yes, it's related to what we were talking about before. It's related, especially, to the question of instrumentality, to what good it is that reading can do in a non-instrumental way. And this is related, too, I think, to what the collection, I think, unsettles in its very way of settling in, to what good Cavell has done for us, Cavell "after Wittgenstein," as the collection's title says. Because there is a difference between Cavell and Wittgenstein in their understanding of non-instrumental value, a polarity, even, between which the essays hover.

Look, for instance, at Wittgenstien's asceticism, not only in his life but in his writing, the sparseness of his sentences compared to the almost luxuriant foliation of lines of thought in Cavell. For Wittgenstein, he even says it: thinking is a problem. By which he means doing philosophy. Doing philosophy is the highest form of thinking. And he wants to bring himself to a place where he doesn't have to think anymore. He says that, right? The problem with our thoughts is that our thoughts construct various kinds of things that move us away from the way in which we ordinarily speak when we speak naturally. And that's the disease of mankind. Mankind has that disease—that's what it is to be human. And so the aim of philosophy of the kind Wittgenstein wishes to practice is to cure the disease, to bring us back from thinking which carries us away from where we are really living and to bring us back to our certainties, to where we really are living.

Cavell is somebody who does not want to stop thinking. Rather, he wants to live *in* the thinking about his thinking. He doesn't want a place of rest. Exactly what he wants is to go over and over again the life you are thinking about, the life that you don't have. And this seems good, the more literary approach, anyway. This is also, however, where I find Cavell problematic. Cavell—I mean, I think he's right about that, I think he's more human than Wittgenstein is, insofar as he wants to live that human condition rather than cure it. To put it in other terms, there's a way in which Wittgenstein wants to cure the human pain of having to reflect on yourself ... the pain of that self-consciousness without which we wouldn't be quite human, after all. It is essentially self-consciousness, right, that he wants to cure himself of. To get back to the grounds on which you do things unthinkingly, in some ways. Cavell doesn't want that. Cavell wants to *live* in that human condition of a problematical self-consciousness. But that also means that Cavell, again and again, refuses to rest, refuses to acknowledge the desire for rest, which is also human. And this includes denying places where he himself might have rested.

There's a really interesting scene in the autobiography [*Little Did I Know*] where he talks about being in a music composition class. He's a really talented musician, right? And the teacher plays something from Bach on the piano, changing something—some little thing—in a way that is apparently compositionally perfectly acceptable ... and then the teacher says to the class, "Sounds good?" Yes, they say. Sounds good. Now, says the teacher, let me play you what Bach actually wrote. And he asks the class, do you hear the difference in tonality that makes? Who can actually hear it? Cavell is the only one in the class who hears it. He really hears the difference. And the teacher praises him for having heard it. Cavell's response to that—and this is one of the reasons why he decides that he doesn't want to be a musician or have a life in composition—is that he finds he was not interested in the talent that he had, in the fact that he heard it. But he was interested in the conditions which would enable one to hear it or not hear it. One of the things he rejects is his own talent, his own ability, as a resting place. He wants the ability to always be *thinking* about his own talents.

EVANS: So what's wrong with that? Because it is more interesting, isn't it?
DAUBER: Yes. Much more interesting. And why should one rest in one's talent? What if your talent is what you have but not what you particularly enjoy or think especially valuable? I'm thinking of my mother, who decided not to be a concert pianist. "What's wrong with that?" ...Well, let me say what's right about it. What's right about it

has to do with Cavell's notion of perfectionism. I've been thinking about that... You see the books? [*points to a tall stack of Cavell's many books on the desk*] I've been reading through Cavell, you know, one after the other....

EVANS: Why?

DAUBER: Well, maybe I'm thinking of writing something for the volume....

EVANS: Good! Are you going to? You better get on it!

DAUBER: Well... [*shrugs*].

EVANS: Kenny! You can't do that. Look. Look. Think of the people who don't have the stack there. And who haven't read all of those books, and who maybe can't *read* those books. And who write something....

DAUBER: Okay, okay. I hear you. Anyway, this moral perfectionism that Cavell keeps talking about. What is perfectionism?—because it doesn't mean being perfect. It seems to be a responsiveness, an openness to absolutely everything. Cavell wants to be ... I mean Henry James talks about wanting to be somebody on whom nothing is lost. For Cavell, the perfectionism that one is striving for is to be someone on whom nothing is lost, to be *responsive* to everything—and responsiveness can include rejections, as well, but total responsiveness is the idea. That's the positive side. And it's an attractive view of mankind. Of a kind of sociality. But what I find troublesome about it is that, you know, part of being human is being more responsive to some things and less responsive to other things. To "get down directly to the work at hand," what Cavell finds problematical about the essays in the collection. One has friends. One has children. One has loves. And that's not an accident. And that's not like, "Well of course one has friends but really I should be responsive to everybody...." Actually, no. One should be more responsive to the people one loves. At least one *is* more responsive to the people one loves. And the ability to be so intensely responsive to this is just precisely given to us by our not being responsive to something else. There's a certain rest in that which might seem like just a kind of giving up, but it's a rest that proceeds not from tiredness but from commitment. So I'm thinking about the way Cavell will say something and then say "or not." Isn't that a certain refusal of commitment? I mean, you know, put your money down.

EVANS: I see what you mean about there being some peril in Cavell's unwillingness to rest, and how it gives a kind of precariousness to his work. Certainly Cavell's responsiveness to absolutely everything feels costly in some of his writing, when for instance he says something absolutely magnificent—life-changing—and then immediately thereafter seems to go too far, or go in too many directions, or include too many voices, and you just think, ugh, you've detracted from that marvelous thing you were doing, because now I can't teach this essay, for example, because you just couldn't stop. In a way, what is meant to make the writing feel more inclusive and more capacious sometimes only makes it feel more personal and idiosyncratic and therefore limited in scope.

But you know, one of the things I re-read for our discussion this morning is Cavell's foreword to *Must We Mean What We Say?* and he says something there that speaks directly to this point you're making, I think. Cavell begins by denying the distinction between philosophy and metaphilosophy, philosophy's taking of itself for one of its own topics, because for him questions about philosophy's motivations, or its audience—doubts about philosophy's relevance, etc.—are, precisely, the stuff of philosophy. And even though he is essentially promoting *and staging* the way philosophy is ill at ease with itself or unduly aware of itself, he goes so far as to say that philosophy's self-consciousness gives him pause. It even gives *him* pause! "No doubt there is a danger of evasion in this spiraling self-consciousness," he writes; "perhaps one should indeed search for more congenial work."[9] All the same he doubles down, because what interests him most about philosophy is precisely the way it becomes its own subject, "as if its immediate artistic task is to establish its own existence." For Cavell, philosophy's self-consciousness is what allows it to be a kind of performance—what turns it into an *art*, an expression of human creative skill and imagination even more compelling, presumably, than a career in music.

Now, to go back to that story Cavell tells about being in composition class. You read it as an example of his refusal to rest, which you read as a refusal to commit. Cavell finds the conditions for hearing the music more interesting than the fact that he could hear it. In your retelling it sounds like you are finding fault with this. Secretly I don't believe you are! It's almost as if you are wrapping up something you find admirable and compelling, if exhausting, in the form of a complaint. Either way, though, isn't Cavell basically saying that this refusal to rest is the condition of being a philosopher? I think that is the reason why, in the foreword to *Must We Mean What We Say?*, he ties being a philosopher to being a teacher. I want to get back to this, and I want to read out loud the passage I'm thinking of, but first I want to mention that although Cavell's own writings challenge any neat or given distinction between the genres of literature and philosophy—although his work champions and puts into practice what he calls "a new literary-philosophical criticism"—he is pretty open about the fact that there *are* differences between literature and philosophy and also that he does not (that we do not) understand these differences.

I hope this isn't too personal, but Cavell's commitment to questioning the divide between literature and philosophy, coupled with his refusal to efface it, not to mention his acknowledgment of what he doesn't understand about it, is of some importance to people like me who think of "literature and philosophy" as their chosen field. I mean, what happened to it? To the possibility of it? And if Cavell was a kind of spokesperson for the field of literature and philosophy—the field I was trying to work in, which doesn't even seem like a field any more, Cavell's immense efforts notwithstanding—what should we conclude from the fact that the difference between philosophy and literary criticism was not something even he could understand? This is a separate question, of course, from what Cavell certainly *did* understand: the need for students in either discipline not to be satisfied with what somebody else has achieved or with ready-made answers to age old problems.

DAUBER: Yes, you are quite right. And the vagueness, the refusal of ordinary language-style criticism to offer a methodology, to institutionalize itself by making hard distinctions, as, say, between literature and philosophy, is both its attraction and a prime reason for its occlusion. And Cavell, as you've described, gives voice to this, too. Yet I can't help feeling that this voicing is the result, all the more, of his own refusal to…

EVANS: … Make a distinction that shouldn't have been made?

DAUBER: Well, but we do make it. Cavell, as you say, makes it. And I want to know, since we do make it, what the grounds of its making are. I want to give voice to that, as well.

EVANS: That's very interesting. Because I usually think of Cavell as working to deepen the differences between literature and philosophy but doing that in a fruitful way, as if those disciplines need to remind each other of their differences. But in the foreword to *Must We Mean What We Say?* Cavell says explicitly that he does not *understand* the differences between philosophy and literary criticism, even though at various moments he is led to emphasize them. But here's the thing we do know. You, when you read literature, you turn the reading into something that is philosophical. You do. You've never not done it.

DAUBER: Is that so? But don't I—don't we all, we literary critics interested in literature and philosophy—more significantly, turn philosophy into literature? This is what you do with Plato, isn't it? And here may be a difference between literature and philosophy worth marking. They both seek truth, seek to express the truth they see. And that means a certain spiraling, a moving from one thing as it is "responsive," to use Cavell's concern, to every other thing. But the responsiveness in literature is not upward and outward, as it tends to be in philosophy, but on a dead level of this thing and that thing on the same plane. And here, as in your favorite, Melville, the whole movement of his great book is to gather even the outward-boundedness of his own philosophical speculations back into the bounds of the dead level of this thing next to that thing. It is to reckon by dead reckoning, to use a nautical term your Melville would have liked. The matters of fate and free will are no higher or broader or wider than the matters of harpoons and bowsprits. And that is what guarantees that they are no lower, either, as people who think philosophy is a waste of time think.

Cavell likes Emerson's "Circles." I think it's one of Emerson's most wrong-headed pieces, not even true to Emerson himself. And in it, Emerson's prose, usually so sharp and hard, becomes just impossibly vague. Because when we're reading well, we don't draw larger and larger circles. Our business in reading what somebody says is not to outdo him. It is to learn what he is saying and then go on and say something of our own, which will be a truer thing to say not because it is more capacious than what the other guy has said, but because it will be a way of thinking and saying which we feel we can live more truly or, perhaps, which we think is truer to the way people do or can or should live.

That is the trouble with Cavell's interest in the conditions of hearing a piece of music rather than in the piece of music. As Wittgenstein would have said, conditions have to end somewhere. As Cavell's Emerson did say, in the line Cavell himself made us all look at as an Emersonian touchstone, "I would write on the lintels of my doorpost, *Whim*. I hope it is better than whim at last, but we cannot spend the day in explanation."[10] At some point, you have to declare that what you see and what you say stop with themselves. It may only be whim. But if that makes it something that has no conditions, it also makes it something that is unconditional in the other sense of that word. Your seeing and your saying are ultimately their own conditions.

That is why Emerson's prime unit of composition is the aphorism. An aphorism is a saying whose authority is its own wording. That is also why it is so hard to know what, in Emerson, is a metaphor and what is straight referential talk. In the metaphor, the outside of the referent is recaptured internally as the reference itself. And this is what happens in literature as it does not, typically, in philosophy, and it's why we need to read philosophy literally, to bring it back to us. Both literature and philosophy spiral. But philosophy spirals outward. Literature takes what is out there and spirals it inward. In lyric poetry, it spirals it toward the voice, in novels, toward the characters, perhaps. Literature makes everything ordinary.

EVANS: Well, I'm pretty sure you are right about that. And I also think that your way of describing the pull of truth on literature as a dead reckoning of this thing next to that thing gets right to the heart of why novels considered in terms of what their characters do and say—what the book's author has her characters do and say—have always been "machines to think with" as someone has said. Recently there seems to be a movement afoot among high-powered critics (formerly unconcerned with any question that has to do with characters and their motivations, or authors and their motivations) that attempts to get back to the experience of thinking with characters. It's about time. But we shouldn't forget the other side of the coin. Because if, as you rightly say, the work of the literary critic is to turn philosophy into literature—or more precisely mark out a certain subset of philosophy that can really only be meaningfully read when it is read *as* literature (and in this way discover a very different Plato than the one philosophers go on about, for example) then isn't it also the case that the literary critic who is also an ordinary language critic must bring something similar to the reading of literature? I mean, reading literature *philosophically* is what you do. And I think that's what you did to me. [*Laughs*] Because the funny thing that kept happening to me at my first job in an English department was that I'd hear the students saying things to one another like, "Oh, you're taking a Kim Evans class." I'd hear them say that. And I'd ask, "What is a Kim Evans class?" What constitutes a Kim Evans class? And the answer would be something like, "I'm not sure, but your classes are not like other classes in the English department." And that happened at my next job too. And I *think* it has to do with the fact that whatever it is that I do in class—whatever it was you taught me, and let's say it has something to do with both Wittgenstein and Cavell—isn't strictly literary criticism as it has come to be thought of in English departments, even with the very wide range of practices that term obviously encompasses. And I'll admit that when I do find myself in the class of someone teaching literature, I generally find myself thinking, "What is this? What are we doing? I don't know what this is. Why does it feel so much like history? Or political theory? Or some kind of conversation about foreshadowing, or whatever. But, whatever it is, it isn't *reading* in a way that feels transformative." And I think that this comes from philosophy—really from moral perfectionism, in its right sense or in its useful sense. I think that us folks in literature and philosophy believe that reading in this different way is world saving. That it changes *who* is reading, what kind of person they are or could become. And that is the reason why you do it! You know, a friend of mine who I taught a class with last summer, a professor of literature at Cornell, at one point turned to me, hands on the table, and said: "You think that we should be teaching the students to be, you know, better people." She said it like an accusation! Like, *You* think ... And I said, "Yeah ... Don't you ...? [*Laughs*] And she said, "No. I don't."

DAUBER: [*Laughs*] Really?

EVANS: Yes. Now, *I* think that wanting people to become better is not an inherent part of the study of literature. Not these days, at any rate. But it is of philosophy—at least, as Plato envisioned it.

DAUBER: Ahh... That it's not an inherent part of literature but it is of philosophy, because philosophy is the love of the good, of wisdom.

EVANS: Yeah. In the old world. You can't be interested in doing philosophy unless you are somehow invested in the project of ...

DAUBER: ... the good.

EVANS: The good. And I think that is perhaps the source of the difference between what students found in my classes and in their other classes in literature.

DAUBER: Yes, but we also shouldn't forget that what they find in your classes is Plato read as literature. So let's compromise. Because isn't a love of the good also an inherent part of literary criticism, if not exactly of literature, an inherent part of, let's say, the reading of literature? It's just that literary criticism would locate the good somewhere else than where philosophy locates it. It would locate it not in what might be said, but in what we do say, in what, in fact, we mean when we say. Call literary criticism of this sort philosophy, if you will—hence the field, your field, of literature and philosophy. But it's philosophy in a new key, for a new age. The literature that Plato banished from the city ruled by the philosopher king because it wasn't interested, as the king was, in the good, has returned to capture the city by becoming the only philosophy that is now really possible in an age when there are no kings and where the good is democratic rather than aristocratic.

We could say that to read philosophically is to be interested in how does this make you better. How an engagement with what you are reading makes you better. But maybe the thing to say about reading literarily is that it makes you see that you are already better or have in you already the possibility of being better. Because to learn to judge a work is to learn to practice your judgment in difficult cases. To like or dislike it is to measure the application of your likes and dislikes. To understand it is to reach deep into what you do already understand and apply it.

EVANS: And perhaps that has something to do with why Matthew Arnold never wanted literary critics to become a professional class. In any event, professional literary criticism no longer seems to be interested in what it is to learn to practice your judgment in difficult cases. Nor does it get its grounding in the desire to be good or to help people be better. I don't know what it's grounded in ... cleverness,

I suppose. At least that would explain why there are so few ... why it feels like there are so few people ... I mean you know, when you run into someone who is doing 'literary theory' with this philosophical inflection. They stand out, you feel an affinity.

DAUBER: [*Under his breath*] Don't you want this to make you better ...? Or to give you some awareness of the possibilities of being better—of what being better might *be*? ... Something of that sort?

EVANS: [*Laughs*] Well. It is the thing that was right in front of our noses. That was too obvious to say. But you do, don't you? Want them to be better. Isn't that the point?

DAUBER: [*Laughs*] Well, yes. And it's too obvious to say. It goes without saying. And Cavell talks about that too. He talks somewhere about the problem of not wanting to say the obvious. And yet the obvious has to be said! And you always feel the double bind of worrying, "Am I just saying what everybody knows? So why bother to say it?" And yet you've got to say it. Yet this is just why I can't help but go back to Cavell's hearing Bach, which shows him not quite happy with saying what—to him, anyway—is obvious, a sort of 'aha' moment in his career. And this time, let me compare it to my own 'aha' moment in music. I took piano lessons as a kid, like so many other kids, especially of that day. I had no talent—of any sort, not the talent of my mother, let alone the talent of Cavell. But when I was a senior in college, having finished my requirements, decided on my own career, and having so to speak in Melville's way of speaking, nothing particular to keep me in class, I thought I might enroll in a one-on-one piano teaching course with a master professor in the music department.

He asked me to play something as a kind of audition, and I obliged with a Clemente sonatina, one of those little pieces that everybody learns to play in the third year or so of piano lessons. After I had played for about fifteen seconds, the professor stopped me and said "you're playing as if there were only two octaves worth of notes there." "But there are only two octaves in the piece," I said. "Yes," the professor answered, "but the piano has 88 keys." His point was that you can't know this piece of music if you don't know music. And maybe, we might say that you can't know music if you don't know art, and art if you don't know politics and sociology, and all there is to know. Sure, knowing is infinite. You have to learn everything. But what you really learn from learning everything isn't everything, but the two octaves that are nearest and dearest to you. This is the difference between Emerson and Thoreau. At a certain level, Thoreau seems to particularize more than Emerson. He lies on his back on the ice and counts the bubbles. But it's as if he thinks that by counting he might count his way to infinity, which is where he wants to get and which is why, since you can't ever get to infinity by starting with number 1, he is always disappointed and ultimately has to leave Walden for somewhere else, to start counting again. Or, on the other side, he sounds the depths of Walden Pond and is disappointed when he finds it actually does have a bottom. Emerson, on the other hand—that is, Emerson at his best, when he's not being woolly as he is in "Circles"—is content if he can learn to skate on the surface, as he phrases it. He faces his corpse or his debts. He doesn't want to move beyond them. And Cavell, after all, knows this, too, which is why, I think, he shifts in his career from Thoreau as his main man to Emerson. You have your two octaves before you. But you learn the 88 keys, and then you see those octaves as you've never seen them before. The greatest value of seeing everything is that it enables you to see something, which however much you've stared at it, you can't possibly see as well unless you've seen everything else. And it is that something, after all, that is your motivation for seeing everything, its grounding, what makes the attempt to see everything more than simple idle curiosity. Cavell, it seems to me, doesn't want to ground himself in his two octaves.

Well, Cavell's curiosity isn't at all idle. But, then, he's a philosopher. And his philosophical genius is precisely not two octaves but everything. That's what makes him a philosophical genius. He, like ordinary language critics in general, would bring the meta back home. But his home just *is* the meta. And it is so large that it can look a lot like homelessness to other people with other geniuses. Too Jewish, as he says, to find a proper reception in America. Too American, as he says, to find a proper reception in the world of philosophy at large. This is his Emerson's 'aspiration for immigrancy.' But as Cavell notes, he often wonders what his immigrant father would have made of that aspiration, his immigrant father who wanted nothing more than to find a home for a genius that wandering could not satisfy.

EVANS: Right. Yes. And I wonder if the danger you've proposed is evident in that passage I wanted to read from Cavell's foreword. I think I now see more clearly why those two features I've associated with philosophy, *in contrast* to literary criticism—spiraling self-consciousness, on the one hand, and on the other, an assumption that philosophy contributes to the climate of ideas about how to live, to "goodness," as we say—are also features of ordinary language criticism. Call it "literary criticism after Wittgenstein and after Cavell." (Though for me, "Dauber" has to be in that line-up too.) Anyway, the bit I wanted to read from Cavell is when he expresses unhappiness about the *absence* of spiraling self-consciousness in his own beloved teacher, J. L. Austin. Cavell characterizes himself as "in effect complaining simultaneously of a lack in his philosophizing and of a failure in his teaching." Then Cavell writes this:

> These complaints have their proper weight only against the recognition of how powerful a teacher he was; for it was in part because Austin was devoted to teaching, according to a particular picture of what teaching can and should be, that he avoided certain ranges of what the teaching of philosophy perhaps must be—the *personal* assault upon intellectual complacency, the private evaluation of intellectual conscience.[11]

For Cavell, "a major motive for wishing to leave the field of philosophy, for wishing relief from it, from one's periodic revulsions from it, would be to find something which could be taught more conveniently, a field in which it was not part of one's task to vie with one's students, nor to risk misleading them so profoundly."[12] Despite his enormous admiration for Austin, I take it that Cavell is drawing an important distinction between a "powerful" teacher like Austin, and the kind of teaching that can only come by way of an elaborate, tireless (and so exhausting), unduly self-aware philosophical procedure or *performance*—the kind of philosophy/art that is a "*personal* assault upon intellectual complacency," that is a "private evaluation of intellectual conscience." The kind of performance found in the great and revolutionary works of instruction, for example Wittgenstein's *Philosophical Investigations*.

Is Cavell right about this? I think he must be. But I also want to say that in you I found a teacher who modeled a "*personal* assault upon intellectual complacency" and who never, not once, avoided "certain ranges of what the teaching of philosophy must be." However, in contrast to Cavell's sketch of himself, or of the kind of teaching he received, I also never felt in danger of being misled. Nor was I ever *vied* with, for that matter, for there was never so much as a hint of crossing swords in your kind of instruction. I'd say this is a very important point of difference, one I am hugely grateful for. And I suspect that the combination of not being eagerly competed with and concomitantly feeling invited to undertake an assault on intellectual complacency (in regard to both "the falseness in one's character" and the "needless and unnatural compromises in one's institution," as Cavell writes) is practically a requirement for anyone who hopes to actually *live* as an ordinary language critic—that is, who takes as given the connection between the words we use and the lives we have.

Notes

1 Kenneth Dauber and Walter Jost, eds., *Ordinary Language Criticism: Literary Thinking after Wittgenstein after Cavell* (Evanston: Northwestern University Press, 2003), xv.
2 Ibid., xii.
3 Ibid., xiii.
4 Ibid.
5 Ibid., xii.
6 Ibid, xiii.
7 Ibid., iv.
8 Stanley Cavell, "Foreword: An Audience for Philosophy," *Must We Mean What We Say?* (New York: Charles Scribner's Sons, 1969; Cambridge: Cambridge University Press, 1976), xxiv; italics in original.
9 Ibid., xxiii.
10 Emerson, "Self-Reliance" (1841) as cited in Stanley Cavell, "The Philosopher in American Life," *Emerson's Transcendental Etudes*, ed. David Justin Hodge (Stanford: Stanford University Press, 2003), 54.
11 Cavell, "Foreword," xxiv.
12 Ibid.

10

Monsters and Felicities

Vernacular Transformations of the Five-Foot Shelf

LAWRENCE F. RHU

I FIRST MET STANLEY CAVELL one Sunday morning in June 1980. William Alfred and I were taking a walk on Brattle Street near Longfellow Park in Cambridge. Bill had just pointed out a large window in front of Longfellow's house and remarked that the poet liked to write in view of whoever passed by. Since he was not very tall, Longfellow used to stand before his study window on a wooden podium to make himself appear taller. Thus, he looked like a man in full, engaged in the art whose skillful practice won him renown. I am not sure whether that's true about Longfellow, though Bill was a charitable man, to say the least, and, if anything, kind to a fault. Still, he had grown up worlds away from Harvard, in Brooklyn, where his father worked as a brick mason and his mother as a telephone operator; and he had acquired a keen ear and eye for pretenses inspired by success and good fortune. In this regard, he would have agreed with Cavell's observation that the problem with importance in academia is that it may lead to self-importance.[1] Moreover, I hear a kindred spirit in Cavell's earliest essay in defense of ordinary language philosophy, "Must We Mean What We Say?," which gives voice to impatience with a philosopher's "laborious questioning" in an effort to discover what native speakers say in certain contexts. "I might just ask *my landlady*," Cavell writes at one turn (emphasis his). At another, he expresses hope against hope that philosophy might be spared "having to think up *special brands* of meaning," though it seems too far gone into entanglements of unusual terminology to effectively reclaim the vernacular (emphasis mine).[2]

On that June day in 1980, Stanley, as he would later become known to me, was walking along Brattle Street with his wife, Cathleen, and they stopped to exchange greetings with Bill, who introduced me to the Cavells. Later I would learn that Bill and Stanley were among the few Harvard faculty members recruited by the College dean, John U. Monro, to teach for a few weeks during the summer of 1964 at Tougaloo College, a historically black college just north of Jackson, Mississippi. In *Little Did I Know: Excerpts from Memory*, Stanley explains how decisively those weeks during what became known as Mississippi Freedom Summer affected him. He summons the idea of an identity crisis and elaborates on his exhilaration at discovering a sense of membership in a particular generation—or two: "The sense of identification, even modified to include partial identification with each of two actual generations, was earnest that there was someone not merely to whom to write, but for whom to write, to speak for, to justify my sometimes unappeasable wish or need to say 'we' and know whom I meant, or wanted to mean."[3]

Stanley also discerns the beginnings of such exhilaration in "Must We Mean What We Say?," which he calls "the first of his published philosophical papers of continuing significance for [him]." There, his endorsement of appeals to ordinary usage in everyday contexts expresses an openness to a wider community of speakers. When Benson Mates issues a challenge designed to trivialize such appeals by making them seem as though they could go on "ad infinitum," Stanley asks, "Isn't this just another of those apostrophes to the infinite which prevents philosophers from getting down to cases?" He thus defends his "heavy reliance on the idea of *context*" with the same down-to-earth candor that would prompt him to ask his landlady about everyday speech in ordinary circumstances. From early in his career, Stanley seeks to practice philosophy of a kind that may shed some light and inspire some confidence about how *we* ordinarily proceed in thinking. In fact, we may already be in the habit of making such advances, though we may need some reassurance of both their reality and our own presence of mind to appreciate their value in doing philosophy, if that's what we call thinking.

My first encounter with Stanley was an unrecognizable prelude to what would happen exactly a year later, when I first read *Pursuits of Happiness*. Bill Alfred had asked me to house-sit for him in Cambridge while he stayed in Manhattan during the summer of 1981 because he was involved in preparations for the New York production of his play *The Curse of an Aching Heart*. It was a typically kind invitation, for Bill knew how much I missed Cambridge since I'd recently moved to New Orleans to take a teaching job there. In his living room Bill had a painting of his house entitled

"Lucky House," and 31 Athens Street was just such a place for many people who had the good fortune to become acquainted with Bill, wherever their paths happened to cross. The prospect of that summer in Cambridge was part of such luck for me, which only increased after I arrived and began seeing *Pursuits of Happiness* in store windows. I first saw it in, of all places, the window of the Cambridge Trust Company, and I quickly bought my first copy down the street at the Harvard Bookstore. Soon I was having the time of my life reading that book and seeing the movies discussed in its pages—all of which (both the pages *and* the movies) I'd never seen before. Thanks to Stanley's book, all seven of those remarriage comedies were being screened in Cambridge and Brookline at three different venues that summer.[4]

Besides the pleasures of those films and Stanley's prose, what engaged me in that summer experience was a sense that Stanley had accomplished the difficult feat of inheriting and transmitting the sort of culture mainly on offer at Harvard in its Program in General Education when I was an undergraduate in the mid-1960s. A clear example of his achievement appears in his chapter on *His Girl Friday* (1940, dir. Howard Hawks), which brings to bear ideas of the state of nature and the social contract, as presented in Thomas Hobbes and John Locke, on his discussion of that Hollywood film. I had struggled hard to make pertinent sense of such "monsters of fame," as Stanley calls the likes of Hobbes and Locke, and my efforts often seemed in vain and usually went unappreciated even at their best. But Stanley's readings of those films in the light of such texts made differences between elite and popular culture less of an obstacle to democratic understanding at a time when such differences were becoming politically explosive and often seemed insurmountable in the wake of the Vietnam War, the Black Power movement, and feminism.

It is worth noting that other Harvard professors were beginning to use film in their courses during the 1960s—none more memorably, in my experience, than Erik Erikson, whose essay on *Wild Strawberries* (1957) remains a profound exploration of both Ingmar Bergman's film and crises of integrity and despair in late adulthood and old age.[5] But *Young Man Luther* (1958), Erikson's first sustained "study in psychoanalysis and history," pertains more directly to Stanley's way of thinking as it evolved to include reflections on Luther and on his own "identity crisis." Indeed, Erikson's growing prominence in American culture during the 1960s is difficult to overestimate as that particular book and Erikson's other writings became increasingly part of our public conversation. *Gandhi's Truth: On the Origins of Militant Nonviolence* (1969), which Erikson jokingly dubbed a study of "middle-aged Mahatma" and thus a sort of sequel to *Young Man Luther*, won both the Pulitzer Prize and the National Book Award in 1969. Soon the National Endowment for the Humanities invited Erikson to deliver the Thomas Jefferson Lectures in 1973.

Lawrence J. Friedman calls his thorough and perceptive biography of Erikson, *Identity's Architect* (1999), and Erikson could arguably be considered the *inventor* of the "identity crisis" as a concept through his earlier work both on Luther and, more generally, on youth and early adulthood in the stages of the human life cycle, as he observed and conceived of them. Of course, the idea of "invention" warrants both historical and philological interrogation in such a context, just as Stanley's brief appeals to Erikson's terminology in the process of exploring his own life experience suggest further routes of pertinent interest, since they involve reading and reflecting on Luther's three treatises of 1520, which Stanley regularly assigned his students in Humanities 5 for the better part of two decades. In his memoir *Little Did I Know*, Stanley summons this phrase from Erikson on Luther: the discovery of "a life's work."[6] Moreover, Stanley connects that phrase, via Erikson (and somewhat mystically, it strikes me), to a particular age—thirty-three—when such a discovery often takes place. Still, I cannot help thinking of "a life's work" as both an invention and a discovery, because, taken together, invention and discovery include both subject and object—the worker and the work, you might say, as in Stanley's increasing reluctance to separate autobiography from philosophy, or, in "Thinking of Emerson," moods from objects: "This very evanescence of the world proves its existence to me; it *is* what vanishes from me. ... [T]his is not realism exactly, but it is not solipsism either."[7]

In Stanley's reference to Erikson on "a life's work," the precise synchronicity of obvious parallels—Luther, Jesus, and Stanley, all at age thirty-three—does not interest me much, but I do have a hunch about a particular passage in Erikson that Stanley may be calling to mind. It is part of the remarkable chapter in *Young Man Luther* entitled "The Meaning of 'Meaning It'." The title itself rhymes with Stanley's earnest and virtually simultaneous expression of concern about whether we must *mean* what we say. "Must We Mean What We Say?" (the essay that gives Stanley's 1969 book its title) and Erikson's book were both published in 1958; but, here again, synchronicity needs not preoccupy us. Specifically, Erikson writes, "Luther accepted for *his life work* (my emphasis) the unconquered frontier of tragic conscience, defined as it was by his personal needs and superlative gifts. '*Locus noster*,' he said, in the lectures on the Psalms, '*in quo nos cum Deo, sponsos cum sponsa, habitare debet ... est conscientia.*'" Erikson renders Luther's Latin this way: "Conscience is that inner ground where we and God have to learn to live with each other as man and wife ... where our self can either live in wedded harmony with a positive conscience or is estranged from a negative one."[8] Luther's marital simile represents the moral stakes of the inner life figuratively as a marriage of true minds, the individual's and God's; and, of course, he shook the foundations of Christendom not only via such interpretive gestures. He also decided to abandon his priestly vow of celibacy and marry Katharina von Bora, formerly a nun at the Cistercian cloister of Marienthron.

In the passage above, Erikson is citing a sentence from Luther's lectures on the Psalms, which invokes the higher authority of conscience and uses the idea of "marriage" in an allegorical sense. Stanley's references to Luther mainly derive from *The Pagan Servitude of the Church* and Nietzsche's *On the Genealogy of Morality*, both of which he regularly included on the syllabus in Humanities 5. Those works both seek to release marriage from the confines of established authorities—the church in Luther's case and conventional morality in Nietzsche's—and whatever claims they may traditionally exert upon individual conscience. In *Pursuits of Happiness*, the belated series of epigraphs, which appears after the introductory "Words for a Conversation," includes the passage in the *Genealogy* about "Luther's wedding," a subject that preoccupied Wagner during "the finest, strongest, happiest, *most courageous* period of [his] life."[9] Thus, Nietzsche registers his keen disappointment in the composer's failure to elaborate on that theme and demonstrate through his music that there is "no necessary antithesis between chastity and sensuality; every good marriage, every good love affair transcends this antithesis."[10]

Soon thereafter, in the second chapter of *Pursuits of Happiness*, Stanley addresses the other side of that alleged antithesis via a crucial passage from John Milton's *Doctrine and Discipline of Divorce* (1643). The passage contributes to Stanley's argument the idea of "meet and happy conversation" as a modern definition of true marriage, which is more readily open to the possibility of divorce for such spiritual reasons as emotional incompatibility—in other words, for the failure to achieve a marriage of true minds.[11] Milton's pamphlet petitions Parliament to include considerations of "household unhappiness," beyond the sole predicate of carnal infidelity, as a legitimate premise for divorce.[12] Thus, Milton helps to expose the false alternatives of chastity and sensuality, and he becomes a useful voice in appeals for the conversation of marriage as a dialogue that honestly includes body and soul.

The Doctrine and Discipline of Divorce eventually appears on the reading list for Cavell's Core Curriculum course on Moral Perfectionism, in which I had the good fortune to work as a teaching fellow during the spring of 1996 and lead a weekly discussion section. The passage on "household unhappiness" joins the four pages of epigraphs in *Cities of Words* (2004), a book that makes the conversation between movies and "monsters of fame" more explicit by interweaving Stanley's "letters" on the "monsters" with more summary accounts of the films. Of course, those letters derive from Stanley's lectures, and he hopes to keep "something of the sound" of their delivery in the classroom on the pages of his book.[13]

In *Pursuits of Happiness*, as we have seen, Stanley's initial mention of Luther appears among the belated epigraphs via Nietzsche's *On the*

Genealogy of Morality and his reflections on Luther's wedding and Wagner's failure to compose music on that theme and produce a "nice, plucky Luther comedy."[14] Stanley's subsequent discussion of that passage from the *Genealogy* leads him to allude to the *Pagan Servitude of the Church*, where Luther challenges the legitimacy of the Church of Rome's treatment of marriage as a sacrament; and, ultimately, in the final chapter of *Pursuits of Happiness*, Stanley cites this version of another sentence from that treatise: "All our life should be baptism," which, of course, derives from Luther's attack on the church's monopoly of another sacrament.[15] Unlike marriage, baptism satisfies Luther's criteria for the status of a sacrament, but his arguments in all cases, pro and con, rely heavily and continuously on biblical exegesis. They thus reflect the Reformation rallying cry of *Sola Scriptura*, or "Scripture alone," as the basic predicate for claims of true Christian faith and practice.

Simply put, a sacrament is an outward and visible sign of an inward and spiritual grace, as Luther insisted.[16] He attacked the church and its functionaries for mistaking signs and ceremonies for the grace they symbolize and thus nullifying the desired affirmation of a spiritual process. Stanley, in his way, continues this Lutheran pursuit in his discernment of the spirit's presence or absence on-screen in remarriage comedy, among other places; and Arnold Davidson justly describes him as a "diagnostician of the spirit in which things are said."[17] Stanley employs Luther's high expectations of the drama of everyday life—its pathos and fear and joy and laughter—to point out spiritual possibilities that reflect his own convictions about Hollywood comedies of remarriage and amount to ordinary American epiphanies regardless of ecclesiastical rites and ceremonies.

Specifically, Stanley is seeking to demonstrate that Lucy Warriner (Irene Dunne), the estranged wife in *The Awful Truth* (1937, dir. Leo McCarey), acknowledges her genuine love for her husband Jerry (Cary Grant), by remarking: "We had some grand laughs." Moreover, that avowal demonstrates the validity of their marriage, or "meet and happy conversation," and leaves the opportunity for *re*marriage open. Even as they are in the process of getting a divorce, they may still get back together and enjoy more grand laughs again. Every day may indeed become a baptism. Recognition of the possibility of sharing such an experience matters more than whatever you call it—baptism or grand laughs or household happiness—so long as you know what you are talking about when you see it. But calling it baptism or household happiness and thus connecting those terms in Luther and Milton to *The Awful Truth* worked like a revelation on me when I first encountered such movies from *their* perspective. My experience of highly touted changes in the 1960s and 1970s had seemed to bring me into one era and out the other with no such revolutionary consequences, but Stanley's way of thinking and writing about these particular movies made a world of difference to me, as would his later book about Hollywood melodrama. Both made emotional sense to me and filled me with hope that our country is a place in which happiness can be found and unhappiness can be acknowledged and transcended.

From the solemnity of sacraments to laughter in Hollywood comedy, that roundabout journey through examples of Luther's role in Stanley's thinking indicates the unconventionality of his writing as far as orthodox scholarship is concerned. In my experience, however, such writing abounds in fresh insights. His surprising claims sound like the best one could achieve as a humanist of the sort General Education at Harvard sought to produce, but that achievement was just the beginning. If we follow Luther through the mere four mentions indexed in *Pursuits of Happiness*, we find him thus in the third: "It is part of our understanding of our world, and of what constitutes an historical event for this world, that Luther redefined the world in getting married, and Henry the Eighth—one of the last figures Shakespeare was moved to write about—in getting divorced. It has since then been a more or less open secret in our world that we do not know what legitimizes either divorce or marriage."[18] In my early adulthood, I had never thought of marriage and divorce in such sweeping yet historically specific terms, and I had never seen *The Philadelphia Story* (1940, dir. George Cukor) either, though I had taken a few Gen Ed courses at Harvard and read *Young Man Luther*. Such bold assertions about "monsters of fame," like Luther and Henry the Eighth (and Milton and Nietzsche), rang true in ways that enabled me to proceed and put history to more immediate and less tentative uses. Stanley was showing us how to inherit European thought without a crippling sense of obligation to the whole edifice of its various traditions. Such claims can serve as a point of departure from which an American scholar can set forth from Wittenberg and London to Philadelphia without automatically regretting real or imagined details of history and theology left behind or overlooked. Maybe certain details will turn out to matter more than we initially appreciate, but we cannot anxiously spend the day in laborious explanations.

Moreover, as classroom instruction such claims may register with an indelibility that few professors manage to achieve in their lectures. In the mid-1990s, when I told my friend Jon Levenson that I was beginning to write about Stanley's essays on Shakespeare, he promptly summoned from memory the gist of an observation he had heard as a freshman in Hum 5 during one of Stanley's lectures on *King Lear* over a quarter of a century earlier. "Machiavelli's knowledge of the world is present [in *King Lear*]; not just in his attitudes of realism and cynicism, but in his experience of the *condition* to which these attitudes are appropriate—in which the inner and the outer worlds have become totally disconnected, and man's life is all public, among strangers, seen only from the outside. Luther saw the same thing, at the same time, from the inside" (emphasis mine).[19]

The sound of the classroom, which Stanley pointedly seeks to maintain in his writing, clearly registered in Jon's case: his memory of the last sentence above was virtually word-perfect. Moreover, I remain struck to this day by that passage inasmuch as it has made me ever after want to clarify for myself what Stanley's assertion means. In 1512, Machiavelli lost his government job due to the return of the Medici. Since the Florentine Republic, in which he had served, no longer existed, he wrote *The Prince* to demonstrate his qualifications as a strategically amoral advisor in the new monarchical context of a principality. Little more than a year earlier Luther journeyed south as the *socius itinerarius*, or traveling companion, of a senior member of the Augustinian order in Saxony. He was seeking to petition their prior general on behalf of seven more strictly Observant cloisters, including the one at Erfurt where Luther resided. They were averse to amalgamation with their more lenient brethren. Luther's accounts of his pilgrimage through Renaissance Italy and his encounter with the scandalous reality of Rome as the Borgias had left it for the warrior Pope, Julius II (who would soon be succeeded by Leo X, the Medici Pope) are mostly composed well after the fact. By then Luther had perfected his polemical invective against the Church of Rome and registered his absolute sense of the emptiness and corruption of the Papacy, whose power is merely self-serving and worldly in its ambitions, like that of any other Renaissance prince. That is what Luther saw, from the inside, as an individual with a spiritual vocation. Machiavelli saw from the outside, as a political operative trying to maintain his chosen career in an altered world under a new regime.

In an elegant way, Erikson turns his account of Luther's journey into pertinent lessons in cultural history. The secular worldliness of Italian humanism becomes a revealing context for Luther's spiritual ordeal, especially when Erikson highlights the hypocrisy of priests who rush suppliants through the sacrament of the Lord's Supper and make snide remarks about the host in the process.[20] Thus, *hoc est corpus* ("this is my body") became *hocus pocus* in Protestant eyes. Stanley's stylishly provocative succinctness achieves a similar contextualization via Luther and Machiavelli for students of Shakespeare's most agonizing tragedy—Lear's agon, and Gloucester's too, featuring that consummate Machiavelli, Edmund the bastard, as an unforgettable and almost unforgivable villain. Before embarking on *King Lear* in Hum 5, students were assigned only two other books, *The Prince* and *Three Treatises* by Martin Luther, which collected his chief clarifications and defenses of his positions after he had posted his ninety-five theses on the church door in Wittenberg. Those three treatises include *The Pagan Servitude of the Church*, *The Freedom of a Christian*, and *To the Christian Nobility of the German Nation*, and they were all written in 1520.[21] What is most striking in Stanley's comparison, if not his assimilation, of Luther to Machiavelli is the way he appeals to the *condition* of what prompts a response of realism and cynicism, which are both attitudes we would immediately associate with Machiavelli. That condition is the world as each of these two "monsters of fame" found it. Via that premise, Stanley offers a basis for a surprising comparison between Machiavelli's *real politik* and Luther's theology of grace—or between pragmatism and transcendentalism, if you jump ahead roughly half-a-millennium.

Such thinking foreshadows and illuminates Stanley's reading of the final paragraph of Emerson's "Experience," which begins, "I know the world I converse with in the city and in the farms, is not the world I *think*." Stanley refers to that sentence as a "transcription of the vision of Kant's [*Foundations*]," and students in Stanley's 1990s Core Curriculum course on Moral Perfectionism would readily associate it with Kant's "two standpoints" in *Foundations of the Metaphysics of Morals*: the intelligible world and the world of sense. Moreover, when Stanley sets out a series of epigraphs for *Cities of Words*, he starts with Emerson's version of this Kantian distinction between these two worlds, and he follows it with a passage from the *Foundations* about the realm or kingdom of ends as "a useful and permissible idea for the purposes of a rational faith." Immediately thereafter comes the passage from Plato's *Republic* that gives *Cities of Words* its title and makes a similar distinction between going into politics (in "the world [one sees]") and describing an unearthly utopia as a model laid up in heaven for the government of the soul ("the world [one thinks]").

This sequence of epigraphs continues and pertinently represents the daunting "monsters of fame" assigned in Stanley's course on Moral Perfectionism. So, as we anticipate such intellectual trials, it is with some relief that we hear these thinkers characterized as "guardians or guides at the entrance to this book," in Stanley's first sentence, as he begins to introduce them in his book in precisely that sequence: Emerson, Kant, and Plato. Stanley thus proceeds with a primary task that Emerson assigns to the American scholar, "the gradual domestication of culture"; and it corresponds to ways of thinking Stanley was memorably prompting his students to consider three decades earlier as a useful prelude to reading *King Lear*. Both Luther and Machiavelli inhabit (or "see") the same world inasmuch as Luther, when he travels to Rome, seems entirely oblivious to Renaissance culture; and Machiavelli only finds time for it when he is out of a job—and, even then, he most memorably celebrates Cesare Borgia's brutal *virtù*, not Cicero's civic version. In a way, Luther and Machiavelli *are* like Cordelia and Edmund, only *she* sees the same thing, at the same time, *from the inside* that he sees from the outside. But the connection that Stanley seeks to make between Kant and Emerson emphasizes the latter's point of departure from Kant's unanswerable question: how do we make reason practical? Initially, Emerson does not find that much is gained "by manipular attempts to realize the world of thought." "[P]atience, patience" then becomes Emerson's response, and he meets the challenge of realizing his world "not by action but by suffering, of which Emerson's continuous example is his writing, which continuously and patiently gives expression to his aversion to the way things are, that is, to the ways he and his countryman keep things."[22]

Moreover, Stanley makes a further advance upon the realm of ends. Via Emerson's embrace of inclination, which Kant shuns as an incentive for moral action, Stanley proceeds with the task not only of domesticating culture but of realizing his world as well. Though inclination may seem mere whim or even the voice of the devil, Emerson is willing to risk it, and Stanley follows his lead in reimagining Northrop Frye's idea of the Green World in Shakespearean comedy as it reappears on-screen in remarriage comedy. It serves as a place of perspective where lovers sort out their problems, a place where desire is acknowledged instead of distorted or repressed in reason's effort to rise above it, if not to disown it. Such films call that allegorical place Connecticut in five of the seven examples of the genre that Stanley explores; yet, *It Happened One Night* (1934, dir. Frank Capra), the film that he pairs with Kant's *Foundations* in *Cities of Words*, represents the Green World as three nights on the road—or, as Emerson puts it in "Experience," "Everything good is on the highway."[23] By the third night, Peter Warne (Clark Gable) is able to acknowledge his desire, and alert moviegoers will notice how closely it resembles what he and Ellie Andrews (Claudette Colbert) experienced together the night before, which they spent outdoors under the stars. Such viewers will also take note of these alternative perspectives on their first night on the road together. The "grand laughs" they share arise from their pretending to be married, and they improvise their parts so convincingly that onlookers *in* the movie ironically reach that judgment about them. In those strangers' eyes, their fake fight confirms skeptical commonplaces about the reality of marriage. But the movie lets its viewers in on a secret, which Peter and Ellie themselves have not yet discovered. The obvious pleasure they take in their spontaneous performance and the easy give-and-take of their acting suggest the unacknowledged chemistry between them. By their third night together, it becomes clear to both of them that they want similar things. Moreover, in the utopian dimension of Stanley's thinking, their mutual intelligibility becomes a sign, or a promise, not only of their possible "remarriage" but also of a further possibility: an eventual community, which Stanley invents or discovers, via Kant and Emerson—and Capra. This realm of ends, or new yet unapproachable America, can be entered, or realized, however, only in pairs.

In *Little Did I Know*, Stanley describes the differences between teaching at a major state university and teaching at a top-tier private one. Of course, he is drawing on his experience at the University of California, Berkeley, and at Harvard, respectively, to make this comparison. In the late summer of 1957, once Stanley has settled in at Berkeley, he is "free, or rather forced, to face the reality of preparing [his] eight lectures a week for [his] three fall courses." Or, as he bills the pages about this showdown with reality in the table of contents: "How may one roughly sanely commence a life of teaching, where this means appear to give 120 lectures over the first semester of one's first year?" In answering that question, he is most candid and funny when he recounts his first (and only) experience of calling in sick and not *appearing* at all. One night during the wee hours, when he is still trying in vain to subdue a monster named Kant for a large lecture class at nine in the morning, Stanley fantasizes various scenarios of banishment and shame as a result of his possibly not showing up at all, until, irresistibly, he falls asleep on the floor at home. Fortunately, he wakes up early enough to make the necessary call to the department secretary and cancel his classes for the day. Soon thereafter, his Kantian crisis solves itself, and he can proceed with preparation for his other classes as well. "But," he realizes, "this cure would only work once."[24]

As Stanley describes it, the main difference between teaching at Berkeley and Harvard boiled down, by and large, to the number of lectures one must *appear* to give. Stanley's course load at Berkeley amounted to eight classes per week for fifteen weeks; at Harvard, it amounted to four classes per week for twelve weeks. The word from Stanley's table of contents that I have italicized warrants parsing a bit. "Appear" probably means "show up" there, but it could be construed as "seem" and thus taken as a little joke Stanley is making at his own expense in order to suggest the impossibility of such a task for most first-year philosophy professors who have not entirely become products of what we may call, in its worst manifestations, the intellectual industrial complex known as graduate school education. Stanley's potential play on the word "appear," or my misprision of it, can help us get at some major points about Stanley's experience of teaching at Harvard and his students' experience of learning from him. In *Little Did I Know* and elsewhere, Stanley celebrates the quality of Harvard graduate students in philosophy who assisted him by teaching sections in Humanities 5 and Moral Reasoning 34 and the undergraduates whom he came to know during his decades of teaching these introductory courses. Further, he elaborates on the diverse population that a Harvard auditorium draws as "[constituting] as perfect a set of occasions for the public exploration of great philosophical texts of our tradition (eventually including literary texts and films) as I could wish to imagine ... No comparable experience has had a greater effect on my quest for a sound philosophical prose that I could place conviction in, nor has been more heartening to it."[25]

Such prose as Stanley's quest led him to write has an unforgettable sound for many. Thus, my friend Jon Levenson's memory of a thought from Stanley's lecture on *King Lear*, decades after he had heard it given voice, made me want to see if it had made its way onto the page, but it also made me wonder about "perfect occasions" that initially enabled such thoughts to be spoken. Lectures were rarely recorded in the 1960s but miscellaneous papers— syllabi, essay assignments, mid-term and final exams—were preserved. So, I went to look through those from Hum 5 in the Harvard archives, and I can report the following relevant discovery. In the spring term of 1969, the first paper assignment in "Ideas of Man and the World in Western Thought," as Hum 5 was more fully called, required "3–5 double-spaced typewritten pages" in response to this claim and these questions: "Both Machiavelli and Luther hold certain views about what should be the relation of the people they address to ordinary morality. What do these passages reveal about their respective views, and what considerations might have led them to take them?" These are the excerpts from Luther and Machiavelli, respectively:

> It is clear, then, that a Christian has all that he needs in faith and needs no works to justify him; and if he has no need of works, he has no need of the law; and if he has no need of the law, surely, he is free from the law. It is true that "the law is not laid down for the just" [1 Tim 1:9].[26]

> ... [F]or how we live is so far removed from how we ought to live, that he who abandons what is done for what ought to be done, will rather bring about his ruin than his preservation. A man who wishes to make a profession of goodness in everything must necessarily come to grief among so many who are not good.[27]

In reckoning with the relationship between works and faith in biblical theology, Luther's potentially suicidal scrupulosity risked a passage through the most dangerous depths of a crisis of conscience at the beginning of the sixteenth century. For Luther, in certain straits, reassurance of personal justification seemed impossible to come by, so it is no wonder that Erikson invokes the pathology of a negative conscience, or a relentless superego, and describes Luther in the grip of self-destructive energies from which psychoanalysis seeks to free individuals in the process of self-understanding. Stanley's turn toward moral perfectionism requires a similar reckoning with dark forces, such as the devil in Emerson's "Self-Reliance" or bad citizenship and potential tragedy in Nietzsche's "Schopenhauer as Educator" (in *Untimely Meditations*), texts regularly assigned in Moral Reasoning 34: Moral Perfectionism. Moreover, Stanley's sense of the audience for this sort of philosophizing resonates with Erikson's approach to the stages in the human life cycle in two significant ways. First, he has chosen to explore the crisis of Luther's youth, and the perfectionist philosophers whom Stanley singles out—Emerson and Thoreau, Kierkegaard and Nietzsche—specifically address their words to students and the young. Second, Stanley understands youth not only as a stage of life that we pass through at a particular time, once and for all, but also as a dimension of the self. Erikson calls this way of understanding human development "epigenesis": we grow and change, but we also circle back, not necessarily in regression, but also to return to the bedrock of fundamental strengths, tried and tested along the way.

In the psychopharmacology of our era, recent editions of *The Diagnostic and Statistical Manual of Mental Illnesses* specify "perfectionism" as a symptom that legalizes prescribing certain medications rather than as a philosophical tradition in which reflection and conversation can open pathways both to the consolation of established strength and to the liberation of fresh energy, even when we reach a most stubborn impasse. Fortunately, these alternatives are not mutually exclusive nowadays in the practice of psychiatry or the principles of medical ethics. Often caregivers offer some combination of psychotropic drugs and therapeutic conversation in whatever proportion they deem advisable and medical insurance is obliged to cover. Through a forthright acknowledgment of the darkness and the light—from Shakespearean tragedy to Emersonian onwardness and becoming—Stanley's embrace of perfectionism invents, or discovers, ways of thinking through texts that recuperate presently beneficial traditions of philosophy; and he compounds them with a voice of his own that inspires others to join in. We may consider the moment when an object of interpretation becomes a means of interpretation as a victory over "the anxiety of influence," but Stanley's relationship with many texts is less adversarial than Harold Bloom's theory of literary inheritance generally maintains. Stanley not only acknowledges his occasional need for the friendship of the reader. Often, in the process of interpretation, he extends his friendship *as* a reader in a scrupulous effort to understand, even though he acknowledges that the assertion of his right to speak may require the arrogation of voice. In the *Pagan Servitude*, Stanley finds a warrant for such reading and interpretation in Luther's adaptation of the Augustinian maxim: *Crede ut intelligas*. In order to understand, you must believe.[28] Stanley's domestication of "monsters of fame" brings to life therapeutic possibilities in philosophy that not only console but also prepare us for the ongoing unforeseeable eventfulness of ordinary life.

I first became acquainted with Erikson's work during my senior year at Harvard when I took his course on the Human Life Cycle in the fall of 1966. "The Avoidance of Love," Stanley's essay on *King Lear*, unforgettably registers his contemporary response to the American tragedy then underway both at home and abroad. Its republication in *Disowning Knowledge* twenty years later prompted Stanley to observe that this essay "bears the scars of our period in Vietnam; its strange part 2 is not in control of its asides and orations and love letters of nightmare."[29] My section leader in Erikson's course was Robert Coles, who later made his own remarkable contribution to the public conversation about the war in Vietnam. For a week in July 1970, he hosted Father Daniel Berrigan at his home in Concord, Massachusetts, while the priest was a fugitive from the FBI for his involvement in the destruction of selective service files in federal offices in Catonsville, Maryland. Their tape-recorded conversations became *The Geography of Faith* after first appearing in *The New York Review of Books* as "A Dialogue Undergound."[30] Coles had been active in the Civil Rights movement down south, mainly as a reporter and researcher. His medical specialty as a psychiatrist sometimes involved him in court proceedings where such expertise gave him some influence on the treatment of activists in jail and on trial. His research focused on how individuals respond to political crises, and it constituted part of his own response to the struggle for civil rights in the South. Yet, his role as a participant observer did not preclude taking sides. The detachment and objectivity prized by social science did not immunize him against moral and political passions aroused by social crises.

On the Wednesday before Thanksgiving, Coles scheduled our section meeting in his small basement office behind Claverly Hall on Mount Auburn Street because many students would have already headed home for the holiday by then. Among those few who attended that day, the conversation turned to the anti-war protest that had detained Secretary of Defense Robert McNamara during his recent visit to Harvard. Protesters first blocked his departure from Quincy House; then, on Mill Street behind Lowell House, they forced a confrontation. Coles sensed how upset I was by news of that event, and perhaps he had already discerned how troubled I was overall in those days. Though we had not spoken personally before that small group meeting in his office, he phoned me out of the blue on the Friday after Thanksgiving and asked how I was doing. He was upset too, as it turned out, though it took me a long time to fully realize the truth of that fact, which he was quite willing to share from the beginning of our conversations. At Harvard I had encountered nothing before like his candor and his political passion, and nothing like his kindness either, in the way he reached out to me that day. Gradually our friendship blossomed and became an inspiration for me thereafter. Thus, when Stanley discusses the need for an alternative response to the criticism of his colleagues "who were so fiercely contemptuous of the behavior of our distressed students" in April 1969, when SDS organized the occupation of University Hall, I feel lucky that I met Robert Coles in that hour of my distress over two years earlier.

Bob, as I had begun calling him soon after that fateful Thanksgiving, was editing the journal *DoubleTake* thirty years later when he agreed to my proposal to interview Stanley for an article. I was teaching a course at Harvard that summer, so Stanley and I arranged to get together each week for lunch and conversation. When my wife, Karen, would drop me off Wednesdays at noon at the Cavell's home in Brookline, she'd explain to our kids, then three and five, "Your Dad is going to play with Stanley." Sometimes, as Stanley and I were leaving for a nearby Chinese restaurant, he would lift his voice to make it reach upstairs and say goodbye to his adult son, Ben, by name, adding "sweetheart" to this tender everyday farewell. Though I had a pacemaker successfully installed three years ago, this behavior shows why I still consider Stanley my favorite cardiologist. He became my heart specialist decades earlier, first with *Pursuits of Happiness* and then with *Contesting Tears*, and so he remains. That summer I became comfortable calling my son Danny, "sweetheart."

I have no wish to sentimentalize the personal effect of such a moment. My good fortune enabled me to become friends with teachers mentioned in this essay and witness their behavior both at work and at home. They became pedagogical and intellectual and literary *heroes* of mine, if you will—and colleagues too, inasmuch as I worked as a teaching fellow in courses they taught. But they also became older friends whose personal conduct brought to life aspirations of mine that others at Harvard had not so effectively encouraged. Just as Stanley didn't "identify" with Jesus and Luther when they were all thirty-three years old, I didn't identify with those teachers so much as I appreciated their companionability and their willingness to let me get to know them in the process of our doing something together: conversing, collaborating, breaking bread.

Bill Alfred used to lament the influence that "we" (his word) had on students' critical writing at Harvard: "[It's] absolutely ghastly, but ultimately that's our fault. We've got so used to bad writing that when an occasional essay comes that is graceful, we suspect it of being shallow."[31] In Bill's dismay I hear the same emotion that prompted Stanley to consider his landlady the likeliest resource for understanding what *we* ordinarily say in particular circumstances; for Bill had a knack for letting the air out of inflated speech and intellectual pretensions. Such concern also moved Bob Coles to get down on the floor and draw pictures with children while he listened carefully to what they and their families and their fellow citizens across our country had it at heart to say about being caught up in crises caused or exacerbated by racism, poverty, and neglect. All three of them discerned and appreciated candor and clarity, which convey a certain "grace"—the savor of the salt of the earth, to put it proverbially.

When I started working as a research assistant for Bob Coles in the summer of 1968, I went out to his home in Concord to sort through piles of pamphlets about places he had visited in Appalachia and the Deep South to meet with people he had become further acquainted with in the process of writing the second volume of *Children of Crisis: Sharecroppers, Migrants, and Mountaineers*. While I worked in Bob's study, he sat under a tall tree in the backyard and filled a remarkable number of yellow pages on a legal pad with his longhand scrawl. We then enjoyed sandwiches that his wife, Jane, prepared, and, though she expressed sympathy for my having to sift through Bob's enormous pile of miscellaneous brochures and papers, I was glad to have such work and said so too. After lunch their four-year-old son, Bobby, showed me their chickens and explained, "The red thing on their head is a 'comb,' but not like the comb we use for our hair." Later, I sat talking with Bob under the same tree where he had written so much in such a short time. As their two-year-old son, Danny, focused his efforts sharply on moving his modest fleet of toy dump trucks and steamrollers and other heavy earth-moving equipment into our immediate vicinity, Bob quietly remarked, "He makes his presence felt."

Stanley called philosophy the "education of grownups," and people justly say that he was a towering figure, an intellectual giant. But he also made his presence felt by reminding us of our own, as his friends and companions, when we were with him and when we read him with enough presence of mind to hear his voice and catch the tune. For example, the final paragraphs of "Knowing and Acknowledging" actually brought tears to my eyes when I reread them recently. Since we can fairly describe *Little Did I Know* as, among other things, a story of "professional formation," we have some idea of what it took for Stanley to become a tenured professor of philosophy. Thus, I am especially susceptible to the remarkable accomplishment of Stanley's early essays since I arrived at their pages late, via Hollywood comedy and melodrama. He strikes me as a moral philosopher who, like Montaigne, not only knew that virtue was wisdom's goal but also that "you can get there, if you know the way, by shady, grassy, sweetly flowering roads." Without stint, I am grateful that Stanley guided me in that direction via the Green World of Connecticut in remarriage comedy.[32]

Notes

1. "A vice of generally recognized importance is the attraction to self-importance." Stanley Cavell, *Little Did I Know: Excerpts from Memory* (Stanford: Stanford University Press, 2010), 275.
2. Stanley Cavell, "Must We Mean What We Say?," *Must We Mean What We Say?* (Cambridge: Cambridge University Press, 2002, updated edition), 1–43, 4–5, 11.
3. Cavell, *Little Did I Know*, 432.
4. I write about this experience in *Stanley Cavell's American Dream: Shakespeare, Philosophy, and Hollywood Movies* (New York: Fordham University Press, 2006), 26–30.
5. Erik H. Erikson, "Reflections on Dr. Borg's Life Cycle," *Daedalus*, vol. 105, no. 2, Spring 1976, 1–28.
6. Cavell, *Little Did I Know*, 384–5.
7. Stanley Cavell, "Thinking of Emerson," *Emerson's Transcendental Etudes*, ed. David Justin Hodge (Stanford: Stanford University Press, 2003), 10–19, 13.
8. Erik H. Erikson, *Young Man Luther: A Study in Psychoanalysis and History* (New York: W. W. Norton, 1958), 170–222, 195.
9. Stanley Cavell, *Pursuits of Happiness: The Hollywood Comedy of Remarriage* (Cambridge: Harvard University Press, 1981), 43.
10. Friedrich Nietzsche, *On the Genealogy of Morality* (Cambridge: Cambridge University Press, 1994), 73.

11 See Cavell, *Little Did I Know*, 316. In discussing his divorce from Marcia, Stanley's use of the words "admit" and "impediment" echoes the first sentence of Shakespeare's Sonnet, 116: "Let me not to the marriage of true minds / Admit impediments," which itself echoes a key word of the marriage ceremony in the Elizabethan Book of Common Prayer: "impediment." The preceding paragraph in *Little Did I Know* gives an account of an autobiographical episode, which resonates with the seaside memory of the lovers in *Conte d'hiver* (1992, dir. Éric Rohmer), which Stanley calls a "meditation" on *The Winter's Tale*, Stanley's primary Shakespearean antecedent for the genre of remarriage comedy.

12 Cavell cites Milton's pamphlet on both these topics: "conversation" and "household unhappiness." See Cavell, *Pursuits of Happiness*, 87 and 150–1, respectively.

13 Stanley Cavell, *Cities of Word: Pedagogical Letters on a Register of the Moral Life* (Cambridge: Harvard University Press, 2004), ix.

14 Nietsche, *On the Genealogy of Morality*, 73.

15 Martin Luther, "Pagan Servitude," *Selections from His Writings*, ed. John Dillenberger (New York: Doubleday, 1961), 249–359, 303.

16 Notably this definition of a sacrament also appears in Henry David Thoreau's *Walden*, a crucial text for Stanley's sense of his own writing and thinking as a continuation of the transcendentalist tradition in American philosophy. Thoreau understands customs of the Mulcasse Indians and the Mexicans in a proto-anthropological way. He compares the efficacy of their "casting the slough annually" and their purification rituals, or at least the idea of them, with his Concord neighbors' accumulation of useless "trumpery," which they never shed but merely *auction* off (punning on the Latin root of that word, which means "increase"). "Casting the slough" also rhymes pertinently with another image in Thoreau that Stanley brings to bear in relation to what he calls having "a nervous breakdown" or "more politely, [suffering] an identity crisis": "Our moulting season, like that of the fowls, must be a crisis in our lives. The loon returns to the pond to spend it." Cavell, *Little Did I Know*, 222–6.

17 Arnold I. Davidson, "Beginning Cavell," *Pursuits of Reason: Essays in Honor of Stanley Cavell*, ed. Ted Cohen, Paul Guyer, and Hilary Putnam (Lubbock: Texas Tech University Press, 1993), 230–41, 232.

18 Cavell, *Pursuits of Happiness*, 141.

19 Stanley Cavell, *Disowning Knowledge in Seven Plays of Shakespeare* (Cambridge: Cambridge University Press, 2003, updated edition), 67–8.

20 Erikson, *Young Man Luther*, 174.

21 Stanley inherited Hum 5 from Morton White, and he initially followed his predecessor in using the text published by Fortress Press, *Three Treatises from the American Edition of Luther's Work*. But he soon adopted John Dillenberger, *Martin Luther: Selections from His Writings*. Thus, in *Little Did I Know*, the reading list for the course includes "Preface to the Letter of St. Paul to the Romans" and does not include "Appeal to the Ruling Class,"

an alternative translation of the 1520 treatise, which Stanley seems to have emphasized least in his teaching (421).

22 Cavell, *Cities of Word*, 139.
23 Ralph Waldo Emerson, "Experience," *Emerson: Essays and Poems*, ed. Joel Porte (New York: Library of America, 1996, college edition), 480.
24 Cavell, *Little Did I Know*, 333–6.
25 *Harvard Radcliffe 361* (Cambridge: Harvard Yearbook Publications, 1997), 70.
26 Martin Luther, "Freedom of a Christian," *Selections from His Writings*, 42–85, 58.
27 Machiavelli, from chapter 15 of *The Prince* in the Modern Library Edition.
28 Lawrence F. Rhu, "Stanley Cavell: An American Philosopher at the Movies," *DoubleTake*, vol. 7, no. 2, Spring 2001, 115–19, 116.
29 Cavell, *Disowning Knowledge*, x.
30 Robert Coles and Daniel Berrigan, *The Geography of Faith: Conversations, Conversations between Daniel Berrigan, When Underground, and Robert Coles* (Boston: Beacon Press, 1971).
31 Henry S. Miller, Jr. "A Conversation with William Alfred," *Harvard Magazine* (November–December 1979), 50–6, 51.
32 Michel de Montaigne, "Of the Education of Children," *The Complete Essays of Montaigne*, trans. Donald M. Frame (Stanford: Stanford University Press, 1957), 106–32, 119.

III

Cinema, Music, Art, and Aesthetics

11

The Idea that Films Could Have a Bearing on Philosophy

Robert B. Pippin

THE IDEA THAT FILMS COULD HAVE A BEARING ON PHILOSOPHY, and especially that there could be a form of cinematic, reflective thought that deserved the name of philosophy itself, remains quite a controversial one. When Stanley Cavell began teaching philosophy seminars on Hollywood films in 1963, it was even more controversial. Indeed, the very idea was outrageous. In *Little Did I Know*, Cavell reports, "There was, I do not deny, a certain pleasurable indecorousness in the idea of taking film into a philosophy classroom, anyway in the English-speaking dispensation of the subject."[1] Cavell explains why he thinks this was an important and appropriate thing to do in a number of different ways, some of which are quite general and involve an inspiring resistance to the idea that philosophy is exclusively what academic philosophers do. Instead, he argued that philosophy in some form is instead a part of everyone's life, is at work in any thoughtful response to living a life as the distinct creatures we are. Other accounts are more specifically addressed to the problem of skepticism, treated by Cavell not as a puzzle that needs (and always lacks) a solution, but an unavoidable aspect of human life that can either be borne well or can become a kind of philosophical neurosis, a narcissistic retreat from the world and a form of resistance to, rather than acknowledgment of, the other people with whom we interact. Still others, especially in his book on melodrama, involve psychoanalytic contributions to philosophy's general task, "clarifying concepts," say. I found especially inspiring in his memoir, and clarifying about why his work on film and literature has been so important to me, this passage:

This makes the medium of film inherently philosophical. (Philosophical here contrasts, as explicitly in Wittgenstein's *Philosophical Investigations*, with the scientific, on the ground that philosophy does not seek to tell us anything new but rather to understand what human beings cannot on the whole simply not already know. Yet we are shown repeatedly in the *Investigations* that one cannot tell another something unless it is news to that other. It follows that philosophy takes place before or after we tell things to each other, in art or in rumor or in confidence or as information. So what moves philosophy to speak?)[2]

All of these accounts intersect with the concerns of a philosopher who, for one reason or another (as much chance, the dispensations that determine where one goes to school, who one's teachers are, what colleagues one happens to have), never seemed important to Cavell, Hegel, the center of my philosophical interest for over forty years. The terms "sociality," "Geist," "the state," "the Absolute," "the struggle for recognition," "logic as a form of metaphysics," "contradiction," or even "history," in the sense in which Hegel made it a philosophical topic for the first time, are certainly not Cavellian terms of art. But there are analogues and echoes of most of Hegel's concerns throughout Cavell's work, and not just his work on film. I can say what I found inspiring in Cavell, given an interest in Hegel, by drawing back from the terminology somewhat and posing the issue in a term that best fits his melodrama book, *Contesting Tears*.

Assume (and it is a very safe assumption) that among the most obvious human needs are two that Hegel links with his most important topic, freedom, understood by him not just in the sense of an escape from domination by the will of others, the absence of external constraint, but as the positive realization of some objective and subjective conditions thanks to which I can experience my life as my own, as the expression of who I take myself to be, to stand for, while also experiencing recognition by others as having such standing. These two needs are the desire to love and be loved (Hegel's most frequent examples of the positive realization of such freedom, called by him "being with oneself in others") and the desire for status, standing, acknowledgment as equally worthy—a respect from others that is indispensable in self-respect. Understanding the realization of our independence as involving the proper acknowledgment of our dependence on others is already a paradoxical ("dialectical") notion, and it is made more complex by the intersection of such desire with the need for some standing in the world as a worthy participant in the communal exercises that constitute living a human life, in romantic love, marriage, the family, the production of wealth, and the organization of social and political power. It becomes more complex because these great desiderata can and frequently do conflict, do not seem compossible. This is especially so because criteria of such recognition can become deformed in ways that could be called, indifferently, pathological or ideological or simply wrongs. These mostly have to do with inequality, unequal standing, a situation that renders both the giving and receiving of recognitive status unsatisfactory to both sides ("both" being Hegel's great innovation)—a form of suffering. Lacking such standing when judged by such deformations is a serious human lack, an injury, and the results of that injury can infect and distort the understanding of love and its fulfillment. In *Stella Dallas* and *Now, Voyager*, these deformations involve both socioeconomic class and patriarchy. Stella is deeply distressed by the meanness, in effect the ugliness, of her working-class home life and aspires to rise in class, not, interestingly, ever for the sake of money and the power it brings, but for the beauty and elegance of the upper class lives she sees in movies—in order to be, as we say, classy, refined. She finds that aspiration incompatible with marriage as she experiences it; it requires a sacrifice of spontaneity, independence, and genuineness that she is not willing to make, and she senses that it is a sacrifice any man would require of her, so she withdraws from the game, devoting her life to her daughter instead. (She says that no man "could get her going" again.) Conventional readings of the film would have it that Stella's self-sacrifice at the end of the film involves her complicity in her own erasure as a mother, and would see the film as an expression, rather than critique, of the patriarchy that requires it. Cavell seeks to rescue the film from such a reading, offering instead a view of Stella as canny, the subject of her life, not the unknowing object of a manipulative world. It is a part of a general resistance he complains about in the book.

> But to assume that the technology and economy of motion pictures emerged in Western civilization, perhaps especially in the Golden Age of Hollywood, exactly and rigidly to reiterate the worst gestures of that civilization, is beyond me.[3]

In this essay especially, we see especially clearly why for Cavell films can bear on philosophy. The main issue to be discussed—how to interpret what we have seen—is deeply tied in all great films of exceptional emotional power to philosophical questions. The interpretive task and the philosophical assessment are inseparable. Stella is working out how her dependence on men for her happiness and security, and the dependence of her daughter on her, is or is not compatible in this kind of a social world with her desire for independence, her insistence that she lead her own life, not playing a role assigned to her by others, a question that is immediately tied with how we should understand this dialectical relationship in order to interpret and assess what Stella does—whether it is good or bad, reasonable or not, responsible or not, whether she is free or manipulated unknowingly. This issue—properly understanding her emotional life—is in itself and for Cavell inseparable from understanding the social world in which she comes to have those emotions—the world stratified into social classes, including gender roles. And "inseparable" also means that we would not have understood the philosophical issue of independence and dependence, knowingness and unknowingness, or what skepticism about what we know of others amounts to, were we not able to explore the issue as it actually "lives." Any cinematic universality we find expressed in the film will be exemplary or typic, a matter of "perspicuous representation," or of a "concrete universal," or even of an "ideal type," but our sense of things will be all the better for that. This all corresponds to the task Hegel set for modernity in the preface to his *Phenomenology of Spirit* in 1807, something often ignored in criticisms of Hegel's abstractness.

> Nowadays the task before us consists not so much in purifying the individual of the sensuously immediate and in making him into a thinking substance which has itself been subjected to thought; it consists instead in doing the very opposite. It consists in actualizing and spiritually animating the universal through the sublation of fixed and determinate thoughts.[4]

And in Cavell's treatment of *Now, Voyager*, his demonstration of the powerful role played by cinematic irony also seeks to rescue the film from conventional readings. These would have it that a woman's lack of acknowledgment, her social invisibility, is a function of her appearance. She is fat and ugly, and the road to higher social status is the beauty industry. And again, her independence seems to require a great sacrifice, indeed of her life itself, again for the sake of motherhood (if here surrogate), treated as incompatible with female independence, and the sacrifice seems to require yet again a great self-de-sexualization. Cavell again brilliantly "rescues" the film from such readings. And he sums up his reading with a fine statement of what Charlotte Vale (Bette Davis) is rejecting, one of his most insightful in the book.

> There is surely a sense of sacrifice in this group of films; they solicit our tears. But is it that the women in them are sacrificing themselves to the sad necessities of a world they are forced to accept? Or isn't it rather that the women are claiming the right to judge a world as second-rate that enforces this sacrifice; to refuse, transcend, its proposal of second-rate sadness?[5]

All of these treatments resonate with Hegelian themes, as well as with Hegel's confidence that art works are an indispensable modality of collective self-knowledge. This is resisted by some who argue that Cavell treats the human dramas he explores in apolitical terms, that he is insensitive to the role that the struggle for power, and the results of unequal power, play in human life. This has always seemed to me short-sighted, and demands that any interrogation of such issues must be recognized by appeal to some particular set of terms and to some particular theoretical structure before it can qualify as an appropriate treatment. Cavell is well aware of the issue, and we can see in what he says that his awareness of the political concerns what he generally calls "the public."

> A recurrent theme of the course, following the consequences of recognizing that Emersonianism provides the intellectual texture of remarriage comedies, is the perpetually contested relation of public and private.[6]

and

> I might say of novels that they are meant to make private what is public and private business, make them mine. In these terms, film brings an unprecedented, if not unanticipated, medium into play that questions the distinction between public and private.[7]

I find this commitment carried out throughout the work on film. It is behind what he calls the "taint of villainy" in the male heroes of both the comedies and the melodramas, and in his account of the manifold barriers to mutual acknowledgment, treated by him as primarily a matter of some form of psychological resistance (mainly an unwillingness to be known, disguised as a worry about what one can ever know of others) but the social bases of such resistance are never far from view, even if expressed in terms that do not explicitly invoke power, privilege, self-interest, greed, or even injustice. But the concerns, and their Hegelian resonances, are there. There is even, throughout the film books and articles, *The World Viewed*, and *Must We Mean What We Say?*, an inherent and sometimes explicit theory of Western modernity, and what such modernization means for us, does to us, psychologically. (It largely calls us away from ourselves, makes us forget what we somehow know, encourages a kind of willed thoughtlessness.)

When Dr. Jaquith (Claude Rains) tells Charlotte in *Now, Voyager* that "if you want people to be interested in you, you have to be interested in them," he is expressing a version of Cavell's understanding of the relation between knowing and being known, as well as what is for me the underlying Hegelian problematic of seeking recognition from those whom you recognize as recognizers, in a world where a mutuality of such status should be institutionally secured, but is not. That seems to me the heart of Cavell's treatment of movies, and it will stand as a permanent contribution, forever altering our sense of the potential of both film and philosophy.

Notes

1   Stanley Cavell, *Little Did I Know: Excerpts from Memory* (Stanford: Stanford University Press, 2010), 424.

2. Ibid., 204.
3. Stanley Cavell, *Contesting Tears: The Hollywood Melodrama of the Unknown Woman* (Chicago: University of Chicago Press, 1996), 26.
4. Georg Wilhelm Friedrich Hegel, *The Phenomenology of Spirit*, trans. Terry P. Pinkard (Cambridge: Cambridge University Press, 2017), 21.
5. Cavell, *Contesting Tears*, 129.
6. Ibid., 203.
7. Ibid., 229.

12

Words Fail Me. (Stanley Cavell's Life Out of Music)

WILLIAM DAY

STANLEY CAVELL ISN'T THE FIRST TO ARRIVE AT PHILOSOPHY through a life with music. Nor is he the first whose philosophical practice bears the marks of that life. Jean-Jacques Rousseau "testifies to the harmony between his musical work and his philosophy in his *Dialogues*."[1] Friedrich Nietzsche saw himself as "the most musical of all philosophers"—presumably more than even his musico-philosophical mentor Arthur Schopenhauer—and asserts in all seriousness that "without music, life would be an error."[2] Ludwig Wittgenstein tells his friend Maurice Drury, "It is impossible for me to say in my book one word about all that music has meant in my life. How then can I hope to be understood?"[3] (That these are all philosophers Cavell wrote about and cared about shouldn't go unnoticed.) I can't recall when exactly Stanley told me that a highlight of his high school years was playing lead alto sax in an otherwise all-black jazz band; or when I heard the story of his performing at Berkeley in the premiere of an opera by Roger Sessions during which the English horn player had some mishap and Stanley, seated next to him playing clarinet, transposed and played the English horn solo on the spot; or when he confessed to me late in his teaching career, after the first iteration of his opera course, his nearly unbearable, silent anxiety or fear (somehow traceable to his mother's perfect pitch) that in humming or singing an excerpt from an aria in class he might be reproducing the melody in the wrong key.[4]

Much of Cavell's life with music is confirmed for the world in his philosophical autobiography *Little Did I Know*. The place of that life for Cavell is best captured, to my ear, in the anecdote of what he calls his "impotent gallantry." On leaving a New Year's Eve party in Greenwich Village as 1948 became 1949, he offered to escort an African American singer-friend to her apartment up in Harlem. Recalling her unease and eventual admonishment as they walked together north of 125th Street—"Don't you see that you are in far greater danger here than I am? Please go back"—Cavell writes, in partial echo of Wittgenstein's despairing remark to Drury: "It had evidently never occurred to me that a black person would not know by looking at me what my life with music had been and therewith comprehend that that life of mine exempted me from participation in the tragedy of racial injustice."[5] It's possible to read the autobiographer here as admonishing his younger and naive Juilliard-student self. (The autobiographer calls his book, after all, *Little Did I Know*.) But on what account? Naivete isn't a philosophical error. Self-ignorance, however, is. What strikes the older Stanley in this memory, I think it's clear, is the younger Stanley's youthful failure to recognize that this crucial aspect of his identity doesn't show itself with every step and breath he takes. It is a gentle, convivial admonishment, the kind that a musico-philosophical mentor might give, smilingly, to a student he or she is fond of.

The numerous scattered anecdotes of Cavell's early musical career in *Little Did I Know* are capped off by an entry, April 10, 2004, describing his eventual realization that he was to leave that career behind—for what exactly, he did not yet know. As his description makes clear, it would take the better part of a lifetime for the leaving to arrive at an end:

> Yet this laborious path to nowhere had, I laboriously came to understand, been essential for me. Music had my whole life been so essentially a part of my days, of what in them I knew was valuable to me, was mine to do, that to forgo it proved to be as mysterious a process of disentanglement as it was to have been awarded it and have nurtured it, eliciting a process of undoing I will come to understand in connection with the work of mourning.[6]

Readers of Cavell may well be surprised by the implication that the concept of mourning, a master tone of Cavell's writing from his reading of Thoreau's *Walden* through his essays on Coleridge and Wordsworth and Emerson's "Experience," should have as one of its originary sites the memory-shock of his leaving his musical life behind.[7] There is no mention of mourning, notably, in Cavell's description of his family's move, just before he turned seven, from the south side of Atlanta to its north side—an event often highlighted (including by me) in discussions of *Little Did I Know*.[8] But mourning will become for Cavell an emblem of the perfectionist work of philosophy itself, which "has to do with the perplexed capacity to mourn the passing of the world."[9] If the emblem of that emblem for Cavell is the abandonment or transformation of his life with music for a life of philosophy, a life dedicated to "the repetitive disinvestment of what has passed,"[10] then Cavell's life with music and thoughts about the nature of music ought to be revelatory of Cavell's philosophical life and thoughts.

Is that promising too much? It can seem to overlook the simple, undeniable truth that Cavell's musical performance and improvisational and compositional abilities were after all, pretty completely, when all is said and done, *abandoned*. It is also true that the singular musical experience Cavell writes about most often—his composing, while at Berkeley, the incidental music for a student production of *King Lear*—had its greatest impact on him, as he discovered "not without considerable anxiety,"[11] for the thoughts it engendered about Shakespeare's play rather than for the music it drew out of him. But then unsurprisingly, as Cavell acknowledges, what leads him into *Lear's* world is exactly his writing and rehearsing and conducting this music "in response to the play." My concern, in any event, isn't to resuscitate Cavell the musician (though some amateur recordings of him at the piano improvising on popular songs near the end of his life are, I found on the distracted occasions of my hearing them, intriguing). It is to become even more familiar with the philosopher Cavell that our interest in Cavell the musician matters.

The thought I want to follow in these remarks is that Cavell's distinctive orientation in philosophy—call this his lifelong coming to terms with his abandoning a life in music—is guided in part by an interest in those moments in experience where words seem to run out, or veer toward nonsense, leaving in their wake touchstones of ecstasy.

I was introduced to the name "Stanley Cavell" by a musician. John Harbison, the American composer and a long-time friend of Cavell since their meeting in Princeton in 1962, was in the summer of 1981 composer-in-residence at the music festival in Santa Fe, where I was an undergraduate at St. John's College. We met up at one point to talk about music and philosophy (I was making plans, despite or because of St. John's classical curriculum, to write a senior essay on jazz improvisation), and I asked Harbison if he could recommend any contemporary writing on the philosophy of music. That's how I first came to know Cavell's writing voice, a voice I would soon enough learn was indistinguishable from his speaking voice, through the pair of essays Harbison directed me to, "Music Discomposed" and "A Matter of Meaning It."[12]

Seven-and-a-half years later, on leave from my graduate studies at Columbia to spend a year at Harvard,[13] I asked Stanley about musical ineffability. More specifically, I asked whether passages from "Music Discomposed" like the following—passages that picture the scene of exasperation in our trying to explain to someone what we value in some music or other—are depictions of the unsayable:

> One is anxious to communicate the experience of such objects. ... I want to tell you something I've seen, or heard, or realized, or come

to understand, for the reasons for which *such* things are communicated (because it is news, about a world we share, or could). Only I find that I can't *tell* you; and that makes it all the more urgent to tell you. I want to tell you because the knowledge, unshared, is a burden—not, perhaps, the way having a secret can be a burden, or being misunderstood; a little more like the way, perhaps, not being believed is a burden, or not being trusted. ... It matters, there is a burden, because unless I can tell what I know, there is a suggestion (and to myself as well) that I do *not* know. But I *do*—what I see [or hear] is *that* (pointing to the object). But for that to communicate, you have to see [or hear] it too.[14]

I remember asking Stanley my question with some urgency, since I had pressed the same question, possibly only days earlier, over lunch with Jim Conant—Jim was about to make his philosophical reputation disabusing readers of the *Tractatus* who mistakenly find in it a "hidden teaching" that is "inherently inexpressible"[15]—and he had all but persuaded me that the category of the unsayable was a null set.

Stanley was, I'll say, less resolute than Jim in rejecting my suggestion. Still, my reading was off, and in responding to it he offered what I wanted, a rare and detailed gloss on his first essay on music. Stanley's response—I wrote down the gist of it at the time—carried two lines of thought:

1. He said that part of what he was thinking when he wrote that passage was how the imperative "You have to *hear* it" can discount another's claim to have described what is going on in a piece, even if the other person mouths the same words you would use to say what is going on in it. Cavell's recalling this motive turned my focus to the following two excerpts from the same section of "Music Discomposed":

What I know, when I've *seen* or *heard* something is, one may wish to say, not a matter of *merely* knowing it.... Perhaps "merely knowing" should be compared with "not really knowing": "You don't really know what it's like to be a Negro"; "You don't really know how your remark made her feel"; "You don't really know what I mean when I say that Schnabel's slow movements give the impression not of slowness but of infinite length." You merely say the words.

The paragraph goes on to discuss what place knowing *has* in these contexts:

The issue in each case is: What would *express* this knowledge? It is not that my knowledge will be real, or more than *mere* knowledge, when I acquire a particular feeling, or come to see something. For the issue can also be said to be: What would express the acquisition of that feeling, or show that you have seen the thing? And the answer might be that I now *know* something I didn't know before.[16]

Knowing in these (moral and aesthetic) contexts doesn't have the shape of a proposition to which is added the appropriate grounding or justifying experience; it has a quite different shape. Knowing here is more like cases of sudden recognition ("I know that face," "I know that move") that can change in a flash every element of one's perception.[17] To express *this* knowledge requires that one *give expression to* those features or that gesture, to that sight or sound. In that light, this section of "Music Discomposed" is not so much about what cannot be said or expressed as about what we mean when we say that we know (or see or hear) a something of this sort. What "Music Discomposed" *does* say about expressing this knowledge is contained in a single sentence: "Describing one's experience of art is itself a form of art; the burden of describing it is like the burden of producing it."[18]

2. Stanley also pointed out, as his teacher J. L. Austin had done, that there is a perfectly trivial sense in which the smell of coffee or the sound of a clarinet,[19] say, can be put into words. (Just like that.)[20]—But those words, of course, standing by themselves, are hardly an expression of knowledge, at least of the kind of knowledge we are tempted to declare beyond words. *Expressing* what we know—or showing it, Tractarian-wise—comes easier in some matters than in others.

And yet: Cavell recounts early in *Little Did I Know* a peculiar gesture of his mother's that seems to serve him as a touchstone for what one might well call music's expressible-but-unsayable aspects—"the great secrets," he writes, "I knew I craved to have" and that his musically gifted mother "seemed to divine." The instance he reports occurred at a recital by the great violinist Fritz Kreisler, for which Stanley (aged ten or eleven) traveled with his mother to San Francisco from their home in Sacramento. At various moments during the recital, particularly at the ends of each of Kreisler's encores, his mother would "suddenly produce (a gesture I knew well and would glory in when directed to something I had done) an all but inaudible high cry and silently snap the fingers of her hand nearer me and thrust it toward her face, which was turned as if to ward off a blow."[21] (Is there an epistemology that gives us a complete account of this species of knowing, a knowing that is neither propositional nor a mere familiarity nor a knowing-how?) If you were to attempt to translate or reduce Stanley's mother's gesture to words—"It is obviously an expression of approval"; "It means, in effect, 'exactly right' "—you would thereby invite the response, "But you have to *hear* it." Part of what that command expresses, we will see, is an awareness that music-making is itself already a kind of saying (for those who have ears to hear). The point is alluded to in Cavell's description of what he took away from Kreisler's playing that day:

> There was a way he stood listening when the piano was playing a solo passage, especially I suppose in a slow movement, his head and body absolutely still, which I retain as an image of total concentration, ending in a single unhurried gesture that brought the violin back beneath the chin and the bow back to the strings at the instant of the violin's next entrance—as if music had been induced to utter itself.[22]

I grant that the "as if" here ("as if music had been induced to utter itself") matters, as the modifier "a kind of" does in my description of music-making as "a kind of saying." But just as the suggestion of a link between music and speech is an ancient and seemingly innocuous one, so is it neither flippant nor mere analogy, not peculiar to Kreisler's somewhat singular and memorable preparation before an entrance. (I clarify or forge the link between music and speech that I associate with Cavell below.)

Words appear to run out at other moments and in other contexts. Twice in *Little Did I Know*, having said all that seems fitting about a particularly striking experience, Cavell is left sensing that not enough has been said to fully convince his reader, and he concludes by simply affirming his conviction, but without any fear that he has thereby undermined it. I am struck by where these moments occur. Taken in tandem, they appear to link the mysteries of sexual awakening and musical ecstasy. The first—in which, admittedly, the moment of wordless knowing is somewhat whimsical—concerns the unspoken connection that the not quite seven-year-old Stanley felt between himself and "a girl of crushing beauty" nearly twice his age who, like him, appeared in a children's talent review in Indian dress, but not before appearing before him backstage undressed:

> I think that is what I saw, although it took some time for me to understand that she had taken off really all of her clothes, upon which recognition I was propelled from the room by an invisible force of nature, something like a consuming wave of aromatic mist. ... I tried once or twice during the ensuing week of two shows a day to interest this mythical being in the cosmic fact that we were both Indian royalty, by leaving my costume on and stationing myself by the stairs down to the men's dressing room until she walked off the stage and had a chance to remark the closeness of our connection. Evidently I had failed to place myself in clear enough view for that. But I knew what I knew, and it was satisfactory.[23]

The second occasion concerns the particular, polished, professional sound of the all-black (except for a guitarist and himself) rehearsal jazz band in which the fifteen-year-old Cavell played the lead alto saxophone, a band he claims could rival the sound of the best jazz bands of its day:

When he counted off the tempo for a downbeat the ensuing force of sound was so strong that I feared the house could not withstand it, and I was so thrilled by it that I felt I could barely continue playing. ... Everything we played that morning ... was an original composition of Wiley's, not simply an arrangement; and the ideas were more advanced than any I had heard outside of the Ellington band.... I can readily imagine that someone will think my story remembering our sound in Wiley's arrangements for his black band, as it were invoking comparison with the Basie band of that era, belongs on the side of the delusional. I have to say that on somber reflection I do not really or fully believe that. I place it among those experiences of my life about which I am moved to say: I know what I know.[24]

Finding these passages in a philosophical autobiography called *Little Did I Know*, the reader is all but required to consider how it is that "I know what I know" ("I knew what I knew") says what it does, avoiding triviality.

We can grant that Cavell's story of a secret connection to the Indian princess registers little more than a child's impression, and that the majesty of Wiley's band (absent recorded evidence) is no better than an impression. Given that, the absence of further words, while understandable, can seem protective, even dismissive of doubt, as if the book's title meant, "Little did I know, but I knew *this*." But these invocations of "I know what I know" should be compared to a remark in Wittgenstein's *Investigations* to which Cavell often turns. In it, Wittgenstein gives voice to that moment in any explanation of my apparent certainties when my justifications appear exhausted: "Then I am inclined to say: 'This is simply what I do.'"[25] Cavell (reading Wittgenstein) interprets the one so inclined not as dismissing the questioner or voicing despair over the possibility of communication, but as holding that inclination in check, perhaps through an awareness of what our understanding each other, after all, rests on. Taking a cue from Cavell's reading, I want to suggest that "I know what I know" in these passages is not intended by Cavell to silence doubters or to mark where words end. Rather, he employs these words to flag a memory, to draw our attention to it, and to acknowledge where a next question must lead—namely, further down the path of such incandescent experiences, with the aim of discovering how these "detours on the human path to death" might help Cavell "achieve my own death."[26] In the wake of these recaptured memories, in other words, words do not come to an end out of necessity, as if in the presence of something ineffable. They simply stop, awaiting the impulse to more speech (whether from himself or, in reading, from his reader).

But to return to music: What I take to be culminating thoughts on the burden borne by words and their failure appear in Cavell's late essay on music, "Impressions of Revolution."[27] There the sense of our failure to articulate—or more exactly, to conceptualize—what we hear in music draws inspiration from Walter Benjamin's mid-1920s work *The Origin of German Tragic Drama* (*Ursprung des deutschen Trauerspiels*). In this study of German baroque tragedy (*Trauerspiel* literally means "mourning-play") Benjamin declares at one point that "the spoken word [as opposed to music on the one hand, and to written language on the other] is only afflicted by meaning, so to speak, as if by an inescapable disease" so that "meaning is encountered, and will continue to be encountered as the reason for mournfulness," and that "the phonetic tension with speech in the language of the seventeenth century leads directly to music, the opposite of meaning-laden speech."[28] Cavell ties these remarks to his long-posited idea that what is known as philosophical skepticism is fueled by our alternating fear of and wish for inexpressiveness. He then offers this succinct summary of Benjamin's claim and its resonance with his own: "Music allows the achieving of understanding without meaning, that is to say, without the articulation of individual acts of reference on which intelligibility is classically thought to depend."[29] I find in this formulation or epigram a guide for clarifying not only Cavell's thinking about music but the place of musical experience in his thinking about the expressibility of words.

The picture of human understanding ungrounded in individual acts of reference is more than reminiscent of the picture of language that emerges from Wittgenstein's *Investigations*. In that picture, our ability to speak to one another, and to understand one another, does not rest in some fact of language or some fact about a world that our words attach to, as the philosophical tradition to which Wittgenstein is responding argues. Cavell notes elsewhere that the effort to apply the traditional picture to concepts of experience—Wittgenstein "remembers someone striking himself on the breast in the heat of a philosophical discussion, crying out, 'No one else can have THIS pain' "—appears to make sense only if the referring term ("this") remains mysteriously unspecified, "an absolute demonstrative absolutely pointing to an absolute object."[30] Absent such absolute connections, understanding happens, and it happens in a world whose actual mystery we overlook. To give the merest indication of Wittgenstein's picture of that mystery: understanding happens through the human ways or forms of life that we inhabit and find ourselves attuned to, and that we also find ourselves desiring (broadly speaking)—ways or forms of life into which we are inaugurated together with language, and that enable language to work on us and to move us (broadly speaking).

But Cavell's epigram is explicitly characterizing music, not language. And it draws its inspiration from Benjamin, who had implied a contrast between music's happier expressivity and that of (spoken) words, which are "afflicted by meaning," "meaning-laden speech" being "the reason for mournfulness."

Rather than a grief brought on by our words falling short of capturing our experience, Benjamin's concern is with the grief and mourning that follows from speech itself. What we say, we must mean. And yet, what I do with my grief or mourning, my attitude toward words, is not spelled out in this extract from Benjamin's text.

As I read "Impressions of Revolution," we should take "the achieving of understanding without meaning" to be as instructive of the workings of language as it is of music. What happens when we let go of the idea that the primary fact of communication is that words carry meanings (the ones found in a dictionary), or the idea—more to the point—that my understanding you rests on my associating your words with objects in the world, and similar feats of absolute translation? We might, in that case, rethink the following analogy, pitched by someone bearing a life with music: "Understanding a sentence is much more like understanding a theme in music than one might believe" (Wittgenstein's words, quoted by Cavell in the penultimate paragraph of "Impressions of Revolution").[31] Wittgenstein continues: "Why is just *this* the pattern of variation in intensity and tempo [in a musical theme, or in its performance]? One would like to say: 'Because I know what it all means.' But what does it mean? I'd not be able to say."[32] The sense of Wittgenstein's remark, and of Cavell's interest in quoting it (he counts it among the "revolutionary" things Wittgenstein has to say about "the nature of our agreement in speech"),[33] is not to mark where the ineffable or unfathomable enter into our understanding of a musical theme or a sentence. The point is rather to underscore a fact of unending surprise, that "the impress produced in you by things as they pass and abiding in you when they have passed"[34] —that is, your attending, in just these surroundings, with whatever relation you bear to them, and with what has gone before, to just this tone and mood—is the necessary but sufficient condition that structures our understanding (or our failing to understand) one another. —And so similarly, my capacity to mourn the passing of the world (as of time, or a friend and mentor, or the fact of meaning-laden speech itself) does not depend on something fixed in speech or in the world to which I might still return, but is akin to my ability to follow a musical theme without losing the thread.

Notes

1 John T. Scott, "The Harmony between Rousseau's Musical Theory and His Philosophy," *Journal of the History of Ideas*, vol. 59, no. 2, 1998, 287.

2 Georges Liébert, *Nietzsche and Music* (Chicago: University of Chicago Press, 2004).

3 Maurice O'Connor Drury, "Conversations with Wittgenstein," *Recollections of Wittgenstein*, ed. Rush Rhees (Oxford: Oxford University Press, 1984), 160.

4   Cf. Stanley Cavell, *Little Did I Know: Excerpts from Memory* (Stanford: Stanford University Press, 2010), 73–5, 183; Andrea Olmstead, *Conversations with Roger Sessions* (Boston: Northeastern University Press, 1987), 107–8.
5   Cavell, *Little Did I Know*, 172.
6   Ibid., 225; cf. 209.
7   Cavell doesn't make explicit Thoreau's "morning/mourning" pun in his book on *Walden*—the word "mourning" doesn't appear there—but see Stanley Cavell, *The Senses of Walden* (New York: Viking Press, 1972), especially chapter 2, "Sentences," where "morning" is paired with "moulting" (and "metamorphosis" and "leaving"); *In Quest of the Ordinary: Lines of Skepticism and Romanticism* (Chicago: University of Chicago Press, 1988), 44–5, 72–3, 171–2; and *This New Yet Unapproachable America: Lectures after Emerson after Wittgenstein* (Albuquerque: Living Batch Press, 1989), 83–4; see also David LaRocca, "In the Place of Mourning: Questioning the Privations of the Private," *Nineteenth-Century Prose*, vol. 40, no. 2, 2013, 227–42.
8   See my "A Soteriology of Reading: Cavell's Excerpts from Memory," *Stanley Cavell: Philosophy, Literature and Criticism*, ed. James Loxley and Andrew Taylor (Manchester: Manchester University Press, 2011), 76–91; James Conant, "The Triumph of the Gift over the Curse in Stanley Cavell's *Little Did I Know*," *MLN*, vol. 126, 2011, 1004–13; Timothy Gould, "Me, Myself and Us: Autobiography and Method in the Writing of Stanley Cavell," *Conversations: The Journal of Cavellian Studies*, vol. 1, 2013, 4–18; and Chiara Alfano, "A Scarred Tympanum," *Conversations*, vol. 1, 2013, 19–38.
9   Cavell, *This New Yet Unapproachable America*, 84.
10 Ibid.
11 Cavell, *Little Did I Know*, 215.
12 Stanley Cavell, "Music Discomposed" and "A Matter of Meaning It," *Must We Mean What We Say? A Book of Essays* (New York: Charles Scribner's Sons, 1969; Cambridge: Cambridge University Press, 1976), 180–237.
13 I was by then well on my way to the better part of a lifetime of conversation with Cavell, and also with the remarkable cadre of graduate students studying with him in the mid- to late-1980s at Harvard, a group he would later describe to me, and then in print, as "permanently inspiring" and "providing a continuity of intellectual purpose unmatched in my decades of teaching" (Cavell, *Little Did I Know*, 476).
14 Cavell, "Music Discomposed," 192–3.
15 James Conant, "Throwing Away the Top of the Ladder," *The Yale Review*, vol. 79, Spring 1990, 328–64, 329; see also "Must We Show What We Cannot Say?," *The Senses of Stanley Cavell*, ed. Richard Fleming and Michael Payne (Lewisburg: Bucknell University Press, 1989), 242–83.
16 Cavell, "Music Discomposed," 192.
17 Experiences of sudden (visual or auditory) recognition are the explicit topic of Wittgenstein's late remarks on aspect-seeing, remarks that figure prominently

in Part Four of Cavell's *The Claim of Reason* and that he returned to late in his career. See Stanley Cavell, *The Claim of Reason: Wittgenstein, Skepticism, Morality, and Tragedy* (Oxford: Oxford University Press, 1979), 354ff.; and his "The Touch of Words," *Seeing Wittgenstein Anew*, ed. William Day and Victor J. Krebs (Cambridge: Cambridge University Press, 2010), 81–98.

18 Cavell, "Music Discomposed," 193.
19 Cf. Ludwig Wittgenstein, *Philosophical Investigations*, trans. G. E. M. Anscombe, P. M. S. Hacker, and Joachim Schulte, rev. 4th ed. (Chichester: Wiley-Blackwell, 2009), §610, §78.
20 "Nearly everybody can recognize a surly look or the smell of tar, but few can describe them non-committally, i.e. otherwise than as 'surly' or 'of tar.'" J. L. Austin, "Other Minds," *Philosophical Papers*, 3rd ed. (Oxford: Oxford University Press, 1979), 85.
21 Cavell, *Little Did I Know*, 53.
22 Ibid.
23 Ibid., 21–3. Stanley's contribution to the review was a piano piece entitled "Indian Drums," which our autobiographer says, "I can still play flawlessly on demand," thereby making a rare and explicit gag out of the truth.
24 Ibid., 77.
25 Wittgenstein, *Philosophical Investigations*, §217.
26 Cavell, *Little Did I Know*, 4.
27 Stanley Cavell, "Impressions of Revolution," *The Musical Quarterly* 85, no. 2, 2001, 264–73.
28 Walter Benjamin, *The Origin of German Tragic Drama*, trans. John Osborne (London: NLB, 1977), 209, 211; quoted both more and less extensively by Cavell in "Impressions of Revolution," 270.
29 Cavell, "Impressions of Revolution," 270.
30 Stanley Cavell, "The Wittgensteinian Event," *Reading Cavell*, ed. Alice Crary and Sanford Shieh (London: Routledge, 2006), 11.
31 Wittgenstein, *Philosophical Investigations*, §527, as quoted by Cavell, "Impressions of Revolution," 272. (The translation in the revised fourth edition of *Investigations* reads: "Understanding a sentence in language is much more akin to understanding a theme in music than one may think.")
32 Ibid. For the later Wittgenstein's conception of language as revealed through the lens of his life with music, see my "The Aesthetic Dimension of Wittgenstein's Later Writings," *Wittgenstein on Aesthetic Understanding*, ed. Garry L. Hagberg (London: Palgrave Macmillan, 2017), 3–29.
33 Cavell, "Impressions of Revolution," 272.
34 Augustine, *Confessions*, trans. F. J. Sheed, 2nd ed. (Indianapolis: Hackett, 2006), 253 (*Conf.* XI, xxvii).

13

Cavell's Ear for Things

Andreas Teuber

Home is where one starts from.
—T. S. ELIOT, *Four Quartets*

I FIRST MET STANLEY CAVELL IN THE DINING HALL of Adams House. Adams is part of the university house system that is modeled after the college system at Oxford and Cambridge but without the gardens or quite the tradition. Adams is just south of Harvard Yard and still some distance from the Charles River. It was there in 1963 that I met Stanley, which is how those of us who were his students knew him and how I remember him—by his first name. At that particular moment, there was a small group of students seated with Stanley at one of the long tables in the dining hall. Someone waved and I went and sat down on the side opposite Stanley, to his left, some distance from him, but not far. I noticed he tilted his head ever so slightly in my direction as he listened to the person across the table from him, as if he were favoring his right ear. I asked Tim—I believe it was Tim—about this afterward and he looked at me quizzically, "What?" he said, "Don't you know?" and I said, "Know what?" and he said: "About the accident?" and he told me about Stanley's chasing a ball down the driveway at a friend's house, when Stanley was six, out into the street, only to be hit by a car, damaging his left ear. This was the first I heard of it, albeit everyone else at the table already seemed to know.

Stanley was amazed by what he called his mother's "uncanny capacity to sight-read" on top of having "perfect pitch," a condition that we learn from Joan Richardson only one in ten thousand have.[1] The fact that his uncle had it too prompted Stanley to wonder about the fairness of God's distribution of talents and think of himself as one of the unfortunate. Years later, long after the family left Atlanta, when Stanley was at Juilliard, thinking he might pursue a career in musical composition but beginning to have doubts, he thought "there must be something [he] was meant to do that required an equivalent of the enigmatic faculty of perfect pitch."[2] His own uncanny ability to sight-read not only music but words on a page he came to believe may be "some attestation of this prophecy."[3]

Every so often he would remind us that he learned to read music before he learned to read words. The three literary texts he writes about first, other than works of philosophy, are plays—*King Lear*, *Endgame*, and *Othello*—that come to life in performance and in words that are spoken, not written. So, too, whenever I happened upon Stanley in his office when he was reading, he seemed to be sight-reading. As Thoreau on the track and the trail of "a hound, a bay horse, and a turtledove" would call out to them, knowing "what calls they answered to,"[4] Stanley appeared to call out to the texts he read fully expecting they would speak back to him.

As I recall, reading, for Stanley, was always a matter of voice, of listening for a text's distinctive sound. It was impossible for me as a student of his—listening to his readings of Wittgenstein and having him as a reader and advisor of my undergraduate thesis in philosophy—not to think of him as someone who had "an ear for things." Once you know the story of his childhood accident, of his having damaged his left ear, it is also hard not to notice how many words throughout his writing evoke sounds and music.

Open *A Pitch of Philosophy*, halfway through the first chapter, and you hear: "Certain questions of ear run through my life ... become in these pages ... questions of the detection of voice."[5] Certain questions of ear? Detection of voice? Then turn to "Thinking of Emerson," where Stanley will tell us: "I was trying to get Emerson's tune into my ear, free of Thoreau's."[6] Tune? Into my ear? And in speaking of the task of reading *Walden*, Stanley notes that "what is before you is precisely not, if you catch Thoreau's tune, something in the future; what is before you, if you are, for example, reading, is a text."[7] Thoreau's tune? A text? And if we look to the preface of *A Pitch of Philosophy*—a preface Stanley calls, not "a preface," but, "an overture"—we learn that the title for the lectures on which the book is based and that Stanley originally submitted and subsequently delivered at Hebrew University in 1992 was "Trades of Philosophy," which makes the title of the lectures sound as if it came from someone with no ear at all. What was Stanley thinking? Trades of philosophy? What was he hearing? He does admit that "no one seemed to take pleasure in that title," because "it failed," he speculates, "to invoke the wind it names."[8] Or perhaps, one might add, because the title invoked the idea that philosophy runs the risk of being thought of as a business and if and when that happens philosophy loses its power to provoke wonder.

But then he hits upon the title *A Pitch of Philosophy* and bang, just like that, a host of meanings flood into play: baseball, music, peddling, and lurch (as in lurch out of the way of those within the discipline who see themselves as gatekeepers and tell you what you can and cannot say). But even without these reverberations that Stanley pulls from "pitch," the title alone, *A Pitch of Philosophy*, puts us in the company of someone with an ear for things.

And he not only heard things we missed, he listened. He listened to his students. He asked us questions. He was curious about what we thought and what we, in our garbled manner of speaking were trying to say. For those of us who were with him (then) in Adams House, who sat with him in the dining hall, at breakfast, lunch, and dinner, sometimes all three, his listening came as something of a surprise. As the teacher in our small "family," a number of us thought he ought to be the one to do the talking and *we* the ones to listen. While that may be the usual order of things, even when Stanley talked, he seemed just as surprised by what he said as we were by his listening to us.

So too, I believe, what I have been calling Stanley's "ear for things" was deeply connected to his style of reasoning—although "style" is not quite apt. "Mode of inquiry" would perhaps be better. If and when he himself spoke of his "style," Stanley called it "his way of philosophizing" or his "manner." "Sensibility" is perhaps most fitting, since he put his whole being into his philosophy, and it was his sensibility that drew many of us to him. Yet 'sensibility' does not easily modify 'reasoning' and it is Cavell's reasoning that I wish to say more about since it's often thought to be idiosyncratic or as Stanley was inclined to put it, "esoteric." Already in 1968 when he wrote the foreword to *Must We Mean What We Say?* he fortified himself with a reply to what he anticipated would be a criticism: "If philosophy is esoteric that is not because a few men guard its knowledge but because they guard themselves against it."[9]

For someone like myself who was an early student of Stanley's, his "way of philosophizing" was hard to distinguish from the way he taught. His philosophy grew directly out of his teaching: a characteristic he shared with the later Wittgenstein. It is tempting to think of Stanley and Wittgenstein's ways of philosophizing as pedagogical rather than polemical or argumentative. Hilary Putnam, who was also a faculty member when I was a graduate student, was not only a friend of Stanley's, he was deeply affected by this aspect of Stanley's work: "All philosophy does not have to be argument; and all arguments do not have to be in the analytic style. Kierkegaard, for example, does have arguments, although analytic philosophers will never recognize it. It is the same with Wittgenstein; his arguments often have a pedagogical character, the objective of which is not to explain something to the reader, but to get the reader to work things out for himself. This, I think, is the true purpose of philosophy."[10] It is also easy to forget that Wittgenstein left philosophy in 1919 and after a year of training applied for a teaching job in a small village in the mountains south of Vienna, twelve miles from any train. He taught elementary school for six years. He returned to philosophy and wrote what became the *Philosophical Investigations*. There are any number of examples of teaching children throughout the book. From the few reports we have from those who lived in Trattenbach, and the children Wittgenstein taught, it is evident that he was passionate about his teaching. When I think of Stanley, I think of him as a teacher first, as someone who engaged us in conversation in the dining hall, in his office, in seminar, at tutorial and in lecture. He taught by offering examples, by hinting at rather than by explaining his subject, with parables, stories, and analogies. His "manner" was different in this respect from the style of others in the department who taught us to think syllogistically, from premises to conclusion. Our job was not to engage in top-down reasoning but to become adept at to "seeing" the point, and "getting" the example, at knowing how to "take" a hint, pick up a thread, or and "draw" on an analogy.

Henry James talked in the prefaces to his novels that he wrote late in life of the "germ" that gave rise to the story. In *The Art of Fiction* he wrote of an English novelist whom he much admired, whom he praises for her depiction of French Protestant youth and whom when asked how she knew so much about "this recondite being," replied she had ascended a staircase in an apartment complex in Paris and spied through an open door a gathering of "some young Protestants seated at a table round a finished meal" and that was enough "to create a reality and produce a story,"[11] a "germ" theory James cannot help but praise: "The power to guess the unseen from the seen, to trace the implication of things, to judge the whole piece by the pattern, the condition of feeling life, in general, so completely that you are well on your way to knowing any particular corner of it—this cluster of gifts may almost be said … to be the very air we breathe."[12]

Stanley too comes to quote this very same passage from *The Art of Fiction*, recognizing that James has described "that younger version of myself, playing hooky from Juilliard and in the poverty of his formal education, reading all day and spending half the night in theaters, already taking to heart Henry James's most memorable advice to aspiring writers." The passage I quote from James above and that Stanley cites in "The Thought of Movies" ends on a most commendable note: "Try to be one of the people upon whom nothing is lost."[13] Stanley, took the hint, only to discover there are hints here and there and everywhere, just waiting to be taken.

In *Little Did I Know*, Stanley wrote about many such moments from early on in his life that he remembers and from which he later, sometimes much, much later, took his cue. Two such events occur not far from the Sierra School where he was installed shortly after he and his parents arrived in Sacramento. They both involve sounds. The first takes place in a vacant lot a number of blocks from a work site where Stanley had been helping workmen. The work complete, Stanley wanders around and finds at the bottom of a shallow ditch a large heavy glass jar with a cap screwed on it, empty but for the residues of disuse. The cap had been inexpertly punched with several holes, I imagined to hold insects without suffocating them, conceivably fireflies which were a common summer fascination on Atlanta Avenue [back in Georgia], although I do not recall ever having seen one in Sacramento. ... I unscrewed the cap and filled the jar with each different thing I came across in the field, a twig, crumbling leaves, assorted bugs various kinds of stones, perhaps a marble, a gum or candy wrapper, a soda bottle cap, a piece of torn tennis ball, to which I added a penny and a duplicate stamp from my stamp collection, enclosed in an envelope which I found in my pocket. Then I filled the remaining space of the bottle with dirt and grass, closed it tightly and contemplated it, feeling I had completed something important, even solemn. Something will be discovered to grow from this, if it is well preserved and we wait long enough.[14]

Stanley then borrows a shovel and buries the jar and as he is sitting on top of the mound of earth under which he has hidden the jar, he hears "a faint low hum, as if produced by the ground, which [he] explicitly said to [himself] others could not hear." He remembers this event, although it is small and asks himself what keeps the memory of it coming back "perhaps every other year."[15] It could be Henry James's admonition doing its work: "Try to be one of the people upon whom nothing is lost."

And the humming does not end here. Stanley recalls another moment that occurred that very same year. He was listening to the radio, to the announcement of the execution of John Dillinger and Bruno Hauptmann, who were convicted of killing the Lindbergh baby. Stanley remembers: "As the announcer spoke of execution in the electric chair, the radio gave out a hum that I understood as the sound of electrical execution. It may have been an imperfection in the radio transmission, or the station's attempt at a reenactment of the moment. Either way it was a comment on the world of retribution. I was, as I recall, alone in the house, and it seemed to help to control my fear, to go outside, if just to see live people walking around somewhere."[16]

Stanley admits that both these moments are not the sorts of impressions that demand expression, let alone cry out for expression at all. Yet they were not lost on Stanley. Nearly sixty years later, while Stanley was teaching a class on film and opera, he found himself describing the overture to Mozart's *The Marriage of Figaro* "as expressing the hum of the world, specifically the restlessness of the people of the world, ... associating the impression of restlessness (not as an item within Locke and Hume's inventory of experiences) with what [is called] the modern subject, sketched in Wittgenstein's *Philosophical Investigations*, the subject perpetually seeking peace, therefore endlessly homeless."[17] These tales of the three hums are tales of someone who knew how to take a hint, who took hints throughout his life to become someone upon whom nothing was lost. He wondered at the time that he was digging that hole whether he: "was burying [his] life, perhaps to preserve it for some time in which it might be lived or chosen."[18]

To live a life of one's own and make it one's own is a theme that runs throughout Stanley's writing from the beginning. It includes the problem of postponement and the lesson he took away from his chasing a ball down a driveway into the street into the path of an oncoming car: a wariness of becoming too exuberant. On almost every occasion that he was offered a chance to postpone something that mattered to him, he leapt at the opportunity, enabling him to put off having to think, to speak, or to act before he was ready, before he was confident enough that it was *his* thought he was expressing, *his* remark he was making, *his* desire he was acting on. Already in the acknowledgments to *Must We Mean What We Say?*, published fifty years ago, he thanks the Harvard Society of Fellows for giving him a three-year leave of absence from his dissertation; thanks the Society for what he calls "the most precious benefit of those years ... the chance to keep quiet, in particular to postpone the Ph.D., until there was something I wanted, and felt readier, to say."[19] He was grateful for these moments of "postponement" or, as he also described them, these "moments of silence." Postponement, Stanley believed, "is what distinguishes the human, the crossover from instinct into reason. To interpret silence as delay—that is, to refuse to see that sometimes there is nothing to say—is tragic."[20] These moments of silence also become the main focus of interest in his reading of *King Lear*.

I close on two notes. The first is a reminder of Stanley's having scolded his teacher, J. L. Austin, for not being more forthcoming about the "radicality" of his "method." I put method in inverted commas because, as I have already said, there are good reasons to think that Stanley, following in Austin's footsteps, would not have been altogether pleased to hear his way of philosophizing described as a "method." There is, perhaps, a case to be made for the word as a description of the sort of thing Austin did, but whatever we call it, Stanley scolded Austin for his "refusal," as Stanley saw it, "to draw consequences from [his] innovations that did justice to their radicality."[21] A similar sort of complaint, of course, might be lodged against Stanley, who was hesitant throughout his life to claim too much for his mode of inquiry, preferring to do what he did and to go on doing it, and let others come to their own conclusions.

In rereading much of Stanley's writing in anticipation of pulling together a contribution for *Inheriting Stanley Cavell*, I was struck by the many things in this world and in ourselves that Stanley's way of philosophizing is able to bring to light, things we have come to take for granted, that habit has made dull, and, not so unsurprisingly, we overlook or, more aptly, no longer hear because they have become so familiar and so ordinary. Cavell's work took its cue from the way he taught, non-polemically and non-argumentatively, by "articulating the conditions which allow a coherent utterance to be made, or a purposeful action to enter the world, or else to provide an explication or elaboration of a text—sometimes of the merest fragment, sometimes one of [his] own—that accounts for, at its best increases, which is to say appreciates, [his] interest in it,"[22] a manner whose philosophicality is as revelatory, if not more so, than reasoning from premises to conclusions.

On a second, and final note, picking up on Stanley's predilection for postponement, he once confessed that "the way, or space within which, I work, which I can put negatively as occurring within the knowledge that I never get things right, or let's rather say, see them through, the first time, causing my efforts perpetually to leave things so that they can be, and ask to be, returned to. ... Put positively, it is the knowledge that philosophical ideas reveal their good only in stages."[23] From this double reading of the gifts of delay, and of returning, I suspect, we should all take a hint, that Stanley's work is not done. There is more to do and this something more has now been bequeathed to us, to those of us who have taken a shine to his work, in one way or another. Now it is up to us, to pick up where he left off and run with it.

Notes

1   Joan Richardson, "Thinking in Cavell," *Stanley Cavell: Philosophy, Literature, Criticism*, ed. James Loxley and Andrew Taylor (Manchester: Manchester University Press, 2011), 205.
2   Stanley Cavell, *A Pitch of Philosophy: Autobiographical Exercises* (Cambridge: Harvard University Press, 1994), 21.
3   Cavell, *A Pitch of Philosophy*, 21.
4   Stanley Cavell, *The Senses of Walden: An Expanded Edition* (Chicago: University of Chicago Press, 1992), 51
5   Ibid., 30.
6   Stanley Cavell, "Thinking of Emerson," *Emerson's Transcendental Etudes*, ed. David Justin Hodge (Stanford: Stanford University Press, 2003), 15.
7   Stanley Cavell, "The Philosophy in American Life," *Emerson's Transcendental Etudes*, 47.
8   Cavell, *A Pitch of Philosophy*, ix.
9   Stanley Cavell, *Must We Mean What We Say?* (Cambridge: Cambridge University Press, 2002, updated edition), xxiii.
10 Gioanna Borradori, *The American Philosopher: Conversations with Quine, Davidson, Putnam, Nozick, Danto, Rorty, Cavell, MacIntyre, and Kuhn* (Chicago: University of Chicago Press, 1994), 69.

11 Henry James, "The Art of Fiction," *Henry James: Essays on Literature, American Writers, and English Writers*, ed. Leon Edel (New York: Library of America, 1984), 4.
12 Ibid., 8.
13 Stanley Cavell, "The Thought of Movies," *Cavell on Film*, ed. William Rothman (Albany: State University Press of New York, 2005), 90.
14 Stanley Cavell, *Little Did I Know: Excerpts from Memory* (Stanford: Stanford University Press, 2010), 98.
15 Ibid., 99.
16 Ibid.
17 Ibid., 100.
18 Ibid., 99.
19 Cavell, *Must We Mean What We Say?*, x.
20 Cavell, *A Pitch of Philosophy*, 16.
21 Cavell, *Must We Mean What We Say?*, xxiv.
22 Stanley Cavell, *Philosophy the Day after Tomorrow* (Cambridge: Harvard University Press, 2005), 6.
23 Cavell, *Must We Mean What We Say?*, xvii.

14

How to Mean It

Some Simple Lessons

TIMOTHY GOULD

> *We speak of understanding a sentence in the sense in which it can be replaced by another which says the same; but also in the sense in which it cannot be replaced by any other. (Any more than a musical theme can be replaced by any other.)*
> *In the one case, the thought in the sentence is something common to different sentences; in the other, something that is expressed only by these words in these positions. (Understanding a poem.)*
> *... Words can be hard to say. ... (Words are also deeds.)*
> —LUDWIG WITTGENSTEIN, *Philosophical Investigations*[1]

CHARACTERIZING STANLEY CAVELL'S LEGACY is probably hopeless but not necessarily thankless.[2] His influence reaches out from philosophy to literary criticism and history, film studies, political science, and psychoanalysis. He was president of the Eastern Division of the American Philosophical Association and his work was recognized by the Shakespeare Association and the Psychoanalytic Society of New York.

Cavell was born in Atlanta and died in Brookline, Massachusetts, at the age of ninety-one. On his own account, he grew up in two provincial capitals, Sacramento and Atlanta. This was, among other things, his way of saying he was not a New York intellectual, though he shared with them some important influences and preoccupations. He leaves a tightknit and talented family, four or five academic generations of (nonexclusively) students, readers, and friends, and more than fifteen books, ranging in topics from Wittgenstein and Austin to the movies and Shakespeare, to Emerson, Thoreau, Freud, and Nietzsche as well as to museum collections, mass society, opera, jazz, and quilts.

Since Cavell's work seems increasingly less known among academic aestheticians, it might be useful to sketch in some of his basic themes and arguments, as well as something of his place in recent American thought. In aesthetics, he was of a generation with Arthur Danto and Richard Wollheim, both of whom he had known from fairly early on. Like them, he wrote about the arts and literature as near the center of philosophy and not as ornamental. This perspective is not out of order within Continental philosophy, but it remains somewhat alien to mainstream American philosophy. In a wider historical context, which included the majority of his colleagues at Harvard, Cavell was part of the counterrevolution against the still persistent scientific conception of knowledge promulgated by positivism, including the shadows that positivism still casts on ethics and aesthetics.

An early stage of this project is Cavell's critique of the widespread idea that ethics and aesthetics have no "cognitive meaning" or that poetry is a series of pseudostatements. His response was not to provide such terms with some new logic or some special variety of aesthetic, ethical, or poetic meaning. Rather, he looked at the forms of utterance and discourse in which certain terms occur. He looked less at our physical positions in the world and more at our "standing" in the world. He wanted us to focus on our being in a position to understand a situation and in a position that allows us to make an appropriate claim on others, even if the claim is denied. For instance, "You ought to keep that piano tuned." This imperative "ought" depends on no more special sense of words than the one that occurs because of my relation to the piano, to the act of keeping it tuned and to the person I am holding responsible.

This more general defense and revision of elements of aesthetic and ethical discourse began already in his dissertation, the middle sections of which became chapters of his most ambitious book, *The Claim of Reason: Wittgenstein, Skepticism, Morality, and Tragedy* (Oxford, 1979). This work led Cavell to revisit and to clarify certain specific aesthetic and ethical terms (like "intention," "paraphrase," "form," and "rules"). His approach to ethics and aesthetics was blended into his early essays on Austin and Wittgenstein, which in turn became the first chapters of his first book, *Must We Mean What We Say?* (Scribner, 1969). And that book in turn was part of a decades-long rereading of Wittgenstein as everywhere contesting the grip of a skeptical understanding of knowledge and its success and failure.

Cavell's account of skepticism paints it as a consequence of our disappointment in the success of knowledge. It is as if we would rather deny knowledge than accept such a fragile, human thing as what we know of the world and of others. Skepticism must not simply be defeated but allowed to play out its story—and not just in philosophy but also in the world of human culture. It is in literature and above all in Shakespeare that we see the consequences of demanding and disowning knowledge (the "ocular proof") but also the possibility that what we sometimes have is what knowledge is like in a world of artifice and accident.

The keystone of this project is hinted at in "Knowing and Acknowledging" (in *Must We Mean What We Say?*). The utterance "I know you are in pain" is relayed back from knowledge to the acknowledgment that the sentence more immediately expresses. Put more strongly, it is only under very specialized circumstances that "I know you are in pain" is merely a proposition about my cognitive relation to the state of your being well or ill. Uttering the sentence acknowledges my relation to your pain—in particular, that I have one—though it does not dictate what I go on to do or feel. I can construct a purely cognitive meaning for this sentence, independent of the fact of my response (or lack of response): "I know you are pain but I can't give you an anesthetic until the doctor checks your lungs." To reduce the utterance to stating a purely cognitive state and strip it of the component implication that I stand in a relation to you as well as to your pain is not just to distort language but to distort what my knowing your pain is.

Knowledge without the substance of acknowledgment is not the knowledge of pain. Such an assertion of knowledge would have nothing to be about—nothing that is not the concoction of philosophers. Investigating why ordinary humans are so quick to resort to the same empty assertions about others as philosophers tend to do is what leads Cavell to the concluding sections of *The Claim of Reason* and to a large part of his work in the next several decades. It is one place to begin to think about Cavell's relation to politics, perhaps especially to the work of feminism and of anti-racism, undoing pictures of the other and of ourselves.

This insight about the priority of expression continues to spread throughout Cavell's work. It shows up centrally in his reconstruction of Wittgenstein's private language argument. That words do not mean something by an act of referring prior to human expression is, of course, one of Wittgenstein's signature moments. But Cavell takes this further by making explicit the need to explore the requirement of expression—or what he later names the "voice"—as prior to reference. For Cavell this is one of the paths that leads directly to literature, as if philosophy must learn from poems, paintings, and novels how we may refer to the simplest things—indeed, how we learn to name at all.

That human nature—like language—is partly composed of wishes, partly of conventions, and partly of aspirations (transcendental and otherwise) is an essential part of what opened up Cavell's interest in Kant, Thoreau, Emerson, and film. The possibility of a composite nature becoming intermittently whole (in a sense, complete or perfect) is what he calls perfectionism. But his work on Shakespeare and film also follows out some of the ways in which the drive to perfection or integrity can destroy itself or invite other forms of destructiveness. (His chapter on *Coriolanus* is central to this account.) Perfectionism is not for angels (or brutes), though it may be for those who have not yet seen the dangers of that desire for perfection.

Over the years—but especially in the months since he died—friends and students have been remembering stories and offering testimony of Stanley's apparently inexhaustible gifts for friendship and endless generosity toward other people's work. I have benefitted from both of these traits. I also confess I once made him laugh by reminding him, in roughly the words of Barbara Stanwyck in *The Lady Eve*, "I'm not your student for free, you know."

Once, when I was eighteen, he invited me to watch a movie from the projection booth at the Carpenter Center. Thrilled but desperate to say something of interest to him, I said, "Isn't it kind of strange to watch a movie from a projection booth?" And he leaned toward me, out of the hearing of the others, and said, "Do you think we murder to dissect?" It was clearly a quote but I did not know from whom. It was also clear that he was inviting me to enjoy a privileged moment and not to let my sense of propriety—my uptightness—get in the way. (Later I learned the line about dissection was from Wordsworth. Much later I learned that one of Stanley's preoccupations was not letting our knowledge of how moments got made spoil our sense of their significance.)

There is also a side of Stanley that is less reported, a kind of sternness in his conversation that was passed down to me from a handful of graduate students in Emerson Hall, among other places. I am thinking of a remark of Stanley's that I think I heard from Allen Graubard: "The unexamined life is probably not worth examining." There is a high level of fierceness as well as fun in that sentence (though not necessarily fiercer than in Socrates's original). Both appealed to my youthful anger at human torpor, partly no doubt at my own.

But it is the sweet spots I remember most. Sometimes it was his praise (which, like his smile, was well worth winning) and sometimes it was his rescuing a moment of disappointment with a brighter piece of his mind.

Returning from an interview for a Rhodes scholarship that I was pretty sure I wouldn't get, I deflected my disappointment by telling Stanley that they had made it clear that volunteers and draftees could have their scholarships held over, but draft resisters could not. Anxiously and not without anger, I asked Stanley, what do I say to that? That is when I first heard him tell the once-famous Austin story about the bribe. Supposedly it was R. M. Hare who said, "If someone offered me a bribe, I would say 'I do not take bribes on principle.'" Austin responded, "That's very odd. I should have said, 'No thank you.'" Stanley paused and said to me: "That's what you say to the Rhodes people. 'No thank you.'"

I did not take it as a put down of my moral principles or my political anger, nor of (all) academic moral philosophy. (I was months away from almost certainly being reclassified as 1A—eligible for the draft—and Stanley knew it.) I took it as a lesson about how and when you learn to say what you know you have to say—and to a very particular audience. He was teaching me how to decline something: how to say "no." I am very glad that not all that much later I had a chance to show him that when you learn how to say "No thank you," then "Thank you" becomes a lot easier to say.

Notes

1 Ludwig Wittgenstein, *Philosophical Investigations*, 3rd ed., trans., G. E. M. Anscombe (Englewood Cliffs: Prentice Hall, 1953), §531, §546.
2 This essay first appeared in the Winter 2018 newsletter of the *American Society for Aesthetics*, vol. 38, no. 3.

15

Stanley Cavell's Doubling

Rex Butler

THERE IS AN EXTRAORDINARY MOMENT in Frank Capra's well-known and much-loved *It Happened One Night* (1934) that takes place when newspaperman Peter Warne (played by Clark Gable) and heiress-on-the-run Ellie Andrews (played by Claudette Colbert) find themselves staying at a motor inn overnight. The recently out-of-work Peter has met Ellie after she boarded a bus seeking to get to her just-married husband against her father's wishes, and for various reasons the two decide to travel together. Peter for his part wants to keep the story of Ellie's disappearance to himself so that he can taunt the editor who sacked him and perhaps get his job back, while Ellie for her part needs Peter's help to get to the husband her father disapproves of and has forbidden her to see. Of course, *It Happened One Night* is a romantic comedy—perhaps the inaugural one, at least in the newly arrived medium of sound cinema—and the couple soon find themselves attracted to each other. But, needless to say, this being a romantic comedy, they cannot so easily admit it, either to the other or to themselves. Peter because he is filled with a masculinist contempt for Ellie's unworldly ways, and Ellie perhaps a little more unwillingly because Peter is so frequently rude to her. Meanwhile, as the two catch a series of buses and stay at a variety of stopovers, Ellie's father hires a team of detectives to look for his runaway daughter (not the police because he suspects that his behavior in stopping his daughter seeing her husband might not stand up to scrutiny). Armed with a photo of Ellie, they trawl motels and auto camps looking for her. Finally one morning they arrive at the one where Peter and Ellie are staying, and accompanied by the flustered and unwilling manager they stand outside Peter and Ellie's cabin door while they are having breakfast.

At the time Peter and Ellie are having one of their usual semi-good-natured fights, with Peter patronizingly teaching Ellie the "authentic" way to dunk a donut in coffee, while Ellie pretends not to understand exactly in order to annoy him. But realizing the seriousness of the situation as he sees the detectives about to enter, Peter suddenly switches modes. Rushing across the room in a seemingly unmotivated and vaguely threatening manner, he brushes Ellie's usually elegant fringe across her forehead and, raising his voice several decibels and adopting an ersatz Midwestern accent, starts yelling nonexistent family news at her. Ellie, after a brief moment of incomprehension—barely jerking her head back in surprise—picks up on Peter's lead and begins herself, in an even bigger surprise, to shout back in a strident Okie accent. The following is an excerpt of their conversation as it takes place in front of the bewildered detectives and the at first embarrassed and then angry (at the detectives for making their mistake and disturbing paying customers) motor inn manager:

> PETER: [To Ellie.] Come here, you little fool! Sit down! [He musses her hair.] Yeah, I got a call from Aunt Betty. She says if we don't stop over at Wilkes-Barre she'll never forgive us.
> ELLIE: What are you talking about?
> PETER: [Hand over her mouth.] The baby is due next month and they want us to come. [Ellie looks into his eyes.] She says she saw your sister Ethel the other day and she's doing swell.
> ELLIE: [To door.] Come in!
> PETER: I hope Aunt Betty has a boy, don't you?
> ELLIE: [To Peter.] There's a man to see you, sweetheart.
> PETER: Who? Me?
> DETECTIVE: [To Ellie.] What's your name?
> ELLIE: You addressing me?
> DETECTIVE: Yeah. What's your name?
> PETER: [Stepping in front of detective.] Hey, wait a minute! You're talking to my wife. [Peter and Ellie then start arguing among themselves.]
> MOTOR INN OWNER: [To detective.] Now look what you've done!
> DETECTIVE: Sorry, Warne. But you see, we're supposed to check up on every couple.

After being so sure that they had finally tracked down their client's daughter, admittedly in this unlikely place, and even holding up a photo of an elegantly dressed Ellie against the apparently disheveled and lower-class woman currently involved in a domestic dispute with her husband (Peter and Ellie necessarily checked in to the motor inn as husband and wife), the two detectives accompanied by the manager beat a hasty retreat.

For them, they have come across an unfortunate moment of working-class life that they (and movie audiences) usually avoid. But when they finally leave the cabin, shutting the door behind them, Peter and Ellie collapse with shared laughter at their mutual deceit. Peter in his still patronizing way says to Ellie: "Say, you were pretty good. Jumping in like that. You got a brain, haven't you?" He is clearly impressed at the way she was able, without anything explicit being said, to pick up on his cues and suddenly enter the game. She immediately recognized that things were being said in a different register, that Peter was not merely speaking to her but speaking *about* his speaking, setting out the new rules that henceforth would govern their discourse. And it is this playful moment, one of apparent discord and disagreement, that is the beginning of their true love for each other (although once again they cannot admit it, and it can even appear to take the form of its opposite). Peter is newly respectful of Ellie for her "wifely" ability to pick up his hints, as well as convincingly acting like a lower-class woman, and Ellie is pleased that Peter chose to involve her in his game in this way. Again, without him actually saying anything, she realizes that he must always have believed that she was capable of doing what she did.

Of course, all those who read the work of Stanley Cavell know that this sequence is discussed in his classic book on Hollywood romantic comedies, *Pursuits of Happiness: The Hollywood Comedy of Remarriage*. Indeed, even though it is not actually the first film he takes up there, it is chronologically at least the earliest he addresses. It is not only, that is to say, a decisive film in Hollywood history—it was the first whose commercial success convinced the moguls that the new sound technology could prove attractive to audiences—but the inaugural film in that new genre he identifies as the "comedies of remarriage." The "comedies of remarriage," as we now know, are that particular strand of classic Hollywood romantic comedies of the 1930s and 1940s, in which, as opposed to the usual story of a young couple falling in love and getting married for the first time, a slightly older and more experienced couple falls in love again after breaking up and gets married for the second time. The couple, that is, decides to get married not with the usual romantic illusions but overcoming a prior disappointment and yet nevertheless trying again. For Cavell, it is an allegory of that overcoming of skepticism that for him is the essential condition of modernity. Marriage is not—or no longer—something that can be taken for granted, whose rules and conventions are unchanging and that we can simply follow, but something that must constantly be worked at and whose rules and conventions must continually be brought up to date in the light of contemporary conditions. This is Cavell in his chapter on *It Happened One Night*, "Knowledge as Transgression," on the way that the "remarriage" seen in the sequence of films he identifies is no longer something unquestioned but is a consciously created convention:

> But this natural relationship [between couples] is a kinship from which the freedom to marry is precisely to be won. Without the kinship, the eventual marriage would not be warranted; without the separation or divorce, the marriage would not be lawful. The intimacy conditional on narcissism or incestuousness must be ruptured in order that an intimacy of difference or reciprocity supervene.[1]

To put this another way, Cavell's point about the Hollywood comedies of remarriage is that not only are they "modernist art" in the proper sense of the word because it is a matter of them maintaining their own artistic conventions over the historical period in which they are made, but they also show marriage itself as modern. Marriage today, they suggest, is no longer traditional, able to be unthinkingly assumed, something in which we are unhesitatingly able to repeat the same customs, conventions, and even conversations and have it survive. Rather, as that conversation between Peter and Ellie reveals, marriage is now a matter of improvisation, of conventions having to be made up and kept responsive. Peter and Ellie's pretend marriage is absolutely a model for proper marriage—and, fittingly, at the end of the film, after Peter wins both Ellie's and her father's approval, when they are officially married, it is in a sense their remarriage or "second" marriage. Cavell's point in *Pursuits of Happiness* is that all marriages nowadays—even if actually a first—are second marriages, insofar as they take place only across or against the ever-present possibility of their breakup. That is, the conventions holding together even "traditional" marriages are no longer able to be taken for granted, but always have to be reinvented, founded, or indeed refound again after they have been lost, or at least potentially lost. All marriages are second marriages in the sense that "first" marriages are now over, impossible, no longer able to be entered into.

Doubt and Its Overcoming

Pursuits of Happiness is not only a great book on Hollywood cinema, providing a brilliant and unexpected "philosophical" take on some of the most popular cultural objects of all time—with the striking sense after Cavell has written on them that no one has properly seen them before—but an equally brilliant and unexpected "popularization" of the philosophical system he had been working on since the publication of his first book, *Must We Mean What We Say?* For Cavell's ultimate point about the comedies of remarriage, the meaning of there being a second marriage and suggesting that all marriages now are second marriages, is that marriage today is the overcoming of a prior doubt or skepticism. What the possibility of divorce or separation indicates, the fact that it might take place at any point in a marriage, so that marriage in effect is the continual getting back together after a prior break, is that it is always possible to doubt or misunderstand another, and therefore the world itself. And that even when we think we understand this other, we still potentially misunderstand them. It is just this that we see dramatized in the comedies of remarriage: one of the couple misunderstands the other, and the other attempts to clarify, only to further exacerbate the misunderstanding, driving them further away. So that in the end the two have nothing in common, no way of talking to the other, no way of clarifying things or making the misunderstanding up and they end up getting divorced. But it is exactly something like this that characterizes modernism more generally: the ever-present possibility that we do not understand the other or they do not understand us. This is always the case, even when we think we are making sense and the other understands us, as in being married.

Cavell, as we say, finds this situation or possibility dramatized in a series of Hollywood romantic comedies of the 1930s and 1940s, which he emphasizes evidence a certain American modernity—the advent of sound technology, the rise in the status of women, the economic upheaval of the Great Depression—and even the beginning of cinema itself as a modernist medium. But elsewhere in Cavell's work he identifies a number of other cultural and historical markers of modernity, some of which are significantly earlier. He speaks of the scientists Copernicus in the early sixteenth century and Galileo in the early seventeenth century, who posited a heliocentric conception of the universe. He points to the political theorists John Locke in the late sixteenth century and David Hume in the mid-eighteenth century, who theorized forms of political democracy. He writes at great length on Shakespeare, whose plays, particularly the tragedies, dramatize the consequences of the misunderstandings between people. However, the thinker we want to concentrate on here, who is perhaps most widely identified with the question of doubt and its overcoming, is the early-seventeenth-century René Descartes, who in truth is not elaborated in great detail or at least systematically so by Cavell. Cavell does nevertheless write on him in the section "Skepticism and the Existence of the World" of *The Claim of Reason: Wittgenstein, Skepticism, Morality, and Tragedy* and in the lecture "Being Odd, Getting Even (Descartes, Emerson, Poe)," now republished in the collection *In Quest of the Ordinary: Lines of Skepticism and Romanticism*, and it is from these texts that we draw here. As is well known, the great story of Descartes's *Meditations* is that of its author being drawn into a form of "madness," in which everything is able to be doubted: the external world, what people say to him, even the existence of God. It is a descent that is halted only when Descartes is able to pause and say to himself that he is able to *think* this doubt. There must be, he realizes, some point outside of this doubt from where it is able to be thought, or to put this another way there must be some position outside of this doubt so that there can be doubt. Thus doubt in the *Meditations* exists only as an episode, which can be narrated only in retrospect. Descartes would certainly not be able to write a book in which he was actually experiencing what he writes of. This "madness" can be grasped only in the past, at the beginning of a narrative that has its overcoming as its endpoint.

This is certainly the conclusion—which is also the prevailing philosophical consensus—Cavell reaches when he writes on Descartes. Descartes's doubt is merely, as Cavell describes it, a "hypothesis" that cannot actually be experienced, or cannot be thought as it is experienced.[2] It can be spoken of only from a place of certainty, after it has passed. Indeed, the very thinking of it is the doing away with it. Skepticism in this sense is self-contradictory or self-defeating. As Cavell writes in "Being Odd, Getting Even": "Emerson goes the whole way with Descartes' insight—that I exist only if I think— but he thereupon denies that I (mostly) do think. From this it follows that the skeptical possibility is realised."[3] And this has always been Cavell's attitude toward the famous philosophical problem of skepticism. It cannot be asserted as such, insofar as its assertion does away with it. It cannot be taken too far before it turns upon itself. Therefore the true "refutation" of skepticism is not simply to oppose it, but rather to let it run out to its limit, when its inherent inconsistency is revealed. Again, as Cavell writes in the later section "Skepticism and the Problem of Others" in *The Claim of Reason*: "In speaking of [the unknowability] of other minds, the skeptic is not skeptical enough: the other is still left, along with his knowledge of himself; so am I, along with mine."[4] And this also is the subtlety of his characterization of those thinkers of skepticism he points to as inaugurating modernism. They do not so much assert skepticism as think its possibility.

However, this is to make the point that, if skepticism is self-refuting, it also cannot entirely be refuted. This again is the subtlety of Cavell's treatment of the major figures of the thinking of skepticism, and where he will often differ from their usual characterization and even on occasion their own self-understanding. For if skepticism cannot form a consistent philosophical doctrine, so equally cannot the *refutation* of skepticism, for broadly similar reasons. It is this that explains why Cavell so often approaches the question of skepticism through art and not philosophy, for art does not so much seek to solve the problem of skepticism as to speak of or dramatize it. But what exactly do we mean here? The real point of Descartes—and this is the point emphasized by Cavell in all of his various treatments of him—is that the true refutation of doubt is to be found not in anything he actually says but in the very possibility of thinking (or saying) doubt itself. This, indeed, points toward the complexity, difficulty, or even self-contradiction of Descartes extracting the lesson he has learned as his famous Cogito, the statement "I think, therefore I am." It is actually only during the writing of the *Meditations* itself that he is free of doubt. And, once more, Cavell is very clear on this, and it is undoubtedly why, given his overall philosophical problematic, there is surprisingly little "philosophical" treatment of Descartes (or indeed of any of the other major thinkers of skepticism) in his work: because it is not their philosophical doctrines but their philosophical *practices* that he is interested in. Words can always be misunderstood. Descartes can even misunderstand himself. As soon as he looks back in retrospect at what has happened, he can get it wrong, misunderstand it, not make clear, even to himself, what he went through. And this is the true self-contradiction that is at stake here: Descartes's doubt does not exist as doubt until it can be spoken of from some position outside of it, which is also the overcoming of doubt. It is while he is actually in its grip—and here the coming together of skepticism and anti-skepticism—that there is no doubt, but also not yet the overcoming of doubt. With the result that, if skepticism is self-contradictory because it cannot be formulated except from a position of certainty, so is anti-skepticism because it can formulate itself only as doubt (or formulate itself only through doubt).

In fact, it is through Ludwig Wittgenstein that Cavell conducts this debate in greatest detail. More specifically, it is Wittgenstein read through or at least read alongside J. L. Austin—Austin, of course, being Cavell's first great philosophical encounter and influence. For undoubtedly one of the innovations of Cavell's reading of Wittgenstein—it is what makes him "available" in Cavell's early essay "The Availability of Wittgenstein's Later Philosophy"—is his emphasis on the question of skepticism in his work, and particularly in relation to language. For Wittgenstein it is the necessity of language that makes our relationship both to the external world and to others doubtful or uncertain. Once expressed in words, our intentions can always be betrayed. We can misunderstand others or they can misunderstand us, and it is possible that we can even misunderstand ourselves. Upon inspection, it is apparent that words do not carry a stable meaning, do not correspond to an unchanging essence, but are always open to change according to use and context. It is quite obvious that in ordinary speech the same word does not unfailingly correspond to the same thing. But it is nevertheless possible that, if it is not one object or quality that a word refers to, it is a set or series of objects or qualities that all the uses of a word share and that these can ultimately be unified under a single head. This is, as is well known, Wittgenstein's notion of the "family resemblance" of words as outlined in his *Philosophical Investigations*, and it is taken up by Cavell at several points in his work. Here he is in his essay "The Wittgensteinian Event" pointing to the different uses of the word "table": "What does a tall, small round table at which two bar stools are drawn up have in common with a table of numbers displayed on a page, and both with a water table?"[5] And here he is later setting out the test that such a "family resemblance" theory of language would have to pass:

> Well, the instances do all have something in common with a common library table—its horizontal stretch of flatness fits the surface of water;

that it is mounted on legs (one or more) fits the round bar table; its rectangularity fits the table of numbers. But is *this* what we thought we meant in insisting that they *must* have something in common? Didn't we mean something more like: they have it in common *in a common or essential way*—a *same* something that calls out for the concept *in each case*?[6]

According to the prevalent reading of Wittgenstein, he believed it was a matter of defeating skepticism in this way: not by showing that it is self-contradictory, but by actually demonstrating that truth or truth effects could be attained despite the potentially misleading qualities of language. And this is even more the case with Austin. Austin is widely known for his dismissal of skepticism as a proper philosophical question, his belief that it is possible to distinguish between "serious" and "nonserious" uses of language and more generally his characterization of many of the long-standing questions of philosophy (not just skepticism but also a priori concepts and theories of action) as "over-simplification, schematisation and the constant obsessive repetition of the same small range of jejune 'examples.'"[7] And Cavell himself largely follows this reading of him. His early essay "Austin at Criticism" is a criticism of a particular reading of Austin and an assertion that Austin's work is about criticism in the sense of the judgment and refutation of competing intellectual positions. As Cavell writes of both Austin and Wittgenstein in this regard: "Their work is commonly thought to represent an effort to refute philosophical skepticism, as expressed most famously in Descartes and in Hume."[8] And yet even from the beginning, Cavell also opens up a certain distance onto this anti-skeptical reading, both of Austin's own belief that it is possible simply to refute skepticism and those readings of Wittgenstein that suggest he understands this of himself. With reference to Austin, this is the thrust of Cavell's many returns to the well-known Derrida-Austin debate, most notably in *Philosophical Passages: Wittgenstein, Emerson, Austin, Derrida*, but also in *A Pitch of Philosophy: Autobiographical Exercises*. Derrida's reading of Austin in "Signature Event Context" is of course notorious for its "deconstruction" of the distinction Austin seeks to draw between "serious" and "nonserious" uses of language. Cavell throughout defends Austin in insisting that Derrida has not read those texts of Austin in which this distinction is not drawn as sharply as he alleges. But in a way that Cavell cannot see—or it is the only form in which he would allow this criticism to be made of his old teacher—this point also goes against Austin, for Austin certainly *did* think that we could draw a distinction between the serious and the nonserious. And, indeed, more than this—and this is in fact Derrida's real point and the point we are trying to make here ourselves—it is possible that the two positions are not ultimately irreconcilable: if against Austin it is the attempt to draw a distinction between the serious and the nonserious that produces a kind of recursive loop in which we are always having to make up for a certain "nonseriousness," against Derrida, or at least a certain reading of him, the "nonserious" does not exist as such but only within or as the failure of the serious.[9]

We see something similar in Cavell's treatment of Wittgenstein. As we say, in a first reading of Cavell it is certainly possible to argue that Cavell sees him much as Austin, as simply seeking (if necessarily failing) to defeat or overcome skepticism. But on a number of occasions in his work Cavell makes it clear that, if Wittgenstein's "ordinary language" approach means anything, it does not involve any direct refutation of skepticism in the "critical" or argumentative manner of someone like Austin. Rather, if anything—and here just as Cavell disagrees with Austin's belief that he can refute skepticism, with regard to Wittgenstein he does not so much disagree with him as suggest that he does not properly see the consequences of his own theoretical breakthrough—it is a matter of paying attention to the *practice* of language, to not so much what is said as how it is said, or indeed just the simple fact that it *is* said. It is from the *practice* of language that ordinary language philosophy should draw its lessons, just as it is not in anything it argues that we might follow it—this is Cavell's great insight in relation to Wittgenstein that he tries to give expression to in his own work—but in its actual way of speech.[10] And we might return at this point to Wittgenstein's notion of "family resemblance," but this time supplying Cavell's "answer" to the question he previously left us with. As we suggested before, the usual reading of "family resemblance," including Wittgenstein's own, at least at the time he initially proposed it, is that it is a kind of "practical" solution to the fact that a word like "table" does not appear to have any common meaning or reference: that instead there is a series of similar although not identical meanings that are shared and understood according to purpose and context. Thus, sometimes "table" means X and sometimes Y, and although there is sometimes an overlap or intersection—Cavell speaks of this in terms of metaphor—these meanings are not the same or unifiable in any kind of public agreement, with both speaker and listener being able to state outside of the conversation the meanings being referred to.[11] However, as Cavell makes clear on a number of occasions, if this notionally loose and less rigorous approach appears both closer to everyday practice and an example itself of "ordinary language" philosophy, in fact it merely defers or avoids the problems that bedeviled previous theories of language. For, it might be asked, if we speak of the different "contexts" that require and allow the different meanings of a word, how might these contexts themselves be demarcated? Are we even able to call these contexts "different" without some way of comparing them, which seems to imply a word or concept that carries the same meaning across them? A form of infinite regress is implied here, in which we need something common in order to speak of different contexts, a word or a concept that would itself need its defining context, and so on.

It is at this point that we might turn to Cavell's "solution" to Wittgenstein's family resemblance problem, which is also to make Cavell's argument about the real consequences of "ordinary language" philosophy. Cavell in *The Claim of Reason* contends that, in order properly to know the meaning of a word, it is necessary to be able to use it in a different context from that in which we originally learned it: "To know the meaning of a word, to have the concept titled by the word, is to be able to go with it into new contexts."[12] Indeed, although Cavell leaves this merely implicit, it is to suggest that *every* use of a word takes place in a new context, that we are *never* able to repeat its original context. The same word is always different from itself, even from the beginning. But—and this is the paradox that Cavell draws on, which pays attention to the fact that these skeptical questions can be asked and that what was previously taken to be an objection to family resemblance is its proof, at least of a different version of it—this would not be possible unless there were something of the "same" meaning across all of its various uses. In other words, the answer to the skeptical problem of words not having any underlying meaning is the very problem itself, the fact that the "same" word can mean so many different things. For precisely the word cannot enter different contexts, cannot take on different meanings, unless the two people using it believed they were using the same word. That is to say, in that way we began trying to explain, the meaning of a word lies in its saying and not in what it says. At the time of its speaking two people believe they understand each other, are using the same meanings, but any attempt to explain this would produce a misunderstanding, employ words with other meanings (but again this could be only said because of a certain impossible "sameness").[13] If we were to compare Cavell's treatment of family resemblance to something else, or at least find some literary equivalent to it—one that is not pursued to our knowledge by Cavell himself—it would be to Jorge Luis Borges's famous essay "Kafka and His Precursors." The essay is best known for the idea that "every writer creates his own precursors,"[14] but there is an even more brilliant insight that perhaps has some bearing on what we are speaking of here. After listing the extraordinarily heterogeneous series of authors who now become evident in the light of Kafka, Borges writes: "If I am not mistaken, the heterogeneous pieces I have enumerated resemble Kafka; if I am not mistaken, not all of them resemble each other."[15] To put this otherwise, if we are able to speak of the "Kafkaesque" in literature, it is not any particular quality that is compared, but just this very possibility of comparison itself. Kafka is nothing in himself—and this is in a way how we actually do think of the "Kafkaesque" in literature—but only the possibility of thinking the relationship between all these authors so widely separated in time and space. We could no sooner say what Kafka is than he turns into one of his precursors, but Kafka is, as it were, just the fact that they can now be seen to speak to each other.

Finally, all of this is connected to the way Cavell speaks of artistic medium in his work. The distinctive aspect of Cavell's conception of medium—it is what allows, for example, Michael Fried to break with Clement Greenberg—is that it has nothing to do with any physical properties or even teleological reduction or end point. Rather, as Cavell insists in his essay "A Matter of Meaning It" in *Must We Mean What We Say?*, the significant artistic objects that make up a medium are not able to follow any simple tradition in which they all have something in common, but each must be different from the others. The history of a modernist medium is not determined by any commonality of materials or techniques or attempt to find its underlying truth, as in Greenberg, but is made up of the sequence of artistic objects that have "convinced" at some moment in time, and again for this reason must be different from each other.[16] For in the modern world, we do not convince by repeating what has come before. That is to say, the history of any particular medium is made up of objects that are "different" from each other, but only because each artist attempts to live up the standard of what has come before. Just as in the Borges story (and, indeed, we might speak of "Kafka" or the "Kafkaesque" there as a kind of medium), the history of any particular medium in modernism consists of a series of objects that have nothing in common with each other, but each has something in common with its medium. The history of art, as enunciated, reveals only a series of differences, while the making of this history, its moment of conviction or enunciation, is always the same.

The Doubling of Philosophy

To conclude, let us return to that extraordinary moment in *It Happened One Night* when Peter and Ellie suddenly become aware that Ellie's father's detectives are outside looking for them. Without anything explicit being said, Peter and Ellie suddenly switch roles and demeanors, first Peter and then Ellie. But, in fact, we are not even able to say that Peter started unless Ellie follows. Whatever it was that Peter does, some sign he makes to indicate that he is changing registers, it does not exist until it has been taken up by Ellie. Of course, in this particular case, this is a sign of the empowerment, the making-equal, of women that characterizes the remarriage genre, but more than this we would say that whatever Peter is saying exists only in his conversation with Ellie. If in one way Ellie imitates Peter, in another she imitates no one. And this is indeed Cavell's ultimate point here, and how his interest in the comedies of remarriage comes out of his involvement in the rigors of post-Wittgensteinian "ordinary language" philosophy. For what we want to say here is that, if on the level of what is said Peter and Ellie disagree with each other, do not understand each other, as we see in the sequence they yell at each other, on the level of their saying they are actually in agreement. And what is said for all of its difference is not possible without this shared saying (as is literally the case in the film: Peter and Ellie argue the way they do only insofar as Ellie realizes what Peter is trying to say to her—that they must pretend for the detectives—even though he is unable actually to say this, and even if he could, we can predict that they would end up disagreeing about what to do).[17]

In other words—and this is Cavell's Wittgensteinian point here—at the same time as Peter and Ellie are speaking to each other, they are also setting out the conventions that make possible their speech. They are not only speaking to each other but also speaking about speaking to each other. And this is modernism in art and philosophy: not only do the conditions require the constant rethinking and reestablishing of the conventions by which we communicate and make sense of the world, but our thought and language—to the impossible extent they can be—must also be about this. Modernist art and philosophy are *about* their very saying, seek to think that moment when communication takes place, which is not in anything said but its saying. This is Cavell in *The Claim of Reason* putting forward the notion that in modernism convention takes place not in anything said but in the saying of it, or to put it another way that, even though what is said between two people is inevitably misunderstood, this would not be possible, the conversation would not take place, unless the two in some sense do understand each other. It is this that is the "overcoming" of skepticism: not any actual doctrine of anti-skepticism but the self-contradiction of skepticism: "If there are no rules or universals which insure appropriate projection, but only our confirmed capacity to speak to one another, then a new projection may be made appropriate by giving relevant explanations of how it is to be taken."[18] And this is also the idea that it is in the act of speaking that conventions are produced, and that modernist language attempts to speak of this, but always fails to, so that the only real convention is the act of speaking itself. Again, as Cavell says in *The Claim of Reason*:

> Since we cannot assume that the words we are given have their meaning by nature, we are led to assume they take it from convention; and yet no current idea of "convention" could seem to do the work that words do—there would have to be, we could say, too many conventions in play, one for each shade of each word in each context. We *cannot* have agreed beforehand to all that would be necessary.[19]

Each act of speaking, that is to say, is the attempt to overcome a prior skepticism, which is also a skepticism that does not exist until the act of speaking. But, again, what do we mean by this? What is this doubt or skepticism that is the basis of modernism and where does it come from? Or to give this its proper sense of historicity, what explains this sudden eruption of doubt or skepticism at the origins of modernity? Of course, again, although Cavell is no social or cultural historian, there are any number of reasons he gives in his work for this moment of modernism (or moments of modernism, because it appears to take place at a number of different occasions in history). With Copernicus and Galileo, it occurs with the rise of scientific enquiry and the decline of theistic explanations of the world. With Locke and Hume, it corresponds with the thinking of forms of democracy and the advent of the Industrial Revolution. With Shakespeare, it comes out of the rivalry between the British monarchy and parliament. In the comedies of remarriage, it is the effect of the growing demand for sexual equality in America and the crisis in modern capitalism with the Great Depression. But, in fact, what we want to suggest, accompanying these and making them possible (because history itself, as opposed to tradition, is possible only after modernism), is a pure philosophical "doubling" of what is, a radical surmise or assumption—indeed, we are tempted to say, something of an Austinian prescriptive—which is finally nonempirical and nonhistorical, and after which nothing is the same. For let us go back for a moment to *It Happened One Night* and the sudden shift in register into another realm we see there. Peter and Ellie are no longer speaking to each other, but speaking about their speaking to each other, about what makes possible their speaking to each other. Suddenly it is as though they are not actually able to speak to each other unless they also speak about how they speak to each other, unless each statement they make is also (and also is about) the new convention that allows them to speak to each other. It is as though we were henceforth in the realm of *remarriage*, where tradition no longer applies and how people relate to each other has to be worked out afresh at every moment.

What we ultimately want to suggest here—and we see Cavell allegorize this in the film he is speaking of, what he speaks about in his speaking—is that for Cavell "philosophy" has the same kind of inaugurality. "Philosophy" in the proper sense is always modern, which is to say that "philosophy" also inaugurates modernity. Now, of course, in saying this, we realize that philosophy, the question of whether Cavell does philosophy, is a contested subject in Cavell scholarship. Precisely "ordinary language" philosophy as carried out by Wittgenstein and Austin, and even more so given Cavell's emphasis on the "practice" of their work, appears to avoid or do away with the classic task of philosophy, which is the making of statements that are universally true. Nevertheless, we would insist that Cavell does do philosophy, and that "ordinary language" philosophy, far from being any kind of anti-philosophy, is one of philosophy's highest accomplishments. And what fundamentally is philosophy in the sense we are speaking of here? It is the positing of a transcendental condition that explains everything, for which everything stands in, but—this is its distinctive, "modern" twist—this condition can never be seen as such, but only through what stands in for it. To put this more simply, Cavell posits, following Hobbes, Locke, Shakespeare, and Descartes, a certain condition of skepticism, which is "original," and which everything attempts to overcome, stand in for, take the place of. We never, as we say, actually have this doubt. As with Descartes, it is arrived at only in retrospect. But we speak, communicate at all, only because of this doubt, only to overcome this doubt. Doubt, although never seen, is what motivates us to speak and to keep on speaking, to try to make ourselves clearer—but this doubt is never seen as such. Nevertheless, the very proof of this doubt is the fact that we do speak and keep on speaking, which can now only be understood as the attempt to overcome a prior doubt.

The one certainty we have here is our speaking, the fact that we speak. But we can no sooner try to speak of this, which of course is the fundamental task of "ordinary language" philosophy, than we fall once again into doubt, from the "certainty" of enunciation to the doubt of the enunciated. But this again only from a new position of "certainty." There is thus a kind of continual recursivity, a speaking about speaking about speaking ... which is also just speaking, speaking to another. But this unattainable, always lost, "transcendental" condition of doubt or skepticism as the basis for our understanding each other is exactly what Cavell means—in one of his signature phrases, adopted from Henry David Thoreau—by the "extraordinary" nature of the ordinary, which is to speak of both how impossible the ordinary is as the overcoming of skepticism, how it is no sooner spoken of than lost, and how the extraordinary as skepticism is the condition of possibility of the ordinary, which takes place only as the unceasing attempt to take the place of the extraordinary: "Part of *Walden*'s answer is we have to learn what finding is, what it means that we are looking for something we have lost."[20] And, indeed, it is this recursivity that is behind Cavell's revivifying of the American transcendentalist doctrine of perfectionism. Perfectionism is usually characterized as the mere moral progress toward a better self, following such thinkers as Thoreau and Ralph Waldo Emerson. Of course, we are right to see it this way, but perfectionism is also the very model of thought in modernism. It is the repeated attempt to state the conditions of speaking that allow the overcoming of doubt, which, as soon as they are stated, can only be doubted again.[21] We see this, for example, in Michael Fried's art history with the inevitable fall of absorption back into theatricality. We see it also in Cavell's idea of the "unknown woman" in Hollywood melodramas, when as soon as we identify any actual woman to embody this she is unknown no longer. And we see it in the "progression" of any modernist artform. Perhaps with this caveat added—but this is the paradox of the whole of modernism—that at once we are in an infinite recursion and we are always at exactly the same moment, confronting doubt for the first time.

Notes

1. Stanley Cavell, *Pursuits of Happiness: The Hollywood Comedy of Remarriage* (Cambridge: Harvard University Press, 1981), 103.
2. For Cavell on doubt as a "hypothesis" in light of Descartes, see *The Claim of Reason: Wittgenstein, Skepticism, Morality, and Tragedy* (Oxford: Oxford University Press, 1979), 141.
3. Stanley Cavell, *In Quest of the Ordinary: Lines of Skepticism and Romanticism* (Chicago: University of Chicago Press, 1988), 108.
4. Cavell, *The Claim of Reason*, 353.
5. Stanley Cavell, "The Wittgensteinian Event," *Reading Cavell*, ed. Alice Crary and Sanford Shieh (London: Routledge, 2006), 12.
6. Ibid.
7. J. L. Austin, *Sense and Sensibilia* (Oxford: Oxford University Press, 1962), 3.
8. Stanley Cavell, "Psychoanalysis and Cinema: The Melodrama of the Unknown Woman," *Images in Our Souls: Cavell, Psychoanalysis, and Cinema*, ed. Joseph H. Smith and William Kerrigan (Baltimore: Johns Hopkins University Press, 1987), 21. In fact, Cavell goes on immediately after the passage quoted to qualify this: "And an essential drive of my book *The Claim of Reason* is to show that, at least in the case of Wittgenstein, this is a fateful distortion, that Wittgenstein's teaching is on the contrary that skepticism is not exactly true, but not exactly false either."
9. Cavell writes in "What Did Derrida Want of Austin?": "Hence Austin's tethering reverses Derrida's picture of philosophy's concept of writing as *extending the limits* of the voice or breath; turns it so to speak into one of limiting the inevitable extension of the voice, which must always escape me and will forever seek its way back to me," *Philosophical Passages: Wittgenstein, Emerson, Austin, Derrida* (Oxford: Blackwell, 1995), 64. It would be interesting to relate the "human voice" (69), which Cavell at once credits Derrida for bringing out in Austin and holds up against Derrida, to the moment of enunciation and the "overcoming" of skepticism, as opposed to Derrida's "writing," which might be understood to correspond to the enunciated and the fall into skepticism. Cavell will later relate this voice to the "ordinary" (74).
10. For an excellent essay bringing out this aspect of Wittgenstein with regard to Cavell, see Sandra Laugier, "Rethinking the Ordinary," *Contending with Stanley Cavell*, ed. Russell B. Goodman (Oxford: Oxford University Press, 2005).
11. Cavell, *The Claim of Reason*, 190.
12. Ibid.
13. For a new approach to the problem of "family resemblance" that bears some similarity to this, see Odi Al Zobi, "Wittgenstein and Austin on 'What Is Common': A Neglected Perspective?,'" doctoral dissertation, University of East Anglia, 2014 (https://ueaeprints.uea.ac.uk/53445/1/odai1.pdf).

14 Jorge Luis Borges, "Kafka and His Precursors," *Labyrinths* (Harmondsworth: Penguin, 1970), 201.

15 Ibid.

16 See on this Stanley Cavell, "A Matter of Meaning It," *Must We Mean What We Say?* (Cambridge: Cambridge University Press, [1969] 2002), 219–22.

17 To complete this point, when is it that couples do not speak to each other and end up getting divorced? When they are no longer able to argue with each other, when "nothing in common" is unable to be remarked as "something in common." This is Cavell's "fantasy of necessary inexpressiveness" (*The Claim of Reason*, 351), and why so much of his work—for example, his discussion of the "unknown woman" in melodrama—is a way of turning nothing into something, understanding inexpressiveness as the deliberate hiding of expression. This is also what is at stake in Fried's "absorption": not mere indifference, but the refusal or holding back of the acknowledgment of the spectator.

18 Cavell, *The Claim of Reason*, 192.

19 Ibid.

20 Stanley Cavell, *The Senses of Walden* (New York: Viking Press, 1972), 97.

21 On this "doubling" aspect of perfectionism, see Stanley Cavell, *Conditions Handsome and Unhandsome: The Constitution of Emersonian Perfectionism* (Chicago: University of Chicago Press, 1990), xxxv. See also *The Claim of Reason*, in which Cavell speaks of the fact that after the "hypothesis" of skepticism at once "nothing is different and everything is different" (451) and of the history of skepticism (and perhaps history as such) as a history of skepticism's "imagined overcomings" (470). Finally, Cavell describes modernist works of philosophy as what would "split their audience into insiders and outsiders" (xx), which is also a split that occurs at every moment within the same audience.

IV

The Significance of Everyday Life

16

The Importance of Being Alive

Sandra Laugier

Remarks given at a memorial event, "Celebrating the Life and Work of Stanley Cavell," convened in Emerson Hall, Harvard University, November 2018.

LITTLE DID I KNOW, WHEN I ARRIVED as a visiting student from the École Normale Supérieure de Paris at the Department of Philosophy at Harvard University in 1984, in order to study what was beginning to become known as "analytic philosophy" (I was writing my PhD on Quine) that I would end up translating most of Stanley Cavell's work into French, and dedicating (as I realize since Stanley's passing) most of my work and life to understanding, presenting, and discussing his work. And loving it.

I just happened to walk into one of his classes, to hear his voice, and that was it. I had never read Cavell's work before, and in order to make the moment last, I went to Robbins Library and began to read *The Claim of Reason*, then *Pursuits of Happiness*. It was a turning point: and at this important moment of my life, Cavell's work became the most important thing in my intellectual life, giving it its continuity and strength. So all these years of work, from the publication of my dissertation on Quine under the too-obviously-Cavellian title *L'apprentissage de l'obvie* [*The Learning of the Obvious*], until the translation of *Little Did I Know*, built up to creating a scene, and a background, a context, in France, for this voice.

We have all noticed how Cavell's autobiography *Little Did I Know* elicits the autobiographical drive in all of us, and makes you rethink the turning points, or the unexpected turns, in your life. *Little Did I Know*, as the title registers, is about this unseen importance of moments in a life. The first teaching by Cavell: to understand what matters to you. The second: to make use of yourself to make it matter.

We are here today because—having encountered him, and his work—Stanley Cavell has had this kind of importance—a tremendous importance, not only in our work but also in our lives not in an abstract sense, but in our way of being alive, of "bearing" life.

Stanley taught us how to be an intellectual as a form of life in both senses, by teaching each of us (here in this room), what *importance* is, that is, what is important to us (to me, to you).

By making us understand how work, and writing, can bear on our lives, and how our lives get their significance from what we think and say and write. By teaching us a specific way of being alive and being a human being. This is what he meant by one of his discoveries, the sense of forms of life (in the Wittgensteinian "social" sense of understanding) as lifeform, ways of being alive, of "bearing" life.

He taught us and is still teaching us, by his life and his immense work, about learning from ourselves what is important to us. And by teaching each of us, what *importance* is, that is, what is important to us (to me, to you). In other words, he teaches us about learning from ourselves what is important to us. This is the core methodology of Cavell's teaching: getting you to learn what is important to you, what matters (to you, hence to anyone). The revelation of one's own relevance, of the possibility and the necessity of making use of who one is, is something that we all, all of Cavell's readers and students owe him. As he said in his first book, about Socrates: "This discovery about himself is the same as the discovery of philosophy, when it is the effort to find answers, and to permit questions, which nobody knows the way to nor the answer to any better than yourself."[1] And as he adds also about himself in the autobiography: "Austin's philosophizing allowed me—demanded of me—the use of myself as the source of its evidence or the measure of its effect. Whatever philosophy's pertinence to me, I felt for the first time my pertinence to philosophy."[2]

Use of yourself, to be useful, you as source of evidence: this is a kind of radical empiricism. I think all of us have felt *useful* in this sense, *because* we loved Stanley's work; he made us forever relevant to philosophy. Useful also in the sense that all work, though hard, was a sort of fun. Going to the movies was ... work. Watching television shows still is, thanks to Stanley, both fun and work. I am especially grateful to him for that.

Translating Cavell's work was always hard work, but this difficulty pointed to the specificity and importance of his philosophy to the contemporary world. Like Emerson, Thoreau, but unlike the majority of contemporary Anglophone philosophers, Cavell used English as a *language*, a philosophical tongue, rather than as an international, dominant, and transferable medium. This meant that his writing was based on terms that were "untranslatable" from English (i.e., from "American"—the cover of the translation of *The Claim of Reason* says "translated from the American"), as I came to see when I revisited them for Barbara Cassin's *Dictionary of Untranslatables*. When Cassin undertook this dictionary project in the late twentieth century, the great philosophical languages, Greek and German, were well represented in it. What happened is that Cavell's words ("claim," "mean," "acknowledgment") instantiated English as an opaque tongue, as a medium in which the transformations of philosophy were operated, in particular those forced by Wittgenstein's work.

It so happened that over the last decade I translated, consecutively, *Must We Mean What We Say?* (*Dire et vouloir dire*, 1969, trans. 2011), Cavell's first book, and his last book, *Little Did I Know* (littéralement *J'étais loin de me douter*—the title was ultimately rendered *Si j'avais su* (2010, trans. 2015). Even without being obsessed by the coherence and themes in Cavell's work, one is constantly amazed by the continuities at forty years of distance. Unlike Wittgenstein, whose thinking mutated significantly over the years, Cavell's thought was always consistent, even as it took on the most unexpected objects, which he allowed to transform it.

The question that strikes me as most persistent is "what is it to mean anything?"—not as would be given in a theory of meaning, but in terms of meaningfulness, of significance. To mean what we say is to know, or to tell, what matters, what we *mind*. So the question of what matters becomes the question of what it is to *tell* anything. Much has been written in the field of pragmatics, and since *Must We Mean What We Say?*, about relevance. Cavell, however, remains the only philosopher to have offered an actual theory of relevance, or pertinence, that takes into account "the total speech situation"—everything that is involved in speaking (especially the question: to whom?). Austin writes: "The total speech act in the total speech situation is the *only actual* phenomenon which, in the last resort, we are engaged in elucidating."[3]

Cavell's analyses of passionate utterance, as well as the writing of *Little Did I Know* (and its method, defined at the beginning), are the most recent actualizations of Cavell's project in *Must We Mean What We Say?*, to define relevance, and find his own relevance, by understanding how *telling* is done, both in context and by giving a context. Austin tirelessly demanding the context (he would often call this the story) of an utterance, Wittgenstein repeatedly asking to whom an utterance is made, "How is *telling* done?" What it is to *Say Anything?* one of my favorite titles (and a movie I love especially because Cavell has written about it). Film turns out to be a modern technique for giving a context to words. If telling and recounting what is important is the task Cavell assigns to philosophy, the difficulty of the task, expressed blatantly and systematically in *Little Did I Know*, is that the unimportant (the trivial, the accessory, the detail) is sometimes, and maybe often, what is most important.

> The obvious point in dating the times of writing was to keep separate the two necessary temporal registers in a narrative, the time of a depicted sequence of events and the time (or place/time) of depicting them. Formally this portrays the fundamental importance granted to the time and context of utterance in the work of Austin and of the later Wittgenstein that has meant so much to me. My stress on the time, or time and place, of depiction is meant to capture what Austin means in tirelessly demanding the context (he would often call this the story) of an utterance and what Wittgenstein means by repeatedly asking to whom an utterance is made. When Wittgenstein asks, "How is *telling* done?" he is in effect asking how it is that saying something, speaking, is done; how it is that someone is in a position to *be* told something. This turns out to be a good question.[4]

This descriptive project clarifies the idea, expressed in the title of chapter 3 of Cavell's *Pursuits of Happiness*, of "The Importance of Importance." The phrase comes, again, from Austin: "What, finally, is the importance of all this about pretending? I will answer this shortly, although I am not sure importance is important: truth is."[5]

Focus, or attention, connects words to world—and film teaches us how to focus, how to *see* what matters or to understand what we have missed: "In this crosslight the capacities and salience of an individual are brought to attention and focus."[6] The connection between language and reality (words and world—maybe Cavell's most basic pun, together with morning and mourning) rests on the *seeing* and *telling* of details, differences, bringing them into focus. Attention (to what we say) is then how we get to know the world. Or as Austin said, "We are using a sharpened awareness of words to sharpen our perception of the phenomena."[7] So how is importance important?

Cavell follows up, parenthetically, on an Austinian parenthetical point, again in *Pursuits of Happiness*. Austin, in his essay "Truth," reflects on defining something, say an elephant: "[For defining an elephant is] a compendious description of an operation involving both word and animal (do we focus the image or the battleship?) and so speaking about 'the fact that' is a compendious way of speaking about a situation involving both words and world."[8] For Cavell, in order to define truth, we must examine what Austin calls in his essay a "compendious way of speaking about a situation involving both words and world." Cavell writes: "(J. L. Austin was thinking about the internality of words and world to one another when he asked, parenthetically in his essay "Truth," "do we focus the image or the battleship?")."[9] This reciprocal internality of words and world is called by Cavell and Austin, *focus*. Focus, or attention, connects words to world—as film teaches us how to focus, how to *see* what matters. To matter is also to make a difference, and Cavell insists in *Little Did I Know* on Austin and the elucidating power of differences, or distinctions, reminding us that "in this crosslight the capacities and salience of an individual are brought to attention and focus."[10]

The connection between language and reality (words and world) rests on the *telling* of differences, bringing to focus. Attention (to what we say; our care for the self) is then the way to get to know the world. Austin says: "We are using a sharpened awareness of words to sharpen our perception of the phenomena." This awareness is the perception of what matters. Importance and truth are both important and internal to each other. This importance of mattering appears in *Little Did I Know*, at a quite painful moment of conversation with Austin when Cavell, to a question concerning whether something must be common to things sharing a common name, says something like: "If people want to say there are universals, let them. It doesn't matter as long as they know the facts." Cavell reports: "I was sitting next to Austin, and he turned toward me as if startled, and said hard, straight between the eyes, 'It matters.' I felt an utter, quite impersonal, shame—shame, and a kind of terror."[11] In so many ways, *Little Did I Know* describes both this kind of terror (connected to the terror of an abusive father figure) of missing what matters and the methods found to overcome it, alternative ways of finding, and expressing, importance—methods that include human conversation, "being interesting," finding your own voice.

Putting importance first means transforming our idea of what is important. Cavell follows Wittgenstein here: "Where does our investigation get its importance from, since it seems to destroy everything great and interesting?"[12]

We need a shift in our ideas of what is important, of what we are asked to let interest us.[13] We have a "distorted sense of what is important (call it our values) that is distorting our lives."[14] In this way, *relocating importance* becomes the new task Cavell defines for philosophy, and this is where Cavell helps us to be feminists and activists—his aim is to show how the socially negligible actually matters, to give a voice to the voiceless, as in *Gaslight*.

Telling, as Cavell often reminds us throughout his writings, is counting (and knowing what counts). The identification of telling and counting, importance and truth, is claimed by the presence of pawnbroking in the depiction of Cavell's early life, and his task in his father's pawnshop— "counting up the monthly interest owed, upon redemption."

> The concepts of grace and of redeeming are only beginning suggestions of the poetry of pawnbroking. Counting, especially counting up the monthly interest owed, upon redemption (I mean upon the pawner's returning with his ticket to redeem his pledge), was another of my responsibilities. Here we encounter certain opening suggestions of the philosophy of the concepts of pawnbroking. The concept of what we count, especially count as of interest or importance to us, is a matter fundamental to how

I think of a motive to philosophy, fundamental to what I want philosophy to be responsive to and to illuminate. Something like the poetry and philosophy caught intermittently in the ideas of redemption and grace and interest and importance (or mattering) was of explicit fascination to me before I stopped working in the pawnshop, the year I graduated high school. The first stories I tried writing were stabs at elaborations of such connections.[15]

In *Little Did I Know*, Cavell states for the first time a connection between these "ideas of redemption and grace and interest and importance (or mattering or counting)." The motif of counting as redemptive is important in Cavell's work—the idea of a literary redemption of language by telling—in *Walden*, or his comments on the perfectionist moment in *It Happened One Night* when Clark Gable makes a very precise account of the sum Claudette Colbert has cost him, which Cavell correlates to the way Thoreau gives an accurate account of the cost of his cabin: "The purpose of these men in both cases is to distinguish themselves, with poker faces, from those who do not know what things cost, what life costs, who do not know what counts."[16] What counts is what matters to us. *Knowing what counts* defines importance and truth by accuracy, *exactness*—these words define Cavell's autobiographical project. To tell things right, to find the right, relevant word (the pitch) is a task that articulates the search for importance, for perfection, and for the right tone as in the passage of *Little Did I Know* about the pieces of coal—"to determine the point at which, if I hit it just right, it would, instead of chipping or crumbling further, split apart cleanly into two intact pieces."

An unseen passage or detail that encapsulates Stanley's method and life is as follows:

After the event of a coal delivery, I would sometimes go down to the basement to look at the new mound of this substance of mysterious origin some of whose black pieces would shine with particular brilliance just then before shoveling had dislodged some of them onto the dirt floor and thrown up recent dust. If, as generally was the case, near the foot of the mound a few isolated large pieces would have tumbled free as the coal was being delivered, I would take the ax standing next to the shovel against a short wooden wall, perhaps part of a small tool shed, and with the blunt end of the ax head, tap the side of a piece at first too lightly to affect it, but then strike with increasing force, to determine the point at which, if I hit it just right, it would, instead of chipping or crumbling further, split apart cleanly into two intact pieces. Evidently I had first seen this effect happen inadvertently. The satisfaction of the sound of the ax tapping the coal, rather as if to test its soundness, and then on lucky occasions the sight of the lump splitting open, perhaps one or both of the halves falling over under its own newly discovered imbalance to rest on a new facet of itself, produced in me a primitive equivalent of the almost silent shout of appreciation with which my mother would greet a perfectly managed musical ornament or cadence, as during the Kreisler recital. In rehearsing the high school dance band I would quite often come up against the ingrained conviction of some of its members that to swing meant never to hit notes exactly on the beat but something like to syncopate perpetually and to bend notes at unpredictable moments, so that I might sometimes say to them roughly, "Don't anticipate the beat here, and don't be tempted to play louder when the notes increase in speed. Just split the notes cleanly and let them fall." But I never confided in them about the ax and the larger pieces of coal.[17]

Cavell's reminds us in *A Pitch of Philosophy*: "there is an internal connection between philosophy and autobiography, that each is a dimension of each other."[18] To tell things right, in context, to find the right, relevant word (the pitch) is a task that articulates the search for importance, and of truth, making awareness of importance part of the task of knowing the world. But it also transforms our ideas of importance. Wittgenstein's point is also that the importance of the grammatical investigation is precisely in this, in "destroying everything great and interesting," displacing our interests, our hierarchies. Here the "fervor" early identified and expressed in Cavell's reading of Wittgenstein (as in *This New Yet Unapproachable America*), its specificity, may be seen, heard, as a refusal of a kind of male (or paternalistic) assertiveness in finding the right words, and the all-too-easy identification of the important with the masculine.

Stanley's tone—with women and men—was never paternalistic, virilistic: he was just sweet and kind. The conversion required in putting aside competing ideas of the important, in destroying our ideas of the important, is the condition for the possibility of a place for women's voices (accomplished in *Pursuits of Happiness* with the emergence of women's voices in conversation, and in *Contesting Tears*). More deeply, Wittgenstein makes it possible to give up, or minimize the importance of, the male/heterosexual tone in language. Cavell was among the first philosophers to give and enforce appropriate attention to women's voice, style, and subjectivity, to pursue "philosophy's aspiration to exchange intimacy without taking it personally."[19] "I suppose that what I am expressing here is the fact that I am from time to time haunted—I rather take it for granted that this is quite generally true of male heterosexual philosophers—by the origin of philosophy (in ancient Greece) in an environment of homosexual intimacy."[20] It is strange that compared to the clearly elegiac, even melodramatic tonality of the many autobiographical moments in Cavell's earlier work—often, but I won't pursue that, connected to the relation to the mother, as at the end of the *Stella Dallas* essay or at the end of *A Pitch of*

Philosophy—and after being among the very first philosophers to give and enforce the appropriate attention to the feminine voice, style, and subjectivity, Cavell finds in *Little Did I Know* (despite the total absence in the book of mention of homosexuality, except about Bette Davis and *Now, Voyager*, an absence to be contrasted with its recurring focus on legendary friendships) this kind of *impersonal intimacy*, thus achieving a nonheterosexual tonality of language that may be sought after in Wittgenstein, and could be at stake in *ordinary* language philosophy. *Little Did I Know* acknowledges importance by pursuing the experience and reading of film in autobiographical writing. Cavell notes, about the ontology of film, that its "source of data" is: "The appearance and significance of just these objects and people that are in fact to be found in the succession of films, or passages of films, that matter to us."[21]

The importance of film lies in its power to make what matters emerge: "to magnify the sensation and meaning of a moment." Film cultivates in us a specific ability to see the too-often invisible importance of things and moments, and emphasizes the covering over of importance in ordinary life.

For importance is essentially what can be *missed*, what remains unseen until later, or possibly, forever. The pedagogy of film is that while it amplifies the significance of moments, it also reveals the "inherent concealment of significance," teaching us:

> If it is part of the grain of film to magnify the feeling and meaning of a moment, it is equally part of it to counter this tendency, and instead to acknowledge the fateful fact of a human life that the significance of its moments is ordinarily not given with the moments as they are lived, so that to determine the significant crossroads of a life may be the work of a lifetime.[22]

What Cavell describes is something else than attention or inattentiveness—it is "an inherent *concealment* of significance, as much as its revelation." Experience reveals itself as defined by our quasi-cinephilic capacity for seeing detail, reading expressions. The structure of expression articulates the concealment *and* the revelation of importance, and such is the texture of life (our life form). This is the difficulty that Cavell describes when he speaks of the temptation of inexpressiveness and of isolation, and shows the essential vulnerability of human experience (another name for skepticism). We experience "the appearance and significance" of things (places, faces, patterns, words), but only afterward, after words.

Knowing Stanley has been such a privilege; we all have the feeling that we spent incredibly important moments with him, conversing, or just hanging out. Now that he is gone, we understand the privilege was that we were perfectly aware that it was important; he taught us to be aware: "an inherent *concealment* of significance, as much as its revelation." Here the structure of expression articulates the concealment *and* the revelation of importance. Such is the texture of our life form.

This is the difficulty or reality that Cavell describes when he speaks of the temptation of inexpressiveness and of isolation, and shows the essential vulnerability of human experience (another name for skepticism, missing the subject): "[T]o persist in missing the subject, which may amount to missing the evanescence of the subject, is ascribable only to ourselves, to failures of our character."[23] Failure to pay attention to importance, it turns out, is as much a moral failure as it is (in Austin's words) a cognitive one. Yet we discover importance not only through accurate and refined perception, but through our suffering and misperception, in other words, through our failures to perceive. Because "missing the evanescence of the subject" is constitutive of our ordinary lives, it is also at the core of writing an autobiography—as well as being the ultimate truth of skepticism. Robert Chodat has analyzed beautifully the expression "little did I know":

> The phrase suggests a moment of being *startled* by such understanding—a realization that our lives extend beyond us, into circumstances that are present all the time yet mostly obscure to us, recognized only through gradual revelation or renewed attention. Little did I know that my colleague could be so witty; little did I know when talking to him that his son had died just last year; little did I know that my next-door neighbor held those political beliefs. And little did I know the range of affiliations, unrecognized commitments, forgotten influences, and obscure desires that have constituted my life.[24]

What I don't know (what I couldn't possibly know) is also part of what I *mean*. It is possible now to reverse the brilliant move made in the opening of *The World Viewed*, where moviegoing is defined as autobiography. Just as in *Little Did I Know*, by telling and detailing scenes and details from his past life in the context of his present life, Cavell finds the words to break the blessing and curse film is the name of, to express the hidden importance of past moments of his life; and to express the hidden importance, or uncanniness, of moments of his life, past and present—"Like childhood memories whose treasure no one else appreciates, whose content is nothing compared to their unspeakable importance for me."[25] The "unspeakable importance" is put before our eyes, reveals itself: "We involve the movies in us. They become further fragments of what happens to me, further cards in the shuffle of my memory, with no telling what place in the future. Like childhood memories whose treasure no one else appreciates, whose content is nothing compared to their unspeakable importance for me."[26]

Acknowledging this consequence of skepticism, this failure, would be "taking yourself seriously." Stanley was serious (he says about his father: "He was a serious man"). Again: we all remember being perfectly aware (at the time) of the importance of these moments with him. Because he took himself, and us, seriously. "I do not, I think, know what people mean when they accuse others, so often and easily, of taking themselves too seriously. Why in the world should one not take oneself with utmost seriousness?"[27] In which sense am I important to myself? *Little Did I Know* answers (finally) the question of *Must We Mean What We Say?*—the question of *my relevance* to myself is the question of "true importance" (if there is such a thing as fake importance, and it is evoked in the same passage—obviously, yes). What sounds like dogmatism (e.g., in the ordinary language philosopher's claims about the uses of language, or about film tastes) is a claim about a cause (such as race, or gender) having to be taken seriously. "I think that air of dogmatism is indeed present in such claims; but if that is intolerant, that is because tolerance could only mean, as in liberals it often does, that the kind of claim in question is not taken seriously. It is, after all, a claim about our lives."[28]

This relevance is something that the great filmwriter, Arnaud Desplechin, has perceived. He uses a passage from Stanley's autobiography (on its last page) in a scene in his wonderful film *Ismael's Ghosts* (*Les fantômes d'Ismaël*, 2017), where the heroin Carlotta (Marion Cotillard) says farewell to her father (László Szabó) at the hospital. It's not an adaptation; these are literally the words of the passage.

"Do you understand me?"

"You mean can I hear you? Yes."

"No, I mean am I making sense to you right now? I know sometimes I get confused."

"You are perfectly clear. Why do you ask?"

"I have to ask you something."

"Ask me."

"Why are these doctors and nurses and the family running in and out of my room as if there is an emergency?"

"You know they had to place a pacemaker for your heart."

"That's what I mean. How old am I?"

"About eighty-three."

"It's enough. It's natural. What is the emergency? If a child is seriously ill, it is an emergency. To run in and out of the room because an eighty-three year old man may die is not an emergency. It is ugly to behave this way."

"They are just doing their job. Placing a pacemaker has become a standard medical procedure."

"You mean I don't have a choice?"

"I don't know."

"Tell them to stop."

"That's not my job."

I remember seeing this film in Stanley's company in Paris two years ago. How lucky is that? Probably Desplechin has best understood what was at stake in *Little Did I Know*, namely, that:

1. "telling one's life ... becomes a way of leaving it ... given that it is a human life."
2. "human death is not natural, confirming the formulation I have come upon so often in my efforts to describe passages of the human life-form, namely, that the human is the unnatural animal."

Short of that, I have, I find, now closing this writing from memory, been drawn to exemplify, still with some surprise, the condition that telling one's life, the more completely, say incorporating awkwardness, becomes one's life, and becomes a way of leaving it. And now that seems to be as it should be, given that it is a human life under question. The news is that this awkwardness, or say, self-consciousness, or perpetual lack of sophistication, stops asserting itself nowhere short of dying. ... (Which suggests that, as throughout the progression of human life, human death is not natural, confirming the formulation I have come upon so often in my efforts to describe passages of the human life-form, namely, that the human is the unnatural animal.)[29]

Maybe because I saw Stanley quite frequently these past few years, including just two months before his death, at his house in Brookline, Massachusetts, his absence still feels like a painful anomaly. It is also certainly because he remained *himself*—gave meaning by his life to the phrase *being oneself*—through to the end, both attentive to detail and fun; and because he teaches us the human importance of being alive and of having a life, one's life. The feeling of being alive, which the early Wittgenstein would have called a species of nonsense, is something Stanley Cavell exemplified so well, and this is why his absence is so unnatural.

Notes

1 Stanley Cavell, *Must We Mean What We Say?* (Cambridge: Cambridge University Press, 1976), xxviii.
2 Stanley Cavell, *Little Did I Know: Excerpts from Memory* (Stanford: Stanford University Press, 2010), 323.

3   J. L. Austin, *How to Do Things with Words* (Cambridge: Harvard University Press, 1975; William James Lectures, 1955), 148. Italics in original.
4   Cavell, *Little Did I Know*, 60.
5   J. L. Austin, "Pretending," *Philosophical Papers*, ed. J. O. Urmson and G. J. Warnock (Oxford: Clarendon Press, 1979), 271.
6   Cavell, "Austin at Criticism," *Must We Mean What We Say?*, 103.
7   Austin, *Philosophical Papers*, 130.
8   Ibid., 124.
9   Stanley Cavell, *Pursuits of Happiness: The Hollywood Comedy of Remarriage* (Cambridge: Harvard University Press, 1981), 204.
10 Cavell, "Austin at Criticism," 103.
11 Cavell, *Little Did I Know*, 325.
12 Ludwig Wittgenstein, *Philosophical Investigations*, ed. G. E. M. Anscombe (Englewood Cliffs: Prentice Hall, 1953), §118.
13 Stanley Cavell, *The Claim of Reason: Wittgenstein, Skepticism, Morality, and Tragedy* (New York: Oxford University Press, 1979/1999), xxi.
14 Stanley Cavell, *Cities of Words: Pedagogical Letters on a Register of the Moral Life* (Cambridge: Belknap Press of Harvard University Press, 2004), 40.
15 Cavell, *Little Did I Know*, 115–16.
16 Cavell, *Pursuits of Happiness*, 5–6.
17 Cavell, *Little Did I Know*, 134–5.
18 Stanley Cavell, *A Pitch of Philosophy: Autobiographical Exercises* (Cambridge: Harvard University Press, 1994), vii.
19 Stanley Cavell, *Contesting Tears: The Hollywood Melodrama of the Unknown Woman* (Cambridge: Harvard University Press, 1996), 158.
20 Cavell, *Contesting Tears*, 159.
21 Stanley Cavell, "What Becomes of Things on Film?," *Themes Out of School: Effects and Causes* (San Francisco: North Point Press, 1984).
22 Cavell, "The Thought of Movies," *Themes Out of School*, 11.
23 Ibid., 14.
24 Robert Chodat, *The Matter of High Words: Naturalism, Normativity, and the Postwar Sage* (New York: Oxford University Press, 2017), 212.
25 Stanley Cavell, *The World Viewed: Reflections on the Ontology of Film* (Cambridge: Harvard University Press, 1971, enlarged edition, 1979), 154.
26 Ibid.
27 Cavell, *Little Did I Know*, 297.
28 Cavell, *Must We Mean What We Say?*, 96.
29 Cavell, *Little Did I Know*, 547.

17

Impression, Influence, Appreciation

STEVEN G. AFFELDT

An initial version of this essay was prepared for a memorial event, "Celebrating the Life and Work of Stanley Cavell," convened in Emerson Hall, Harvard University, November 2018.[1]

EARLY IN MY JUNIOR YEAR AT BERKELEY, Janet Broughton introduced me to the work of Stanley Cavell with a recommendation that, given my interests in both skepticism and Wittgenstein, I read *The Claim of Reason*. When I found myself initially unable to advance with that work, I turned instead to the essays collected in *Must We Mean What We Say?* There was much in those essays too, of course, that was beyond me. And yet, in reading the foreword "An Audience for Philosophy," I knew immediately that I was discovering both a vision of the stakes of philosophy and a voice expressing that vision that resonated deeply with the feelings and aspirations that had led me, the unbelieving son of a fundamentalist Protestant pastor, to its study. By the time I had completed the foreword, a process of formation had begun that continues to decisively shape my sense of philosophy and my attitude toward it. An initial stage of this process was my setting myself to read all of the work of Stanley's I could find—a manageable, but still significant, commitment at that point in the early 1980s. In addition to completing the essays in *Must We Mean What We Say?*, moving on to *The Senses of Walden* and *The World Viewed*, and eagerly devouring the essays on Hollywood comedies and plays of Shakespeare that were then appearing with some frequency in journals such as *Raritan* and *Critical Inquiry*, this commitment included returning to *The Claim of Reason*, which ended up systematically informing my senior honors thesis on the philosophical relevance of Wittgenstein's appeal to "what we do" in *On Certainty*. By the time I had completed the thesis, and with warm encouragement from Warren Goldfarb who was visiting Berkeley during the final semester of my senior year, my fervent hope was to pursue my graduate studies at Harvard and to work with Stanley. (In fact, although I applied to—and was accepted into—most all of the then leading graduate programs in philosophy, I couldn't actually imagine myself happily studying anyplace else.)

In a moment I'll speak more specifically to some of what so powerfully attracted me in Stanley's work both then and now. But I want to say immediately that it is one of my life's great joys that those hopes were not only met but the reality exceeded anything I had imagined. I not only had the pleasure of studying at Harvard and working with Stanley (as well as with Warren Goldfarb and Hilary Putnam most closely among others) but also of becoming dear friends with Stanley and being welcomed into, and befriended by, the entire family. (My experience was by no means unique. The extraordinary kindness and generosity of Stanley and the Cavell family led them to welcome and befriend many of Stanley's students and readers from across the globe. And, since Stanley and Cathleen brought these various friends together, these friends of theirs become friends of one another in turn so that through Stanley and Cathleen a remarkable, and enduring, network of friends was created reaching across generations and locations.) Especially during the eleven years I spent in graduate school (something that, for better and worse, would not now be allowed), I was blessed to spend many hundreds (and more likely thousands) of hours with Stanley. Naturally, plenty of this time was spent in his classes and seminars or in meetings related to my work as one of his teaching assistants or as his research assistant. However, countless hours were also spent together walking the family dog, or strolling the few blocks from the house to collect takeout from the local Chinese restaurant (from which, since we shared the pleasure of routine, we ate an alarming number of meals), or while working over two successive summers to bring some order to the avalanche of books and papers that buried his home office, or sitting on the front stoop during a break from work while I smoked a cigarette and Stanley, having long since quit but positioning himself so as to enjoy my smoke secondhand, told tales of both the pleasures of smoking and the pain of quitting, or, to mention only one more treasured type of occasion, years after leaving Harvard and joined by my wife (and later our young daughter), enjoying a chicken dinner with Stanley and Cathleen on their back deck during which the rhythm of conversation would be punctuated by pauses as the Green Line trolley passed just beyond the backyard.

In light of the riches of my personal experience with Stanley, with the exception of the eulogies delivered at his funeral, in the days immediately following his death I deliberately avoided reading any of the many formal and informal obituaries and remembrances that came my way—many written by, or shared by, friends. Although I welcomed the comfort of companionship in remembrance, I wanted first to allow space for my memories to come without being diverted by the recollections and impressions of others. However, in the event, and to my growing alarm, the kind of communion with my memories, and so with Stanley, for which I had hoped didn't occur. Instead, I suffered a kind of chaos of fragmented memories. Memories came, but only to be immediately interrupted and eclipsed by others so that none brought any past into stable presence. Or, when memories came more calmly, many of those that came struck me as, if not trivial, inconsequential—often enough sweet and full of pleasure, but none seeming to support the impact of Stanley's work and friendship on my life. (One apparently trivial, but actually quite consequential, fragment that kept asserting itself forms my first vivid recollection of Stanley's personal presence. At the close of the second of his Beckman lectures delivered at Berkeley in 1983, and as seen from my vantage in one of the last rows of a packed Wheeler Auditorium, Stanley leaned over the podium and, as though taking the audience into his confidence, remarked: "Next time I'll talk about Heidegger's essay 'The Thing,'" and then, following a brief pause, impishly added, "some of you may have seen the movie."[2] Although my determination to study with Stanley didn't rest solely on my delight in that moment, it did rest, in no small part, on my deep appreciation of the sensibility behind the joke—on Stanley's willingness to weave together the philosophical and the ordinary, the high(brow) culture of European letters and the low(brow) popular culture of Hollywood, as well as on his suggestion of some illicit pleasures and terrors (like and unlike those produced by Hollywood horror films like *The Thing from Another World* [1951]) that the weaving might produce.)

There are, no doubt, several ways in which this symptomatic failure of memory might be accounted for clinically. Beyond recognizing it as a fairly typical expression of shock and grief, I came to think of it as manifesting a resistance to mourning—a resistance that consisted in a refusal to allow memories to settle and be worked through. What is important here, however, is that I found that the condition was relieved by reading Stanley's work. Dwelling with the words on the page and, through them, reexperiencing Stanley's exacting but unlabored modes of attention, his invariably revelatory ways of forming or taking a question, his characteristic ways of unfolding and layering a thought, his depth of seriousness matched by his delightful humor—all of this returned me to my experience of Stanley.

This experience of Stanley's words opening access to my memories of him no doubt has something to do with the character and quality of our friendship—a friendship that was, after all, shaped not only by our shared love of philosophy but also by deep affinities of philosophical sensibility. However, I think it ultimately speaks less to anything unique in my relationship with Stanley than to the kind of integrity that he achieved between his life and his philosophical writing. I mean the idea of integrity here to convey a pair of thoughts. First, without denying the artistry of his writing or the importance of that artistry to its work, the voice and character on the page are, to a remarkable degree, continuous with Stanley's voice and character in ordinary conversation—a fact that is also, to be sure, a function of the artistry he brought to ordinary conversation. Indeed, no small part of the artistry of his writing consists precisely in the intimacy with which his writing conveys a distinctive persona. Even without having met him, in reading the work it's easy to feel that you are coming to know Stanley quite personally. Second, this continuity of voice and character reflects something essential about Stanley's relation to philosophy—I mean the way in which he was continuously engaged in philosophy and yet was never withdrawn from ordinary life. This is integral to the form of ordinary language philosophy lying at the heart of all of his work. For if philosophy is most essentially a mode of attention to our words and actions—to what they are and are not, and to what they mean or fail to mean—then, as Stanley put it in an early essay, "there is no point at which [philosophy] must, or even may, stop."[3] The call for philosophical attention is, and must be, perfectly continuous with the ordinary actions and events of our lives. Stanley often cast this continuity of the call for philosophical attention with each ordinary moment of our lives as a kind of unrelenting and inescapable philosophical demand—picturing the philosopher, in echoes of Socrates and Thoreau, as a kind of hero of watchfulness who is awake when all others sleep.[4] Without wishing to deny the accuracy or force of this image, for me, Stanley's achievement of a deep continuity between his life and his writing is emblematized in the more domestic image of him working at the family's dining room table and so in the midst of the daily life of the household. Of course, Stanley also worked in his large home office and it was exclusively there that he typed or, later, used the computer. But in my time with him, it was much more common to find him sitting at the dining table, with books spread open around him (along with the morning newspapers and assorted mail), filling the pages of his familiar yellow notepads while Ben and David played or watched television in the adjoining living room.

Although my personal crisis of remembrance lifted, in light of the way it lifted through reading Stanley, I want to devote most of the remainder of my reflections here to reading part of a passage from Stanley's work. In addition to allowing me to share the pleasure of the sound and texture of Stanley's writing and its capacity to activate the experience of his presence, this will also allow me to honor Stanley's having taught me (and others, of course) to understand philosophy as a practice of reading. Consider that, although the idea had been present both implicitly and explicitly in much of his earlier work, when Stanley "introduced [himself]" in the second paragraph of *The Claim of Reason* by announcing that he "wished to understand philosophy not as a set of problems but as a set of texts," he was claiming that reading texts is itself a philosophical activity—rather than simply, at best, preparatory to the real philosophical activity of developing theories or solving problems.[5] And as Stanley's readings from across the range of his authorship demonstrate, not only does reading demand the clarity, precision, and rigor of thought traditionally associated with philosophical argumentation, but the practice that he came to call reading as allowing yourself to be read by the text carries the liberating and redemptive power that philosophy has claimed for itself since Socrates.[6]

The passage I've chosen to read is from late in Stanley's autobiography, *Little Did I Know*, and is dated August 11, 2004. I'll note immediately that it isn't on its face one of Stanley's more bravura passages and, apart from some special reason to hold up over it, it might not make a particularly striking impression. That is itself something that interests me about the passage. However, I've chosen this passage precisely because it's about what makes an impression, what impresses us, and how our convictions are shaped by what impresses us. More specifically, the passage begins with Stanley reflecting on the nature of philosophical conviction and how what he calls his "manner" of writing is connected to conviction in his work and it ends with him considering how we, individually, determine what we want of philosophy—how we determine how we want to go on. This struck me, then, as an especially apt passage to consider as part of reflecting on how Stanley's work has shaped my convictions and helped me to determine how I want to go on.

Here, then, is the passage—from which, with pangs of various kinds, I've omitted several parenthetical remarks so characteristic of the ways Stanley modulates a thought and reveals its various stands or strata.

> My manner, so far as I could judge it, or even perceive it, did not seem to me arbitrary or imposed, or put positively, it was the ground and guide of my conviction.—But then that is perhaps the problem, and the reason it is intractable. Shouldn't my philosophical convictions be based on rational argument, not upon personal manner? That seems unarguable.
>
> And yet. Questions, for example, about whether we do or do not know the world as it is, do not present themselves to me as resolvable by argument, anyway by what may be recognized as argument in dissociation from tracing a web of assumptions, pictures, myths, prejudices, cravings, presentiments, intimidations, impositions (all elements of the ordinary) that determine the locus of argument and are not ordered by it. Nor do I suppose questions to be resolvable by argument that concern ... the way the classical empiricist distort or stylize experience. Suppose I say that the classical empiricist idea of experience as made of impressions creates a stylization of the concept of impression, specifically isolating the picture

of making a physical impression ... from that of being (psychologically, sensibly, intellectually, spiritually) impressed. Letting the latter idea, that of being impressed, say, struck, by what you find impressive, continue its palpable relation to the concept of an impression ... ties the idea to that of being interested ..., [to] articulating what matters, what counts. ... The picture of impressions as an unremitting patter upon consciousness makes mysterious what moves the human to utterance, or keeps it silent ....

One can say, in opposition to the suggestion that experience is stylized by empiricists, that the attempt to keep the fullness of the concept of impression makes it unwieldy for scientific purposes. So here philosophizing requires determining what one wants of philosophy. Then how can philosophizing become part of a university curriculum? Can one allow, even encourage, students to determine what it is they want of philosophy? What is the alternative?

The only serious answer to determining the course of philosophizing lies in your relation to the works you care about. And this means to me, in your relation to what allows you to work productively, to think further.[7]

I don't recall this passage standing out for me when I first read it soon after the book was published. These pages of the book were virtually unmarked. And yet, when I came upon it some months ago while rereading the text in connection with a writing project, I was more than struck. In fact, to recall one of Stanley's favorite passages from Emerson's "Experience," I believe that I quite literally clapped my hands in infantine joy. Although my joy crystalized around a specific moment of the passage, it was also importantly a function of realizing that this brief passage about the source and nature of philosophical convictions epitomizes many of the characteristics of Stanley's work that have most decisively shaped my own philosophical convictions. The apparent casualness of the passage disguises a surprising density so that the characteristics of Stanley's work I find epitomized are not all equally obvious. I'll excavate and briefly unfold some of these characteristics, focusing initially on the portion of the passage in which Stanley links, and also distinguishes, the ideas of impression and of being impressed.

Perhaps the most evident feature of this passage, and certainly a first source of my delight and gratitude in rereading it, is simply Stanley's attentiveness to ordinary language—his openness to hearing and his letting us hear, in the quasi-philosophical and quasi-scientific term 'impression,' a "palpable relation" to the ordinary idea of being impressed—of finding something or someone impressive. Part of the pleasure here lies in the power of this particular observation, which I'll turn to next. But it also lies in the way this observation reminds us of the riches that our ordinary language provides and of their philosophical importance. Here, for example, Stanley doesn't argue against the empiricists' picture of experience or assert a philosophical "thesis" regarding the function of being impressed in the constitution of experience. Rather, he takes up the idea that experience is a function of impressions and reminds us that the grammar of 'impression' includes a relation to the idea of our being impressed. In refusing argument and leading us back to grammar, Stanley isn't, of course, asking us to forgo reasons. He is reminding us of the ground of reasons embodied in our ordinary language and confronting us with our (philosophical) temptation to ignore or evade its rigor.

But much of the specific depth of this passage rests on the force of Stanley's grammatical reminder and its implications. In particular, as he elaborates it, the distinction between the classical empiricists' conception of impressions that impinge upon us and what we find impressive is not a matter of the force of the impact—as though it were always what scored us most deeply that we found most impressive. Rather than being pressed upon with great force, Stanley reminds us that to be impressed is to be *attracted* and *drawn toward* something. Both registers of the concept of impression share a focus on our human pliability. But where the empiricist conception of impression focuses on our capacity for being indented, Stanley's attention to our being (psychologically, sensibly, intellectually, spiritually) impressed reminds us of our capacity to expand. To find something or someone impressive, he suggests, is to be drawn out, enlarged, or expanded rather than pressed upon. This is the domain of what Stanley, following Emerson, calls provocation— the awakening and enlivening of our sense of our own capacities, our own interests and desires, by an impressive exemplar. In highlighting this dimension of our capacity to be impressed, Stanley's grammatical reminder calls for a reorientation in our conception of experience and in our relation to our experience—a reorientation that places our interests and desires at the heart of the formation of experience and that challenges us to attend not simply to what impinges upon us but also to what draws us or attracts us.[8]

This call for a reorientation in our conception of experience points toward a third dimension of Stanley's work epitomized in this passage. For to recognize that our experience is structured by the ways in which we are interested and attracted is to recognize that a central philosophical task is to determine our interests—to discover what (truly) draws us, what counts or matters to us, and how it matters. (If the classical empiricist conception of impression makes philosophy's primary task that of discovering the structure of the world outside me based on the imprints that it leaves, here the philosophical task is, in the first instance, to learn about myself and how I am drawn to attend to the world and to the others with whom I share it.) This is a prime example of the kind of philosophical task that leads Stanley to emphasize that philosophy, as he understands it, is not an esoteric discipline examining its own special class of problems, but a practice of giving undivided attention to questions that no one can simply avoid. As he puts it in a memorable formulation, what "makes philosophy philosophy" is "a willingness to ... learn to think undistractedly about things that ordinary human beings cannot helping thinking about, or anyway cannot help having occur to them, sometimes in fantasy, sometimes as a flash across a landscape."[9] At the same time, a great deal of Stanley's work—and especially his work on and from Wittgenstein—involves showing how the task of determining our own interests is at once epistemological, ethical, and political and forms an important nexus of connection among these areas of philosophy.[10]

I can hardly do more than glance down this path here, but the nodal point is Stanley's explication of Wittgensteinian criteria as expressing what counts. Linking the sense of 'counting' as expressing what matters to us (what stands out, interests us, has worth or value for us) and the sense of 'counting' as expressing identity conditions (what determines whether something falls under a concept), Stanley argues that the criteria that tell what things are and that control the application of concepts express the structure of our interests. They reflect what matters to us and the ways in which they matter. Our coming into language and its forms of life turns on our naturally sharing (enough of) this structure of interests and it is through our inheritance of language that we come into ourselves, our world (with all that it includes), and into community with those with whom we are agreed in judgment on what counts.[11]

Wittgenstein's philosophical methods of grammatical investigation and of asking what we would say when raise this inheritance to self-consciousness. They allow us, that is, to come to a more explicit understanding of our criteria—and so of what matters to us and how it matters—as well as of ourselves, our world, and the extent and depth or intimacy of our community with others. This is why Stanley describes these methods as methods for acquiring self-knowledge.[12] These methods also, and importantly, allow us to diagnose what Wittgenstein shows to be our perpetual temptation toward emptiness of speech—where emptiness is understood not as a matter of violating rules of grammar but as a matter of wishing to speak apart from, or without expressing, any interest. For it is only through expressing some interest, revealing what counts for us, that we say anything.

There is, however, a further level to the philosophical task of determining our interests. It is a level beyond that which is achieved through grammatical investigation but it is also importantly epistemological, ethical, and political. At this level, we are not uncertain of our shared criteria or whether and how they apply in a given circumstance. Rather, we are uncertain how we stand with respect to our criteria and to the structure of interests and values they embody. We are unsatisfied with the language we have inherited, restive in our words and in the self, world, and community they grant us. Stanley hits off this experience of dissatisfied restiveness as arising from being asked questions by a child—that is, by one not yet fully initiated into, or not yet fully at home in, our inherited language. The questions he imagines include "Why do we eat animals? or Why are some people poor and others rich? or Do you love black people as much as white people?"[13] Echoing a formulation of Wittgenstein's, Stanley describes this as a level at which "my reasons come to an end and I am thrown back upon myself, upon my nature as it has so far shown itself."[14] It is a kind of crisis in which I am divided against (parts of) my culture and against (parts of) myself. I am uncertain whether I (any longer) agree with the agreements that structure some of our concepts, whether some of the interests that I have inherited with our language are interests that I truly share, or whether they "were merely imbibed by me" in coming into language.[15]

In such a circumstance, Stanley says that "I require … a convening of my culture's criteria, in order to confront them with my words and life as I pursue them and as I may imagine them; and at the same time to confront my words and life as I pursue them with the life my culture's words may imagine for me: to confront the culture with itself, along the lines in which it meets in me."[16] This image of a confrontation of the culture with itself along the lines in which it meets in me suggests a process of discernment through which I seek to determine *my true interests* and, with them, to determine who I am, or want to become, and the structure of the world and community I desire. I (imaginatively) renounce any stable ground and stand alternately inside and outside of myself (and my words and life as I imagine them) and my culture (and the words and life it imagines for me), seeking through the confrontation of self and culture with one another to discover a path or paths to new or altered ground on which I can (more) happily stand. There is no assurance I will succeed, and the stakes of the undertaking are high. I may become lost, unintelligible, to myself and to my culture or I may retreat to my former assurances and seek to put the crisis out of mind. It is in this context that Stanley speaks of philosophy as "the education of grownups" and emphasizes that, for grown-ups, education is not natural growth but change. In recognition of the deep existential stakes in play and the profound difficulty of the change at issue, Stanley characterizes this education as a matter of conversion and remarks that "conversion is a turning of our natural reactions; so it is symbolized as rebirth."[17]

With the emergence of the idea that philosophy is essentially connected with conversion (with a depth of reorientation or a level of human transformation that calls for the concept of conversion), I have reached a point at which my reading of the passage from *Little Did I Know* opens onto matters beyond those contained within the passage itself. In particular, the idea of a philosophical call for conversion takes us, quite directly, to Stanley's work on moral perfectionism and, only slightly less directly, to his insistence on a therapeutic dimension of philosophy.

Although these are two areas of Stanley's work that have most systematically informed my own, I won't discuss them here. Instead, I want to bring these reflections to a close by returning to the experience of

Stanley's impact on my life and work. However, rather than recounting any of its autobiographical details, I will draw upon the experience in order to sketch, at a more general level, a few thoughts about the broader issue of philosophical influence.

In terms of the concepts my reading of Stanley's passage has highlighted, I can say that Stanley's work, and later Stanley himself, impressed me. That is, they spoke to and activated interests and desires that attracted me and drew me toward them. In part my attraction was rooted in ways in which Stanley's work—both its topics and its manner—was connected to philosophical interests and aspirations that I had already begun to form. Some of these were clear to me apart from encountering Stanley's work, but a deeply important source of my attraction to Stanley's work lay in my sense that it was showing me my own interests—helping me to discover or acknowledge interests and aspirations that I didn't quite, or fully, realize I held and granting permission and encouragement to pursue them. And, of course, I was also attracted to the many new directions and possibilities for philosophical thought that Stanley's work opened. In following my attraction to Stanley's work, then, my own interests and aspirations were clarified while, at the same time, the geography of my interests, my sense of philosophy, and my investment in it were also fundamentally altered.

This experience is, of course, familiar to many. For those with a taste for it, to read Stanley's work is to feel—often simultaneously—both that you are discovering reaches of your own interests that you had not recognized or allowed yourself to be drawn by and that your interests are being fundamentally transformed and expanded. This simultaneously clarifying and transformative or expansive power of Stanley's influence is a tribute to the exemplary force of his work. His work is clarifying, at least in part, in its representative "thinking undistractedly about things that ordinary human beings cannot help thinking about" and it is transformative in its extraordinary ability to convey both the interest of the individual topics and objects that happened to occupy him and conviction in his various ways of pursuing those interests.[18] Both of these effects were, surely, part of Stanley's aims in writing. He clearly wanted to return us to ourselves (both to our common human concerns and to our individual interests) and he, no less clearly, meant to recommend the objects of his attention to ours (in the hope that we too might be inspired to take them up) and, more generally, to affect our vision of philosophy—of its nature, importance, methods, and possibilities.

However, this is fraught terrain. Stanley's capacity to awaken interest in the objects/topics that he engaged together with the radical departure from most of professional Anglo-American philosophy that his work represented (a departure marked not only by the range of objects and topics he invited us to explore but also by his call for a new character of personal investment in those objects and topics—allowing them to interrogate our lives and allowing our lives, in turn, to inform our interrogation of them) meant that, for those of us drawn to it, his work could come to represent a kind of horizon for the practice of philosophy. And while this horizon, like any horizon, enables work, it also raises concerns. During my time in graduate school, these concerns were often voiced as fears of professional marginalization—and Stanley himself sometimes expressed such a concern for his students. However, without discounting the reality of that risk, it could also cover a deeper concern—deeper philosophically and personally. Namely, Stanley's extraordinary ability to convey the richness of his interest *and* to present himself as representative (to show those interests to be natural, inevitable, the kinds of things that ordinary humans can't help thinking about) necessarily complicates the distinction between his work helping you to discover your own interests and your being caught by the force of Stanley's fascinating developments of his own. Among those of us who feel the power of Stanley's influence, then, the deeper concern about it might be put this way: Has the force with which we have been impressed by Stanley, been attracted to and drawn by the possibilities of philosophy that he and his work exemplify, enabled us to find and pursue our own (true) interests or have we been caught by its gravitational pull and made satellites circling his star?[19]

In this light, it's understandable that some who have been most powerfully drawn by Stanley's work have also felt a need to move away from it—as though hoping to solve the problem of influence by finding a fallow field to till. (I have certainly felt this temptation and recognize it as a part of what motivated my work on Rousseau—work in which concepts and themes I had acquired through Stanley's work opened illuminating perspectives on a figure that Stanley had not engaged in detail.) But this is obviously no real solution and, in so far as it does nothing to work through the specific form and character of Stanley's influence, it risks leaving the depths and details of the influence insufficiently recognized and acknowledged—to oneself and to others. Furthermore, in my own case, this expedient was hardly workable since too many of my own deepest interests are shared with Stanley. Accordingly, coming to terms with my sense of Stanley's pervasive influence has meant reflecting more generally on the nature of philosophical influence and, among other matters, thinking through what is involved in having an interest and in that interest being mine.

In this thinking too, I've been guided by Stanley's work. To point to only two areas for consideration: the nature of philosophical originality is central to everything that Stanley has done in and from ordinary language philosophy—where the force of a philosophical claim depends upon its *not* being original, in at least one sense, but expressing knowledge that any competent speaker of the language must recognize—and all of Stanley's considerations of the representativeness of the Emersonian or Perfectionist exemplar bear directly on issues of influence and originality.

Here, however, I want to frame a few thoughts by taking off from a passage appearing near the close of "The Availability of Wittgenstein's Later Philosophy."

In this early essay, and, I suspect, partly reflecting his efforts to think through his relationship to his own charismatic teacher, J. L. Austin, Stanley broaches the issue of philosophical influence as a question of discipleship. And strikingly, while he clearly recognizes dangers of discipleship—dangers both philosophical and existential—he does not simply condemn it. Speaking of the depth at which Wittgenstein's writing seeks to influence its readers—a depth that "penetrates past assessment and becomes part of the sensibility from which assessment proceeds"—Stanley remarks that "in asking for more than belief it invites discipleship, which runs its own risks of dishonesty and hostility. But I do not see that the faults of explicit discipleship are more dangerous than the faults which come from subjection to modes of thought and sensibility whose origins are unseen or unremembered and which therefore create a different blindness inaccessible in other ways to cure. Between control by the living and control by the dead there is nothing to choose."[20] It isn't entirely clear how we should take "nothing to choose"—whether it suggests that the choices are equally problematic so there is, literally, no basis for choice or whether, on the contrary, it suggests a clear preference for control by the living. But even if the remark expresses a preference for control by the living rather than control by the dead, Stanley clearly isn't *advocating* for explicit discipleship. More importantly, though, he is also not treating the contrast between the living and the dead as a matter of the present versus the past. The idea of control by the dead speaks to those influences on our modes of thought and sensibility that are not present to us—whether because they have been forgotten, or buried by repression, or simply become part of the unquestioned background or embedded in institutional norms. Rather than advocating for control by the living, then, Stanley is pointing to the ubiquity of influence and emphasizing that influence by the living has the relative advantage that the nature and shape of the influence may more easily be recognized and negotiated—perhaps self-consciously affirmed, perhaps contended with, moderated, or the like. However, control by the dead—by more or less unconscious and ingrained disciplinary norms, by settled questions and modes of response, and the like—is less evident and, therefore, more difficult to recognize as a form of control and to negotiate.

Overcoming control by the living or the dead and achieving control of your own mind—making your interests and your ways of following those interests your own—is not, then, a matter of *escaping* influence. Since influence is ubiquitous (and, in happy cases, to be celebrated), to imagine that you have escaped it is simply to be under control by the dead. Rather, coming into control of your own mind requires moving toward and into your influences rather than away from them. It is a matter of ongoing work of discovering your influences—bringing them into the light of the living—and of assuming responsibility for your interests and for the character of your investments in them.[21]

Although I can't provide here a complete account of what I mean by the work of assuming responsibility for your interests, I want to briefly identify three moments or elements of the idea that I see as constituting core parts of its structure.

In part, then, the work of assuming responsibility is investigative or archeological. It is seeking to discover and to make apparent (to yourself at least) the sources of your interests as well as why those interests draw you—what it is about them that inspires and provokes you, that activates your desire.

In part, it is determinative. It involves, that is, an effort to discover and to acknowledge (to yourself at least) the ways in which your particular constellation of interests and the character of your investments in those interests determine who and what you now are. And this determinative moment also involves an effort to discover and to acknowledge (to yourself at least) the ways in which who and what you now are determines how you take up the interests you hold—how, that is, the development or elaboration of those interests is inflected by your ways of holding them. Neither of these directions of determination is rigid, of course—we remain open to what Emerson calls a "new degree of culture" that can "revolutionize the entire system" of our pursuits.[22] However, this determinative moment does involve acknowledging that new developments will likely take only some forms or directions and will unfold within a specific horizon. This (sometimes chastening) acknowledgment of limits is part of accepting our finitude, part of growing up. But it is also, and equally, a realization of our character.[23]

The final element or moment that I see as central to assuming responsibility for your interests and so coming into control of your own mind is appreciative.[24] 'Appreciation' speaks of a combined cognitive and affective or sympathetic understanding ("I appreciate the difficulty of his situation") and it speaks of a combined intellectual and sensuous enjoyment that is rooted in understanding while also fueling the desire for richer understanding ("I am developing an appreciation for Bluegrass"). 'Appreciation' also speaks of prizing or valuing and so of holding in regard or esteem ("I appreciate the craftsmanship evident in the joinery"). And, the most important dimension of the concept for my purposes here, 'appreciation' speaks of growth or increase in value ("The property has appreciated considerably since they bought it"). In identifying appreciation as a moment in the work of assuming responsibility for your interests, then, I mean to suggest that to hold an interest, to take it on as yours, is to invest yourself in its appreciation. This will involve cultivating the development of your understanding and enjoyment of the interest and doing so because you value the interest and regard it as worth the investment. And it will also involve working to add to, enrich, elaborate, or take the development of the interest further. It is this appreciative moment of assuming responsibility for our interests that I hear in Stanley's concluding thought in the passage I've read from *Little Did I Know*: what determines your course in philosophy, determines what is yours to pursue, is whatever allows you to work productively, to think further—whatever, as I might put it, solicits your appreciation.

Part of what makes *Little Did I Know* a powerful work of moral perfectionism is the extraordinary richness, detail, and systematicity with which it exemplifies Stanley's own work of assuming responsibility for his interests and so coming into control of his own mind—work that he characterizes in terms of achieving his own death and achieving his own birth.[25] He not only recounts many of the pivotal events, episodes, and encounters—the fateful accidents—through which he came to his interests, but he also provides an accounting of how they have determined who he is, have informed his character, and how his character, in turn, shapes his ways of investing in these interests. Further, and importantly, he exhibits his commitment to the daily practices of writing through which he continues to invest in these interests, to cultivate them, and to seek whatever increase he can help them yield. However, in the light cast by *Little Did I Know*, we can see that all of Stanley's work exemplifies the kind of work of assuming responsibility for our interests that I've been outlining. It's what is at stake in his recurrent recounting of how he has come to some topic or text, in his often elaborate and detailed explanations of how and why a topic or text is his to address or to invest in, and in his accounts of how he hopes his contribution to the topic or text will be profitable—productive for his thinking and for ours.

These are at one and the same time forms of what Stanley calls the philosophical and perfectionist demand to make ourselves intelligible (to ourselves and others) and forms of achieving ourselves. They are among the lessons from Stanley, points of his influence, that I will continue to appreciate.

Notes

1 I am grateful to Richard Moran and Cathleen Cavell for their invitation to participate in this wonderful event. I also had the pleasure of presenting portions of these pages as part of the group meeting of the American Society for Aesthetics at the Central Division Meetings of the American Philosophical Association in February 2019. I am grateful to Timothy Gould, the organizer of the session, for his invitation and to Adam Leite, Jerold Abrams, Peter Fosl, and Arata Hamawaki for raising questions that have helped me to think further. I should note that, given the context for which they were originally composed,

these pages are in places explicitly autobiographical and are, throughout, more personal and less formal than a typical academic paper. I am grateful to David LaRocca for his invitation to contribute these pages to the present volume and for his assurance that these features of the paper would be welcome in this context as well.

2 My impression at the time, and in recollection, was that this impish quip was a spontaneous improvisation rather than being included in the text from which Stanley was reading. In any case, it was not included in the published text when the lectures were published in *In Quest of the Ordinary: Lines of Skepticism and Romanticism* (Chicago: University of Chicago Press, 1994).

3 Stanley Cavell, "Existentialism and Analytic Philosophy," *Themes Out of School: Effects and Causes* (Chicago: University of Chicago Press, 1984), 213.

4 See, for example, Stanley Cavell, "Introduction," *Emerson's Transcendental Etudes*, ed. David Justin Hodge (Stanford: Stanford University Press, 2003), 3.

5 Stanley Cavell, *The Claim of Reason: Wittgenstein, Skepticism, Morality, and Tragedy* (New York: Oxford University Press, 1979/1999), 3. The attention drawn by the opening paragraph of *The Claim of Reason* seems to have resulted in this extraordinary second paragraph receiving less attention than it deserves. Having said that he wants to understand philosophy as a set of texts, this paragraph constitutes the beginnings of an examination of the concept of a philosophical text—of what constitutes a text (whether, for example, a text must be written, how long or short it can be, etc.), of what makes a text philosophical (whether it must, for example, contain arguments), and of how different types of texts position us as readers and philosophers. About the matter of what constitutes a text, Stanley takes Descartes to have shown that the self, at least as clearly and distinctly perceived, represents a text and claims that "in philosophy" to find the idea that the self is a text "incredible may well amount to disbelieving that one could oneself contribute a philosophical text," 4.

6 For the idea of reading as allowing yourself to be read, see, for example, Stanley Cavell, "The Politics of Interpretation," *Themes Out of School*. The definitive treatment of this idea is Timothy Gould's *Hearing Things: Voice and Method in the Writing of Stanley Cavell* (Chicago: University of Chicago Press, 1998).

7 Stanley Cavell, *Little Did I Know: Excerpts from Memory* (Stanford: Stanford University Press, 2010), 497–8.

8 Stanley doesn't develop this reorientation in our conception of experience in the passage I'm reading and neither will I. My interest here is less in developing an altered conception of experience than in tracing a few implications of granting a central place for attraction and desire in our conception of experience.

9 Stanley Cavell, "The Thought of Movies," *Themes Out of School*, 8–9.

10 In emphasizing Stanley's work on Wittgenstein, I don't want to obscure the fact that discovering our true interests is also a central axis of his work on both Thoreau and Emerson and, there too, the task is shown to be at once epistemological, ethical, and political. Indeed, this is a point of deep

connection that Stanley traces among these thinkers and each is invoked in parenthetical remarks I have omitted from the passage I am reading. My comments here will be restricted to Stanley's work on Wittgenstein.

11 Stanley elaborates this dependence of language upon "shared routes of interest and feeling" most memorably in a famous passage from "The Availability of Wittgenstein's Later Philosophy."

> We learn and teach words in certain contexts, and then we are expected, and expect others, to be able to project them into further contexts. Nothing insures that this projection will take place (in particular, not the grasping of universals nor the grasping of books of rules), just as nothing insures that we will make, and understand, the same projections. That on the whole we do is a matter of our sharing routes of interest and feeling, modes of response, senses of humor and of significance and of fulfillment, of what is outrageous, of what is similar to what else, what a rebuke, what forgiveness, of when an utterance is an assertion, when an appeal, when an explanation—all the whirl of organism Wittgenstein calls "forms of life."

Stanley Cavell, *Must We Mean What We Say?* (Cambridge: Cambridge University Press, 2002, updated edition), 52.

12 Ibid., 66.
13 Cavell, *The Claim of Reason*, 125.
14 Ibid., 124.
15 Ibid., 125.
16 Ibid.
17 Ibid.
18 An important task, which I cannot undertake here, is to account for both of these dimensions of the power of his writing—to identify and describe, that is, the features of his work on which they rest. The dimensions are linked in that both turn on Stanley's gifts as a critic—his capacity for directing our attention to the object under consideration and to our own experience of the object rather than to him or to his particularity. A few features of his work connected with this critical power include his capacity for illuminating description of the objects to which he attends; his ability to establish suggestive connections among objects/topics and to create constellations among objects/topics in which each energizes the others; his willingness to be provisional and suggestive; and, to note only one further feature of this kind, his production of charged moments of reading/textual interpretation that radiate lines of continuation beyond themselves.
19 I trust it's clear that the concern I'm expressing about Stanley's influence is a form of the danger inherent in the dynamics of attraction to an Emersonian/ Perfectionist exemplar. For if the true object of our attraction to an exemplar is our own as yet unrealized possibilities, the danger is that our attraction will become fixed to the exemplar himself—that we will regard the other not as an exemplar (which is necessarily connected to us and our possibilities) but

as a kind of apotheosis that we should devote ourselves to celebrating. The sometimes dizzying turns and reversals of Emerson's "Uses of Great Men" are, largely, determined by his efforts to chart the forms of this danger while also providing assurances against it.

20   Cavell, "Availability of Wittgenstein's Later Philosophy," 71–2.

21   To say that this work is necessarily ongoing is to acknowledge that we are always, in various ways and at various levels, subject to influences both living and dead and, hence, there are always influences of which we are, to varying degrees and for various reasons, unaware. The point, however, is to work toward clearer self-understanding and the assumption of greater responsibility.

22   Ralph Waldo Emerson, "Circles," *Essays and Lectures* (New York: Library of America, 1983), 408.

23   Each of these first two moments is wonderfully captured in a set of instructions suggested by Nietzsche in the opening section of "Schopenhauer as Educator." Beginning from a perception that we are lost to ourselves, not living our own lives, and yet that we desire to be "responsible to ourselves for our own existence" and "the true helmsman of our existence," Nietzsche asks, "But how can we find ourselves again?" and, in response to this question, offers the following admonition: "Let the youthful soul look back on life with the question: what have you loved up to now, what has drawn your soul aloft, what has mastered it and at the same time blessed it? Set up these revered objects before you and perhaps their nature and their sequence will give you a law, the fundamental law of your own true self." "Schopenhauer as Educator," *Untimely Meditations*, trans. R. J. Hollingdale (Cambridge: Cambridge University Press, 1983), 128–9.

24   The concept of appreciation, as I am using it here, bears comparison with the concept of inheritance as it figures in the title of this volume. Cavell often speaks of his work with and from Wittgenstein, Emerson, and Thoreau as inheriting, or seeking to inherit, their work. In doing so he registers that he is seeking to accept and come into possession of their gift, their bequest, but also that he is assuming responsibility for passing on the inheritance by continuing the work in his own way. I am grateful to David O'Connor for conversations that have helped me to see the specific importance of appreciation in this context. O'Connor has frequently emphasized that the measure of our inheritance of a writer/thinker is less a matter of our *application* of the work than of our appreciation of it—where the concept of appreciation includes all of the elements I will note.

25   In the sense in which Stanley uses these ideas, they are quite closely linked. Achieving your birth speaks of coming into, claiming, your identity, your (own) life and that is the condition for being able to achieve your (own) death. The following couple of passages from *Little Did I Know* are especially relevant. In explaining his decision not to structure his autobiography as a straightforward chronological narrative, Stanley remarks:

> Such a narrative strikes me as leading fairly directly to death without clearly enough implying the singularity of this life, in distinction from the

singularity of all others, headed in that direction. So the sound of such a narrative would I believe amount to too little help to me or others. What interests me is to see how what Freud calls the detours on the human path to death—accidents avoided or embraced, strangers taken to heart or neglected, talents imposed or transfigured, malice insufficiently rebuked, love inadequately acknowledged—mark out for me recognizable efforts to achieve my own death. (4)

And in speaking of the stakes he placed on achieving overwhelming success on the PhD qualifying exams since they represented for him a ratification of his move from a life of music to a life of philosophy, Stanley says:

I was no longer asking for admittance but for confirmation that I had found what I wanted to become of my life, the basis on which I would be able—as Plato and Aristotle both have ways of saying—to choose my (next) life. The issue for me was not to prove that this further life was better than another, but to prove that it was mine, that I was born to it, that I was born. (284)

18

Taking an Interest in Interest

RICHARD DEMING

He is bequeathing it to us in his will, the place of the book and the book of his place. He leaves us in one another's keeping.
—STANLEY CAVELL, *The Senses of Walden*

RECENTLY, AT ONE OF THOSE LONG PROFESSIONAL DINNERS with colleagues and visitors that writers and academics so often find themselves attending, I was asked in reference to my work, "How do you move from Ralph Waldo Emerson to movies?" Often such a question seems motivated by a pervasive suspicion of cross-disciplinary work, a sense that it is merely a breezy and perhaps trendy dilettantism rather than serious intellectual engagement. My usual answer for that kind of question is a demure sidestep: "I'm profligate in my preoccupations." This particular night, however, the question didn't come across either as disdain or as passive-aggressive judgment; it was disarmingly earnest. For that reason, I confess that I didn't have an answer at hand. It isn't often that I don't have some way, however tentative, of explaining why I do things—decades of self-analysis as well as time spent "on the couch" have made me generally attentive to my conscious and unconscious motivations. Nevertheless, for a minute I was speechless. I couldn't offer a clear rationale that justified and explained how these points of investigation actually were for me in dialogue.

To stall, I immediately offered models, immediately gave the names of some of my intellectual heroes: Richard Wollheim, Arthur Danto, George Steiner (to name a few). Even if these wouldn't make obvious connections, they would offer examples in defense of capaciousness. These are philosophers who, in different ways, trace lines of thought no matter where they traverse boundaries of method and discourse. The person with whom

I was chatting is an art historian by training and an archivist by profession and these names, other than Danto, did not quite seem to signify to her. I then mentioned Cavell, and said specifically, he was a philosopher who showed that Emerson, old films, Fred Astaire's dancing, and skepticism were all interrelated insofar they all flow into and from the life, this human life, that we daily live, and so such subjects are fair game, so to speak. More than casting around for worthy topics, what stands as most important is finding one's way to pressing questions. It is not exactly enough that I simply am interested in the topics, but that interest serves as a point where attention takes root deeply enough to take the focus of attention seriously. I mentioned how Cavell, in the essay "The Thought of Movies," cites a passage from the novelist Henry James's "The Art of Fiction" wherein we find the platitude to which James himself points: "Try to be one of those people on whom nothing is lost."[1] That line rhymed with a bit of ongoing advice Cavell says his father was quick to give: "you can learn from anybody."[2] We might describe that widening of attention as an active generosity, yet it is self-serving insofar as the broadened receptivity means there are more ideas, possibilities, more potentialities to work with and from. Cavell's own body of work provided a kind of permission to take seriously the idea that there is something to be learned from anything, if we give ourselves to deep, careful consideration of it. Offering Cavell's name as a form of context did the trick in that my interlocutor knew him as a representative figure, even though ultimately it wasn't an answer that I gave her so much as an analogy. The only answer I could offer was that my interests came to me before I saw in them something to write about.

My own love of both Emerson's essays as well as American films, not to mention stand-up comedy, photography, and other subjects, didn't come from Cavell. Indeed, these interests—as well as literature and then, eventually, philosophy—were things that had, from early on, been generative possibilities for understanding or at least acknowledging the warp and woof of my own subjectivity. Whatever was to be found would be a way of understanding not only my subjectivity but subjectivity broadly conceived. In Emerson I had found, even before I had such conscious sensibility of what I was looking to find, a thinker who wrestled with authenticity and argued for art and action as a way of reading the world by means of an active engagement of its terms as revealed by—as realized in—its materials. Emerson assures us that in looking at the things of the world, one sees not just the things but also one's own act of looking. In that I have long wrestled with depression, the idea that an attention to how things such as events, objects, and even my very environment were shaped by my own acts of perception (rather than necessarily the other way around) offered a kind of imperative of hope. If I came to be conscious of how I perceived things, I would be able to respond with new or deepened awareness of the world and of other people and my relationships to such things. I would, in other words, be responsible to and for my responses. In *Nature*, Emerson puts it this way:

> Yet it is certain that the power to produce this delight, does not reside in nature, but in man, or in a harmony of both. It is necessary to use these pleasures with great temperance. For, nature is not always tricked in holiday attire, but the same scene which yesterday breathed perfume and glittered as for the frolic of the nymphs, is overspread with melancholy today. Nature always wears the colors of the spirit. To a man laboring under calamity, the heat of his own fire hath sadness in it. Then, there is a kind of contempt of the landscape felt by him who has just lost by death a dear friend.[3]

As Emerson indicates, delight and melancholy are both indwelling rather than caused by material things. In some ways, this understanding that one's own mood or spirit shapes the world—that anyone of us can say at any moment, as Emerson puts it in his essay "Character," "I am always environed by myself"—could lead to despair, that is, to the resignation or even shame that "it's my own fault things are like this."[4] For a depressive, that is no small threat. On the other hand, from that perspective arises the possibility of an alternative, one that suggests that if I change my thoughts, my ideas, if I change myself, the world I live in will change as well. This speaks for the creative and potentially recurring *re*creative power of the imagination in terms of perception.

In his journals, Emerson describes the potential power of the imagination and insists that it helps shape the reality within which one dwells, if we think of "reality" as the order we bring to, the sense we make out of, the materiality around us. "There are two powers of the imagination, one, that of knowing the symbolic character of things and treating them as representative; and the other ... is practically the tenaciousness of an image, cleaving unto it and letting it not go, and, by the treatment, demonstrating that this figment of thought is as palpable and objective to the poet as is the ground on which he stands, or the walls of houses about him."[5]

We could take this to suggest that the imagination finds a capacity for meaningfulness in things and then forges an association of a particular meaning to a given thing with such insistence that the association comes to feel intractable. Given the strength of that insistence, it is not, then, merely whim or fancy that can get us to change perception, even or especially one's own perception, but rather what is required is an active reeducation. It is in this sense that perhaps we can understand Cavell's characterizing philosophy as "education of grown-ups." Such a conception necessitates that education, self-formation, needs to be ongoing and not become fixed perspective. We have to find a way, Emerson's Romantic tendency will posit, to see anew in order to be freed from the habitus of habit, or at least to be able to see the most ordinary things with vivid experience and detail because even there significance is waiting to be found—waiting, paradoxically, right where each of us have left that significance to be found.

As powerful as that thinking has been for me, Emerson, somewhat notoriously, does not often tie such claims to specifics, and Cavell, despite how abstract he can be, no matter how baroque his prose can turn, looked to particular occasions and sites for tracking thought in a way that was more than compelling to me. It felt liberating as well as illuminating. Cavell, for one, helped show that philosophy need not be—perhaps ought not to be—a closed discourse, but could encompass a range of occasions of experience as being worthy of sustained attention. What struck me from the very first time I began reading him was Cavell's investment in the proposition, as Emerson describes it in "The Poet," that "[things] admit of being used as symbols, because nature is a symbol, in the whole, and in every part."[6] If this is the case, anything that is held long enough within the field of attention, analytic attention, could be plumbed and tested for what it might be made to signify. These objects of attention need not be grandly philosophical thought experiments and subjects, but the stuff of everyday life or, perhaps more to the point, might be the language we use to express our relationships to and with everyday objects. In that, Cavell's method of philosophy echoed a psychoanalytic approach, without, however, also resorting to pathologizing the subject of inquiry.

In light of this, Cavell, at least in my reading, gave a license for finding how one's life was always to be intertwined with philosophical issues. The ordinary could thus be revelatory, if its complexities were taken up. I have in mind a very particular moment among Cavell's range of books and essays, one that occurs in his memoir *Little Did I Know*; it is a moment that I find haunting and seems to bear out what I have been saying about Cavell's methods. Whenever I visited his home in Brookline and the weather was accommodating, we would walk over to a nearby Japanese restaurant for lunch. It was one of his usual haunts, especially when he had visitors. On one such walk, we discussed how he was in the midst of writing his memoir and what it felt like for him to be not only recalling memories but actually reimmersing himself in them to such a degree that particular moments opened themselves up as insight and in so doing, to use Emerson's language, "admit of being symbols." One memory from his childhood, from when he was about seven, that he described for me as we talked struck me as particularly compelling and it turned out to be, as far as I could remember it, almost word for word how it appeared in the book itself.

> I evidently kept my feelings to myself and wandered around trying to take an interest in the combination of familiar and strange objects in the living room. I recognized an ornamental object on a table at the side of the sofa, a purple glass bowl, somewhat wider but less deep than a drinking

tumbler, set into a molded dull silver stand and covered with a dome top of matching silver inset with glass purple panels. I lifted the silver dome off the bowl to discover that it was filled with small chocolate-covered mint wafers whose tops were sprinkled with tiny white dots of hard candy, a treat I loved to sample when these used to fill this container in anticipation of company coming to the old house. I noticed that I was not alone in the room. My father was standing silently in the semi-dark at the other end of the sofa, apparently looking out of a window. I do not know if it would have crossed my mind before then that I had almost never been in a room alone with him, indeed, that I knew him much less well than I knew everyone else who had lived in the house I grew up in.[7]

Already the father is a looming, threatening presence. He himself is familiar yet unknown. The story continues:

As I took one of the speckled wafers from the purple bowl, I said aimlessly, but somehow to break the silence with my father, "I didn't know we had these here." He lurched at me, wrenched the dome top and the wafer out of my hands, and said in a violent, growling whisper, "And you still don't know it!"

Concluding the anecdote, Cavell assigns to this encounter a portentous emotional and psychological significance: "This is the moment I described as dating my knowledge that my father wanted me dead, or rather wanted me not to exist." Those must have been some mints.

In part, this memory stuck in my own mind somewhat ironically. Whenever I would visit Cavell, I would be struck almost anew by the fact that I lived for a time just two blocks or so from his house on Monmouth Court. Maybe a little over a decade before I had ever read him, before I had ever even heard his name, I was living in a small apartment just off Kenmore Square in Boston. At the time, I was a financially and emotionally struggling musician. The feeling would come over me as I rang the doorbell that it is not only possible but in fact probable that we passed each other on the street numerous times back then. How was I to know that years later, I would read every book by some stranger who shopped and ate where I shopped and ate? The feeling that the line "I didn't know this was here" communicated would resonate poignantly with me whenever I thought of that onetime proximity of which I had once been so unaware.

We shared, respectively, an early background of a serious study of music, and we both turned away from it because of a profound interior crisis. That similar experience fueled my wondering about what might have happened had I met him when I was that musician gigging around Boston. Perhaps he could have served as an early model, maybe even a mentor, for making my own transition. As he so often mentioned, Freud was the first "philosopher" to whom he turned, and it was Freud who helped him make the transition from music to his new life trajectory. Mine, as it turned out, was Emerson. I note with interest that that I don't make Cavell into a father figure, either negatively or positively. Perhaps he is, symbolically, the bowl that encloses the mints (which actually are my own favorite flavor). Without the bowl, there is no discovery and in the story, it is the discovery rather than the mints that is the source of pleasure.

Freud's providing the early foundation for Cavell's approaches to thinking philosophically is evident even in the passage from *Little Did I Know* that I have cited. For instance, we can see in Cavell's description the archetypal Oedipal agon between father and son.[8] Yet, what is intriguing is the very idea that the memory can be a text to be read and interpreted by others, and that this rests on the idea that it is not only the unknown but also the familiar that can reveal new things to us. Cavell shows this by means of analogy in his description of the dish that young Stanley, in his exploration of the strange and familiar, discovers to be filled with candies. Evidently, academic discourse needs to be reminded of this fecundity of personal, subjective experiences if it is to be of value beyond the parameters of the academy. Or, as Thoreau puts it in the opening of the chapter titled "Reading" in *Walden*, "My residence was more favorable, not only to thought, but to serious reading, than a university; and though I was beyond the range of the ordinary circulating library, I had more than ever come within the influence of those books which circulate round the world, whose sentences were first written on bark, and are now merely copied from time to time onto linen paper."[9]

This acknowledgment of what anecdote can offer enacts the way that a relatively banal memory itself is a narrative that can be a vehicle for larger emotional and perhaps even philosophical resonance. In this case, the memory of this volatile encounter with his father indicates for Cavell a new context for their relationship. The moment has something to say about a boy's realization at some level of the need to break free from the limiting authority of a parent, and that this break is a necessary part of the maturation process. Yet more broadly, the anecdote offers a metaphor for the process of analysis, in that we can read it as illustrating not only that exploration of the familiar can yield surprises and insights *and* reveal what was always available yet unknown but also that there is a force within us that seeks to deny that revelation, to repress any insights that come from that realization. In Cavell's story, the father then is an external force as well as an internalized one. That internal force of limitation, repression, and self-denial needs, finally, to be acknowledged if it is to be ever overcome precisely because that repression seeks to overwhelm the grounds of that knowledge. In Cavell's anecdote, the power of authority is represented in the form of the parent who proclaims he knows better than the child what the child knows. The violent growl underlines that the threat is real and that the power seeks to negate opposition by any means it needs to employ. This threat is certainly how political power works; this is how patriarchy sustains itself. Yet as we internalize these paradigms, that fear of change, that wish to please a parent, that insistence on the preservation of a self as it is plays out in that scene that Cavell describes in regards to the father's response, all begin to police one's subjectivity. To a certain extent, this desire to overcome that dialogue of the self with self- and other-imposed limitation, that ironic and ironizing negotiation with the very process of repressing an unearthed knowledge about where one lives could lead us to think about Cavell's ideas about the fraught nature of skepticism that denies the very world within which we live. No wonder that this memory fixed itself in Cavell's mind: it offers us a way into the very heart of his thinking.

I want to be quick to say that what interests me is not necessarily what this event meant to Cavell in terms of his emotional life. The personal element matters to the extent that I knew him, of course. More abstractly, however, yet more generally valuable is the ways that it provides a self-reflexive text by which we can read how we locate something (an event, an object) as being able to hold meaning and then how we determine what it seems to represent. As Cavell himself writes in an essay on the relationship that psychoanalysis shares with philosophy, "In Freud's practice, one human being represents to another all that that other has conceived of humanity in his or her life, and moves with that other toward another all that that other has conceived of humanity in his or her life, and moves with that other toward an expression of the conditions which condition that utterly specific life."[10] Cavell as a reader, as a critic, as a philosopher, reads his own memory and determines its significance, thereby converting it into a text that his readers then in turn read and interpret. By way of the "utterly specific," we can glean the shape of the larger conditions of the utterly human conditions by which we can recognize one another.

There is a perspective that would argue that analyzing a bit of autobiographical writing is presumptuous and even appropriative, yet in bracketing off the specific personal associations we are left with—or given, depending on one's view—a text with which to work. If it is only a matter for Cavell himself to recall and interrogate, what value would it have to others? What are we to gain from it? This last question seems to me tied to how we inherit not only an idea or concept but actually also how we might determine the process for how to inherit—that is, learn and/or learn from—approaches to interpretation. Tied up in this inheritance and the intersection of psychoanalysis and philosophy are thorny philosophical questions of ethics (what is the text of another's life to me?) and epistemology (what value can be attached to the interpretation of another's life experience and/or psychological moments?).

I am brought back then to that opening question about what the link between and among my interests might be. To a certain extent, I perhaps cannot actually answer such a question. It may be better to see them as places on a map rather than a unified field of inquiry. What is being mapped is a large enough question unto itself—a map of the mind trying, as it can, where it can, to find itself. This is something I have gained in reading and rereading Cavell's books and essays, in remembering e-mails and conversations. In Cavell's work, again and again, that attempt to burrow into the ordinary, however determined, is propelled by the sense that interest is a beginning of knowledge, and, like love, is an action, revealed through its active expression, and thus never finds its conclusion, but opens ever outward, bringing everything before the world's astonished and astonishing eyes.

Notes

1 Stanley Cavell, *Themes Out of School: Effects and Causes* (San Francisco: North Point Press, 1984), 6.

2 Ibid., xii.

3 Ralph Waldo Emerson, *The Collected Works of Ralph Waldo Emerson, Vol. 1: Nature, Addresses, and Lectures*, ed. Robert E. Spiller and Alfred Riggs Ferguson (Cambridge: Belknap Press of Harvard University Press, 1971), 10–11.

4 Ralph Waldo Emerson, "Character," *The Collected Works of Ralph Waldo Emerson, Vol. 3: Essays: Second Series*, ed. Alfred Riggs Ferguson, Joseph Slater, and Jean Ferguson Carr (Cambridge: Belknap Press of Harvard University Press, 1983), 58.

5 Ralph Waldo Emerson, *The Journals and Miscellaneous Notebooks of Ralph Waldo Emerson*, vol. 9, ed. Ralph H. Ort and Alfred Riggs Ferguson (Cambridge: Belknap Press of Harvard University Press, 1971), 369–70.

6 Ralph Waldo Emerson, "The Poet," *The Collected Works of Ralph Waldo Emerson, Vol. 3: Essays: Second Series*, ed. Alfred Riggs Ferguson, Joseph Slater, and Jean Ferguson Carr (Cambridge: Belknap Press of Harvard University Press, 1983), 8.

7 Stanley Cavell, *Little Did I Know: Excerpts from Memory* (Stanford: Stanford University Press, 2010), 18.

8 James Conant offers an incisive reading of the symbolic agon within this passage from Cavell's memoir in "The Triumph of the Gift over the Curse in Stanley Cavell's *Little Did I Know*," MLN, vol. 126, no. 5, 2011, 1004–13.

9 Henry David Thoreau, *Walden and "Resistance to Civil Government,"* ed. William Rossi (New York: Norton Critical edition, 1992), 67.

10 Stanley Cavell, "Psychoanalysis and Cinema: Moments of *Letter from an Unknown Woman*," *Contesting Tears: The Hollywood Melodrama of the Unknown Woman* (New York: Columbia University Press, 1992), 97.

19

Philosophy and Autobiography

TORIL MOI

Remarks given at a memorial event, "Celebrating the Life and Work of Stanley Cavell," convened in Emerson Hall, Harvard University, November 2018.

I AM GRATEFUL TO CATHLEEN CAVELL and Dick Moran for inviting me to speak here as an interloper, a literary critic among philosophers. Before I begin, I must explain that I come from Norway. I studied at the University in Bergen, and lived in Oxford for a decade, before I ended up at Duke around 1990.

Stanley Cavell once asked me if I remembered what text first attracted me to his work. I certainly did: "Philosophy and the Arrogation of Voice," the first of the three essays making up *A Pitch of Philosophy: Autobiographical Exercises*. He was surprised: he hadn't met anyone who had come to his philosophy through that essay. And no wonder. For a newcomer in Cavell's world, "Philosophy and the Arrogation of Voice" is almost impossible to read. It explicitly sets out to do a "recounting" of some of Cavell's work. To someone who missed the original "counting," this makes it both forbidding and foreboding. On my first reading, I only understood the odd sentence here and there. But that was enough. The essay grabbed hold of me and wouldn't let me go. It convinced me that this man, this Stanley Cavell, had something to say, something I desperately needed to hear.

In my hardback copy of *A Pitch of Philosophy*, I have written the date "September 1994." The book was published on June 20, 1994. This is the first book by Cavell I ever bought, and I clearly bought it as soon as it was published. Why?

In September 1994, I was beginning my first sabbatical ever. I was forty, had written a couple of books, one on feminist theory and the other on Simone de Beauvoir, and I was looking for a new departure, a different way to think about feminism, and about literature too. That year would turn out to be decisive. I was lucky enough to be at the National Humanities Center at the same time as Dick Moran, George Wilson, and Sarah Beckwith. We had a fantastic reading group on "the everyday." I can't remember reading "Philosophy and the Arrogation of Voice" in that group. But after reading the usual suspects—Bourdieu, Lefebvre, Certeau—we began to read Wittgenstein, and some of Cavell's early essays, and my intellectual life changed forever.

The Pitch

That this text would be so decisive for me was not self-evident. I was not a philosopher. I didn't plan to become one either. I just wanted to think forcefully and clearly about things that matter to me.

What follows is an adventure story: the story of the adventure of reading "Philosophy and the Arrogation of Voice." The book title—*A Pitch of Philosophy: Autobiographical Exercises*—struck me as opaque. Was philosophy the kind of thing one could "pitch"? And if so in what sense? In the preface, Cavell writes that he first wanted to call the book *Trades of Philosophy*, hoping that people would understand that "trades" had to do with "trade winds." But apparently they didn't. He decided to use the idea of "philosophy's pitch" instead. That idea, he writes, takes on "music and baseball and vending."—Music, baseball, vending—that helped. At least a little. There isn't much about vending in the book, unless I am supposed to count the references to his father, who owned a pawnshop and had an unusual talent for storytelling. But maybe it simply means that Stanley Cavell himself means to pitch philosophy, make us take it up, and do something with it. If that was the idea, he succeeded with me.

The themes of pitch and ear, music and hearing, run through the essay. As a child, Stanley ran out in the street to retrieve a ball, and was hit by a car. The accident damaged his ear, and when he was a young man, the ear prevented him from joining the military. His mother, an outstanding piano player, had perfect pitch. But Stanley did not. Pitch and hearing point to attunement, and so to Wittgenstein's *Übereinsstimmung*, and the thought of sharing a language, sharing a world. In the last chapter of the book, "Opera and the Lease of Voice," Cavell returns to pitch, as in singing. And of course, opera conjures up the idea of Ingrid Bergman's "cogito aria" in *Gaslight*, in an essay Cavell first published a few years before he wrote *A Pitch of Philosophy*.

Throughout the essay, Cavell gives voice to his own yearning to *hear differences*. At the very end of the essay, he describes a moment in Ernest

Bloch's music theory class at Berkeley, when Bloch played a short piece by Bach twice, but the second time "with one note altered by a half step from Bach's rendering" (49). "You hear that? You hear the difference?" Bloch would say, full of excitement (50). If you didn't hear it, you could never be a musician. But Stanley Cavell did hear it. Maybe that's why, in the end, he felt free to leave the thought of a career in music and take up philosophy instead.

But what about baseball? Baseball is not widely played in Norway. In fact, it is not played in Norway at all. And of all the American sports, baseball turns out to be the one I remain utterly incapable of understanding. To give you an idea of my ignorance, I will confess that for a long time I thought the pitcher was on the same team as the guy with the bat. To me, then, the baseball connection simply signaled that there was something "American" about the book.

But there was more. For after mentioning music, baseball, and vending, Cavell writes that the pitch of philosophy speaks "not darkly, of a determined but temporary habitation and of an unsettling motion that befit the state of philosophy as a cultural fact always somewhat at odds with philosophy on its institutional guard" (ix). To me, this suggests not just baseball pitching (the unsettling motion) but also the pitching of a tent (the temporary habitation). Cavell was telling me that the kind of philosophy he cared about was on the move, looking to escape the institutional inertia that always threatened to pin it down. This was the kind of philosophy I—who was not a philosopher at all—could respond to.

Philosophy and Autobiography

So much for the pitch. But what got me hooked? On the first page of the book's "Overture" I read that philosophy and autobiography are dimensions of one another. That philosophers don't know anything others do not know, that an education in philosophy is one that prepares us to recognize that "we live lives simultaneously of absolute separateness and endless commonness, of banality and sublimity" (vii).

These themes resonated with me. For if Cavell had made Emerson and Thoreau his tutelary spirits, I had made Simone de Beauvoir mine. And the themes of human separation, the intertwinement of life and philosophy, of autobiography and philosophy are fundamental to Beauvoir. In the preface to the second volume of her memoirs, *The Prime of Life*, she wonders whether there is something egocentric about writing about one's own life: "Not so," she replies, "if an individual—Samuel Pepys or Jean-Jacques Rousseau; a nonentity or a genius—reveals himself sincerely, almost everyone will find that they too have something at stake. It is impossible to shed light on one's own life without at some point also illuminating the lives of others" (translation heavily amended).

By the end of that same first page, Cavell was writing about philosophy's "arrogant assumption of the right to speak for others" (vii–viii). Now *that* spoke to me! For back in 1994, I felt I was drowning in the kind of feminist identity politics in which one could get the impression that every utterance had to be prefaced by long identity strings. Feminists would endlessly rehash the idea that to speak for others was always illicit, always an attempt to subsume the voice of other women under one's own, which led to the further idea that the only solution would always be to speak only for oneself: Not just "speaking as a woman, I ...," or "speaking as a Norwegian woman, I ..." but "speaking as an upwardly mobile rural Norwegian woman in voluntary exile, I ...," and so on. But as Beauvoir clearly saw already in 1949, in *The Second Sex*, if a woman takes that route, she gives up on her claim to simply be speaking the truth. Cavell was right to say that to do philosophy one has to arrogate to oneself the right to speak for all. Now I truly was hooked.

A few pages later I read: "The autobiographical dimension of philosophy is internal to the claim that philosophy speaks for the human, for all; that is its necessary arrogance. The philosophical dimension of autobiography is that the human is representative, say, imitative, that each life is exemplary of all, a parable of each; that is humanity's commonness, which is internal to its endless denials of commonness" (10–11). How true, I thought, and how genuinely democratic! But at the same time I couldn't forget Beauvoir's analysis of how patriarchy makes it impossible for women to gain access to the universal. How hard it is for a woman to be seen as representing the human. Eventually, I went on to write two long essays about all this, called "What Is a Woman?" and "I Am a Woman." But back in 1994, all I knew was that by page 11 in *A Pitch of Philosophy*, I realized that there was no looking back. I needed to understand what kind of philosophy this was, understand the ideas, and the ways of thinking that could lead this man, Stanley Cavell, to such insights.

But there was more. For "Philosophy and the Arrogation of Voice" circles around the theme of access to philosophy. There are fathers blessing sons, giving them their inheritance, or refusing to. And sons choosing their own fathers, claiming the inheritance they needed. And the need to feel authorized to speak, and the discovery that one never is. Or rather: that every one of us is as authorized to speak as anyone else. That all we can do is to arrogate to ourselves the right to speak. But this must surely be true for women too. But who will bless women? Give women their inheritance? These are questions with rich implications for feminist theory.

In short, I could see that this essay was about something of the greatest importance to me as a woman writing in a foreign language, namely: How does one find the courage to speak one's mind? Cavell writes: "Writing philosophy is for me finding a language in which I understand philosophy to be inherited, which means telling my autobiography in such a way as to find the conditions of that language" (38). The story of the struggle to find one's way into philosophy, the struggle to find one's philosophical voice, is a struggle to find a language—a point I took rather literally. But the story of that struggle is also one's intellectual autobiography.

Trying to tell his story, Cavell launches into some rather convoluted invocations of Emerson and Thoreau. I mean convoluted to me, who hadn't read a word of either of them. I didn't understand what Cavell was saying about them. But I understood what he was *doing*: he was looking for a tradition he could inherit as a specifically *American* philosopher. Some of the passages in "Philosophy and the Arrogation of Voice" that connect to this theme almost drove me to despair. There is, for example, a long and opaque sequence about Derrida, which segues into something about Nietzsche, after which Cavell returns to Derrida to pick a fight about how to read a sentence in Nietzsche's *Ecce Homo*. Eventually he returns to Hamlet and Antigone, but not in ways I could easily warm to. Just as I was wondering whether I could stand any more of this, Cavell made me sit up and take note again, by asking the question that was on my mind: "Why, under what conditions, might anyone care about Emerson and Thoreau authorizing a stake in Nietzsche?" (46). Yes, exactly.

Cavell explains that he finds in Emerson and Thoreau an openness to both the German and English traditions of philosophy and a freshness and originality that is all their own. He hopes they one day will be recognized as "reticent, belated founders of some eventual international philosophical culture," talks about their "problematic of the discovery of America," and declares that the human "quest for home" and the "human fact of immigrancy" belong together as "aspects of the human as such" (47).

Suddenly I got it! Here we have Stanley Cavell, the son of Jewish immigrants, asking about his inheritance of world philosophy as an American. To find his philosophical voice in his time and his century, Cavell needed to make his way into philosophy against the odds, which means that he needed to find not just the tradition through which he could speak but also get clear on why other traditions did not, or did not fully, speak for him, why he could not find himself in them.

Cavell speaks for himself, but because he does so with sincerity, he makes me see myself more sharply. I am nothing like Cavell. I am not an American, and not a philosopher either. I am the daughter of generations of Norwegian farmers and fishermen. As far back as records go the two branches of my family have been settled in the same little valley, on the same little island in Norway. Was there a tradition of philosophy or anything else to inherit for me in Norway? Or how about claiming my inheritance of world philosophy? Had the thought ever crossed my mind, I would have dismissed it as absurd.

Yet at the same time I knew that Cavell was right: one simply cannot write if one cannot find one's inheritance and if one cannot find the courage to say what one sees. Only by speaking can we discover if there is a community for us. Muteness is separation, and oppression. And he was right to insist that autobiography and philosophy are "internal" to each other. Now I see that my specific yearning for an intellectual voice has made me both an immigrant and a linguistic exile.

In the end, "Philosophy and the Arrogation of Voice" set me on a path that changed my intellectual life and made me realize that I too could aspire to an education in philosophy. This essay authorized me to look for my own voice, to find, and to claim my own tutelary spirits. For me, they weren't going to be Emerson and Thoreau, and not Nietzsche either. I had already found Simone de Beauvoir. But to find my way to her, I had had to learn French. And now I was finding Stanley Cavell. But to find my way to him, I had had to master English.

When I was granted the good fortune to meet Stanley Cavell, not long after reading "Philosophy and the Arrogation of Voice," he greeted me with friendship and spoke to me as an equal. I felt singled out, encouraged, blessed by him. He even gave me feedback on drafts. He gave me courage. Over the next years, reading and talking to Stanley Cavell dislodged something, opened something up in me. After some years, I discovered that I was ready to acknowledge a third tutelary spirit. I was ready to write about Henrik Ibsen. And to find my way to him, I didn't have to learn any languages. I just had to return home.

20

Autophilosophy

David LaRocca

I mentioned in the introduction to this volume that the volume itself may serve as an introduction to the work of Stanley Cavell. Such a description presumes an audience, that is, readers who are coming to the text wondering what Cavell's work proposes, whether it can speak to them (or under the auspices of a mercenary investigation, what it might *do* for them). Perhaps it will be amusing to discover that the (very) question of an audience for philosophy is one that Cavell takes up on numerous occasions over the course of a half-century of disciplined remarks—indeed, the phrase itself forms the title of the foreword to his first book, *Must We Mean What We Say?*;[1] in his estimation, it is a broad concern, one that agitates for an understanding of the kind of work that philosophy may be claimed to achieve, or aside from that accomplishment may be uniquely suited to undertake, that is, attempt. Cavell's preoccupation with audience fits naturally with his exploration of cinema's audience—what it means to be present to a (past) world projected for us.[2] And he returns perennially to the question of having or making or finding an audience ("the same again, only a little different?") as in *Cities of Words* and *Little Did I Know*—echoing his notion that "the only audience of philosophy is one performing it."[3]

In philosophy, it seems we have to create an audience (rather than presume it); and the audience may be somewhere between one person (perhaps it is one's self) and many others, or may not yet exist (hence Nietzsche writing for "tomorrow and the day after tomorrow," when he, in fact, achieves his audience), or, more soberly, may never materialize. Is being an audience to one's own thoughts enough to warrant their expression in language? What if one's book is for "no one," not even oneself? If philosophical writing begins in the first person, does it always risk ending there as well; or are there ways it can find its measure of public significance beyond personal anecdote and private fantasy? Cavell's practice of philosophizing—his mode of writing it—provides gratifying replies to such questions.

If we have begun here by looking to the beginning of Cavell's first book, it takes little effort to notice that forewords are the sort of apparatus typically undertaken by someone *other* than the book's author—as a moment of path-making or credentialing. Yet here, in the first words of his first book, Cavell seems to be speaking as someone else—or else on his own behalf (as he might if he were "beside himself in a sane sense").[4] If we are now familiar with Cavell's voice, after having listened to it, for it, over the last handful of decades, we may also wish to hear his *voices* (multiplying and radiating as they do over time, as they exhibit themselves notoriously and to exemplary effect in *The Claim of Reason*, but also, to my ear, in the foreword to *Must We Mean What We Say?* and elsewhere in these inaugural addresses to the public; he repeats the practice in *The Claim of Reason*, with another self-authored foreword). Still, as in the spirit of Ludwig Wittgenstein, Cavell's voices are all spoken in the direction of an audience. Hence the paramount issue of finding or making one.

Not surprisingly, given the companionable tone Cavell created and sustained, he postulated that "philosophy is essentially uncertain whom in a given moment it seeks to interest."[5] In this way, philosophy is unlike science, art, and religion. To wit, the question of having or making or finding an "audience for philosophy" abides—perhaps regardless of previous acclaim. Part of its persistence calls us to ask after the very nature of philosophy—how it does its work, how one would know philosophy had expressed itself. If Cavell sought to practice philosophy, it remains a peculiarity of philosophy that it must operate out of and through individual persons. To be an audience to Cavell's thought means, in part, to have or hold an interest in the way philosophy operated through him. Suddenly, the scale of our inquiry becomes quite circumscribed: we, the purported audience, approach an authored volume, and—word by word—undertake an encounter with it. The reader of such philosophy does not so much discover an audience as become one.

On this occasion, as we (individual writers and a community of them) are drawn to the question of the inheritance of Cavell's work—namely, what it would mean to be an audience for its achievements, to read it and write about it, and thus think about it, integrate it into the culture of our thinking now and into the future—there are some points in his writing that appear especially fecund (and for that generativity and abundance, perhaps not at first blush intelligible to even a seasoned reader of Cavell, much less a novitiate). In this concluding chapter, I take up one conspicuous characteristic of his approach to the saying and doing of philosophy, one that can be described simply as asking after what Cavell means when he draws philosophy into relationship with autobiography. Why does he do this? And what should we understand as a few of the salient and enduring reasons for this coupling—one that seems so continuous within and consequential to his work from early to late, across his diversity of selected interests, topics, texts, figures, and problems? And lastly, can we marshal cogent responses to these questions—ones that such a liminal moment, such as this one, wishes to call for? For example, does Cavell offer something like an account (coherent, original, or otherwise) of this relationship—and to what end? And are we in a position to describe or define it in a way that can be made not just shareable so that others can understand it but shareable, heritable, in a way that others might *practice* it—take it on for themselves as an approach or methodology that could become familiar enough to be recognized in their own work, *as* their own work? In what sense does it portend to speak of the relationship between autobiography and philosophy as *Cavellian*?

In the ongoing inheritance of Cavell's work, we have grown used to reflecting on how philosophical writing involves, or intersects with, autobiographical practice. Many informed and formidable scholars, from William Rothman to Timothy Gould, among others, have taken up the topic as essential to any understanding of Cavell's body of work.[6] Gould, for example, notes that when Cavell "begins to insist on the issue of autobiography and the first person pronoun, the first connections he draws are not from philosophy to literature but rather from the philosopher's writing to philosophical method or, indeed we might say, to the authority of philosophy."[7] Hence the very ambitions of Cavell's (philosophical) writing are caught up in the stakes of how it gets written—in what manner, and by what measure of (philosophical) presumption or pretension; and quite consequentially, as Cavell notes, the "quest for authority naturally tends toward the autobiographical."[8] Assuming we know what we mean when we use such (seemingly familiar) terms as the autobiographical and the philosophical (or autobiography and philosophy—for example, discerning one genre from the other), assessing their domains of relevance, and adjudicating their respective claims to truth, reality, and suchlike—would help a great deal, here and more generally. Yet clarity on these matters is rarely on offer—even at moments when the terms are invoked and interrogated. In Cavell's work, the distinction is regularly and spectacularly dissolved, often with profound results that radiate between and disturb fixed definitions. Considering these two categories and their relationship pushes us to consider, as Cavell does at the end of his seminal *The Claim of Reason*, whether and to what extent philosophy is, or may become, a kind of literature (and whether in that state of achievement or anticipation it would or could remain philosophy).[9] Cavell's own questions, then, about the nature, mode, or style of writing that takes place in (or as, or for) philosophy substantiate the concern that underlies the present investigation.

For some philosophers, the very appeal to autobiographical experience is unfounded, a measure of disqualification from philosophy; or if it is warranted, the status becomes a cudgel—evidence of fallacious thinking, category errors, and the like. What should we call this latter response—ordinary language cynicism? How then, by contrast, if we imagine a way of speaking of the writing or thinking self that is not only loyal to personal experience but also assures us that it becomes shareable, testable in some sense to the judgment of others, and thereby, a candidate to legitimate philosophy? From such a disposition, the truth of individual experience finds ratification in a community or readers and interpreters; something, then, needs to be said about how such truth is different from or related to the truths of fiction (i.e., literature) and those of science. To this end, I wish to propose the word autophilosophy.

In this chapter I hope to say why the proposal is not unnecessary or further confounding, but instead, with the assistance of Cavell's own remarks, perhaps helpful as a shorthand for the kind of work he did. It is, in my estimation, worth the risk to nominate and develop such a notion because the relationship between literature and philosophy appears to so regularly confuse both parties—literary theorists and scholars of literature, on the one hand, and philosophers, on the other hand (admitting that philosophers arrive from many precincts, some of which welcome the literary nature of philosophical prose). To better aid and abet the inheritance of Cavell's work by the broadest possible number of thinkers, what if we could have a term that coalesced the traits of the kind writing we recognize in Cavell's prose (which may also, in time, extend to the description of Cavellian offerings by others)? Instead of saying Cavell writes autobiography as philosophy, or that his philosophical work effectuates something like a literary voice, we would more compactly and perhaps more accurately speak of his accomplishment as an autophilosopher—that is, as someone who makes and transforms private experience into a register of such careful reading and puissant formulation that it becomes of vital significance to a public audience. In this way, autophilosophy is not about the self (Cavell's or anyone else's) but rather about the transcendence of the self for the purposes of public philosophical pertinence.

As a measure of Cavell's artistry as a philosopher, I wish to amplify a valence of his methodology, while avoiding the charge of essentialism, since I do not mean this report to offer a definitive or exhaustive account. I will, rather, call out select qualities or aspects of his work—postulating that attributes that lie on the surface of his prose may yet be motivated by deeper recesses of private experience. I appreciate that Cavell himself was not given to the creation of neologisms, but instead interested in the way we put (ordinary) words to use, and more especially, what that use reveals about our thinking and thus ourselves. However, the proposal of a neologism—even if comprised of familiar parts, including ordinary words inherent to Cavell's project—underscores that there are many things I do *not* want to do or say here on behalf of this provisional syntagma: (1) I do not want to defend the merit of a naïve and unqualified claim that "all fiction is autobiographical"[10] and by transposition, "all philosophy is autobiographical"; (2) I do not wish to say that Cavell is *merely* making public what is (or was once) private; and (3) following Cavell, I do not claim that philosophy is only another variant of literature (and nothing else but literature).[11] Rather, I prefer to join the conversation of those who have already written eloquently and convincingly on the subject of Cavell's writing methodology—as noted, Rothman and Gould come to mind as do a host of others—by extending or, as the case may be, reconceptualizing certain lines of approach to Cavell's prose. Thus, my aim is not to rehearse or paraphrase the already accomplished secondary literature on the subject, though it should be taken for granted as informing what I chose to highlight here, but instead to suggest that something of the mystery of Cavell's singularity in philosophy since the 1960s owes itself, in part, to his willingness to practice and commit to what may be deemed autophilosophical modes of expression. What these are, why they matter, and what we can do with them going forward gives order to my motivations for these remarks.

When Cavell asks at the end of *The Claim of Reason* whether philosophy can "become literature and still know itself" (as philosophy), we could take this concluding query—left in a state of conceptual ellipsis—as a rhetorical gesture that functions like a gestalt: a conservative will have a ready reply while an interested experimenter might lean in to ponder a while longer.[12] Philosophy that has *become* literature? What would that look and sound like? Is Cavell proposing that his work may (already) be pointing us in this direction? Was *The Claim of Reason* an illustration of its actuality or a prolegomena for its eventual appearance elsewhere—and perhaps by others? We know that earlier, in his second book, *The World Viewed*, he had written—as early as the first sentence (in that case, not waiting until the very end of his book)—to say (to admit? to insist?) that "[m]emories of movies are strand over strand with memories of my life."[13] Cavell did some excellent service by providing us with a name for the kind of book *The World Viewed* is: "metaphysical memoir." That is to say: Cavell's experience of film—from his earliest hours in the theater as a child to the time, before and during a training in professional philosophy and after, in practicing and innovating it—is relevant to (what he calls) his "reading" of film. In short, to know a film means to remember viewing it, to recall what one felt or thought about it (on each screening), and then, to make a proposal, in writing, to account for that experience (provisional as it may be, demanding further viewings and additional remarks—some of them corrective).

And yet, given Cavell's steady preoccupation with the Wittgensteinian idea of "bringing words back from their metaphysical to their everyday use," it would seem that a better assignation for his writing is something like a memoir of the ordinary, everyday, near, low, common, "that which had been negligently trodden under foot."[14] (It may stump some readers, therefore, to hear Cavell suggest that "the title" of Wittgenstein's philosophy might be "the philosophy of metaphysical language," since it seemed Wittgenstein's world-historical achievement was the invitation [admonition?] to philosophy to take the ordinary seriously—why not then, a motto such as "the philosophy of ordinary language"?)[15] Perhaps Cavell's choice of "metaphysical" to describe his memoiristic approach in *The World Viewed* bore some relation to his sense of its proximity to the "ontology" of the medium he was reflecting upon. Of course, the switch from a metaphysical memoir to, say, a "memoir of the ordinary" does not mean to suggest a hierarchy, but a difference in objective, and perhaps also a difference in style; for example, Cavell is fascinated by Wittgenstein's interest in the obvious (or "perspicuous")—and the paradox that we seem preternaturally and perpetually poised to miss it. In a phrase, how can the obvious fail to be obvious?[16] *The World Viewed*, to be sure, is no ordinary memoir, but it may be understood to show us how it is that one's (everyday) experience of film can motivate (extraordinary) philosophical reflection on the medium and specific instances of the art form; how we may come to see (and think about) what lies in front of our eyes. But the instinct to draw from everyday experience in venturing to constitute philosophical thought is not confined to thinking about film (though, as Cavell has said, "film was as if made for philosophy," and so may be especially conducive to such endeavors[17]). Rather, one of the most startling insights of ordinary language philosophy, as Cavell understands it and inherits it, is that *any* everyday experience may become an occasion for philosophy.

In his first "pedagogical letter" in *Cities of Words: Pedagogical Letters on a Register of the Moral Life*, Cavell says this remarkable thing about his personal experience—conveyed with his own surprise intact—of finding terms for the very possibility of contributing to philosophy; I should like to call this description an early bid toward a definition of what I mean by autophilosophy.

> This sense of being able to speak philosophically and openly about anything and everything that happens to you is an ideal of thinking that first seemed to me possible in contemporary professional philosophy in the work of the later Wittgenstein and in that of J. L. Austin. It is what their redemption of what they call the ordinary from its rejection in much of philosophy has perhaps most importantly meant to me. Without the sense of liberation that [redemption of the ordinary] afforded me, I do not know that I would have persisted in attempting to find a place in academic philosophy.[18]

As I continue here, I hope to explore what such "an ideal of thinking" means, in particular, how it took shape and found expression in Cavell's work; how it may be an ideal that we can appreciate and share beyond the boundaries of his work (e.g., recognize in the writing of others before, during, and after his own receptions and innovations of a life in letters); and how we may be said to practice or participate in the ideal in our own writing, in our own efforts "to speak philosophically and openly about anything and everything that happens" to us. Well, maybe not everything. Rather, Cavell's suggestion seems to be that we could select from that totalizing range, to find what in our experience demands a response from us, and what we may leave alone as unworthy of comment. Since we can never say for sure and once and for all, suddenly the ordinary seems a vast expanse of potential—and thus anything but ordinary.

Earlier, in a book whose title may be taken as a gloss on the present investigation, *A Pitch of Philosophy: Autobiographical Exercises*, Cavell offers kindred remarks (to those quoted above) on the effects of his encounters with the person and pedagogy of J. L. Austin and the philosophical writing of Wittgenstein: "I was unprepared to claim that the interest in the new philosophy lay precisely in the necessity and openness of its arrogance and its autobiographicality, that these are not personal but structural features of the necessity to say what we say, that in thus laying their bodies on the philosophical line, and living to tell their tale, the likes of Wittgenstein and Austin must be tapping a dimension of philosophy as such."[19] Much has been made, by Cavell and others, about the significance of the "arrogation of voice" (in the first chapter of *A Pitch of Philosophy* and in *Contesting Tears*, especially its first chapter), yet, in many such cases, there is an understandable focus on how the individual negotiates the taking or making of that voice: to transform from voiceless to voiced, in effect, from nonexistence and powerlessness to the person capable of giving names to things (a godlike power) and to making claims upon the world one inhabits with others. Self-definition and self-determination are aggregated. What is less often dwelled upon is the notion Cavell describes above as "not personal but structural features" that would make arrogance, arrogation, and autobiography as it were transcend the individual—in effect, obliterate whatever private claim a person might make for property or propriety, for the sacredness of some imagined self.

A challenge lies before us: to understand what Cavell calls "the internal connection between philosophy and autobiography, that each is a dimension of the other," since this too is a structure—one that helps us see that autobiography turns us to philosophy and, likewise, that philosophy turns us to autobiography.[20] Yet before we can get to "structures" and "connections" that bespeak something about universality, we need to see what gets an individual thinking, what would make it seem possible to contribute to philosophy at all. Cavell has described the origins of the personal in terms of the "sound" philosophy makes or takes, for example, "the tone of philosophy and ... my right to take that tone."[21] Note that we are not given this right, nor are we told, once it is taken, how it might sound or what it might be used for. Hence, there is a double bind: for even as we arrogate the right to speak, we are not (cannot be) sure that the things we say will be shareable or intelligible to others. The peculiarity, call it the paradox, of having (or finding or founding) one's own individual voice, means that only then—in that specificity—can it be taken for, considered a candidate for representativeness, which is to say, a "universal voice."[22]

Writing and speaking, nevertheless, must proceed "to some unspecified extent, anecdotally, which is more or less to say, autobiographically."[23] One of Cavell's own worries—and it should be ours too—is the extent to which he confesses: "I am unsure for whose views beyond mine I would be speaking."[24] Why the uncertainty, the lack of confidence (even in the midst of, at the height of a glorious, institutionally sanctioned, professionally feted time of life, such as we find Cavell writing in, in his maturity, in his late sixties)? Because he has been "reminded so often over the last thirty-five years how eccentric my views and ways are."[25] So if Cavell speaks, must speak, from the anecdotal and eccentric, he may be signaling a certain strain of philosophical thinking that is, as it were, not his alone. Hence "the internal connection between philosophy and autobiography." Sharing the evidence for that internal connection—making a case for its reality—can be hampered by prevailing habits and temporary trends that resist its articulation. Indeed, presenting reasons for believing in the intimacy of these forms or modes of thought can seem more like defining articles of faith, a faith no doubt borne out by experience, but still, something implicated in what may be a series of commitments that are foreign, unfamiliar, or off-putting. In this effort, Andrew Klevan has found not only company for Cavell but also lent definition to what can be called upon to characterize the nature of the work he and others place on offer for our consideration:

> [F. R.] Leavis, and more recently, Cavell think that the critic should be present in the writing to *self-consciously* and dramatically enact, and thereby expose, the processes of response, understanding, and evaluation. The moment-by-moment "interior drama," which goes hand in hand with attentiveness towards the work, should be presented to the reader. This "running presentation" might be regarded as an unnecessary and irritating record of deliberations that could be condensed or erased, and too much of an imposition of personality; for Leavis and Cavell though, in their different ways, it "constitutes a clear and open-handed source of authority."[26]

Notice how Klevan links "attentiveness" with "authority," and that such a liaison is, or perhaps must be, predicated on an "interior drama"—a phrase that serves as a euphemism for what precisely is being imposed on the reader, namely, the author. Klevan's astute assessment leaves open the question of audience, for are we speaking here of readers who await a text or readers who must be created for it? What we know in the nearer term, however, is the "structure" of such writing, namely, that the presence or we might say the inscription of personality in or on the prose is, at last, what gives these writers, Cavell and Leavis at the least, cause for speaking. Even then the threat that such promptings are "unnecessary," "irritating," or may be "condensed or erased," leaves an outsider staggering a bit.

"Philosophy," like every person who would hazard the resolution to create it, Cavell tells us, "is essentially uncertain whom in a given moment it seeks to interest" and its "essential uncertainty of its audience is what may appear as its esotericism."[27] Thus, the precariousness of speech culminates in the danger of seeming beside the point or out of the bounds of everyday discourse; philosophy is, for some, a question of why all *this* (whatever it might be) needed saying. Cavell describes the energy of constituting philosophical prose as one of oscillation: "between seeming urgent and seeming frivolous, obscure and obvious, seductive and repellent."[28] It is not easy work, and positioned or portrayed this way, it may be little surprise why the ranks of philosophers continue to dwindle even as those enrolling in computer science courses multiply exponentially. Who would intentionally pursue such uncertainty and esotericism? Who could stand to occupy her days and nights in a perpetual state of such oscillation—all the while accused of being anecdotal and eccentric? —The one for whom thinking such conditions is itself worthy of philosophical inquiry. But then the question remains for whom does one speak? For oneself alone (and is that enough?) and/or for others—and what if they do not listen or care, or actively dismiss and undermine what is said? Again, one wonders why all this needed saying.

Looking back on his evolution from musician to philosopher, Cavell says he "began finding my intellectual voice" in the philosophical methods of Austin and the later Wittgenstein, which, he notes, "demand a systematic engagement with the autobiographical."[29] We could begin, ourselves, by surveying the voice or voices of philosophical writing—for those who "say 'we' instead of 'I.' "[30] How does one make that transition, that transformational step, or as such movement may require, leap? Indeed, on the project of *A Pitch of Philosophy* as a whole, Cavell says that "a formative idea in planning these lectures was to pose the question whether, or how, philosophy's *arrogance* is linked to its *ambivalence* toward the *autobiographical*, as if something internal to the importance of philosophy tempts it to self-importance."[31] My italics are meant to draw together this trinity, which, first, subtends the relationship between authority and authorship, and, second, uncannily directs our attention to the way a philosopher speaks (must speak?) for herself *and* for humanity.

Most times it is hard enough to write what we think of as our own thoughts; it is another degree further to contend that such words should have any hold, much less validity or vitality, beyond the perimeter of one's private interests. And yet, since antiquity, this is precisely what we find philosophers doing—especially those who operate as critics of culture, call them philosophers of the value of human life, or borrowing Cavell's old job title, "the general theory of value," which, after Wittgenstein, includes both ethics and aesthetics. There is plenty of what Cavell calls "ambivalence" to the autobiographical foundation (or "structure") of philosophical work—but there is also much outright repudiation of the move as well, where any such appeals are dismissed to other realms of inquiry. Consequently, "philosophers who shun the autobiographical must find another route to philosophical authority ... (logic, as Kant says, is such a route)."[32] Indeed, in Cavell's own day, his colleague in Emerson Hall, Willard Van Orman Quine said "philosophy of science is philosophy enough."[33] Needless to say, in the 1960s, Cavell was, as he readily admits "unprepared—and not just intellectually—for the intensity of hostility [such work as Austin's] inspired." Cavell is thinking, in part, of positivists and others in this mold who, as it were, merely "find another interpretation of [philosophy's] arrogance (philosophy's inherent superiority, in intelligence or purity, is always a convenient such route)."[34] One need not go far to find the philosophical enemies of the autobiographical. Whether this is less the case today, or differently the case, in part because of Cavell's writing, remains a persistent question of this inquiry.

Among Cavell's own earliest work, his essay "Must We Mean What We Say?" is a defense of remarks made by his teacher, Austin, against dismissals of his postulations as "unscientific"—and by means of this epithet justifiably denied "as a contender in the ranks of philosophy at all."[35] As Klevan has noted, in the context of film studies (one of the areas that Cavell made seminal *philosophical* contributions to), the notion of "close reading" was tied to a methodology that might "help legitimate arts subjects challenged for being too unscientific and lacking discipline."[36] Earlier in this volume, Susan Neiman's contrast between the legacies of *Geisteswissenschaften* and the humanities reminds us of the encoding of scientism and positivism in the German composite, and the presuppositions about the varying validity and worth of intellectual productions that follow thereafter.[37] For those who are readers of a certain lineage of philosophy and wisdom literature—from Confucius, Socrates, the Stoics, and the Gospels, later to Montaigne, and onward through Emerson, Thoreau, Kierkegaard, Nietzsche, Wittgenstein, Heidegger, and Derrida—the notion that philosophical remarks must attain to universality, verification, and scientific ratification (falsification?) could seem misplaced, a category mistake unto itself. And yet, scientism of the sort that would see claims from autobiography as courting and confirming fallacy abounds. Cavell's response in that early paper was to "get out of the way of the charge, to construe it as largely impertinent, or too late," which is a lovely way of reminding us of the *sound* philosophy can take or make—its tone.[38] And likewise, that in sounding a certain way, we necessarily convey or embody decorum. Cavell's addendum "too late" is also very funny, since the charge of, say, lack of verifiability, has been there since Greek and Roman antiquity. In effect, no one can reach back far enough to outflank the lovers and users of autobiography for pertinent philosophical practice. As Cavell concludes: "The question of verification was exactly made to miss the interest of the new work [by Austin], of its new claim to philosophy's old authority, one whose power would reside in a certain systematic abdication of that authority (without resigning it to science, or to anything else)."[39]

As a measure of where you stand on these matters, ask yourself whether the following is a rhetorical question or not: "Who beside myself could give *me* the authority to speak for *us*?"[40] (The irony that we must rely on Cavell's question, that is, his *asking* of the question is not lost on me, but only draws further interest in the very citationality of thinking, luring us back to, among other places, Emerson's "Quotation and Originality," in which we are meant to consider, or admit, that all thinking is a mode of plagiarism—for what exactly would constitute an original thought or expression? Whose words are these, after all?) Cavell regards his question as rhetorical for "we are each in a position to give ourselves the right [to speak], take it from ourselves, as it were."[41] Thus, in this scene, the arrogation is not predicated on a relationship with, or demand upon, others (who may have a power we wish to acquire) but with ourselves—signaling a latent power we were unaware of possessing. A particular vein of classical liberalism underwrites Cavell's sentiment here—from John Milton to John Locke, from Thomas Jefferson to Thomas Paine—where the "constitutional amending" we do is somehow endogenous.[42] We "hold these truths to be self-evident," we believe these rights are "inalienable," because they are always existentially prior to their (possible but not necessary) exercise. When Cavell asks of philosophers such as Austin, "with what justification?" can he move from "I" to "we," and "by whose authority?" he makes his answer plain:

> Their basis is autobiographical, but they evidently take what they do and say to be representative or exemplary of the human condition as such. In this way they interpret philosophy's arrogance as the arrogation of the right to speak for us, to say whatever there is to say in the human resistance to the drag of metaphysics and skepticism; and authorize that arrogation in the claim to representativeness, expressed autobiographically. There is a humility or poverty essential in this arrogation, since appealing to the ordinariness of language is obeying it—suffering its intelligibility, alms of commonness—recognizing the mastery of it.[43]

We can ascribe a shape to the two models of arrogance on offer here, namely, that the philosophers who "shun the autobiographical … find another route to philosophical authority" in the methodological purity of their work. Claims to universality happen in generic thought experiments, or behind a "veil of ignorance" where all traits are stripped away. There may be truth but there isn't much content. Compare, then Quine's "philosophy of science is philosophy enough" with Cavell's "sense of being able to speak philosophically and openly about anything and everything that happens to you."[44] And what happens to Cavell happens to us all—that is, our encounters with and inhabitation among the low, common, near, everyday, and ordinary, in the very time and space of "humility and poverty." Such is the realm of the hyper-specific, the gloriously finite, and the aggressively circumscribed. Yet, burrowing in this direction, we find a new condition for *daring* to believe that "what is true for you in your private heart is true for all men."[45] So when it comes time for each to "authorize [her] arrogation in the claim to representativeness," it is and must be "expressed autobiographically." It is by means of individuality that we discover universality—though not by reference to "identity," personal or otherwise (to those phenotypical attributes that would seem to distinguish us one from the other), but precisely in studying the ordinary for its revelations of continuities and commonness. In this way, we find something of our bearing to the human.

How can we think of the dismissive adjectives leveled at Cavell's work—that it is idiosyncratic, anecdotal, eccentric, pretentious, and the like—and yet somehow find ourselves thinking about the viability of achieving representativeness (as if learning from those very same means)?[46] Is this a paradox that lies, must abide, at the heart of the autophilosophical? In one of Cavell's assuring responses, in *A Pitch of Philosophy*, he notes that the "autobiographical dimension of philosophy is internal to the claim that philosophy speaks for the human, for all; that is its necessary arrogance. The philosophical dimension of autobiography is that the human is representative, say, imitative, that each life is exemplary of all, a parable of each; that is humanity's commonness, which is internal to its endless denials of commonness."[47] Did you catch the conjunction of "representative" and "imitative," which underwrites if not a paradox, then a tension, perhaps a productive one? We seem forced to contend, moment by moment, with the way our individual lives may be unremarkable (imitative?) and yet for that ordinariness intelligible to others *and also* how our individual lives may be exemplary, yet for that oddness (being odd, standing apart) become figures for something "beyond" the ordinary, perhaps even worthy of its aspiration. For instance, there are times when holding a belief in, say, a human right goes from a private conviction to a public demand to a political reality. "I cannot know in advance," Cavell says of his own attempt at discernment, "which features of my life will be the telling ones" and which will not.[48] Hence the need for perpetual essaying.

In another experiment in autophilosophy, *Little Did I Know*, Cavell concludes—looking back over his manuscript, after two years of steady composition—the telling of these "excerpts from memory" "seemed to me to alternate between the unnoticeably common and the incommunicably singular."⁴⁹ Common, yes (both in the sense of being shared or sharable with others, and of being situated at the level of the everyday or ordinary); and singular, yes. But "unnoticeably" and "incommunicably" so? That such invisibility or impasse could be the result of some 550 pages of autophilosophy places a pause on our confidence in the elastic and assured powers of this mode of writing. In such a position, we are indeed composing "for all and none." If these are our only two options for receptivity, then we are left feeling either bemused at our universal (common) condition or befuddled by its radical, alienating specificity. As a response, we may continually "call upon philosophical reflection," among its most salient moods being "the willingness to find yourself lost."⁵⁰ And in that mood, we may stab at the darkness with an inky pen, attempting to write thoughts into existence by means of the language we are said to possess *and* share. Despite occasional successes, risks and liabilities remain all too present.

There is a headiness to speaking of representativeness; this can seem especially the case when we consider grand ethical or political initiatives, ones in which our lives are on the line. But then, as Cavell noted above, in his seriousness about writing (including listening to human communication in speech), and in the creation of new vocabularies and syntaxes of thought, our lives are still very much on the line, literally, letterally so.⁵¹ As a compelling example, consider how as early as his first book, "a book of essays," *Must We Mean What We Say?* (1969), Cavell already had a keen self-awareness of his style (from work he drafted in the 1950s and 60s), and thus a reasonable guess how the book might be received, perhaps because it had *already* been received in some manner prior to appearing in this new venue. Even before the essays begin, that is, in the acknowledgments, Cavell anticipates a problem—and how intriguing that his remarks in this generic prefatory space are consequential enough to speak of them as marking a beginning— or orientation—to the book.⁵² I mean to illustrate (again, at the outset of his career) that he was conscientious that so much as his *punctuation* would be a matter to deliberate over—and defend. Though we should perhaps not be surprised; after all, we are speaking of a man who wrote music ("Spending my childhood in a musical household—seeming to remember reading notes on a stave before I could read words of my speech"⁵³), and so the punctuation of his prose might be a perfectly fitting place to begin when thinking of cadence and rhythm, of tone, pacing, and pitch. Dots. Parentheses. Dashes. —These are Cavell's obsessions at the outset, and as a modernist artist and jazz improvisor possessed of the capacity to speak of them cogently, he does not disappoint.

Cavell begins tentatively, and apparently with plans to only call out a single issue: "I might mention here one stylistic habit of mine which, in addition to irritation, may cause confusion. I use dots of omission in the usual way within quoted material, but I also use them apart from quotations in place of marks such as 'etc.' or 'and so on' or 'and the like.' My little justifications for this are ... ."⁵⁴ And he continues with two lengthy explanations for his use of dots. But then. Then he cannot help but confess another "stylistic habit": "I can hardly excuse my use of list dots, any more than other of my habits which may annoy (e.g., a certain craving for parentheses, whose visual clarity seems to me to outweigh their oddity)." Dots. Parentheses. But there is more. "A further idiosyncrasy is especially noticeable in the later essays, the use of a dash before sentences." In a keen moment of metaphilosophy, Cavell explains his tic while invoking it: "Initial recourse" to the dash "was a way of avoiding the change of topic (and the necessity for trumped up transitions) which a paragraph would announce, while registering a significant shift of attitude or voice toward the topic at hand." So the dash, like the other punctuation marks, is, in fact, deployed after the talents and instincts of the musician—to cultivate a certain pace and sound. As Cavell concludes: "The plainest use of the device is an explicit return to its old-fashioned employment to mark dialogue.—But there are so many justifications for not writing well."⁵⁵ Who said that? Of course, it is the *dash* that gives us another vote of confirmation for Cavell's prodigious literary skills and his searing wit.

Even before Cavell's first book hits the shelf, before the page numbers leave Roman and head for Arabic, he knows and anticipates something is different about his (style of) writing philosophy; or perhaps just writing full stop. As Klevan noted earlier, bringing this "interior drama" to our attention, allowing the writing or the writer to be "self-conscious" is part of what makes it distinctive—what assures the "imposition of personality." We know someone is there, in the text—wondering and worrying with us; or at least granting us a glimpse of *his* wonder and worry. Hence Cavell's exemplariness as a writer. But does this status *also* confer his representativeness? And for that matter, his philosophicality? Not that Cavell writes in a way that we can (or should) recognize as our own—say, in the way we come to know and love a recipe that gets shared and reproduced year after year. But that Cavell writes so much like himself that we do not mind his idiosyncrasies (whether in matters of punctuation or in point of theorization); indeed, the distinctiveness makes all the difference, which, in turn, means that it confirms his singularity.

Cavell has looked to Emerson to note the continuity between thinking and personality ("Men imagine that they communicate their virtue or vice only by overt actions, and do not see that virtue and vice emit a breath every moment."⁵⁶) It is precisely this logical wholeness that shows we are perpetually charged with the nature of what we do and how we account for it (or say what it counts for, how we value it); such consanguinity helps us recognize the sense of the individual/private/personal launching itself into the realms of the communal/public/universal—as if mimicking the chiastic structure of former Cavell student, Terrence Malick's *The Tree of Life*, where we alternate between scenes of a single mid-twentieth-century Texas family and scenes of the formation of the universe.[57] Cavell has asked "whether serious art does not itself make public matters private?," and yet, in the light of Cavell's work (and Emerson's, and Malick's just mentioned), we seem poised to (also) say the opposite: that serious art—or the art we are calling autophilosophy—has about it the capacity to make private matters public.[58]

The Spirit of the Letter

My choice of the term autophilosophy is, in part, inspired (is it inspired, though?) by certain trends in contemporary literature that go by the name autofiction. I have made the terminological parallel in order to offer exposition on how the two modes are (for the most part) different, if complementary—that is, to find ways that they illuminate one another. A demotic account of the pair could state boldly that autofiction is "lightly veiled" autobiography (thus presuming that autobiography is not itself fiction), and by extension or association, autophilosophy would be "light veiled" autobiography (where the philosopher's life is the crux of the philosophy she espoused). In the latter case, however, our minds are not drawn at once to *writers*, but to the lives of figures of world-historical significance: Buddha, Socrates, and Jesus might stand as exemplars (as they did for Karl Jaspers). But, of course, they wrote nothing. From their lived experience sprung wisdom literature and religious tracts, biographies and philosophies, to be sure, but not by their hands, not from their first-person inscriptions. Autophilosophy, then, will be distinguished principally by its quality as a written exercise culminating in a written artifact. So what then is the nature of such writing?

Partly because of the contemporary attention paid to Roberto Bolaño, Elena Ferrante, Karl Ove Knausgaard, W. G. Sebald, David Foster Wallace, and others—a tradition or approach that often draws on a history reaching back to at least Rousseau and Proust and more recently shares company with Witold Gombrowicz, Wyndham Lewis, Peter Weiss, and those who practice *Sekundenstil*—we are immersed in reflections on autofiction.[59] While the term's provenance is often traced to Serge Doubrovsky's description of his work, *Fils* (1977), the topics that travel under that name have widened markedly, and well beyond its distinctive French incarnations (from Marguerite Duras to Catherine Millet) to include: the nature of truth and reality as we know it in (or as) prose; and the familiar and seemingly endless debate about the authority and truth of a first-person point of view (in so far as it involves a malleable and fallible memory, a perspectival outlook, emotional coloration of experience, and the peculiar—still mysterious—translation of thoughts, feelings, and memories into language).[60] When does, say, autobiography become fiction? Or does the question instead conjure a counterstatement: autobiography is always *already* fiction. What if someone writes literary criticism in the midst of his autofiction, as Knausgaard does, for example, in the sixth book of *My Struggle*; does the work (or only this expositional, even "academic" part) become philosophical? Fredric Jameson, writing on Knausgaard, says "these essays are not narrative, they are opinion—that *doxa* the Greeks so sharply distinguished from *episteme* or 'knowledge.'"[61] Further clarifying his point, Jameson remarks that Knausgaard might have been better served, or served his ideas better, had he "projected [them] in a truly rhetorical and literary form, i.e., the essay. There have been remarkable essays in which the author effectively tells the story of his own opinions."[62] Indeed, Jameson's annotation sounds like a contender for the kind of writing familiar to Cavell's project.

Not surprisingly, when Jameson draws in Toril Moi as a helpmeet for interpreting Knausgaard's significance—and the variations on his kind of thinking—Cavell is invoked. By way of Moi, a Norwegian literary critic who has written on Cavell and Knausgaard, and who is one of Jameson's colleagues at Duke, Jameson comes to see that Knausgaard has adopted "a stance towards life itself, one which is fulfilled in the attention to details of everyday life."[63] Jameson pauses to admire such a stance as requiring a rigorous "life-discipline," a syntagma that encodes the demands of writing, or better, essaying. For Jameson, Moi's approach (perhaps inspired by Cavell and Hölderlin) defines the stance by its capacity for "openness."[64] Such an attribution would be complementary to Moi's notion that "We are always *in* the ordinary" and that far from being alienated from it, "the extraordinary is at home in the ordinary."[65]

It may be given to some to notice the irony that a philosophy of the ordinary (including moral perfectionism), as Cavell has presented it—inspired as it is by founding American thinkers such as Emerson and Thoreau—would find its fame under the name Transcendentalism. Emerson, for his part, explained the matter tersely: "What is popularly called Transcendentalism among us, is Idealism; Idealism as it appears in 1842."[66] But then what Emerson calls idealism we are more likely to call classical realism.[67] The irony, then, lies in thinking that by such names, Emerson and his company recommended us to the elsewhere, when, in fact, they were cultivating a radical philosophy of immanence. So, as we have said that autophilosophy is not about the self, and Cavell has emphasized that perfectionism is not about perfection (and by extension self-reliance is—also—not about the self, at least as we have been taught), so transcendentalism is not about transcending but precisely the stakes of immanent, ordinary life. Why do we create these inversions—or better, perversions—to occupy our conceptual landscape? But they are here, and as my investigation takes for granted, such efforts at naming and defining are worthwhile, for even in their false leads and misleading allusions, they can be clarifying.

Putting aside the irony, then, let us find this element of kindred practice between autofiction and autophilosophy in the notion that both insist upon "a stance towards life itself, one which is fulfilled in the attention to details of everyday life."⁶⁸ If Knausgaard's essaying in the midst of his autofictional enterprise yields *doxa*, it is not a disparagement of his endeavor to note a fitting contrast in Cavell's essaying after *episteme*. In short, Cavell, like Emerson, Thoreau, and Nietzsche before him (along with Heidegger), worries about the "chatter" of the mass of people who "lead lives of quiet desperation," for when they speak "every word they say chagrins us."⁶⁹ Thus, where Knausgaard has turned (according to Jameson) to the only thing left to contemporary writers—itemization—Cavell, I wish to suggest, makes such "accounting" (in the Thoreauvian sense) a matter of vital ethical and existential significance. In this respect, we trade the everyday in its alternation between gossip and tedium for the transcendent ordinary—where random jottings are exchanged for the art of consecutive thought.⁷⁰

When Jameson raises the question about what to call Knausgaard's work (autobiography, confession, novel, essay—are all in the mix), he mobilizes another valence of approach, namely, to wonder about the way one's "stance towards" the everyday matters significantly; perhaps we can anoint this temperament. Whether it is expressive beyond the individual is an intrigue that Elizabeth Hardwick, who herself later tested and innovated autofiction, for example, in her metareferential and still-vital *Sleepless Nights* (1979), explores in "Memoirs, Conversations, and Diaries," first published in 1953.⁷¹ There she writes: "It is very difficult for the English and Americans to compose a respectable *hommage*, to spend a lifetime or even a few prime years on private memoirs, even comfortably to keep a journal, a diary. For these activities the French have a nearly manic facility and energy, but when we grind away at this industry it is as if we were trying to make perfume out of tobacco juice."⁷²

I highlight two consequential insights that issue from Hardwick's discerning analysis of, as it were, national dispositions toward the writing (of) life, first that "if we [viz., the English and Americans] do not practice the memoir or diary with unfaltering confidence, we have the *roman à clef* and satires like Pope's."⁷³ Indeed, there is much to recommend this tradition (rather than the diaristic) as one that Americans and the British have gravitated to, including Emerson and Herman Melville, as they were laboring to discover their own approaches to writing. The assignation (accusation?) that Melville was writing "thinly veiled autobiography" commences his literary career (*Typee*, *Omoo*, *Redburn*, etc.), while Emerson, a fan of much metafiction (Swift, Sterne, Carlyle), was drawn also to the exhaustive experiments in form found in Robert Burton's *Anatomy of Melancholy* and Montaigne's *Essays*.⁷⁴ These circles of literary force anticipate our terms here, with Swift, Sterne, and Carlyle taking up their positions as proto-autofictionalists, while Burton and Montaigne yield early and enduring models for autophilosophy.

If an attraction to the *roman à clef* and satires exposes an underlying (national?) temperament prone to a certain style or tone or mode of writing (both as creators of such work and as an audience for it), the second notion I draw from Hardwick pertains to disposition as well: "In the diary, the private journal, one is relieved of the problem of seeming to debase himself in an undemocratic way before his equals or superiors, but another and more crushing burden of conscience cramps the fingers. This is the fear of outrageous vanity, of presuming to offer simply *one's own ideas* and moods, speaking in one's natural voice, which may appear—any number of transgressive adjectives are exact: boastful, presumptive, narcissistic, indulgent."[75] On this second front, we hit upon another point of conjunction between Knausgaard and Cavell, namely, that both—writing as distinctly different work as they do—have been accused of such vanities. While Knausgaard may be said to address these effects in book six, Cavell, by contrast, makes the very issue of having and "speaking in one's natural voice," courting one's "moods," fearing vanity and debasement, articulating "*one's own ideas*" (as opposed to what? parroting or ventriloquizing them), a central topic of his oeuvre—from his early responses to skepticism and solipsism to his later theorizing of moral perfectionism, indeed, to the very presumption to write seriously about cinema from within the precincts of rarefied analytic philosophy at an Ivy League university a couple of generations ago.[76] What to some readers has seemed Cavell's dauntless intellectual bravery and peerless philosophical virtuosity has to others appeared, well, "boastful, presumptive, narcissistic, indulgent." Could this "fear of outrageous vanity" be not merely an attribute of Cavell's work, but of autophilosophy, so called? And if so, then not just Cavell is at perpetual risk, but anyone who writes (dares to write?) about his work—or, perhaps still worse, who "writes like him" (in attempted emulation or continuation of his art).

Among the many writers and scholars who draw from Cavell and help comment upon his work, Mark Greif may be noted for offering a distinctive inheritance of autophilosophy. As a former student of Cavell's, Greif has written in the pages of the "literary and intellectual journal" he helped found, *n+1*, about his teacher (an essay featured in this volume as Chapter 3).[77] And he has incorporated Cavellian lessons (along with Emersonian and Thoreauvian ones) in his collection of essays, *Against Experience*. As Hardwick situates our thinking in the second half of the twentieth century, Greif motivates another interpretation of our collective relationship with the expression of thinking—one befitting a critic of life in the late capitalism of the twenty-first century, at the dawn of the new social media standard; a standard that has transformed the boundaries of allowable topic (anything goes) and the temporality of response to it (as fast as possible).

In an essay calling upon Emerson, Thoreau, and Cavell entitled "The Concept of Experience," Greif writes: "The need to retell experiences becomes your last means to try to redeem experience from aimless, pure accumulation—and either you cannot find a listener or you realize that you are mute, unfit to communicate the colors of this distant realm of experience in any way adequate to the wonders you found there. Thus everyone longs to tell his story today, but not as literature."[78] Since Greif published this piece, the rise of socio-commercial "influencers" forces us to add *retail* to *retell*, for the redemption of experience becomes a shared and singular concern of the market capitalization of meaning, the monetization of "taste." Indeed, when Jameson assessed why we are fascinated by Knausgaard's writing, "why we take such satisfaction in the notation of all these daily things" (what Jameson calls "itemization" and Greif calls "aimless, pure accumulation"), Jameson concludes that the phenomenon is tied to "what a different post-war theoretical philosophy called redemption; all these insignificant moments of an insignificant life are here redeemed, by the ordinary, undistinctive sentences which write them down."[79] And yet Greif's disquieting "but not as literature." Could we say that Knausgaard's instincts for writing are captivated by the malaise Greif characterizes, and so Knausgaard cannot be said to write literature (at least as we have known it)? Or perhaps, we can embrace Greif's cultural criticism by allowing that redemption may come in other forms and media—say, cinema, even social media. What then of the way Cavell writes philosophy? Is it redemptive—either as we read it, or as we write about it and after it? Greif offers a reply.

He tells us there are two options for contemporary life, both identified under a philosophical title or orientation: *aestheticism* (which "asks you to view every object as you would a work of art") and *perfectionism* (which "puts the self before everything").[80] Greif invokes Cavell as "the major philosophical exponent of perfectionism in our own time," and suggests that for Cavell "the major incitement to becoming oneself turns out to be marriage."[81] I draw Greif in on his tandem set of existential positions to highlight what he names, after Cavell, their "debased" forms: for aestheticism, it is consumerism; for perfectionism, it is self-help.[82] Indeed, it is perfectionism's debasement that helps us see that perfectionism in its proper (moral or Emersonian) sense is not about the self as a *thing* (sometimes called an essence or a soul) but rather the self as a *process*, which is, in fact, to say no self at all.[83] We are not so much human beings as human becomings, since we are not static but always dynamic. Thus, when Emerson writes of the next or "unattained self," and Cavell drafts for us a mood of onwardness, abandonment, and successiveness, we are not courting a cult of authenticity (or fidelity to a "true self"), but a commitment to experimentation beyond our current state. The notion of a "true self" is a fiction we suffer—as exemplified by Polonius's "obligatory, impotent sagacity" and "debased" advice to Laertes ("to thine own self be true"), sure, but also in taking the "auto" of *auto*biography to say something definitive about "the self" writing it.[84] As the produce of the writing self is, by definition, subject to revision, so we should assume (and defend) the same condition for our notion of who does the writing.

The very conceit of trying, putting oneself on trial—*essaying*—in Knausgaard's verb of choice, struggling, creates a crisis for any individual: whether the specificity of one's existence can matter in itself and whether that meaning (hard won, agonistically achieved) bears any significance to the life and world of others. When Daniel Mendelsohn comments on Knausgaard's project, he says that whereas the "life of the narrator" in Proust's *In Search of Lost Time* is "refracted, in a way that enlarges you, gives you a heightened sense of the world itself, its contents and possibilities," Knausgaard's "creation, for all its vastness and despite its serious intellectual aims and attainments, reduces the entire world to the size of the author."[85] If we can marvel at both types of creation—the Proustian and the Knausgaardian—we may well wonder and worry that one is more productive for our own thoughts (beyond the page and in pages of our own). As an agitator and ally for thought, then, when we read Cavell, do we feel ourselves closer to a shared reality or merely nearer to his own? And as a model for methodology, can we adopt Cavell's strategies—his topics but also (assuming we could) his tone, exemplified, in part, by what an anonymous manuscript referee once described to me disparagingly and thus dismissively as his "verbally supple style"—and still find ourselves committed to ideas that lay beyond his purview, and his claim to authorship? These questions will remain with us, haunt our experiments in thinking and writing. Perhaps they are and must be questions asked and answered by each Cavell reader, and ceaselessly.

"The great technical ambition" of Knausgaard's work, according to Mendelsohn, "is the attempt to reconstruct the rich inconsequentiality of our quotidian experience in prose stripped of the usual novelistic devices."[86] The syntax and diction are nearly a match for autophilosophy, but somehow turned inside out, so let us rewrite it with three substitutions rendered in italics: 'The great technical ambition of *autophilosophy* is the attempt to reconstruct the rich *significance* of our quotidian experience in prose stripped of the usual *philosophical* devices.' In short, to write of the everyday in ordinary language. And yet, to do so by making the insights about one's particular existence sufficiently generic to be of use to another in his or her experimentation with his or her everydayness—a move that may demand rare intellectual rigor and perspicacity, as for example when we realize how much and how well Cavell read Kant, and how that education made possible his philosophical legitimation of Emerson, Thoreau, and Hollywood movies. Such an approach to observation and criticism—after Mendelsohn, after Proust—would mean finding our way to prose that helps us find our way back to the world (rather than, say, merely absorbed by the obsessions of one individual account among many, or at that, lost in stratospheric philosophical preoccupations that do not so much as touch ground in the everyday). Admittedly, and importantly then, a lot turns on what one means by "the *usual* philosophical devices," since part of Cavell's offering to philosophy is a reformation of business-as-usual. Yet, in that reconceiving of "what counts" as philosophy, we are conscientious of the fact that we do not want to end up alone, alienated from a tradition (whether neglected or suppressed or otherwise unheard).

We are now accustomed to hearing that part of Cavell's singularity as a philosopher is something that goes by the name of "the personal" or—often owing to his own emphasis on conversation, speech (what we say when), and from musical and operatic lexicons—"voice." The question that abides in Cavell's work from early to late, from the "We" to the "I"—for example, from *Must We Mean What We Say?* to *Little Did I Know*—is whether philosophy (as we have known it) can stand to afford these registrations of the personal, these instantiations of the idiosyncratic; we already know that the pressures of representativeness motivate a movement from the "I" to the "We," that is, when an individual is said to speak for others, indeed, on a Kantian register, to speak for all humanity. Philosophy that would see itself as akin to science, or aspiring to be more than that (mere kin), would likely dismiss the "personal" approach out of hand—and name it something like, well, literature. Depending on how Cavell's work is framed, but taking a cue from his own remarks on the subject, critics on all sides may assent to, or perhaps insist on, the characterization that he *courts* philosophy's proximity to literary expressivity or expressiveness (including the genres and subgenres that are more regularly associated—defensibly so—with that kind of production, namely, autobiography, memoir, diary, journal, correspondence, essay, *belles-lettres*, and similar), while not abandoning his commitment to writing philosophical prose.

As we consider autofiction and autophilosophy in their genre or generic characteristics, we can benefit from Mendelsohn's appraisal that the kind of "unusually intense emotional extremes" that figure in Knausgaard's work reveal the "stuff of many a memoir—a genre that, curiously, doesn't figure at all in the numerous digressions on literature that dot the landscape of intentional quotidian banality here, even though *My Struggle* has far more in common with memoir than it does with fiction."[87] And then Mendelsohn adds parenthetically a theory why: "(I suspect that Knausgaard decided to call his work a novel because memoir continues to be seen as a 'soft' genre, and he's after bigger literary game)."[88] Regularly mentioning and "self-consciously emulating" Proust may be a first point of evidence. But, the comment resonates beyond Knausgaard, since it gives the lie that memoir—perhaps literature in its many incarnations, but especially those types associated with memories and the selves that are said to "have" them—is "soft," or softer than what? Science, of course, "hard" science. "Philosophy of science is philosophy enough" precisely because it brackets any domain of philosophy that might risk its disqualification from inclusion in the scientific pantheon. In such a scenario, to say that philosophy is *more* than philosophy of science, therefore, makes one a target.

If on Mendelsohn's account (at least of this Knausgaardian incarnation of autofiction) the genre is more like memoir than fiction, we either have to counter with the claim that memoir is, in fact, pretty much fiction (despite containing details that align with a historical record), or say that autofiction is, at last, too thinly veiled to justify its proximity to fiction. On this latter front, autofiction, as a term of art, gets half of its appeal wrong; it is something more like autofact (a name that teases with its assonant conjuring of artifact). This apparent fault, however, may serve to highlight a productive resemblance between autofiction and autophilosophy, namely, that they are both immersed in the everyday (as noted above, but with a difference of intention and attitude—some of what has been tracking us under the euphemisms tone and style, the personal and the literary). Mendolsohn says Knausgaard, like other practitioners, "[c]onfidently bestrid[es] the increasingly popular gray zone that lies between fiction and autobiography (the genre the French call 'autofiction')."[89] In this gray zone, we suss out a kinship: Cavellian writing, like Knausgaardian work, "has no plot."[90] There is more of a sense of "little did I know" than of "here is how things happened to me and why." Rather, the focus is on *that* things happen—and the potential significance of that happening (Wittgensteinian description, then, rather than explanation). Both approaches involve meticulous care with the characterization of events and the particularities of thoughts and emotions. The difference, sustaining the contrast drawn above, resolves itself in what a reader can *do* with such accounts. Remain or return to the text, or, as it were go on from it.

Early on in *Little Did I Know*, there is a moment, recorded on Independence Day 2003, when Cavell suggests that autofiction—or the art of the *roman à clef*—might have been an option for him, and an appealing one:

> Trying to fall asleep last night I realized that if I had wished to construct an autobiography in which to disperse the bulk of the terrible things I know about myself, and the shameful things I have seen in others, I would have tried writing novels in which to disguise them. ... To do something analogous to that work I would have to show that telling the accidental, anonymous, in a sense posthumous, days of my life is the making of philosophy, however minor or marginal or impure, which means to show that those days can be written, in some sense are called to be written, philosophically.[91]

What a halting, haunting notion—that "telling the accidental, anonymous, in a sense posthumous, days of my life is the making of philosophy." What *is* a posthumous day of one's life but the acknowledgment of "tomorrow and the day after tomorrow" somehow made alive (again) in the act of looking back? Each night marks a new death (as we lay down to sleep in our recumbent position), and thus each new, each next morning invites a reawakening to life—born again at dawn.[92] The posthumous days (the whole sum of them) become the meat and marrow of what it would mean to write philosophy, to make a claim to it, in the present—for "what is further left explicitly open is precisely what counts as the time of philosophy."[93] We may test and attest for ourselves that constitutionally, as Cavell puts it, we are individually "writing as an emissary from another time."[94] Figuring out what time that would be frames our particular vantage, which, in turn, must be submitted to public scrutiny: "Something this means is that, like poetry, philosophy as I care about it most, exists only in its acceptance, in taking it out of the writer's hands, becoming translated one can say, finding a further life. Acceptance does not mean that it is agreed with, only that disagreement with it must claim for itself the standing of philosophy."[95] And disagreement of this sort is predicated on the successful translation of one's expression of experience to other realms, to the realm of others.

The Grammar and Criteria of Autophilosophy

Cavell writes that the ordinary language philosopher seeks to "discover the specific plight of mind and circumstance within which a human being gives voice to his condition."[96] In the light of such a declaration, which I take as an invitation to say "mind and circumstance" are not interchangeable terms, I would like to follow Andrew Klevan in saying that ordinary language philosophy is much larger than Cavell's take on it and includes many strains that would be allergic to his approach (e.g., the styles and methods of Peter Strawson, Gilbert Ryle et al.).[97] For the sake of announcing characteristics and allegiances, "autophilosophy" would become a way of signaling an especially *Cavellian* mode of OLP (or OLC). To this end, Cavell says conditionally: "If writing philosophy is for me finding a language in which I understand philosophy to be inherited, which means telling my autobiography in such a way as to find the conditions of that language, then I ought even by now to be able to begin formulating some of these conditions."[98] In this scene, inheritance appears to involve (require?) the task of writing in response to existing conditions, where texts beget texts ad infinitum. But then we recall the great teachers who wrote little, or published little, but thought much—and profoundly, not least Wittgenstein, and some of his distinguished students, such as Rush Rhees. As we survey Cavell's "finding a language," we can hear its metaphorical incarnations—that since "in philosophy it is the sound which makes all the difference," an inheritance of philosophy (and Cavell's work in particular) may *also* manifest itself in other modes of expression and expressiveness besides written (and published) prose, among them: teaching, filmmaking, painting, theatrical performance, performance art, the composition of music and its performance, etc.).[99] How much of Wittgenstein's *Philosophical Investigations* is dependent on his abdication of responsibilities at Cambridge, that is, his time away from the academy, and moreover, his teaching young students in Austria and his solitariness in Norway? George Santayana left Harvard for Rome; Nietzsche resigned his Chair at the University of Basel for provisional outposts in Sils Maria and Turin. Harvard's home for Philosophy is Emerson Hall, but Emerson himself spent nearly three decades in exile from his alma mater, much of that time roving on various lecture circuits. Thoreau went to the woods "to live deliberately." We must wonder about the many cases when living at the margin or perimeter, or simply being an outsider, proves salutary for eventual insight. One cannot predict or foreclose the circumstances in which "a human being gives voice to his condition."[100]

As I aimed in my introductory remarks to underscore the manner in which inheritance figures in *our* work as readers and receivers of Cavell's tuitions, so it is constitutional, and thus analytic, to Cavell's own definition of philosophy that inheritance is part of *his* work (however much that labor involves ratios of writing, speaking, and teaching—along with, say, playing music or watching movies—may be left an open question). Call this project in aggregate contending with tradition; however it is taken up, the process invites a particular stance or posture that one must take (or perhaps fail or refuse to take) with respect to intellectual and cultural patrimony; indifference and neglect are also ways of registering one's stakes in an inheritance (including aspects of material life: Wittgenstein, after all, declined to assume a massive fortune). Given what Cavell has said in *A Pitch of Philosophy* and elsewhere, a significant portion of his orientation to past and prior ideas involves autobiography—and the language, thoughts, and sounds it summons—as an ally to his philosophical enterprise. Even though life lacks a plot, life experience motivates the things we can say, or wish to say, about the having of (a) life.

In *A Pitch of Philosophy*, Cavell also characterizes his "conception of philosophy as the achievement of the unpolemical, of the refusal to take sides in metaphysical positions, of my quest to show that those are not useful sides but needless constructions."[101] For a philosopher to stake his claim to the unpolemical may itself invite argument. Let us contextualize the moment by regarding it as a variation on the theme that Wittgenstein "does not advance theses in philosophy"; or that "philosophy does not progress"; or that Cavell wishes to "hold out against the idea that philosophy is science ... or that philosophy is literature" (since "philosophy is not in competition with science but with sophistry").[102] Yet, the unpolemical does not peg Cavell as a Bartleby.[103] Cavell is not advocating neutrality or passivity, but rather a *kind* of activity, or better a measure of it: "What I call slow reading," he tells us by way of example, "is meant not so much to recommend a pace of reading as to propose a mode of philosophical attention in which you are prepared to be taken by surprise, stopped, thrown back as it were upon the text."[104] In a moment of metaphilosophy, such a remark calls attention to itself. Does it not, like so much else in Cavell's oeuvre, take us by surprise, give us pause, orient us anew to what we have just read? The "unpolemical" then is a kind of interpretive affordance so that one comes to appreciate that "a text worth reading carefully, or perpetually, is inexhaustible. You always leave it prematurely."[105] The goal is not to "have a reading" of something, but *readings*—including the terms and features of one's own life, since it too is not a definitive achievement, as noted, a thing with fixed qualities, but instead an ongoing postulation. Each new occasion of encounter positions a reader to be startled afresh, pushed to revise (i.e., re-see, re-flect), and rethink. "What I try to do in my work," Cavell tells us, "is to motivate both gestures of progress, both states of mind, going back and going on."[106] Philosophical progress, then, comes in the form of the *fort-da*.

In thinking of Wittgenstein's writing and Austin's "procedures," Cavell notes that "a certain strain of philosophy inescapably takes on autobiography, or perhaps I should say an abstraction of autobiography."[107] Is autophilosophy a good name for this mode of abstraction? For our purposes, we can say that such abstraction highlights how autophilosophy is not about the self (in the way that, as noted, moral perfectionism is not about perfection). Rather, autophilosophy is a procedure for getting us to think about the relationship between the task of philosophy and the task of being human. One draws upon personal experience in order to find a direction philosophically, which is almost to say, impersonally. For this reason, among others that might be articulated, autophilosophy cannot be a practice of "self-help," "self-care," "care of the self," or cults of authenticity (viz., the "debased" mode that Greif postulates); it is not about the self in its selfness (what has mutated into a perilous politics of identity), but the self in its commonness, as a refraction of the commonplace.

One place culture has allowed for the interaction of personal claim and public contest is the classroom, and Cavell has entertained at length what it would be like "to create a pedagogical environment" for such labors.[108] We may wonder if Cavell can single-handedly (a handsome condition, no doubt) create and establish an environment for autophilosophy, or whether he may do so by means of his invocation and reliance upon savvy associates—from Plato to Montaigne, Shakespeare, Emerson, Thoreau, Nietzsche, Freud, Heidegger, Wittgenstein, and Austin, among others. This environment may be said to exist in the pages of Cavell's books—and, if we are lucky, also in the pages, such as these, that take up Cavell's worth for further reflection. Cavell's prose, in this trope, functions as an atmosphere in which to think. Unlike charges of vanity and self-serving narcissism familiar to autofiction (see Olivier Assayas's film *Non-Fiction* [*Doubles vies*, 2018] for embodiments of this claim), autophilosophy makes one *companionable*, a better citizen, poised to be accountable to oneself, others, and democratic procedure. Let us say it *is* elitist in aspiration and objective, but humble in its demeanor and conduct.[109] In response to John Rawls's harsh assessment of perfectionism in *A Theory of Justice*, Cavell stipulates his "pang of uneasiness" with such an attribution, for instance, that the perfectionist may stand, in Rawls's phrase, "above reproach."

> There is, I argue, no such position to be claimed, so that our question becomes, rather, whether a given dispensation is worth suffering reproach for. To be able to withstand and answer this reproach is a way of seeing the value of perfectionism to democracy, a willingness for change analogous with society's commitment to reform toward greater justice (what is justice to the self? to its desires?) That happiness is possible in the place called America—not by insulation from it (say by wealth or power) but by participation in it—is how I understand the idiosyncratic happiness sought by the principal pairs of the remarriage comedies. ... The perpetual moral risk run by the principal pair of these comedies is that of snobbery. This is a reason the narrative of the films inevitably provides each of the pair with a moment of being humbled, or humiliated, and consequent insight.[110]

Can we any longer hear the name autophilosophy as a call to a celebration of the self? If anything, it must be a banner waved in reminder of the self's service beyond its perimeter and comforts, indeed, to a fundamental reconception of what it means to *be* individual at all. This is to say that if autophilosophy is anti-self, it is also, necessarily, anti-snob. While we have noted prominent points of overlap between autofiction and autophilosophy, the question of self-regard must introduce a chasm. Whether we follow Knausgaard's narcissism or the permutations of vanity in the characters imbedded in Assayas's *Non-Fiction*, we know—in these prominent literary and cinematic instances—that we are very far from the kind of work we should want to claim as autophilosophical.

Often biography and autobiography are subsumed beneath the moniker "life-writing." Or they find traction under the category of the still-expanding art of "the personal essay," where the likes of literary criticism, journalism, culture critique—and sometimes philosophy or philosophical observation—meet. Life-writing and the personal essay—where the personal is the point, instead of the point of departure—are not the kinds of writing Cavell offers. Nor does he write autobiography per se. Rather he braids and blends autobiography with philosophy to achieve something uniquely plaited—hence, the compacted name, autophilosophy. As we continue to ask if such a name can accommodate other voices (at his level of achievement), we can look for salient examples. Yet, where to look? In what library or canon, medium or genre? I have been saying that autophilosophy is kindred with fiction (with signature traces of autofiction), while cautioning that it is not a species or subset of autobiography (a genre that is often understood to report on undiluted or undistorted facts—even if these facts go by the names memories, dreams, and reflections, and include feelings and fantasies).

Cavell's work is autobiographical if and only if autobiography is understood as life transformed, transfigured, which is to say: autobiography as art—that in turn positions autophilosophy as art. When Cavell says he looks for moments in (his) life that "rise to level of philosophical significance," what he seeks is the way the moment is no longer about him, but, as it were, all humans—after Emerson's sentiment that "what is true for you in your private heart is true for all men."[111] In this conversion, writing shifts from anecdote to testament. It becomes art.

Some contend that these traits hold for autofiction—for example, Knausgaard wants his autofiction to protect him from libelous legal proceedings, and the writer Léonard Spiegel (played by Vincent Macaigne) in *Non-Fiction* wants desperately to hide (and have his work hidden) behind a "thin smokescreen." As Giles Harvey observes, "[w]e are given to understand [that Léonard] has a habit of recycling his private life."[112] (Not to be missed is Assayas's broader culture comment that culture-at-large is guilty of a similar "recycling"—what Harvey deems "rehearsing": "Many people, not just those in publishing, spend their workdays anxiously skimming think pieces about the impending obsolescence of their profession, and their evenings and weekends at social gatherings rehearsing what they've read."[113] So again, many of us are, as noted above, ventriloquizing (perhaps not even managing to editorialize along the way.) For Cavell, after Emerson, these phenomenon are classed under the problematic of imitation, of "quotation and originality," and at present may also be known as involving the perilous—but necessary—art of citation-as-endorsement (including the social media "re-post" and "re-tweet").

Hardwick's account resonates, yet again, in the contemporary intellectual landscape, where we retain "the fear of outrageous vanity, of presuming to offer simply *one's own ideas* and moods, speaking in one's natural voice, which may appear—any number of transgressive adjectives are exact: boastful, presumptive, narcissistic, indulgent."[114] Could the method (conceit?) of autofiction be a *response* to such fear, providing as Léonard seems to believe it must, a kind of prophylactic against offense or injury? If the autofiction artist fears being caught out, the readers do too—for when the "key" is provided (à la *roman à clef*), the audience may be suddenly exposed and implicated. Yet the information/art frisson is part of the scandal, much as it was for James Baldwin, Saul Bellow, and Philip Roth among many others—including contemporary writers such as J. M. Coetzee, James Frey (notoriously), Catherine Millet, and also, reaching back to Ernest Hemingway, Henry James, James Joyce, and Henry Miller.

Among the crucial differences between autofiction and autophilosophy, then, is our relation to their centers of concern—namely, that readers of autofiction ask "how much of it is fact?" while readers of autophilosophy ask "how much of it is philosophical?" Thus, while admitting artistry, the autophilosopher strives to make personal life accountable to the history of philosophy (again, not above reproach but subject to ongoing judgment). The autophilosopher may be said to operate in a perpetual state of "surprise at the fact that there should be such an enterprise that measures the value of our lives."[115] To this end, it is permissible for a philosopher to find and cultivate her voice—and explore what can variously feel like the distance from or the proximity to "real life" in what one, in fact, writes. Thus, where autofiction is a distinctive antagonist to fiction, autophilosophy is contrariwise an accomplice to philosophy.

We can assemble a worthy library of autophilosophers, beginning in Greek and Roman antiquity with Seneca, Epictetus, Aurelius; continuing with Augustine, Boethius, Robert Burton, Montaigne; and onward to Emerson, Thoreau, Kierkegaard, Nietzsche, Freud, and as Cavell has attested, Wittgenstein and Austin. Consider as an instance—and an indelible illustration—of autophilosophy a moment when Emerson allows himself to say something that alerts us to the way his work is underwritten by his experience (appearing, as it does, in an essay entitled "Experience"): "In the death of my son, now more than two years ago, I seem to have lost a beautiful estate,—no more."[116] When he speaks abstractly of the "costly price of sons and lovers," we know that Emerson had himself paid very specifically with his own son, Waldo and his first wife, Ellen. Are we in a mood to reread this famous (infamous to some) passage with an eye for the way Emerson makes his personal losses subject to the losses we all face and must bear? I have highlighted, as it were, those elements that biography tells us *are* autobiographical, but the remarks that surround those "facts from life" comprise a serious string of strident philosophical claims that go well beyond the purview of an essayist writing on Lexington Road in Concord, Massachusetts, circa 1844, to make a claim to, or for, all humanity (across time, tradition, territory, and temperament). To help us recognize the alternation between the private and the public, Emerson begins with "people" and "we" (of which he calls himself a member) and from there withdraws momentarily to secure his authority with "I," "me," and "my."

> People grieve and bemoan themselves, but it is not half so bad with them as they say. There are moods in which we court suffering, in the hope that here, at least, we shall find reality, sharp peaks and edges of truth. But it turns out to be scene-painting and counterfeit. The only thing grief has taught me, is to know how shallow it is. That, like all the rest, plays about the surface, and never introduces me into the reality, for contact with which, we would even pay the costly price of sons and lovers. Was it Boscovich who found out that bodies never come in contact? Well, souls never touch their objects. An innavigable sea washes with silent waves between us and the things we aim at and converse with. Grief too will make us idealists. In the death of my son, now more than two years ago, I seem to have lost a beautiful estate,—no more. I cannot get it nearer to

me. If tomorrow I should be informed of the bankruptcy of my principal debtors, the loss of my property would be a great inconvenience to me, perhaps, for many years; but it would leave me as it found me,—neither better nor worse. So is it with this calamity: it does not touch me: some thing which I fancied was a part of me, which could not be torn away without tearing me, nor enlarged without enriching me, falls off from me, and leaves no scar. It was caducous. I grieve that grief can teach me nothing, nor carry me one step into real nature. The Indian who was laid under a curse, that the wind should not blow on him, nor water flow to him, nor fire burn him, is a type of us all. The dearest events are summer-rain, and we the Para coats that shed every drop. Nothing is left us now but death. We look to that with a grim satisfaction, saying, there at least is reality that will not dodge us.[117]

So much for Emerson's much vaunted cheerfulness and optimism, or lack of a tragic sense and "ripe unconsciousness of evil."[118] Yet, if the "office of the scholar is to cheer," then we are positioned to be duly reassured by his confession, and by him drawing us—our fate—into the orbit of his. We are not alone in our suffering, however horrible because deep or horrible because superficial it may seem.[119]

Now, if we have spent a few phrases on a representative example of autophilosophy in Emerson, how does it exemplify something (also) in Cavell? First, by reminding us how such a passage can look and sound, and thereby putting us on intimate terms with the cast and tone of the autophilosophical. Second, by entering into debate about the criteria that constitute philosophy, such as when Cavell writes about the (problematic) reception of Emerson's prose as a "mist" or a "fog":[120] "I do not want a text to be denied the title of philosophy on the ground that it does not exactly take the form you might expect of philosophy. The denial of the title tends to excuse the tendency to refrain from putting much intellectual pressure on Emerson's words, to refrain from accepting the invitation of those words to get past their appearance, if I can put it so."[121] Third, we find Cavell's reflections on Emerson's autobiographical experience, which *Cavell* makes into a moment of philosophical pertinence: "The question whether [Emerson] speaks with philosophical authority—and if not, with what authority—is an undertone, I find, of his prose throughout, connected, I cannot doubt, with the crisis in his life as a result of giving up the questionable, for him, authority of the pulpit. To give up on the question would be to give up following the way Emerson's prose questions itself."[122] In this way, the autophilosophical encodes its status as a perpetual practice of metaphilosophy.

Someone attuned to Cavell's autobiography will feel justified to speculate on it (in his company and apart from it), and in this particular case, on the personal stakes (for Cavell) of such a reading of *Emerson's* autobiography (raised, as it is by Cavell, to philosophical significance). In a word, what it means personally and philosophically "to give up" on an idea or a dream or a vocation—as when not just Emerson walks away from the pulpit and toward the brig *Jasper* carrying him to Europe in the wake of his first wife's death, but when Cavell, a serious musician who played in big bands and jazz ensembles as a teenager, an undergraduate composition student of Ernest Bloch's at Berkeley, and later, a graduate student at Juilliard, finds himself spending his days in Manhattan "mostly ... avoiding my composition lessons" in trade for going to the movies (and reading philosophy).[123] Once again, we are tempted to reread and repurpose lines, though only needing a few minor if crucial adjustments, this time hearing *Cavell's* autobiographical experience percolate to the surface—with substitutions in italics: "The question whether *Cavell* speaks with philosophical authority—and if not, with what authority—is an undertone, I find, of his prose throughout, connected, I cannot doubt, with the crisis in his life as a result of giving up the questionable, for him, authority of *a life in music*. To give up on the question would be to give up following the way *Cavell's* prose questions itself."

While mindfully eschewing tendentious psychoanalytic etiologies and habits of causal explanation *and* readily admitting that for Cavell "Freud" is not a troubling figure or an objectionable frame of reference, once the autophilosophical character of Cavell's work (and Emerson's before it) is thematized this way a veritable stream of associated moments rush in for consideration (no doubt befitting a study of memories, dreams, and reflections), among them, how Cavell's interest in King Lear's disowning knowledge (and love) of his child may be thought of in association with Cavell's struggles with his own father, and perhaps also the general nature of parenting—or the specific nature of paternity (hence skepticism, acknowledgment, and later, in the light of his desire to understand his mother, the "melodrama of the unknown woman," who feels herself variously isolated, contained, voiceless, unheard); how the literal and thematic senses of "immigrant" intersect with his parents' experience, and before and beyond that, to the Jewish experience as such; how his change of surname (from Goldstein to Cavell) in a "moulting season" that marks "a crisis" in his life thereafter gives shape to an aspiration to name himself (to create an "alias" or a "mask" or a "stage name") so that he can find the right words for things and thoughts—call them experiences—and in such calling or naming establish a "furtive legitimacy" for himself;[124] how a childhood ear injury gives rise to an education in musical performance and music composition and also its end, or better, transformation—owing to "my crisis in having left the study of music"—into the notions of "voice," the diction and dialects of everyday speech (including their particular dictations), and the "sound of philosophy" as bona fide philosophical themes—thus suggesting that it were "as if philosophy occurs for me as some form of compensation for, or perhaps, continuation of, the life of music";[125] how arriving at philosophy from music (jazz, in particular) and (the ascendant legitimacy of) cinema might have given him the resources to think about "improvising" on a tradition that often repressed or excluded the voices of others (not just women and people of color but also different or divergent traditions of thought—Shakespeare, Ibsen, Emerson, Thoreau, Freud; and mediums of expression: modernist painting and music, opera, television, Hollywood comedies and melodramas).[126]

Again, the point is not to psychoanalyze Cavell, though he marks Freud as a signal influence and retains an interest in his work throughout his philosophical career (writing of a formative encounter with Freud's *Introductory Lectures on Psychoanalysis* during what he calls a "state of spiritual crisis"), but rather to postulate an alternative reading of similar moments of conjunction.[127] It is not enough, for my purposes here, to make associations that *may* bear out under psychoanalytic treatment, but rather, to look to the work itself: to read Cavell, that is, read his lines, one after another, though some more than others; to find or discover the manner in which he has innovated from (out of, beyond) personal experience in such a way that we, generally speaking, become an audience for his thought. We are not witnesses to a hermetic text, where the author spins a million lines to chase an obsessive interest in daily minutia (which may be an uncharitable way of reading Knausgaard), but instead readers who marvel that a man who only lived one life—as each of us also must—managed to make a series of private fascinations into essential portions of the conceptual terrain of our shared existence.

Cavell as a person *and* as a philosopher presents to us a model for a certain kind of life, but in his singularity *also* a conundrum about reproducibility. What does it mean to heed Cavellian lessons in autophilosophy as we think our own thoughts and write our own words, such as they are "ours"? Cavell's reply might adopt an Emersonian strain—one he ably and amply applies to the moral perfectionism he deems Emersonian in character—namely, that we are, despite distractions and fatigue, invited to trust our relation to something while also trusting our relationship to others (whether that means receiving the world with "shame," at second hand, with "alienated majesty," or by contrast, entering a position in which to "build therefore your own world"[128]). As noted in Cavell's response to Rawls's suspicion, one is not above reproach—just the opposite, for in speaking one's latent (and subsequently informed) conviction, one makes oneself vulnerable to others—to their blame, criticism, and rebuke; and perhaps also, in time, one may become an object of their acknowledgment and praise. In this practice of alternation between the private and public selves (as two horses upon which we ride), straddling the particular and the generic, we see how writing can occupy, as it were, two octaves. A reader's attunement (to one, the other, or both) makes all the difference for interpretation. "As in Emerson, and in

Thoreau," Cavell tells us, the notion that one does not "advance theses in philosophy ... turns out to mean that the philosopher entrusts himself or herself to write, however limitedly, the autobiography of the species; if not of humanity as a whole, then representative of anyone who finds himself or herself in it."[129] Thus, *Cavellian* writing (after Wittgenstein and Austin) requires an "abstraction of autobiography" that is entirely and concomitantly recognized as philosophical. "You've got fires banked down in you, hearth-fires, and holocausts," Mike Connor (James Stewart) tells Tracy Lord (Katharine Hepburn) in *The Philadelphia Story* (1940, dir. George Cukor). And so we have been told many times before, by Emerson and others, to watch for such "gleam[s] of light."[130] Indeed, for the apocalypse itself—or many of them [Gr. *apokaluptein*, uncover, reveal]. Catching or kindling such resources can be daunting, and there is a perpetual risk that for lack of skill, one cannot move beyond the anecdote to some abstract, shareable truth. Writing may mean writing for no one, for a few, or for posterity. But beyond finding an audience, the writing of autophilosophy will always require a willingness to read one's own life "for the lustres."[131] Whether these can be made intelligible to us is a first question, and translated to others, a second.

As William Rothman writes in his contribution to this volume, "The ultimate instance of Cavell reading Cavell is *Little Did I Know*, which tells the story of his life up to *The Claim of Reason*, a story in which the philosophical and the personal are inseparable. Then again, his late turn to autobiography was anticipated in Cavell's early writing. It was already a theme in *Must We Mean What We Say?* that philosophical appeals to ordinary language have an autobiographical dimension."[132] And we know that Cavell spoke, in his second book, *The World Viewed*, about that text being a "metaphysical memoir."[133] While his first book on film along with *A Pitch of Philosophy* and *Little Did I Know* have illustrated, the more explicitly memoiristic aspects of Cavell's writing can announce themselves for all to see. But we should also highlight that domain as one conspicuous subspecies of autophilosophy, only one of its discernible modes. In a taxonomy sketched from the range of his works, Cavell could be said to offer us several distinctive such subspecies, for example, as we find the memoiristic differently present in, say, *The Senses of Walden*, *The Claim of Reason*, *Disowning Knowledge*, and *Emerson's Transcendental Etudes*. When all of his books are held up to the light, however, the catalogue will surely provide instances of "autobiographical exercises" and "excerpts from memory" (that are manifestly autophilosophical), but also a number of less overtly autobiographical methods—where the life has been digested, its incidents all "ground ... into paint"; "as a good chimney burns its smoke, so a philosopher converts the value of all his fortunes into his intellectual performances."[134] Though Cavell does not proceed uniformly, from book to book, essay to essay, by the same means (a varied repertoire of resources and effects many will count virtuous), Cavell's experimentation with autophilosophy would confirm that they are, nevertheless, by the same author. Perhaps such books, many of them, if not all of them, can be thought of as participating in the genre of autophilosophy.

Clarity as False Indicator of Truth; Specificity as Mode of Illumination

Autofiction's attention to the everyday is the best point of overlap with autophilosophy, but, as we have seen (e.g., in Knausgaard and in the film *Non-Fiction*) it leaves the everyday where it finds it, namely, as description (however much or little it is transformed or distorted, as if behind a "thin smokescreen," as we hear in Assayas's film). Autophilosophy goes a step further to *interrogate* the description, to turn it over again, to go back, to back track—to theorize, even. Earlier, I invoked Hardwick, who said of the memoiristic and its variants, "The French have a nearly manic facility and energy, but when we grind away at this industry it is as if we were trying to make perfume out of tobacco juice."[135] Funny, yes, but telling in so far as we are given a clue about what could be named a temperament for autophilosophy (as Hardwick would seem to believe there is for other genres of writing). As a coda to Hardwick's observation, consider *Non-Fiction*'s Alain Danielson's (Guillaume Canet), Léonard's editor, who likens "people sharing witticisms" on Twitter to "intellectual culture under the ancien régime." Thinking of the philosophes and epigrammatists, Alain concludes: "It's very French." Whether one considers the comparison apt or appalling may also depend on one's national context—and temperament. (Follow me @LaRochefoucauld; #autophilosophy).

The question of the Americanness of writing or thought is a theme of Cavell's recuperation and reception of Emerson and Thoreau in the halls of Anglo-analytic academic philosophy, and it could become part of our deliberation on the qualities or characteristics of autophilosophy. In the present age, one is tempted to suggest that Americanness is no longer (never was?) a national/nationalistic trait, but something like an idea in competition with other descriptions of literary-philosophical comportment (as in the Confucian sage, Roman stoic, German mystic, or English empiricist). Given how the thematics of Americanness reside prominently in Cavell's books—especially in *The Senses of Walden, Pursuits of Happiness, In Quest of the Ordinary, This New Yet Unapproachable America, Conditions Handsome and Unhandsome: The Constitution of Emersonian Perfectionism*, and *Emerson's Transcendental Etudes*—we can speculate how autophilosophy might figure in the expression and fulfillment of this line of Cavell's thinking. A persistent preoccupation with the nature and authority of everyday speech—in one's solitary ejaculations, such as we find in journals *and* in one's public expressions—suggest that, for Cavell, writing about American conditions (self, society, democracy, representativeness, constitutionality, community, etc.) call for autophilosophy—summon it.

Scanning for other attributes of autophilosophy, ones that may or may not involve any concern with Americanness, we can look to stylistic tendencies. In writing about the metaphor of voice in philosophical writing, Arthur Danto noted:

> Cavell's asides, his parentheses, are delivered not to the reader but to himself, or to one side of his self from another; the reader, in fact, is ignored. That is why, because internal to the prose, they are so annoying and distracting, keeping the reader's mind off the flow, unable to follow what is action and what is not. Or they are a bit like the patter of the magician, distracting us from seeing how the rabbits are pulled from the hats, with the difference that no one can tell hat from rabbit, action from aside, except that they do not fall into the linearity of good expository prose.[136]

Whatever harshness may be intoned here, there are observations that prove illuminating for an ongoing discernment of (Cavellian?) autophilosophy, namely: that in a work such as *The Claim of Reason*, we may glean few explicitly autobiographical facts (e.g., there are references to speaking with children, perhaps his daughter; physical dimensions of a baseball diamond, perhaps from experience at Fenway Park, or watching Austin give the game a go, etc.), but the autophilosophy is there—and apparent—in the syntax, diction, and punctuation. The autophilosophical voice (whether it is one or two or more) can be heard. Again, autophilosophy is not entirely coincident with autobiography, but rather is a mode in which the transformation of the everyday is necessary, and at that, a transformation that makes philosophical significance an evident part of its presentation.

Toril Moi, whose chapter precedes this one, discusses elsewhere what sort of stylistic elements may cause alarm or trouble for readers of any philosophical text, but especially those who regard ordinary language philosophy as legislating a simplistic or simple-minded approach to prose:

> Nothing is more ironic than [Herbert] Marcuse's idea that ordinary language philosophy must be the enemy of difficult or stylistically challenging writing. If this were true, we would have to begin by denouncing the writing of Wittgenstein (gnomic and startlingly counterintuitive), Austin (those off-putting lists with headings and subheadings, packed with neologisms that usually come to nothing), and Cavell (the self-consciousness! the endless doubling back! the constant effort to say it and qualify it at the same time!). Ordinary language philosophy neither recommends nor forbids any particular writing style. How you write will

depend on who you are, who you are writing for, and what you want to do with your writing. The style of theory or philosophy can't be discussed in general and in the abstract.[137]

In short, "the style of theory or philosophy" must always be particular, concrete, a matter of exploring examples (that on occasion reveal their exemplarity). "How you write will depend on who you are"—perhaps an apposite gloss on autophilosophy as such.[138] Admittedly, an allowance for what might be called the personality of prose—its style—can move in less productive directions: for instance, the passage from Moi comes from a section entitled "Clarity: 'The Bad Writing Contest,'" in which she invokes the journal *Philosophy and Literature*'s (in)famous late-nineties self-defeating, indeed, self-immolating stunt of shame: calling out the "bad" writers (e.g., Homi Bhabha, Judith Butler, Fredric Jameson—the very same critic who offered clarity above).

As we stand, a couple decades on, this "competition" seems a harbinger for the erosion of confidence in the humanities (generally) that has led to its embattled present (made evident in bountiful specifics). Rather than collectively and individually encouraging "better" writing, or, for that matter, reading for the *differences* between complex and convoluted, the default seems to be an assumed privileging of some anonymous author of record who "wrote clearly" (a default without definition) and the others, the naughty narrators, who dissembled in the face of calls for meaning that should be, we are meant to think, merely available at a glance, that is, on the surface of the text (hence the invitation to computational approaches to "reading"—and the emerging promise/threat that artificial intelligence will, in time, also write on our behalf). So these further misleading dichotomies (good/bad, clarity/density, depth/surface, close/distant, etc.) contribute to the long history of academic travails. Moreover, such a debacle signals yet another way that autophilosophy *counters* the prevailing instincts of identity politics to celebrate an individual's traits and, as it were, stop there. Differences in writing style like differences in persons become productive when they become intelligible *beyond* the self. Indeed, if Cavell is a rare exemplar of autophilosophy—that is, a philosopher with an eye and ear for literary expression, who writes "between philosophy and literature"—this may explain why the genre has, or can have, so few fellow practitioners.[139]

Contrary to autofiction, and other forms and genres of writing, as serially emphasized in these pages, autophilosophy demands that one transform—*translate*—individual experience into something shareable, something philosophical. Hence it importunes that a writer can, in fact, make this translation linguistically. One has to know, or come to know, what elements of a life—of one's life—are shareable and also worth sharing. When casting about the annals of contemporary philosophy from the last half-century, or even the last century or more, much if not most of what preoccupies philosophers would strike the average person as irrelevant to, not to say incomprehensible for, the significance of daily life—and a life well lived. As Cavell elucidates the hallmark disposition of philosophical outsiders: "This formulation captures the familiar fact that philosophers seem perpetually to be going back over something, something most sane people would feel had already been discussed to death. A more familiar formulation is to say that philosophy does not progress."[140] Again, by contrast with other modes, autophilosophy might be gleaned in a phrase drawn from *Cities of Words*, namely, that it is the practice of "measur[ing] the value of our lives."[141] Intriguingly, then, you see the elision between *my* life and *our* life. It is precisely in this "volatile transfer point"—where the individual becomes representative—that we find the current and ongoing urgency of any sort of program of autophilosophy.[142]

Since imitation is such a vexing watchword in the Emersonian lexicon, and emulation isn't much better, the question of originality (e.g., having or discovering "one's own voice") would appear to abide deeply within the investigations of autophilosophy. What would it take to mount a satisfying expression of the autophilosophical? Is one capable? Who knows the criteria? Where to begin? —Perhaps by noting that originality, at last, is not as crucial to the project of autophilosophy as we might think, though it may be assigned or associated with Cavell's particular brand. Such questions and replies lead us to ask further not just *can* something be said (by virtue of evidence or reason and thereby achieve a clarity that makes its meaning known to others), but is it important (enough)? As Cavell asked: "Is this worth noting?"[143] In a rare instance of direct advice, he continues this line of questioning in the wake of assessing the worth of what *he* had just proffered: "Can this little radiation from [Robert] Browning's poem ['Incident at the French Camp'] have been intended? By whom? These are questions I know will, even should, arise often. My advice is not to ignore them, but also not to let them prevent your imagination from being released by an imaginative work. To deflect the question of intention you have to say something to yourself about how, for example, just this poem by just this poet is alluded to just here in this work. So if you tell yourself it is an accident, then take that idea seriously."[144] Still, heeding such advice (i.e., having or generating the authority to speak, as an author—as a bid to avoid one's potential encounter with "alienated majesty") may go sideways. Perhaps my private thought—"what is true for [me] in [my] private heart"—is *not* "true for all men," is not majestic, but a fraud, a bit of self-generated drivel shared as a nervous response to Janus-faced shame and narcissism.[145] We need more advice.

> The problem of the critic, as of the artist, is not to discount his subjectivity, but to include it; not to overcome it in agreement, but to master it in exemplary ways. Then his work outlasts the fashions and arguments of

a particular age. That is the beauty of it. ... [P]hilosophy, like art, is, and should be, powerless to prove its relevance; and that says something about the kind of relevance it wishes to have. All the philosopher, this kind of philosopher, can do is to express, as fully as he can, his world, and attract our undivided attention to our own.[146]

Oh, but how to include subjectivity and "master it in exemplary ways"?—that is the work of a lifetime. And, clearly, for some, worthy of a lifetime. Such an inclusion of subjectivity does not proceed by simply providing a "thin smokescreen" and insisting that one's life experience is better as a story, or is just one story among many others (and thus potentially an entertainment, as we find it variously in Knausgaard and depicted in *Non-Fiction*); on this point, again, autophilosophy is decidedly not aligned with autofiction. Nor is autophilosophy history (as say autobiography might be). Autophilosophy, if rendered in response to Cavell's writing, at least, does not lose a grip on its status as philosophy—that is, in its aspiration *to* philosophy.

The themes and questions I have discussed (attempting along the way to offer replies, context, and contenders for further consideration) leave us with still further questions, among them, whether there are heirs for this kind of thinking and writing—assuming it was a tradition to begin with, or could be one (even if in retrospect). Was Cavell one in a series of autophilosophers? Who among us could be looked to as a living companion to Cavell's work? Would such a confederate's writing resemble Cavell's writing—or reveal some related yet distinctively different style? How long must we wait to find the next exemplary autophilosopher? While we ponder replies to these questions, while we wait, reading and rereading Cavell's works and words may yet afford the agitation, acumen, and reassurance we seek.

If the history of letters provides an indication of what work lasts—that is, what remains vital, what remains in print, what remains assigned reading—the achievement of factual truth or the verifiability of claims will not save a book from oblivion. The "undead texts" must be deemed works of ambition—and in this ambition, we find texts of notable style.[147] Can anyone imagine the intellectual bravado it would take at present to write and publish a capacious, erudite field-inventing or field-defining work such as *Mimesis, The Second Sex,* or *The Structure of Scientific Revolutions*? And yet despite faults or mislaid findings, and instead for their conceptual boldness and stylistic ingenuity (and perhaps, for these reasons, as contenders for the category of autophilosophy), we continue to read Erich Auerbach, Simone de Beauvoir, and (Cavell's Berkeley friend and colleague) Thomas Kuhn—and others in this rarefied ilk. Such an observation about "what remains" may say something reassuring about Cavell's positive fate in the near and far term (in the decades to come, in the next century), yet concomitantly lend us misgivings for holding out much hope for all the "specialist" literature that gets produced; perhaps, it is called "secondary" for a reason.

If the core criterion of autophilosophy is personal history (memories, dreams, reflections) raised to the level of philosophy—the cleave point being when the private becomes pertinent to the public—a further criterion may be that the *style* of such writing is distinguishable from other work, and for that reason is also distinguished: work of unusual intellectual imagination and fortitude, writing that feels embodied and therefore possessed of a presence—as if it could not have been written by another, and as if it inclined to membership in the firmament of indelible and indispensable ideas. Though we have heard praise (and complaint) about Cavell's prose, there is (is there not?) consensus on its uniqueness—"a voice like no other in philosophy, today or ever."[148] A "page or two of Cavell—a paragraph or two, in fact—is almost unmistakable," Danto added some years later.[149] Russell Goodman sustains the assessment: "Stanley Cavell writes like no one else, with a range of interests and competencies unmatched by any of his contemporaries."[150]

If there is reason to believe in Cavell's singularity (and who would begrudge such a distinction?), is that status sufficient for sustaining an interest in his work—and thereby assuring a radiating influence yet to be revealed? By way of contrast, Jameson calls Knausgaard's writing formally "undistinguished" even as its content comprises a veritable "itemization" of life's (undistinguished) banalities; and moreover, as we see in Assayas's *Non-Fiction*, the ("successful") writer of autofiction can be undistinguished (in prose and also playfully here, in person), relying desperately on the act of adding a "thin smokescreen" to make and defend his art from those who would say it is otherwise-than-art.[151] But the autophilosopher has a different standard. Indeed, drawing upon a line of Emerson's that Cavell much admired (in part for its Kantian overtones), which Emerson lamentably excised from later editions, we may ask for ourselves, each and every reader, each and every time we read, whether or not we are "constrained to accept his standard."[152] For one person, a constraint is liberating; for another, or at another time, a limit is cause for bridling.[153] We can begrudgingly enjoy the odd fact that a phrase—a notion—that might capture our aspiration to autophilosophy as Cavell practiced it is now no longer part of the official catalogue of Emerson's prose. And yet because Cavell has recovered it—made it essential to his own experiments in autophilosophy—the notion has renewed life. We can adopt it for our ourselves as we come to know and think about the present and future of Cavell's work—as we find it expressed in his personal history, his writing, and his legacy of influence. What becomes of Cavell now? This book constitutes one answer, part of an ongoing chorus of such replies. But there are many years to come. What will we say then? When we say it, perhaps speaking of Stanley Cavell as an autophilosopher will provide further purchase on his distinctive and distinguished contribution to the exhibition of consecutive thought.[154]

Notes

1. Stanley Cavell, "Foreword: An Audience for Philosophy," *Must We Mean What We Say?* (New York: Charles Scribner's Sons, 1969; Cambridge: Cambridge University Press, 1976), xvii–xxix.
2. See, for example, Stanley Cavell, "An Autobiography of Companions" (3–15) and "Audience, Actor, and Star" (25–9), *The World Viewed: Reflections on the Ontology of Film* (Cambridge: Harvard University Press, 1971, enlarged edition, 1979). See also the preface (esp. xxii) and 111.
3. Stanley Cavell, *Cities of Words: Pedagogical Letters on a Register of the Moral Life* (Cambridge: Belknap Press of Harvard University Press, 2004), 331. See also Stanley Cavell, *Little Did I Know: Excerpts from Memory* (Stanford: Stanford University Press, 2010), for among many pertinent instances, two bona fide scenes of inheritance call out—one involving the reception of *Cities of Words* (493–5) and another addressing the reception of *The Claim of Reason* a quarter-century earlier (495–7), both occasions, at the end of his memoir, raising anew the question of audience: for whom is Cavell's work?
4. Henry David Thoreau, "Solitude," *Walden; or, Life in the Woods* (Boston: Houghton, Mifflin, 1893), 211. See also Stanley Cavell, *The Senses of Walden: An Expanded Edition* (San Francisco: North Point Press, 1981), 102.
5. Stanley Cavell, *A Pitch of Philosophy: Autobiographical Exercises* (Cambridge: Harvard University Press, 1994), 5.
6. In William Rothman's writing the relationship is given widespread attention, but one can look to a conspicuous case of engagement in his (and Marian Keane's) *Reading Cavell's The World Viewed: A Philosophical Perspective on Film* (Detroit: Wayne State University, 2000). For Timothy Gould's contribution, look to *Hearing Things: Voice and Method in the Writing of Stanley Cavell* (Chicago: University of Chicago Press, 1998), and "Me, Myself, and Us: Autobiography and Method in the Writing of Stanley Cavell," the first entry in the inaugural issue of *Conversations: The Journal of Cavellian Studies*, no. 1, 2013: *Genesis*, which takes Cavell's autobiographical writing as its theme. See also Áine Mahon, "Fraudulence, Obscurity, and Exposure: The Autobiographical Anxieties of Stanley Cavell," *The Philosophy of Autobiography*, ed. Christopher Crowley (Chicago: University of Chicago Press, 2015).
7. Gould, "Me, Myself, and Us," 4.
8. Stanley Cavell, "A Reply to John Hollander," *Themes Out of School: Effects and Causes* (San Francisco: North Point Press, 1984), 143.
9. Stanley Cavell, *The Claim of Reason: Wittgenstein, Skepticism, Morality, and Tragedy* (New York: Oxford University Press, 1979/1999), 496.
10. See *Non-Fiction* (2018, dir. Olivier Assayas), 00:29:40.
11. On this third point, see Cavell, *A Pitch of Philosophy*, 4.
12. Cavell, *The Claim of Reason*, 496.

13 Cavell, *The World Viewed*, xix.
14 Cora Diamond, "The Difficulty of Reality and the Difficulty of Philosophy," *Reading Cavell*, ed. Alice Crary and Sanford Shieh (New York: Routledge, 2006), 113. See Ralph Waldo Emerson, "The American Scholar," *The Complete Works of Ralph Waldo Emerson*, Concord Edition, ed. Edward Waldo Emerson (Boston: Houghton, Mifflin, 1903–4), vol. I, 110.
15 Cavell, *A Pitch of Philosophy*, 6.
16 Stanley Cavell, "Notes and Afterthoughts on the Opening of Wittgenstein's *Investigations*," *The Cambridge Companion to Wittgenstein*, ed. Hans Sluga and David G. Stern (Cambridge: Cambridge University Press, 1996), 271–2. See also, Diamond, "The Difficulty of Reality," 113.
17 Stanley Cavell, *Contesting Tears: The Hollywood Melodrama of the Unknown Woman* (Cambridge: Harvard University Press, 1996), epigraph and vii. See also "Reflections on a Life of Philosophy: Interview with Stanley Cavell," *Harvard Journal of Philosophy*, vol. 7, 1999, 25; and *The Thought of Stanley Cavell and Cinema: Turning Anew to the Ontology of Film a Half-Century after* The World Viewed, ed. David LaRocca (New York: Bloomsbury, 2020).
18 Cavell, *Cities of Words*, 29.
19 Cavell, *A Pitch of Philosophy*, 10.
20 Ibid., vii.
21 Ibid., 3.
22 Cavell, *Cities of Words*, 31, 124.
23 Cavell, *A Pitch of Philosophy*, 4.
24 Ibid.
25 Ibid.
26 Andrew Klevan, *Aesthetic Evaluation and Film* (Manchester: Manchester University Press, 2018), 113–14; italics in original.
27 Cavell, *A Pitch of Philosophy*, 5.
28 Ibid.
29 Ibid., 6.
30 Ibid., 8.
31 Ibid., 3; italics added.
32 Ibid., 8.
33 Cavell, *Cities of Words*, 8.
34 Cavell, *A Pitch of Philosophy*, 8.
35 Ibid., 9.
36 Klevan, *Aesthetic Evaluation and Film*, 83.
37 See in this volume, Susan Neiman, chapter 4, 95–102.
38 Cavell, *A Pitch of Philosophy*, 9.
39 Ibid., 9–10.

40 Ibid., 9; italics added.
41 Ibid.
42 The phrase "constitutional amending" is drawn from chapter 10 "Emerson's Constitutional Amending: Reading 'Fate,'" Stanley Cavell, *Emerson's Transcendental Etudes*, ed. David Justin Hodge (Stanford: Stanford University Press, 2003).
43 Cavell, *A Pitch of Philosophy*, 8.
44 Cavell, *Cities of Words*, 8, 29.
45 Ralph Waldo Emerson, "Self-Reliance," *Complete Works*, vol. II, 1841, 45.
46 On the charge of pretentiousness, see Cavell, *Themes Out of School*, 7, 18, 239.
47 Cavell, *A Pitch of Philosophy*, 10–11. See also my "Achilles' Tears: Cavell, the *Iliad*, and Possibilities for the Human," *Stanley Cavell and Aesthetic Understanding*, ed. Garry L. Hagberg (New York: Palgrave Macmillan, 2018).
48 Ibid., 11.
49 Cavell, *Little Did I Know*, 9.
50 Ibid., 8.
51 Cavell, *A Pitch of Philosophy*, 10.
52 For more on the role of acknowledgments in Cavell's work, see my "Acknowledgments: Thinking of and Thanking Stanley Cavell" in the commemorative issue of *Conversations: The Journal of Cavellian Studies*, no. 7, June 19, 2019: *Acknowledging Stanley Cavell*, ed. David LaRocca.
53 Cavell, *Emerson's Transcendental Etudes*, 1.
54 Cavell, *Must We Mean What We Say?*, x.
55 Ibid.
56 Cavell, *Cities of Words*, 39; Emerson, "Self-Reliance," 58.
57 For more on Malick and Cavell, see my "Thinking of Film: What Is Cavellian about Malick's Movies?," *A Critical Companion to Terrence Malick*, ed. Joshua Sikora (Lanham: Lexington Books, 2020), 3–19.
58 Cavell, *Cities of Words*, 41.
59 Fredric Jameson writes parenthetically, "the French decided to call it 'autofiction' at one point," "Itemized," *London Review of Books*, November 8, 2018, 5. Daniel Mendelsohn also invokes the term—and the French—when he speaks of the "gray zone that lies between fiction and autobiography," "I, Knausgaard," *New York Times Book Review*, September 30, 2018, 22.
60 For more on memory, see my "Memory Man: The Constitution of Personal Identity in *Memento* (and Some Metaphysical and Moral Implications of Choosing Not to Remember)," *The Philosophy of Christopher Nolan*, ed. Jason T. Eberl and George A. Dunn (Lanham: Lexington Books, 2017); "Memories. In the End, Is That All There Is? (Old Metaphors of Remembrance and the New Nature of Remembering)," *Downton Abbey and Philosophy: Thinking in That Manor*, ed. Adam Barkman and Robert Arp

(Chicago: Open Court, 2015); and "Weimar Cognitive Theory: Modernist Narrativity and the Metaphysics of Frame Stories (after *Caligari* and Kracauer)," *The Fictional Minds of Modernism: Narrative Cognition from Henry James to Christopher Isherwood*, ed. Ricardo Miguel-Alfonso (New York: Bloomsbury, 2020).

61 Jameson, "Itemized," 6.
62 Ibid.
63 Ibid., 8.
64 Ibid.
65 Toril Moi, *Revolution of the Ordinary: Literary Studies after Wittgenstein, Austin, and Cavell* (Chicago: University of Chicago Press, 2017), 115, 162. See also my review, "An Ordinary Investigation, or No Ordinary Investigation?," *American Book Review*, vol. 40, no. 5, July/August 2019.
66 Ralph Waldo Emerson, "The Transcendentalist," *Complete Works*, vol. I, 1842, 329.
67 See K. L. Evans, *One Foot in the Finite: Melville's Realism Reclaimed* (Evanston: Northwestern University Press, 2018).
68 Jameson, "Itemized," 8.
69 Thoreau, "Economy," *Walden*, 15; Emerson, "Self-Reliance," 55.
70 Cavell, *Emerson's Transcendental Etudes*, 85. See also my "'Eternal Allusion': Maeterlinck's Readings of Emerson's Somatic Semiotics," *A Power to Translate the World: New Essays on Emerson and International Culture*, ed. David LaRocca and Ricardo Miguel-Alfonso (Hanover: Dartmouth College Press, 2015), 133n35.
71 Elizabeth Hardwick, "Memoirs, Conversations, and Diaries," *Partisan Review*, vol. 20, no. 5, 1953.
72 Elizabeth Hardwick, "Memoirs, Conversations, and Diaries," *The Collected Essays of Elizabeth Hardwick* (New York: New York Review Books Classics), 5.
73 Hardwick, "Memoirs, Conversations, and Diaries," 13.
74 The phrase "thinly veiled autobiography" and its variants repeat in assessments of Melville's work, from Vernon Louis Parrington, *Main Currents in American Thought: 1620:1800* (New York: Harcourt, Brace, 1930), 261, to Jill Lepore, "Herman Melville at Home," *The New Yorker*, July 22, 2019. See my "Translating Carlyle: Ruminating on the Models of Metafiction at the Emergence of an Emersonian Vernacular," *Religions*, ed. Kenneth S. Sacks and Daniel Koch, vol. 8, no. 8, 2017.
75 Hardwick, "Memoirs, Conversations, and Diaries," 7; italics in original.
76 See Gould, *Hearing Things*; and Adam Gonya, *Stanley Cavell and the Potencies of Voice* (New York: Bloomsbury, 2019).
77 See in this volume, Mark Greif, chapter 3.
78 Mark Greif, "The Concept of Experience," *Against Everything: Essays* (New York: Vintage Books, 2016), 79–80.

79 Jameson, "Itemized," 8.
80 Greif, "The Concept of Experience," 88, 90.
81 Ibid., 91.
82 Ibid., 93. See Cavell, *Cities of Words*, 11.
83 See my "The Opacity of the Initial: Deciphering the Terms of Agency and Identity in 'Self-Reliance' and *On Liberty*," *Nineteenth Century Prose*, vol. 30, nos. 1/2, Spring/Fall 2003; "Unauthorized Autobiography: Truth and Fact in *Confessions of a Dangerous Mind*," *The Philosophy of Charlie Kaufman*, ed. David LaRocca (Lexington: University Press of Kentucky, 2011; with a new preface, 2019); "Rethinking the First Person: Autobiography, Authorship, and the Contested Self in *Malcolm X*," *The Philosophy of Spike Lee*, ed. Mark T. Conard (Lexington: University Press of Kentucky, 2011); and "Not Following Emerson: Intelligibility and Identity in the Authorship of Literature, Science, and Philosophy," *The Midwest Quarterly*, vol. 54, no. 2, Winter 2013.
84 Cavell, *Cities of Words*, 11, 50, 248.
85 Mendelsohn, "I, Knausgaard," 24.
86 Ibid., 22.
87 Ibid.
88 Ibid.
89 Ibid.
90 Ibid.
91 Cavell, *Little Did I Know*, 5–6.
92 See my "In the Place of Mourning: Questioning the Privations of the Private," *Nineteenth-Century Prose*, vol. 40, no. 1, Fall 2013.
93 Cavell, *Little Did I Know*, 9.
94 Ibid., 7.
95 Ibid., 6.
96 Cavell, "Knowing and Acknowledging," *Must We Mean What We Say?*, 240.
97 See in this volume, Andrew Klevan, chapter 2.
98 Cavell, *A Pitch of Philosophy*, 38–9.
99 For more on legible, interpretable texts that are not written, see my "Performative Inferentialism: A Semiotic Ethics," *Liminalities: A Journal of Performance Studies*, vol. 9, no. 1, February 2013.
100 Cavell, "Knowing and Acknowledging," *Must We Mean What We Say?*, 240.
101 Cavell, *A Pitch of Philosophy*, 22.
102 Cavell, *Little Did I Know*, 6; *Cities of Words*, 15; *A Pitch of Philosophy*, 4; and Stanley Cavell, "The Good of Film," *Cavell on Film*, ed. William Rothman (Albany: State University of New York Press, 2005), 340.
103 See my "The European Authorization of American Literature and Philosophy: After Cavell, Reading *Bartleby* with Deleuze, then Rancière,"

     Melville among the Philosophers, ed. Corey McCall and Tom Nurmi with an afterword by Cornel West (Lanham: Lexington Books, 2017).
104 Cavell, *Cities of Words*, 15.
105 Ibid.
106 Ibid.
107 Cavell, *Little Did I Know*, 6. See also my "Changing the Subject: The Auto/biographical as the Philosophical in Wittgenstein," *Epoché: A Journal for the History of Philosophy*, vol. 12, no. 1, Fall 2007; and "Note to Self: Learning to Write Autobiographical Remarks from Wittgenstein," *Wittgenstein Reading*, ed. Sascha Bru, Wolfgang Huemer, and Daniel Steuer (Berlin: De Gruyter, 2013).
108 Cavell, "Moral Reasoning: Teaching from the Core," *Cavell on Film*, 358.
109 See Stanley Cavell, *Conditions Handsome and Unhandsome: The Constitution of Emersonian Perfectionism* (Chicago: University of Chicago Press, 1990), 1, 3; Cavell, *Emerson's Transcendental Etudes*, 184.
110 Cavell, "Moral Reasoning," 356, 358.
111 See my introduction to *Conversations*, no. 7 (June 19, 2019), "Acknowledging Stanley Cavell"; Emerson, "Self-Reliance," 45.
112 Giles Harvey, "Publish and Perish," a review of *Non-Fiction* (2018, dir. Olivier Assayas), *The New York Review of Books*, May 23, 2019, 8.
113 Ibid., 9.
114 Hardwick, "Memoirs, Conversations, and Diaries," 7; italics in original.
115 Cavell, *Cities of Words*, 7.
116 Emerson, "Experience," *Complete Works*, vol. III, 1844, 48.
117 Ibid., 48–9.
118 Henry James, "Cabot's Emerson," *Estimating Emerson: An Anthology of Criticism from Carlyle to Cavell*, ed. David LaRocca (New York: Bloomsbury, 2013), 242; see also my notes on these topics in "A Conversation among Critics," the introduction to *Estimating Emerson*, 10–12; Newton Arvin, "The House of Pain: Emerson and the Tragic Sense," *The Hudson Review*, vol. 12, no. 1, Spring 1959, 38–9; and Sharon Cameron, "The Way of Life by Abandonment: Emerson's Impersonal," *Critical Inquiry*, vol. 25, Autumn 1998, 4.
119 Emerson, "The American Scholar," 100.
120 See selected pieces by James Russell Lowell in *Estimating Emerson*, 138–47.
121 Cavell, *Cities of Words*, 21.
122 Ibid.
123 Cavell, *A Pitch of Philosophy*, 11.
124 Ibid., 24–5, 27–8. "Our moulting season, like that of the fowls, must be a crisis in our lives," Thoreau, "Economy," *Walden*, 40. For more on masks and pseudonymity, see my "Inconclusive Unscientific Postscript: Late Remarks on Kierkegaard and Kaufman," *The Philosophy of Charlie*

Kaufman. For remarks on names and naming, see my *Emerson's English Traits and the Natural History of Metaphor* (New York: Bloomsbury, 2013), esp. chapter 16, "Titles Manifold," and for an account of Cavell's names and naming, see §§12–13, 315–23, and §17, 324–5.

125 Cavell, *A Pitch of Philosophy*, 11; Cavell, "Must We Mean What We Say?," *Must We Mean What We Say?*, 36 n31.

126 See for example, Cavell, "Music Discomposed" and "The Avoidance of Love: A Reading of *King Lear*," *Must We Mean What We Say?*

127 Cavell, *Cities of Words*, 282.

128 Emerson, "Self-Reliance," 45–6; *Nature*, vol. I, 76.

129 Cavell, *Little Did I Know*, 6.

130 Emerson, "Self-Reliance," 45.

131 Emerson, "Nominalist and Realist," *Complete Works*, vol. III, 1844, 233.

132 See in this volume, William Rothman, chapter 12, 103–10. See also my "Reading Cavell Reading," *Stanley Cavell, Literature, and Film: The Idea of America*, ed. Andrew Taylor and Áine Kelly (New York: Routledge, 2013).

133 Cavell, *The World Viewed*, xix.

134 Emerson, "Plato; or, the Philosopher," *Complete Works*, vol. IV, 1850, 43.

135 Hardwick, "Memoirs, Conversations, and Diaries," 5.

136 Arthur C. Danto, "In Their Own Voice: Philosophical Writing and Actual Experience," *The Body/Body Problem: Selected Essays* (Berkeley: University of California Press, 1999), 237.

137 Toril Moi, *Revolution of the Ordinary*, 163; For more from Toril Moi on autobiography and philosophy, see the previous chapter in this volume.

138 See again my "Performative Inferentialism: A Semiotic Ethics," *Liminalities: A Journal of Performance Studies*, vol. 9, no. 1, February 2013.

139 Cavell, *Cities of Words*, 13.

140 Ibid., 15.

141 Ibid., 7.

142 Donald E. Pease, "Re-Mapping the Transnational Turn," *Re-Framing the Transnational Turn in American Studies*, ed. Winfried Fluck, Donald E. Pease, and John Carlos Rowe (Hanover: Dartmouth College Press, 2011), 4.

143 Cavell, *Cities of Words*, 44.

144 Ibid.

145 Emerson, "Self-Reliance," 45.

146 Stanley Cavell, "Aesthetic Problems of Modern Philosophy," *Must We Mean What We Say?* (New York: Charles Scribner's Sons, 1969), 94, 96.

147 I thank Caroline Levine for remarks that inform this paragraph, including notes on her work for the conference "Undead Texts: Grand Narratives and the History of the Sciences," organized by Sharon Marcus and Lorraine Daston, Department of English and Comparative Literature, Columbia University, November 2018.

148 Arthur C. Danto, "Philosophy and/as Film and/as if Philosophy," *October*, vol. 23, Winter 1982, 13–14.
149 Danto, "In Their Own Voice," 237.
150 Russell B. Goodman, *Contending with Stanley Cavell* (Oxford: Oxford University Press, 2005), 3.
151 Jameson, "Itemized," 3.
152 Cavell, *Emerson's Transcendental Etudes*, 165, 257 n35.
153 See my "The Limits of Instruction: Pedagogical Remarks on Lars von Trier's *The Five Obstructions*," *Film and Philosophy*, vol. 13, 2009; "The Education of Grown-ups: An Aesthetics of Reading Cavell," *The Journal of Aesthetic Education*, vol. 47, no. 2, Summer 2013; "Teaching without Explication: Pedagogical Lessons from Rancière's *The Ignorant Schoolmaster* in *The Grand Budapest Hotel* and *The Emperor's Club*," *Journalism, Media and Cultural Studies*, vol. 10, 2016.
154 Cavell, *Emerson's Transcendental Etudes*, 85.

ACKNOWLEDGMENTS

IT IS A MEASURE OF THE PERFORMATIVE AND ILLOCUTIONARY FORCE of language that we deploy it as part of an attempt to expiate our debts. The customary form of this expression, or this effort, on the occasion of presenting a new book is called Acknowledgments, a mode uncannily aligned with certain Cavellian instincts to cross the barrier between self and other—to make a connection, to overcome (or at least live with) skepticism—and all of that by means of language. Thus, as two words uttered—"I do"—become the legal and existential condition for marriage (as it were, binding until death), so two words written—"I thank"—must bring reality to gratitude and let it stand in perpetuity.

What a genuine and perceptible pleasure it is for me to have this opportunity to thank the contributors to the present volume, one and all, who generously shared their memories and dreams of, and reflections on, the life and thought of Stanley Cavell. For your familiarity with Cavell's writing, and in many cases, your candor in speaking about your personal experiences with him, I anticipate that many readers—especially those unfamiliar with Cavell—will find this collection at once a stirring and an orienting introduction to the stakes of his life's work. For those familiar with the texts and contexts in which these remarks are made, they may be heartening and full of hard-won insights.

Thanking Haaris Naqvi never gets old, and indeed, the thanks become richer with each season of collaboration; I remain delighted in my debts to his stewardship. For this project, Haaris offered notes on how to best cast the volume, how it could be given a distinctive conceptual shape; conversations about the nature of the *festschrift*, and ways to innovate from it, were decisive. For their care and attention, navigating production with Amy Martin and Zoë Jellicoe, and in the last stretch, Rachel Walker, has been a pleasure. Production affiliates, including Shyam Sunder, provided necessary expertise for the realization of the book.

I am duly beholden to Boris Dralyuk, executive editor of the *Los Angeles Review of Books*, for his exceedingly generous support of this project and allowing Marshall Cohen's piece to be featured here; that Cohen's remarks occupy the pole position should indicate my esteem for the work and thus my thanks to Boris in being able to share it. In a similarly crucial moment of editorial *espirit du corps*, I turn to Mark Krotov, publisher of *n+1*, for graciously allowing the reproduction of Mark Greif's work.

I extend my gratitude to those who provided the occasions for enriching and extending the content of this collection, including Cathleen Cavell, who kindly put me in touch with Susan Neiman. Relatedly, a number of salient events in recent years availed the conditions for developing content and contributions to this volume, most especially:

"Celebrating the Life and Work of Stanley Cavell," convened in Emerson Hall 105, Harvard University, November 2018, with an assembled crowd of dedicated readers, colleagues, students, friends and family;

The "Think Herzog!" event in April 2019 sponsored by the Colloquium for Unpopular Culture and the Deutsches Haus at New York University, in company with Richard Eldridge, Paul Cronin, Sukhdev Sandhu, and Thomas Elsaesser;

"Le Pensée du cinéma: en hommage à Stanley Cavell," a gathering at the Université Paris 1 Panthéon Sorbonne in June 2019 organized by Sandra Laugier—and her colleagues and co-organizers, especially Elise Domenach—provided a series of stirring scenes of intellectual companionship (recalling in particular conversations with Sandra and Elise as well as Cathleen Cavell, David Cavell, Marc Cerisuelo, Hugo Clémot, Alice Crary, Byron Davies, Piergiorgio Donatelli, Yves Erard, Russell Goodman, Andrew Klevan, Victor Krebs, Paola Marrati, Richard Moran, Kitty Morgan, Stephen Mulhall, Kate Rennebohm, Eric Ritter, D. N. Rodowick, William Rothman, Naoko Saito, and Paul Standish, among others) including the spirited viewing of essential films at Le Champo;

A season later, again in Paris (and before that in Lille), conversations with Branka Arsić and Maurice Lee provided a further complement;

In September 2019, it was a rare treat to welcome Thomas Elsaesser to Cornell University, where he engaged the community on media archaeology and generously screened and commented upon his own remarkable contribution to the field of media archaeology artifacts, *The Sun Island* (2017). I should like to acknowledge the many cosponsors for Elsaesser's visit and principally the partisans who supported and celebrated it, among them: Amy Villarejo, Nick Salvato, Jeremy Braddock, Patrizia McBride, Erik Born, Leslie Adelson, Paul Fleming, and Kizer Walker. Special thanks to Mary Fessenden of Cornell Cinema for hosting the exhibition of Elsaesser's film. Thomas's sudden death a dozen weeks later makes the memory of his visit that much more poignant and precious.

In November 2019, I joined Paul Cronin for a visit to Clinton, New York, where we were welcomed at Hamilton College by Scott MacDonald for an installment of his ongoing Forum on Image and Language in Motion that featured Cronin's epic documentary, *A Time to Stir* (2019). Conversations with Paul and Scott continue to deeply inform my approach to the reception of film as well as Cavell's relationship to that project.

At the time this volume was going to press, I received a gracious invitation from Arnaud Petit to join illustrious others at the "Inheriting Cavell" conference to be convened at the University of Ottawa in June 2020, that is, until the coronavirus pandemic forced its postponement.

And so I recall an earlier series of occasions that proved illuminating, including an invitation to the New Directions conference at the University of Arizona in April 2018, with thanks to Emily Thomas and the community of students and faculty in the Department of English; an invitation to the Docusophia: Documentary Film and Philosophy conference at Tel Aviv University in May 2018, sponsored by the Steve Tisch School of Film and Television and in collaboration with the Docaviv Film Festival, with gratitude to organizers and hosts Shai Biderman, Dan Geva, and Ohad Landesman as well as participants, Linda Williams and Thomas Wartenberg; and an invitation to Lund University in October 2018, where Oscar Jansson and his colleagues at the Centre for Languages and Literatures and the Department of Comparative Literature created a productive space for discussing Cavell, cinematic sound, and *Geschlecht.*

As it happens, there are two recent volumes that feel like genuine companions to the work of this collection, and which, in turn, make conspicuous the way the three projects undertake independent—but still interrelated—researches. First, a commemorative issue of *Conversations: The Journal of Cavellian Studies*, No. 7 (2019): *Acknowledging Stanley Cavell*, which was published open-access on July 19th of that year, that is, on the one-year anniversary of Cavell's death; for this initiative, I remain enormously grateful to Amir Khan, Sérgio Dias Branco, and the Advisory Board for entrusting me with the guest editorship of that special issue. Second, I am thinking of *The Thought of Stanley Cavell and Cinema: Turning Anew to the Ontology of Film a Half-Century after* The World Viewed (2020). So it is that as I convey, here, my first round of thanks to contributors of *Inheriting Stanley Cavell*, I have a chance to reiterate my still-fresh thanks to those who fulfilled the mission of these other investigations. I am keenly appreciative of all these talented contributors for their trust and hard work, and generosity with both.

My memorial thanks to Stanley Cavell, which are as sincerely expressed as they are indelibly felt, have found a place in the aforementioned issue of *Conversations*, in a note entitled "Acknowledgments: Thinking of and Thanking Stanley Cavell."

In recent years, deliberations with colleagues and students at several institutions have been crucial to the development of this and related initiatives, in particular, while I served as visiting assistant professor in the Cinema Department at Binghamton University; visiting assistant professor in the Department of Philosophy at the State University of New York College at Cortland; Lecturer in Screen Studies in the Department of Cinema, Photography, and Media Arts at the Roy H. Park School of

Communications at Ithaca College; and visiting scholar in the Department of English at Cornell University.

Over this same period, the School of Criticism and Theory at Cornell University has for me become a reliable source of provocative reports on the state of the academic humanities. Hent de Vries remains a stalwart presence, and I delight in thanking Emily Apter and members of her "Thinking in Untranslatables" seminar, among other visitors and participants.

I have been lucky to discuss some of the finer points of German lexicography and grammar with Hent de Vries, Kizer Walker, Herwig Friedl, Peter Gilgen, and Mario von der Ruhr—and thank them individually for their kindness and expertise, no doubt saving me from conspicuous errors. Benefiting from their counsel, as ever, does not necessarily mean I avoided trouble; experimental progress is ever by degrees.

My thanks continue to the community of thoughtful, kind, and supportive people who lent good advice and good cheer, and some measure of perspicacity and/or provisions, during the project's development: Steven Affeldt, Diana Allan, Branka Arsić, the Avgar family (Amos and Jan, Ariel and Christie), J. M. Bernstein, Joel Bettridge, Jason and Catherine Blumenkamp, Elisabeth Bronfen, Curtis Brown, Rebecca M. Brown, Giuliana Bruno, Kate and Dave Cavell, Elisabeth Ceppi, Samuel A. Chambers, Timothy Corrigan, Simon Critchley, Paul Cronin, Brunello Cucinelli, Julia Cumes, Jigme and Haven S. R. Daniels, Kenneth Dauber, William Day, Douglas Drake, Andrew and Jane Fitz-Gibbon, William Flesch, Michael Fried, Tarleton and Jenna Lahmann Gillespie, Larry Gottheim, Timothy Gould, Christopher Grau, Vincent Grenier, Paul Grimstad, Garry Hagberg, David and Stephanie Insley Hershinow, Ann M. Hodge, Katherine Kelley, Joshua Landy, Caroline Levine, Giorgiana Magnolfi, John Masters, Richard Moran, John Opera, Joni Papp, Tristan Philip, Robert B. Pippin, Michael Puett, Laura Quinney, Masha Raskolnikov, Lawrence F. Rhu, D. N. Rodowick, P. Adams Sitney, Kristen Steslow, Garrett Stewart, Alessandro Subrizi (and the expanded family, along with dear Tekla and Elio), Gabrielle Tenzer, Andreas Teuber, George Toles, Sarah Walston, Catherine Wheatley, Katja Wessling, and the scullers of Skootamatta (Etheridge, Fitzgerald, Halverson); in conjunction with the production of the film *New York Photographer: Jill Freedman in the City*, Rita Mullaney, Maxwell Anderson, and the late Jill Freedman; members and guests of the Signet Society of Harvard College; and at Cornell University Library, Fred Muratori, bibliographer for English-language Literature, Theater, and Film.

With sustained love and gratitude to Sheldon and Lorna K. Hershinow, Ian M. Evans and Luanna H. Meyer, Frances LaRocca and Roselle Sweeney, David N. and Hi-jin Hodge.

To Ruby and Star, who have recalibrated my sense of success and succession, what it means to succeed and be succeeded, you are marvels fit for awe and admiration, and you have mine entirely. And to Kim, last in the list, first in my heart, what a glory and gift to share this fleeting life with you, making something of substance from ethereal hours. With each new day, you three guide and give shape to my memories, dreams, and reflections. I am grateful to be in your orbits.

CONTRIBUTORS

Marshall Cohen is University Professor Emeritus and Dean Emeritus of the Dornsife College of Letters, Arts, and Sciences at the University of Southern California. He completed his undergraduate studies at Dartmouth College and earned two masters degrees, one from Harvard University and the other from the University of Oxford. With academic interests in jurisprudence; moral, legal, and political philosophy; and the philosophy of art, he has written on a broad number of topics relating to these areas of study, including *Film Theory and Criticism: Introductory Readings*, 8th ed. (edited with Leo Braudy, 2016; first published in 1974), *What Is Dance? Readings in Theory and Criticism* (edited with Roger Copeland, 1983), *Punishment* (edited with A. J. Simmons, J. Cohen, and C. Beitz, 1995), *Ronald Dworkin and Contemporary Jurisprudence* (1984), and *War and Moral Responsibility* (edited with Thomas Nagel and T. M. Scanlon, 1974). He taught at a number of universities, including Yale University and the University of Chicago, before joining the USC Gould School of Law faculty and being named Dean of Humanities at USC in 1983. Cohen is founding editor of the journal *Philosophy and Public Affairs* and is vice chair of the Board of Directors of the American Council of Learned Societies.

Andrew Klevan is Professor of Film Aesthetics at the University of Oxford. He is the author of *Disclosure of the Everyday: Undramatic Achievement in Narrative Film* (2000), *Film Performance: From Achievement to Appreciation* (2005), *Barbara Stanwyck* (2013), and *Aesthetic Evaluation and Film* (2018). He is coeditor of *The Language and Style of Film Criticism* (2011) and is on the editorial board of *Movie: A Journal of Film Criticism*.

Mark Greif is Associate Professor of English at Stanford University. He earned his BA from Harvard, studied British literature on a Marshall Scholarship at Oxford, received his PhD in American studies from Yale, and later taught at the New School and Brown. He is a founding editor of the literary journal *n+1*, in collaboration with Keith Gessen, Chad Harbach, Benjamin Kunkel, Allison Lorentzen, and Marco Roth. He is the author of *The Age of the Crisis of Man: Thought and Fiction in America, 1933–73* (2015) and *Against Everything: Essays* (2017), and coeditor and coauthor of

What Was the Hipster? A Sociological Investigation (2010), *Occupy!: Scenes from Occupied America* (2011), and *The Trouble Is the Banks: Letters to Wall Street* (2012). His work has appeared in the *London Review of Books*, the *New York Times*, *Süddeutsche Zeitung*, and *Le Monde*. A recipient of fellowships from the Institute of Advanced Study at Princeton, the Center for Advanced Study in the Behavioral Sciences at Stanford, and the American Council of Learned Societies, he is a member of the New York Institute for the Humanities at New York University.

Susan Neiman studied at Harvard University with Stanley Cavell and John Rawls, as well as at the Freie Universität Berlin. She was professor at Yale University and Tel Aviv University before becoming the director of the Einstein Forum in Germany. Her books, translated into many languages, include *Slow Fire: Jewish Notes from Berlin*; *The Unity of Reason: Rereading Kant*; *Evil in Modern Thought: An Alternative History of Philosophy*; *Fremde Sehen Anders*; *Moral Clarity*; *Why Grow Up?*; and *Learning from the Germans: Race and the Memory of Evil*. She is also the author of over a hundred articles and essays for academic and general audiences. She is a member of the Berlin-Brandenburg Akademie der Wissenschaften and the American Philosophical Society. The mother of three grown children, she lives in Berlin.

William Rothman is Professor of Cinema and Interactive Media in the School of Communication at the University of Miami. He received his PhD in Philosophy from Harvard, where he was an Associate Professor in Visual and Environmental Studies (1976–84), and was Director of the International Honors Program on Film, Television and Social Change in Asia (1986–90). He was the founding editor and series editor of Harvard University Press's "Harvard Film Studies" series, and for many years was series editor of Cambridge University Press's "Studies in Film." His books include the landmark study *Hitchcock—The Murderous Gaze* (1982; expanded edition 2012), *The "I" of the Camera* (1988; expanded edition 2004); *Documentary Film Classics* (1997); *A Philosophical Perspective on Film* (2000); *Cavell on Film* (2005); *Jean Rouch: A Celebration of Life and Film* (2007); *Three Documentary Filmmakers* (2009); *Must We Kill the Thing We Love? Emersonian Perfectionism and the Films of Alfred Hitchcock* (2014); *Looking with Robert Gardner* (2016); and *Tuitions and Intuitions: Essays at the Intersection of Film Criticism and Philosophy* (2019).

Edward T. Duffy is Emeritus Associate Professor of English at Marquette University. He has also taught at the University of Kansas and the University of California at Santa Barbara. His main area of study has been English Romanticism with a special emphasis on Wordsworth and Shelley and his most recent book, *Secular Mysteries: Stanley Cavell and English*

Romanticism (2013), brings the work of these two poets into conversation with the thought and writing of Cavell. His preoccupation with Cavell's interests—what Cavell once confessed to be the "jungle or wilderness" of them—has given shape to Duffy's own interests for more than forty years, and has informed his essays on subjects ranging from Raymond Carver to the Gospel of Luke. He is currently nearing the completion of a book whose tentative title is *Translating Poetry in Seamus Heaney*.

Charles Bernstein is Donald T. Regan Professor, Emeritus, of English and Comparative Literature at the University of Pennsylvania. A member of the American Academy of Arts and Sciences, he is the 2019 winner of the Bollingen Prize for American Poetry, the major US prize for lifetime achievement. He is the author of the book of poems, *Near/Miss* (2018), and the book of essays, *Pitch of Poetry* (2016), among other books. He studied with Cavell as an undergraduate (1968–72), and his memoir of meeting Cavell was published as part of a Cavell feature in *ASAP Journal*.

Ann Lauterbach is the author of ten books of poetry and three books of essays, including *The Night Sky: Writings on the Poetics of Experience* (2006) and *The Given & The Chosen* (2011); her 2009 poetry collection, *Or to Begin Again*, was nominated for a National Book Award. *Spell*, her most recent collection, was published in 2018. She has written essays on the relation between poetics, aesthetics, and politics, as well as on the work of individual visual artists. She taught critical writing at the School of Visual Arts in New York City and was a visiting critic (sculpture) at the Yale School of Art. Her work has received support from the Guggenheim Foundation (1986), the John D. and Catherine T. MacArthur Foundation (1993), and was the subject of a conference in Paris in 2015. She is Ruth and David Schwab II Professor of Languages and Literature at Bard College, where she has been, since 1992, Co-Chair of Writing in Bard's multidisciplinary MFA. A native of New York City, she lives in Germantown, New York.

Kenneth Dauber is Professor of English at the State University of New York at Buffalo. He is the author of *Rediscovering Hawthorne* (1977), *The Idea of Authorship in America: Democratic Poetics from Franklin to Melville* (1990), and, most recently, *The Logic of Sentiment: Stowe, Hawthorne, and Melville* (2019). He is coeditor, with Walter Jost, of *Ordinary Language Criticism: Literary Thinking after Cavell after Wittgenstein* (2003). His piece, "Ordinary Language Criticism: A Manifesto," appeared in *Arizona Quarterly* (1997).

K. L. Evans is the author of *Whale!* (2003) and more recently *One Foot in the Finite: Melville's Realism Reclaimed* (2018), and coeditor, with Branka Arsić, of *Melville's Philosophies* (2017). A contributor to *Stanley Cavell: Philosophy,*

Literature, and Criticism (2012), she has taught at the University of Redlands, Stern College of Yeshiva University in New York City, the College at Cortland, and for the Telluride Association Summer Program at Cornell University. A Fulbright scholar who conducted research in New Zealand, she completed her doctoral studies under the direction of Kenneth Dauber. She has participated in multiple National Endowment for the Humanities Institutes and twice in the School of Criticism and Theory at Cornell University.

Lawrence F. Rhu is William Joseph Todd Professor of the Renaissance in Italy, Emeritus, at the University of South Carolina. He has published two books, *The Genesis of Tasso's Narrative Theory: English Translations of the Early Poetics and a Comparative Study of Their Significance* (1993) and *Stanley Cavell's American Dream: Shakespeare, Philosophy, and Hollywood Movies* (2006), as well as numerous essays, articles, and reviews. He edited *The Winter's Tale* in the Evans Shakespeare Editions (2011).

Robert B. Pippin is Evelyn Stefansson Nef Distinguished Service Professor of Social Thought, Philosophy, and in the College at the University of Chicago. He is a past winner of the Mellon Distinguished Achievement Award in the Humanities and a Guggenheim Fellowship, and he is a member of the American Academy of Arts and Sciences, the American Philosophical Society, and the German National Academy of Sciences Leopoldina. He works primarily on the modern German philosophical tradition, with a concentration on Kant and Hegel, and has published on theories of modernity, political philosophy, self-consciousness, the nature of conceptual change, and the problem of freedom. He has a number of interdisciplinary interests, especially those that involve the relation between philosophy and literature. He is the author of many books, including *Henry James and Modern Moral Life* (2001); *The Persistence of Subjectivity: On the Kantian Aftermath* (2005); *Fatalism in American Film Noir: Some Cinematic Philosophy* (2013); *Hegel's Realm of Shadows: Logic as Metaphysics in* The Science of Logic (2018); *The Philosophical Hitchcock:* Vertigo *and the Anxieties of Unknowningness* (2019); *Interanimations: Receiving Modern German Philosophy* (2015); and *Filmed Thought: Cinema as Reflective Form* (2019).

William Day is Professor of Philosophy at Le Moyne College (Syracuse, New York). He is contributing coeditor (with Victor J. Krebs) of *Seeing Wittgenstein Anew* (2010), and has published numerous articles and book chapters on Wittgenstein, Cavell, and topics in aesthetics. These include readings of post-1940s films in light of Cavell's study of remarriage comedies and examinations of the moral perfectionist structure of exemplary jazz improvisation. Essays on contemporary remarriage comedies include "I Don't Know, Just Wait: Remembering Remarriage in *Eternal Sunshine* *of the Spotless Mind"* (*The Philosophy of Charlie Kaufman*, 2011) and "*Moonstruck*, or How to Ruin Everything" (*Ordinary Language Criticism*, 2003). Among Day's writings addressing Cavell's thought directly are "A Soteriology of Reading: Cavell's Excerpts from Memory" (*Stanley Cavell: Philosophy, Literature and Criticism*, 2011) and "*Zhenzhi* and Acknowledgment in Wang Yangming and Stanley Cavell" (*European and Chinese Philosophy: Origins and Intersections*, 2013), which one reviewer has called "the very best account of the notion of acknowledgement in any of the literature that I am aware of."

Andreas Teuber studied philosophy as an undergraduate at St. John's College, Oxford, with Paul Grice and at Harvard with Stanley Cavell, who was his senior honors thesis advisor. As a graduate student, he was a teaching assistant for the large General Education course in the Humanities that Stanley taught for many years, each and every spring. John Rawls and Robert Nozick were his PhD dissertation advisors. Shortly after receiving his PhD, he was invited by Albert Hirschman and Clifford Geertz to become a member and fellow of the Institute for Advanced Study in Princeton. He is a recipient of a Fulbright Fellowship and a National Endowment for the Humanities Fellowship as well as two teaching awards, the Michael Laban Walzer Award for Teaching and the Kermit H. Perlmutter Fellowship Award for Excellence in Teaching. His syllabus for the Introduction to Philosophy course that he teaches at Harvard during the summer and at Brandeis in the fall has been listed among the top ten most popular philosophy syllabi in the world. Currently, he is a Professor of Philosophy at Brandeis University and served as department chair from 2006 to 2011. While still an undergraduate at Oxford, he was cast in the role of Mephistopheles in the Oxford University Dramatic Society production of Christopher Marlowe's *Doctor Faustus*, opposite Richard Burton as Faustus and Elizabeth Taylor as Helen of Troy, and repeated his role in the Columbia Pictures movie version (1967, dir. Richard Burton and Nevill Coghill).

Timothy Gould is Professor of Philosophy at Metropolitan State University of Denver and the author of *Hearing Things: Voice and Method in the Writing of Stanley Cavell* (1998). He has written about Wordsworth, Kant, Mill, Nietzsche, Freud, and Wittgenstein, and has incorporated in his essays criticism about Emily Dickinson, George Eliot, Aristophanes, Charlotte Bronte, Shakespeare, Hitchcock, and Jean Renoir. He is working on a manuscript entitled *The Names of Action: Wittgenstein, Austin, Nietzsche, and Cavell on the Issues of Action*, which addresses philosophy, literature, film, and politics.

Rex Butler is Professor of Art History in the Faculty of Art Design and Architecture at Monash University Melbourne. He writes on historical and contemporary Australian art. He has also written books on a number of literary and philosophical figures (Baudrillard, Borges, Deleuze, Guattari, and Žižek), and most recently completed *Stanley Cavell and the Arts: Philosophy and Popular Culture* (2020).

Sandra Laugier is Professor of Philosophy at Université Paris 1 Panthéon Sorbonne, Paris, France, and a senior member of Institut Universitaire de France. She is codirector of the Institut des sciences juridique et philosophique de la Sorbonne (Université Paris 1/CNRS). A former student of the Ecole Normale Supérieure and Harvard University, she has extensively published in French, English, Italian, and German on ordinary language philosophy (Wittgenstein, Austin, Cavell), moral perfectionism (Cavell, Thoreau, Emerson), popular culture (film and TV series), gender studies, democracy, and civil disobedience. She is the translator of Stanley Cavell's work into French and has written extensively on his work. She is a senior member of Institut Universitaire de France (2012, renewed in 2018), member of Academia Europea, and was awarded the Légion d'Honneur. Recent publications include *Why We Need Ordinary Language Philosophy* (2013); *Recommencer la philosophie—Cavell et la philosophie américaine aujourd'hui* (2014); *Le principe démocratie*, with A. Ogien (2014); *Antidémocratie*, with A. Ogien (2017); *Formes de vie*, ed. with Estelle Ferrarese, 2018); and *Nos vies en séries* (2019). She is also a columnist for *Chronique Philosophiques* at the French journal *Libération:* www.liberation.fr/auteur/6377-sandra-laugier.

Steven G. Affeldt is Associate McDevitt Chair in Religious Philosophy and Faculty Director of the Manresa Program at Le Moyne College. He received his BA in philosophy from the University of California, Berkeley, and his PhD in philosophy from Harvard University (where he was a student of Stanley Cavell and, for many years, his research assistant). Deeply informed by Cavell's teaching and writing, Affeldt's research charts intersections of ethics, social/political philosophy, and aesthetics. Drawing on a wide range of figures that include Plato, Augustine, Rousseau, Kant, Emerson, Kierkegaard, Nietzsche, Freud, Heidegger, and Wittgenstein, his work elaborates ways in which philosophy and philosophical texts may be redemptive—possessed of the power to inspire, inform, and effect liberating transformations of both individuals and societies. He has published highly influential articles on Rousseau, Wittgenstein, and Cavell and is currently at work on a monograph explicating, and charting critical ramifications of, what he argues is a decisive turn in Cavell's work following *The Claim of Reason*—the turn from situating philosophy as a Modernist enterprise to situating it as a Romantic quest. Prior to his appointment at Le Moyne College, Affeldt was a junior fellow in the Society of Fellows at the University of Chicago and held teaching appointments at Johns Hopkins, Notre Dame, and the New School University.

Richard Deming is Director of Creative Writing in the Department of English at Yale University, is a poet, art critic, and theorist whose work explores the intersections of poetry, philosophy, and visual culture. His first collection of poems, *Let's Not Call It Consequence* (2008), received the 2009 Norma Farber Award from the Poetry Society of America. His most recent book of poems, *Day for Night*, appeared in 2016. He is also the author of *Listening on All Sides: Toward an Emersonian Ethics of Reading* (2008); *Art of the Ordinary: The Everyday Domain of Art, Film, Literature, and Philosophy* (2018); and *Touch of Evil* (2020). He contributes to such magazines as *Artforum*, *Sight & Sound*, and *The Boston Review*. Winner of the Berlin Prize, he was the Spring 2012 John P. Birkelund Fellow of the American Academy in Berlin.

Toril Moi is James B. Duke Professor of Literature and Romance Studies, and Professor of English, Philosophy, and Theater Studies at Duke University. She has published widely on feminist theory, Simone de Beauvoir, Henrik Ibsen, and modernism. Her book *Henrik Ibsen and the Birth of Modernism* (2006) is inspired by Stanley Cavell's work on theater and modernism. She is the author of *Revolution of the Ordinary: Literary Studies after Wittgenstein, Austin, and Cavell* (2017). Her essay "Rethinking Character," dealing with the belief that literary critics must never treat characters as if they were real people, was recently published in *Character: Three Inquiries in Literary Studies* (2019), a book cowritten with Amanda Anderson and Rita Felski.

David LaRocca is the author or contributing editor of more than a dozen books, and has written over a hundred published articles, chapters, essays, and reviews. Advised by Stanley Cavell during doctoral research, he later edited, annotated, and indexed Cavell's *Emerson's Transcendental Etudes* (2003) and worked as Cavell's research assistant during the time he was completing *Cities of Words: Pedagogical Letters on a Register of the Moral Life* (2004) and *Philosophy the Day after Tomorrow* (2005), and beginning *Little Did I Know: Excerpts from Memory* (2010). He subsequently edited additional books featuring Cavell's work, including *Estimating Emerson: An Anthology of Criticism from Carlyle to Cavell* (2013) and *The Bloomsbury Anthology of Transcendental Thought: From Antiquity to the Anthropocene* (2017), and contributed chapters to *Stanley Cavell, Literature, and Film: The Idea of America* (2013), *Stanley Cavell and Aesthetic Understanding* (2018), and *Understanding Cavell, Understanding Modernism* (2022). He served as guest editor of a commemorative issue of *Conversations: The Journal of Cavellian Studies*, No. 7 (2019): *Acknowledging Stanley Cavell*, and edited *The Thought of Stanley Cavell and Cinema: Turning Anew to the Ontology of Film a Half-*

Century after The World Viewed (2020), *Movies with Stanley Cavell in Mind* (2021), *Metacinema: The Form and Content of Filmic Reference and Reflexivity* (2021), and *The Geschlecht Complex: Addressing Untranslatable Aspects of Gender, Genre, and Ontology* (2022). He is the author of *On Emerson* (2003) and *Emerson's English Traits and the Natural History of Metaphor* (2013) and editor of a trilogy of books on philosophy and film: *The Philosophy of Charlie Kaufman* (2011), *The Philosophy of War Films* (2014), and *The Philosophy of Documentary Film: Image, Sound, Fiction, Truth* (2017). His articles have appeared in journals such as *Afterimage, Epoché, Estetica, Liminalities, Post Script, Transactions, Film and Philosophy, The Senses and Society, The Midwest Quarterly, Journalism, Media and Cultural Studies, Cinema: Journal of Philosophy and the Moving Image, The Journal of Aesthetic Education,* and *The Journal of Aesthetics and Art Criticism*. He studied rhetoric at Berkeley, has held visiting research or teaching positions in philosophy, cinema, and English at Binghamton, Cornell, Cortland, Harvard, Ithaca College, the New York Public Library, the School of Visual Arts, and Vanderbilt, and has participated in a National Endowment for the Humanities Institute, a cinema workshop with Abbas Kiarostami, Werner Herzog's Rogue Film School, and the School of Criticism and Theory at Cornell University. www.DavidLaRocca.org DavidLaRocca@Post.Harvard.Edu.

INDEX

abandonment 14–15, 293, 295
  transformation and 188–9
academia
  fecundity of personal experience for 266
  graduate school education 171
  importance, problem of 161, 176 n.1
  intellectual industrial complex 171
  university curriculum 74–5, 81–2, 247–8
academics
  aestheticians 208
  American 53, 74, 81–2
  defending their interests 261–2
  as managerial class ch. 9 (141–60)
accounting 1, 27, 256, 291.
        See also Henry David Thoreau: economy
Adams, John 83
Adam's Rib (1949) 23, 91
Adorno, Theodor W. 131–2, 134
aestheticism 293
Albritton, Rogers 53
Alfred, William 161–3, 175
Alighieri, Dante 126
America
  as home 83
  idea of 25, 66, 83, 86, 101–2, 232–3, 273, 307–8
  offered to philosophy 81
  place of migration 83
American cinema
  American philosophy and 23, 66, 81, 87
American culture, 100–2, 110, 163, 273
  that there is such a thing as 101
American Dream 34–5
American Philosophical Society 54

Améry, Jean 96–7
Andenken 5
anecdote
  acknowledgment of what it can offer 266
  autobiography and 282–3, 286
  eccentricity and 283, 286
  enduring lesson from 9–10
  public significance of 275–6, 306
  as testament 300–1
Anglo-American analytic tradition 2, 51, 78–9, 81, 91, 95–6, 100, 102, 232, 252–3, 307
  Cavell as reinventor of 100
anoriginality (Andrew Benjamin) 133
Antonioni, Michelangelo 88
anxiety
  of influence 18, 173
  of inheritance 18, 18 n.49
appreciation, concept of 255–6, 259 n.24
Arendt, Hannah 69, 90–1, 94 n.4
Aristotle 22, 85, 259 n.25
  The Lyceum 75
Arnheim, Rudolf 87
arrogance
  arrogation and 74, 272, 281, 283–6
  autobiographicality and 281–6
Arnold, Matthew 20, 155
art
  in the condition of philosophy 110
  describing art as a form of 191
  Disneyfication of 131–2
Ashbery, John 139
aspect-seeing 197 n.17
Assayas, Olivier 299–301, 307, 311–12
Astaire, Fred 56, 115–17, 123, ch. 7 (129–36), 262

attentiveness
  critic and, work of 67, 282–3
  to the everyday, details of 290–1
  inattentiveness and 238
  mode of philosophical 298–9
  to ordinary language 248
  sustained 65
audience
  addressing an 39, 73
  need for the friendship of the reader 173
  ordinary language criticism, why it has no 144
  for philosophy ch. 20 (275–320)
  question of 282–3, 313 n.3
  uncertainty of its, philosophy's 283
  writing to whom 162
Auerbach, Erich 311
Austin, J. L. 11, 13, 23, 52–5, 73, 79, 114, 191
  autobiographical, demands a systematic engagement with the 283
  Hare, R. M., story about bribe 210–11
  at Harvard University 13–14, 73, 78–9, 118
  "Other Minds" 114
  philosophizing of 232
  praising, work elucidates the act of 134–5
  procedures of 299
  skepticism, dismissal of 220
  speech acts and 115, 233–5
  teaching, devoted to 158
  theory of performatives 93, 129, 133–5
  at the University of Oxford 65–6
  verification and, question of 285.
  See also Cavell: Austin
autobiographical
  claim to representativeness 285–7
  drive in all of us 231–2
  exercises 12–13, 306
  experience, appeal to 277–8
  philosophers who shun the 284–5
  quest for authority naturally tends toward the 277

autobiographical (cont.)
  structural not personal 281–3
  writing, reading film in 238
autobiographicality
  arrogance and 281–2
autobiographically
  daring to write, Cavell 97
autobiography
  anecdote and 9–10, 266, 275–76, 281–3, 286, 300–1, 306
  Cavell and 104, 236, ch. 19 (269–74), ch. 20 (275–320)
  moviegoing and 239, 279–80, 306
  philosophy and ch. 12 (187–98), ch. 16 (231–42), ch. 17 (243–60), ch. 18. (261–8), ch. 19 (269–74), ch. 20 (275–320)
  dimension of 270–2, 281, 286, 306
  internal connection with 237, 281
  of the species 306
  writing, core of 239
autofiction 289–91, 295–6, 300–2, 307, 309, 311–12, 315 n.59
  autofact and 296
autophilosopher, task of the 278, 301–2, 311–12
autophilosophy ch. 20 (275–320)
  how to heed Cavellian lessons in 305
  temperament for 307
  as the transformation of the everyday 308
The Awful Truth (1937) 166
Ayer, A. J. 79, 130

Bach, Johann Sebastian 52, 149, 156, 271–2
Bacon, Francis 87
Baldwin, James 301
The Band Wagon (1953) 115–16, 132–3
Basie, Count 193
Batkin, Norton 137
Bazin, André 87
Beauvoir, Simone de 90–1, 97, 270–1, 274, 311
Beckett, Samuel 79, 105–6, 200
Beckwith, Sarah 270
Bell, Michael 67
Bellow, Saul 301

INDEX 337

Benjamin, Walter 106, 130–3, 194–5
Bennett, Joan 63
Bergman, Ingmar 29–30, 37, 88
  crises of integrity and despair
    in 163
Bergman, Ingrid 270
Berkeley, George 99
Berkeley, University of California 6–7,
    52–4, 78, 88, 118, 170–1, 189,
    243–5, 311
  Beckman lectures at 245
  Bloch, Ernest at 6–7, 52, 118,
    270–1, 304
  Cavell performing at 187–9
Berrigan, Daniel 173
Black Power movement 163
Bloch, Ernest 6, 52, 118, 270–1, 304
Bloom, Harold 18, 173
Bogart, Humphrey 86
Bolaño, Roberto 289
Bora, Katharina von 165
Borges, Jorge Luis 222–3
Borgia, Cesare 168–9
Bourdieu, Pierre 270
Bringing Up Baby (1938) 62–3
Brook Farm 75
Broughton, Janet 243
Brown, John 96–7
Browning, Robert 310
Buffalo, State University of New York
    at ch. 9 (141–6)
Burke, Kenneth 130
Burton, Robert 291, 302
Butler, Judith 91, 309

Cage, John 133–4
Calloway, Cab 124
Capra, Frank 22–3, 63, 170, 213.
  See also *It Happened One Night*
Carlyle, Thomas 291
Carnap, Rudolf 79, 96
Cassin, Barbara 233
Cavell, Benjamin 246
Cavell, Cathleen Cohen 162, 244, 256
    n.1, 269
Cavell, David 246
Cavell, Marcia 177 n.11
Cavell, Rachel 137

CAVELL, STANLEY
  accounting 27. See also accounting
  acknowledgement 109, 182, 209
    avoidance and 107
    concept of 27, 77, 80–1, 90
    mutual 185
    praise and 305
    of separateness 121–2.
    See also praise
  adolescence of 52–4, 86, 91, 119–21,
    125, 200, 239, 264–5,
    287, 304
  Afro-American Studies department at
    Harvard, founding of 102
  America as idea, central to his work
    100. See also America
    as American philosophy's Melville 98
    as anti-racist 209
    as apolitical 184–5, 298
    argument, what is and is not
      resolvable by 247–8
    arrival in philosophy 73
  Atlanta, Georgia 52, 86, 98, 119–23,
    188, 199–200, 203, 207
  audience. See audience
  "An Audience for Philosophy" 104–5,
    243, 275–6
  "Austin at Criticism" 208, 220–1
  Austin, J. L.
    passion for 96–7
    as teacher of 13–14, 73, 78, 99,
      118, 157, 204, 219, 232, 254,
      281. See also J. L. Austin
  autobiographical project of 236.
    See also autobiographical
  autobiography, telling his 272–3.
    See also autobiography
  autonomy, ratification of 123
  as autophilosopher 309. See also
    autophilosophy
  "The Availability of Wittgenstein's
    Later Philosophy" 79, 219,
    253–4, 258 n.11
  "The Avoidance of Love" 55–6,
    105–6, 130, 173
  Bach being played by Bloch, scene
    of 52–3, 149, 151, 153,
    156, 270–1

CAVELL, STANLEY (cont.)
  baseball 113, 200, 270–1, 308
  Beckman lectures at Berkeley 245
  "Being Odd, Getting Even" 217–19
  beginning, interest in concept of
    45 n. 88
  Berkeley. *See* Berkeley
  as best reader of Cavell 103–4
  birth, achieving his 259 n.25
  Bloch, Ernest: music lessons at
    Berkeley with 6–7, 52, 118,
    270–1, 304
  Brookline, Massachusetts 75, 119,
    121, 163, 174, 207, 241, 264–5
  childhood of. *See above* adolescence
  coal delivery
    aesthetic judgment,
      touchstone of 124
    scene of 120–1, 123–4, 236–7
  as composer of music 78, 101, 149,
    ch. 12 (187–98), 265–6,
    287, 297
  conversation between psychoanalysis
    and philosophy 32, 267.
    See also psychoanalysis
  crises in the life of 77–8, 265–6,
    303–4, 318 n.124
  critic
    gifts as a 258 n.18
    nature of 282–3
  death, achieving his 259 n.25
  defense of aesthetic and ethical
    discourse 208
  delay, gifts of 204–5
  Derrida-Austin debate 220–1, 227 n.9
  as diagnostician of the spirit in which
    things are said 166
  dissertation of: *The Claim to
    Rationality* 14, 53–4, 80,
    97–8, 104, 106–7, 204, 208
  dismissed by most of the
    profession 101
  divorce from Marcia Cavell 177 n.11
  doctrines of, four central 76–7
  Edinburgh conference on literary
    criticism 113
  education of grown-ups 19, 28–9,
    176, 251, 263–4

ear damage / car accident 52,
  199–200, 270, 304
as Emersonian perfectionist 108.
  See also Ralph Waldo Emerson;
  Emersonian perfectionism
"An Emerson Mood" 108
"Emerson's Constitutional
  Amending" 16, 285
excerpts from memory 11, 30–1,
  286, 306–7
exemplarity of, as exemplar 10–11,
  252, 288, 309. *See also*
  representativeness
family surnames 16–17, 304
father (Irving Goldstein), 52–4,
  119–23, 235–6, 264–7,
  270, 304
  admirer of serious men
    120, 239–40
  heart surgery of 240–1
  as immigrant 157
  inheritance given or denied 272
  learn from anybody 262
  Oedipal agon with 266
  redemption of 120, 239–40
fears of professional
  marginalization 252–3
film
  as if made for philosophy 280
  as if meant for philosophy 33
  began teaching in 1963 181
"Fred Astaire Asserts the Right to
  Praise" 115, 133–4. *See also*
  Fred Astaire
Freedom Summer 102, 162
friendship, gifts for 210. *See also*
  friendship
glass jar, scene of 125, 202–3
"The Good of Film" 105
Harvard Society of Fellows 53, 204
at Harvard University 32, 53, 78, 98.
  See also Harvard University
heart surgery of 121
at Hebrew University 200
high and low culture, weaving
  together 245
horse of thought 13–19, 36, 138, 205
humor and good will 139

CAVELL, STANLEY (cont.)
  identity crisis 162, 177 n.16, 265–6
  immigrancy, concept of 25, 52, 157, 273
  importance, concept of ch. 16 (231–42)
  "The Importance of Importance" 234–40
  impressions and being impressed ch. 17 (243–60)
  "Impressions of Revolution" 194–5
  influence on his students 253–4, 258 n.19. *See also below* as teacher
  inherit
    European thought, how to 167
    philosophy 297–8
    seeking a tradition he could 272–3.
    See also inheritance
  at Institute for Advanced Study at Princeton 53
  Jewish immigrants, son of 273, 304. *See also below* parents
  Jewish Progressive Club (Atlanta) 123–4
  at Juilliard 53, 77–8, 188, 200, 202, 304
  "Knowing and Acknowledging" 176, 209
  "Knowledge as Transgression" 215–16
  life's work, discovery of 164
  "A Matter of Meaning It" 108–9, 133, 189
  measuring the value of our lives 12, 235, 302, 310
  medium, on the idea of a 62, 80, 87, 181–2, 185, 213, 217, 222–3, 232–3, 280
  meta, at home in the 157
  most important American philosopher since Emerson 101
  mother (Fannie Segal), 52, 86, 118–21, 124, 187, 191, 199, 237, 270–1, 304
  as moviegoer 86–7

  music and 93, 153, 156, ch. 12 (187–98), ch. 13 (199–206), 265–6, 304–5
  "Music Discomposed" 133, 189–91
  as musician 52, ch. 12 (187–98), 265–6, 283, 287–8, 304
  "Must We Mean What We Say?" ch. 5 103–10, 284
  name, change of 304
  "North by Northwest" 107
  obvious
    perspicuous and the 280
    saying or not saying the 156
  oddness of 79
  "Opera and the Lease of Voice" 270–1
  the ordinary
    devotion to 118
    the philosophical and 245
    recovery of 77
    redemption of 280–1
    sense of the 137
  ordinary language philosopher, becoming an 78
  ordinary language philosophy and 65–6, 100, ch. 9 (141–60)
  paralysis of spirit 119
  parents of 52, 54, 86, 266–7. *See also above* father; mother
  patrimony of 39, 272
  pawnbroking 16, 52, 119–20, 200–1, 235–6, 270–1
  pawnshop, poetry of the 119–20, 124, 235–6, 270–1
  pedagogical rather than polemical 201–2, 247–8, 298–9
  perfectionism, embrace of 172–3
  Perkins, V. F. and 35, 66
  personal and philosophical 8–13, 104, 121, 247, 252–3, 266, 280–1, 288–9, 306
  pertinence, philosophical 6, 24, 105, 232–3, 278, 303
  a philosopher at all, whether he was 101
  as philosopher
    of the forms of love 93

CAVELL, STANLEY (cont.)
  as philosopher (cont.)
    of the psychological rather than the political 102, 298
  philosophical
    convictions 248
    method 204, 264, 294
  philosophy
    access to 272
    as calling for romanticism 114
    as continuing a life of music ch. 12 (187–98) ch. 13 (199–206), ch. 19 (269–74), 304–5
    did not practice 81
    integrated into ordinary life 245–6, 271
    as practice 275–6
    as practice of reading 246–7
  "Philosophy and the Arrogation of Voice" 22, 73, 173, ch. 19 (269–74), 281
  political, awareness of the 185, 209
  postponement, problem of 204–5
  as professor of philosophy 70, 76. See also below as teacher
  psychoanalyst, idea of becoming a 31–2
  question whether he does philosophy 225
  radio broadcast of execution of John Dillinger and Bruno Hauptmann 203
  redemption, kinds of 119–20, 124–5, 235–6, 280, 293. See also above pawnbroking
  reeducation, need for active 263–4. See also above education of grown-ups
  as reinventor of analytic philosophy 100
  repetitious use of examples by 66–7
  Sacramento, California 16, 52, 119, 125, 191, 202–203, 207
  secret and silent melancholy 33, 56
  Segal family 118–19, 122–3. See also above Fanny Segal
  Sierra School (Sacramento) 202
  singularity as a philosopher 8, 279, 288, 295, 305, 312
  speckled wafers in purple bowl, scene of 264–6
  spiritual crisis 31–3, 77–8, 265–6, 303–5
  as teacher 2, 157–8, 201–2, 205, 211, 231–2, 241
  teaching
    at Berkeley and Harvard 170–1
    "Ideas of Man and the World in Western Thought" (Humanities 5 at Harvard) 164–8, 171–2, 177 n.21
    "Moral Reasoning: Moral Perfectionism" (Humanities 34 at Harvard) 74–6, 104, 165, 169, 171
    at Tougaloo College 102, 162
  "Thinking of Emerson" 15, 108, 164, 200
  Thoreau, Henry David, inheritance of 24.
    See also Thoreau
  "The Thought of Movies" 202, 262
  "Trades of Philosophy" 200, 270
  UCLA, studying at 53, 78
  universal provincialism 20, 22, 24–5
  utopian dimensions of thought 170
  voice
    arrogation of 22, 73–4, 173, 269, ch. 19 (269–74), 281, 285–6
    companionable sound of 276
    continuity of character and 246
    female 237–8
    finding your own 235, 272–3
    giving 298
    of his own 173, 283
    hear differences 270–1
    human 227 n.9
    lease of 270–1
    natural voice, speaking in one's 292
    nonheterosexual tonality 238
    in philosophy 53, 295
    of philosophy 73, 281, 284–5
    reading for the 200
    right to speak 2, 22, 73–4, 173, 272–3, 281–2, 285

CAVELL, STANLEY (cont.)
  voice (cont.)
    singular or plural 283
    speaking for all 272. *See also*
      representativeness
    sound of the classroom 165, 167–8
    tone 8, 91, 236–8, 276, 281–2,
      284–5, 287, 294–6
    unforgettable sound of prose 171
    of women 237–8
    in writing 189, 308
  watching a film at the Carpenter
    Center, scene of 210
  "What Did Derrida Want of Austin?"
    227 n.9
  "What is the Scandal of
    Skepticism?" 104
  "The Wittgensteinian Event" 219–20
  words and world, reciprocal
    internality of 234–5
  work is less and less known among
    academic aestheticians 208
  worldliness of 77
  writing
    academic philosophy and 25–6
    as anecdotal 286. *See also* anecdote
    annoyance in his 288
    aphoristic 80, 105, 153
    autobiographical qualities of his
      12–13, 25, 97, 104, 164,
      231, 236–7, 239, 266–7,
      272, 277, 282–6, 301–8.
      See also autobiography;
      autobiographical;
      autophilosophical
    baroque, how his prose can turn 264
    blockage 107
    capaciousness of 28, 280
    concept-determining status of 21
    commit, refusal to 151
    criticism
      as conduct of gratitude 117
      mode of 67, 105
      philosophical criticism 105–6
      philosophy of 130.
      See also critic; literary criticism
    cure 122
    dialogic quality of 139

writing (cont.)
  as eccentric 54, 282–3, 286
  English as American as jazz, his 101
  as esoteric 105, 108–9, 201, 283
  as not esoteric 249–50
  essayistic qualities of 12. *See also*
    essay; essaying
  evasion, danger of 151
  on film 35. *See also* film; movies
  in the first person 97
  foregrounding of self in 54
  as idiosyncratic 51, 77, 151, 201,
    286, 288, 295
  integrity between life and 245–6
  as interlocutor within his 138–9
  irritation of his 67, 282–3, 287–8
  manner of 143, 201–2, 205, 247–8,
    252, 277, 305
  meta qualities of 157. *See below*
    self-consciousness
  method 8, 20–1, 25, 28, 67,
    138–39, 204, 232–6, 264,
    277–9, 283–4, 294, 306
  mode of 275–6
  mood when 70–2
  motivation to philosophical 74
  about movies 101. *See also*
    film; movies
  nonheterosexual tonality of 238
  novels, as alternative 296–7
  pace of 139
  personal qualities of 8–13, 104,
    121, 151, 247, 252–3, 266,
    280–1, 288–9, 296, 306. *See
    also* autobiography
  praise of his 312. *See also* praise,
    concept of
  precariousness of his 150–1
  pretentious 54, 63, 286, 315 n.46
  punctuation 287–8, 308
  quest for a sound philosophical
    prose 171
  questions itself 304
  reader, need of a 173. *See also*
    audience
  reading film ch. 2 (61–8), ch. 11
    (181–6), 238, ch. 15 (213–28).
    See also reading

CAVELL, STANLEY (cont.)
  writing (cont.)
    reception of 26, 27, 292. *See also* audience
    reluctance to separate autobiography from philosophy 164. *See also* autobiography
    responsiveness to everything 150–2
    rest, unwillingness to 149–50
    returning us to ourselves, aim of 252
    self-consciousness
      in 67, 241, 282–3, 288
      problematical 144, 149, 151, 157–8, 241, 308
    seriousness about 287. *See also* serious; seriousness
    sound
      of the classroom in 165, 167–8
      unforgettable 171
    strategies of 294. *See also above* method
    style of 8, 80–1, 101, 201–2, 237–8, 277–8, 280, 287–9, 294, 296, 308–9, 311–12
    style of reasoning in 201, 205
    unconventionality of his 167
    voice in. *See above* voice
    words seem to run out 189
  Yiddish stories 52
  youth as a dimension of the self 172.
  See also audience; pitch; praise
Certeau, Michel de 270
characters (in novels) 153–4
Chodat, Robert 239
Church of Rome 168
Cicero, Marcus Tullius 169
cinema ch. 2 (61–8), ch. 11 (181–6), ch. 15 (213–28)
  an American motive in 81
  as a fair semblance of ecstasy 34
  irony in 184.
  See also film; movies
cinema studies. *See* film studies

citation
  as endorsement 301
  subconscious 30
citationality
  of interpretation 30
  of thinking 285
Civil Rights movement 173–4
Clarke, Thompson 53
Coetzee, J. M. 301
Cohen, Marshall 25–8
Colbert, Claudette 170, 213–16, 236
Coleridge, Samuel Taylor 188
Coles, Robert 173–6
Columbia University in the City of New York 114, 189
comedy
  as festive abatement of skepticism 115
  as genre 117
  Hollywood 11, 34, 51, 57, 61, 87–9, 93, 101, 116, 166, 176, 183, 215, 245, 294
  of remarriage 57, 89–93, 108, ch. 10 (161–78), 185, ch. 15 (213–28)
    as allegory of overcoming skepticism 215–16
    intimacy of difference or reciprocity 216
    post-Wittgensteinian ordinary language philosophy and 223–4
    women's equality in 223–5
  Shakespeare and 170, 243.
  See also film; Hollywood; movies
common language 81–2, 100, 221, 223, 235.
  See also ordinary language
commonness 80–1, 219–20, 271–2, 285–7
commonplace and 299
community 77, 81
  of learners 75
companionability
  of teachers 175, 299
composition
  teaching 146–7
Conant, James 34, 120, 190, 268 n.8
conformity 83, 85, 131

conscience 164, 292
  crisis of 172
  intellectual 144, 158
  pathology of negative 164–5 172
conversation 57, 65, 77, 80, 90, 92, ch. 8 (137–40), 165–6, 246, 295
  therapeutic 173
Conversations (journal) 5, 8
conversion 51, 55, 100, 105, 122, 118, 237, 251, 301
  conversation and 138
  education as a matter of 251
  philosophical call for 251
Copernicus, Nicolaus 46 n.109, 217, 225
cosmopolitanism 21, 25, 44 n.77, 77
critic
  attentiveness of 282–3
  imposition of personality by 282–3, 288
  inscription of personality by 282–3
  the philosopher as 283–4
  should include subjectivity 310–11.
  See also attentiveness; inattentiveness
Critical Inquiry 243
criticism. *See* critic; literary criticism
Cukor, George 23, 167, 306
culture
  crisis between self and 250–1
  differences between elite and popular 163
  inheritance of 162, ch. 19 (269–74)
  philosophers as critics of 283–4
  weaving together high and low 245
cultural studies 102, 130

dance 56, 115–16, 123–4, 132, 262.
  See also Fred Astaire
Danto, Arthur C. 8, 12, 208, 261–2, 308, 312
Dauber, Kenneth 3–4, ch. 9 (141–60)
Davidson, Arnold I. 166
Davis, Bette 64, 88, 184, 238
Dean, James 86
deconstruction 220
democracy 79, 82, 87–9, 92–3, 139, 163, 217, 225, 272, 308
  value of perfectionism in 299–300.
  See also moral perfectionism
Denkschrift 4
Derrida, Jacques 28, 273, 284
  Austin, J. L. and 220–1, 227 n.9
Descartes, René 57, 63, 72–3, 99, 104, 114, 217–20, 226, 227 n.2, 257 n.5
Desplechin, Arnaud 240–1
diary 291–2, 295
Dickens, Charles 52
Dietz, Howard 132
disinheritance 27.
  See also inheritance
divorce 92, 165–7, 177, 216–17, 228 n.228.
  See also marriage; John Milton; comedy of remarriage
Doubrovsky, Serge 289
dreams 31–9, 99, 122, 300, 304, 312
  memory and 31–2, 34–5, 36–8
  movies and 36–8
Drury, Maurice O'Connor 187–8
Dunne, Irene 166
Duras, Marguerite 289

Eakins, Thomas 86
education
  personal accounting for one's 1
  in philosophy, aspire to 274.
  See also Cavell: education of grown-ups
Eldridge, Richard 27, 113
Eliot, T. S. 120, 199
elitism 299. *See also* snobbery
Ellington, Duke 193
Emersonianism
  providing the intellectual texture of remarriage 185
Emersonian perfectionism 25, 52, 57, 85, 108, 110, 173, 253, 258 n.19, 305
  in films 57.
  See also moral perfectionism; perfectionism
Emersonian perfectionist
  Cavell as 108
Emerson, Ralph Waldo
  aphorism as unit of composition 153

Emerson, Ralph Waldo (cont.)
  as belated founder of international philosophical culture 25, 272
  "Character" 263
  "Circles" 153, 156–7, 255
  "Experience" 18, 33, 302–3
  "Fate" 15
  Kant, Immanuel and 169–70
  Nature 263
  Nietzsche, Friedrich and 12, 23, 85, 102, 110, 118, 172, 273–4, 298
  "The Poet" 14–15, 264
  metaphor in 153
  neglected contribution to American philosophy 130
  philosophical legitimation of, by Cavell 294
  prose that questions itself 303
  "Quotation and Originality" 285, 301
  reception of prose 303
  recuperation of, by Cavell 307
  Representative Men 85. *See also* representativeness
  resurrection of, by Cavell 101–2, 271
  Romantic tendency of 263–4
  "Self-Reliance" 18, 34, 71
  Thoreau, difference between 156–67
  "Uses of Great Men" 258 n.19
  writing as inhabitation 119.
  See also Henry David Thoreau
empiricism
  classical 247–50, 307
  logical 78–9, 100
  radical 232
Empson, William 66
English
  liberal tradition 83
  Romantic poets 81
Enlightenment 81, 89–90
Epicurus 85
  The Garden 75–6
Erie Community College (Buffalo) 146
Erikson, Erik 163–73
  epigenesis 172
  as inventor of the identity crisis 164

essay, as form 290–5, 300.
  See also Cavell: writing
essaying 23, 286, 290–1, 293–4
everyday 31–2, 56–7, 264, 286–7
  attention to details of the 290–1
  autofiction and the 307–8
  autophilosophy as the transformation of the 308
  discourse 283
  drama of the 166
  experience 280, 290, 296
  expressions of the 13
  metaphysical displacement of the 134
  ordinary language philosophy and the 221
  reading group on the 270
  resettlement of the 118–19
  speech 162, 304
  temperament as stance toward the 291
  use of language 279.
  See also commonness; ordinary; ordinary language
everydayness 294. *See also* commonness; everyday; ordinary
exemplar, exemplarity and 11, 20, 85, 138, 253, 258 n.19, 272, 285–7, 289, 309. *See also* Cavell: exemplarity of, as exemplar; representativeness
experience
  experiment and, relation between 137
  fecundity of personal 266
  redemption of 292–3
expressiveness 295, 297.
  See also inexpressiveness

Faust (Goethe) 118
feminism 89–93, 163, 209, 223–4, 235, 237, 270–2
feminist
  identity politics 272
  theory 270, 272
  thinkers 91.
  See also Simone de Beauvoir
Ferrante, Elena 289

festschrift 3–4, 8–9, 11
figurative language 22, 164
  imaginative and 137
  inheritance of 42 n.49
film
  bearing on philosophy ch. 11
    (181–6), ch. 15 (213–28)
  in the classroom 181
  criticism and ch. 2 (61–8)
  cultivates an ability to see the
    important and invisible 238
  as form of philosophical thought
    ch. 11 (181–6)
  as an impulse to philosophy 88
  as inherently philosophical 182
  lambent depths of 61–2
  as if made for philosophy 280
  as if meant for philosophy 33
  medium 62, 87, 181–2, 185, 213,
    217, 280
  reading of, in autobiographical
    writing 238. *See also*
    autobiography; Cavell:
    criticism; critic; literary
    criticism; reading
  teaches us 234
films. *See* movies
film studies 27, 101, 103, 207, 284
Fischer, Michael 27
Florentine Republic 168
Fodor, Jerry 53
forgiveness 92, 120, 258 n.11
Founding Fathers 82
Franklin, Benjamin 83
Freed, Arthur 116
Freud, Sigmund 11, 24, 31–2, 46 n.107,
  53, 58, 66, 100, 208, 259
  n.25, 265–7, 299, 302, 304–5.
  See also psychoanalysis
Frey, James 301
Fried, Michael 53, 133, 223, 226,
  228 n.17
Friedan, Betty 91
Friedman, Lawrence J. 164
friend
  figure of the 58
friendship 18, 22, 58, 85, 145, 173,
  210, 238

Frye, Northrop 170

Gable, Clark 170, 213–16, 236
Galileo, Galilei 217, 225
Gaslight (1944) 235, 270
Gass, William H. 12
Gedankenschrift 4–11, 29–30
Gedenkbuch 4
Gedenkschrift 4, 8
Geisteswissenschaften 96, 284
German baroque tragedy 194
Gershwin, Ira 132
Goethe, J. W. 118
Goldfarb, Warren 244
Goldman, William 20
Gombrowicz, Witold 289
Goodman, Nelson 79
Goodman, Russell 312
Gould, Timothy 277, 279
Grant, Cary 35, 88–9, 101, 166
Graubard, Allen 210
Grazia, Margreta de 130
Great Depression 87, 92, 122, 217,
  225
Greenberg, Clement 223
Greif, Mark 292–3, 299

Hadot, Pierre 12–13
Hammerstein II, Oscar 132
Harbison, John 53, 189
Hardwick, Elizabeth 291–2, 301, 307
Hare, R. M. 210
Hart, Lorenz 132
Harvard University 13
  of the 1970s 96
  Adams House 199, 201
  Afro-American Studies department,
    founding of 102
  anechoic chamber at 134
  Berkeley, compared with 170–1
  Cavell's lectures at 32
  course with Jack McNees at 97
  Emerson Hall 71
  film studies at 101, 103
  seminars at 98.
  See also Austin: at Harvard;
    Cavell: at Harvard
Harvey, Giles 301

Heaney, Seamus 113, 126
Hegel, G. W. F. 94 n.4, 182–5
  the desire to love and be loved in 182
  Hegelian themes in the melodrama of the unknown woman 184–5
Heidegger, Martin 4–5, 12, 66, 69, 81, 94 n.4, 96–7, 291, 299
  Derrida, Jacques and 284
  on dwelling 118
  "The Thing" 245
  Wittgenstein, Ludwig and 55–6
Hemingway, Ernest 301
Henry the Eighth 167
Hepburn, Katharine 35, 62, 89, 306
hermeneutics of suspicion 116
Herzog, Werner 34–5
His Girl Friday (1940) 89, 91, 163
Hobbes, Thomas 163, 226
Hölderlin, Friedrich 45 n.82, 290
Hollywood
  as dream factory 34
  Golden Age 61–2, 89, 183
  movies 11, 34, 57, 87–9, 101, 116, 166, 176, 183, 215, 245, 294.
  See also comedy of remarriage; film; movies
home, quest for 273
homeless and homelessness, tropes of 81, 118, 157, 203–4.
  See also immigrancy; restlessness
Hopper, Edward 86
humanism, Italian 168
humanist, education of the 167
humanities, fate of 309. *See also* academics, as managerial class
Hume, David 72–3, 114, 203, 217, 220, 225

Ibsen, Henrik 11, 35, 57, 274, 305
immigrancy 25, 157, 273
  Jewish 273.
  See also homeless; inhabitation
impersonal
  intimacy 238
  self-hatred 76
impersonality 54

improvisation
  marriage and 216
  musical 189, 287
inexpressiveness
  inattentiveness and 238
  fantasy of necessary 228 n.17
  philosophical skepticism and 194
  temptation of 238–9.
  See also expressiveness
inhabitation 118–19, 286
  as temporary 113, 271
  Emerson and Thoreau's writing as 119.
  See also homeless; immigrancy
inheritance
  of alternative philosophical tradition 110
  American 20, 25
  anxiety of 18, 18 n.49
  Cavellian 27, 297–8
  of Cavell's work, question of 276
  concept of 259 n.24
  of culture 163
  of European thought 167
  finding a language for philosophy's 272–3
  of language 250–1
  learning how to undertake 267
  as philosophers 22
  scenes of 2, 313 n.3
  women's 272
  of world philosophy as an American 273.
  See also Cavell: inherit; disinheritance
interests
  assuming responsibility for one's 255–6, 259 n.24
  capacious 28, 151, 153, 261–2, 280, 311
  discovering our true 257 n.10
irony 27, 58, 267, 285, 290
  cinematic 184
Ismael's Ghosts (*Les fantômes d'Ismaël*, 2017) 240–1
Italian humanism 168
It Happened One Night (1934) 54, 63–4, 89, 91, 170, 213–16, 223–5, 236
itemization 291, 293, 312

James, Henry 14, 130, 132, 134, 301
"The Birthplace" 115
to guess the unseen from the seen 202
a person on whom nothing is lost 150, 202–4, 262
James, William 69
Jameson, Fredric 290–3, 309, 312, 315 n.59
jazz 10, 52, 95, 101, 131–2, ch. 12 (187–98), 208, 287, 304–5
big band 52, 304
Cavell's English as American as 101. *See also* music
Jefferson, Thomas 83, 285
Jesus 99, 164, 175, 289
Johnson, Samuel 99
Jost, Walter 3–4, ch. 9 (141–60)
Joyce, James 133, 301
Jules et Jim (1962) 100
Jung, Carl 29–30, 36
justice
democracy and 93, 300
distributive 79, 93
injustice, racial 188
love and 92
realizing 98

Kafka, Franz 222–3
Kantianism 57
post- 51
Kant, Immanuel 11, 25, 34–5, 57, 72–3, 77–8, 89, 96, 98, 138, 169–71, 284, 294–5, 312
critical philosophy 77
Critique of Judgment 116–17
Critique of Pure Reason 114
Emerson, Ralph Waldo and 101, 169–70, 209
Enlightenment and 81
Foundations of the Metaphysics of Morals 169–70
metaphysics of 54
Katz, Jerrold 53
Kaufman, Charlie 19
Kidd, Michael 132
Kierkegaard, Søren 70, 79, 84, 90, 94 n.4, 97, 172, 201, 284, 302
Klevan, Andrew 282–3, 297

Knausgaard, Karl Ove 289–96, 300–1, 305, 307, 311–12
knowing
and being known 185
the condition of having a self 84
how to go on 123–4
in moral and aesthetic contexts 190–1
what one knows 193
Kracauer, Siegfried 87
Kreisler, Fritz 124, 191–2, 237
Kuhn, Thomas 53, 311

The Lady Eve (1941) 210
language
common 81–2, 100, 221, 223, 235
conditions of 224, 272–3, 297
figurative 137
finding a 272
natural 5, 79, 250
the ordinary, we use to express 264. *See also* everyday; ordinary language
LaRochefoucauld, François de 307
Laugier, Sandra 106
Leavis, F. R. 67, 282–3
Lefebvre, Henri 270
Letter from an Unknown Woman (1948) 66
Levenson, Jon 167–8, 171
Lewis, Wyndham 289
life-writing 300
listening 10, 34, 77, 137, 153, 192, 200–1, 203, 287
friendship and 145
specific intimacy of 137
for a text's distinctive sound 200. *See also* Cavell: voice; music
literalism
living in times of abject 137
literature
extent to which philosophy is, or may become, a kind of 277–9
Kafkaesque in 222–3
philosophy and 98, ch. 9 (141–60), ch. 10 (161–78), ch. 19 (269–74), ch. 20 (275–320)
unlike philosophy 144

literary critic, work of ch. 9 (141–60), 282–83
literary criticism 28, 66, 105–6, ch. 6 (113–28), ch. 7 (129–36), ch 8 (137–40), ch. 9 (141–60), ch. 10 (161–78), ch. 19 (269–74), ch. 20 (275–320)
  forgotten value of 144
  philosophy, differences between 144, 152
  state of contemporary 130.
  See also ordinary language criticism
literary-philosophical criticism, new 151
literary studies 28
literary theory 27, ch. 9 (141–60)
Locke, John 83, 114, 163, 203, 217, 225–6, 285
logic
  metaphysics, as a form of 182
  propositional 79
  teaching of 77
logical
  analysis 78–9
  empiricism 78–9
  positivism 53, 78–9, 96, 208, 284
Longfellow, Henry Wadsworth 161
loss
  being at a 105
  lamenting a 24–5
  of property and other people 302–3
lost
  being 57
  conventions of marriage 215–16
  finding yourself 105, 287
  to ourselves 259 n.23
Luther, Martin ch. 10 (161–78)
  on conscience 164
  on sacraments 166–7
  role in Cavell's thinking 167
  theology of grace 169

Machiavelli, Niccolò 167–9, 172
Malick, Terrence 53, 288–9
Manhattan College's liberal arts program 114
Marcuse, Herbert 102, 308

marriage 23, 57–8, 77, 89–93, 170, 177 n.11, 182–3, 216
  allegorical sense of 165
  conventions of 215–16
  conversation and 92, 165
  divorce and 167
  and the domestic 56
  equality in 89
  idea of true 165
  improvisation and 216
  as incitement to become oneself 293
  The Marriage of Figaro and 203
  as "a meet and happy conversation" 165
  as modern 216
  mutual intelligibility in 170
  perfectionism and 90
  reality of 170
  as sacrament 166
  the task of acknowledgment in 90
  under the conditions of divorce 92
  unhappy 52, 177 n.12.
  See also comedy of remarriage; divorce; John Milton
Marx Brothers 88
Mates, Benson 162
McGann, Jerome 132
McLeod, Randall 132
McNamara, Robert 174
McNees, Jack 97
Medici 168
melancholy 56, 263
  delight and 263
  in Hollywood melodramas 52
  secret and silent 33, 56.
  See also Robert Burton
melodrama of the unknown woman 57–8, 61, 226, 228 n.17, 304.
  See also movies
Melville, Herman 98, 153, 156, 291
  "Bartleby, the Scrivener" 18, 298
  Cavell as American philosophy's 98
  writing veiled autobiography 291, 316 n.74
memoir 11, 53, 124, 264, 291, 295–6, 307
  of the ordinary 279–80

memoir (cont.)
  philosophical 107
  metaphysical 279–80, 306.
  See also autobiography; Elizabeth
    Hardwick
memory
  buried 125
  commemoration and 5
  converted into a text 267
  dreams and 31–2, 34–5, 36–8
  excerpts from 11, 30–1, 286–7, 306–7
  failure of 245
  interpretation of 31
  post-traumatic stress and 38
  as publically pertinent 11
  as self-reflexive text 267
  shuffle of 239
  as text to be read 266
Mendelsohn, Daniel 294–5, 315 n.59
metafiction 14, 291
metaphilosophy 22, 26, 151, 157,
    288, 298–9, 303. *See also*
    Cavell: self-consciousness
metaphor 153, 221
  for analysis 266
  of finding a language 297–8
  of horse 13–19, 36, 138, 205
  of voice in philosophical writing
    297, 308.
  See also Cavell: voice
mind-body
  dualism 79
  problem 99
Mill, John Stuart 57, 89
Miller, Henry 301
Millet, Catherine 289, 301
Milton, John 35, 57, 165–7, 177
    n.12, 285,
misquoting 32–3
misreading 32–3
misremembering 32–3, 36
modernism 51–2, 108–10,
    217–18, 223–6
  in art and philosophy 224
  medium and 223
  perfectionism as model of
    thought in 226

modernist
  art 216, 224
  cinematic medium as 217, 223
  movies as 88
  philosophy 224
  situation 108–10
modernity
  American 217
  condition of 215
  Hegel's task for 184
  skepticism at the origins of 224–5
  theory of Western 185
Moi, Toril 91, 290, 308–9
Monro, John U. 162
Monroe, Marilyn 86
Montaigne, Michel de 12, 176, 291,
    284, 299, 302
moods 72, 164, 287, 292, 301–3
Moore, G. E. 99
moralism
  averting or refusing 134–5
  negativity, as a form of 135
moral perfectionism 25, 32, 35, 57–8,
    85, 150, 154, 165, 169, 172,
    251, 256, 292, 299–300, 305
  Cavell's turn toward 172–3
  as philosophy of the ordinary 290
  as responsiveness 150–2
  sociality and 150.
  See also Cavell: teaching:
    "Moral Reasoning: Moral
    Perfectionism"; Emersonian
    perfectionism; perfectionism
Moran, Richard 21, 269–70
mournfulness 194–5
mourning
  as master tone of Cavell's writing 188
  morning and 196 n.7, 234
  and the perfectionist work of
    philosophy 188–9
  -play (*Trauerspiel*) 194
  resistance to 245
  speech and 195
  Thoreauvian pun on 196 n.7
moviegoing
  autobiography and 35–6, 87, 110,
    232, 239, 279, 298, 304.

See also dreams; memoir; memory
movies (films) 86–9
   actor and character in 88
   bearing of philosophy on ch. 11 (181–6)
   democratic character of 87
   dreams and 36–8
   how to quote 31
   involving them in us 239
   memories of 31, 35, 239, 279
   misremembering 36
   as modernist 88
   philosophy of 86–9
   Plato's cave as allegory of 87
   remembering 31, 36
   as succession of automatic world projections 87
   watching 37, 87, 163, 232, 298
   writing about 100–1, 103–4, 185. *See also* dreams; film; memoir; memory
Mozart, Wolfgang Amadeus 203
Mr. Deeds Goes to Town (1936) 22–3, 63
Mulhall, Stephen 27
music 10, 31, 38, 52, 93, ch. 12 (187–98)
   conditions of hearing 153
   failure to conceptualize what we hear in 194
   as a kind of saying 191–2
   speech and 192
   the unsayable and 191. *See also* Cavell: composer of music; Cavell: music; Cavell: as musician; jazz
musical
   ecstasy and sexual awakening 192
   ineffability 189–90, 193, 195. *See also* unsayable

n+1 292
naming 2–7, 15, 42 n.46, 63, 290, 304, 318 n.124
   how we learn 209. *See also* Cavell: family surnames; Cavell: name, change of
National Humanities Center 270

Neiman, Susan 284
new historicism 129–30, 132
Nietzsche, Friedrich 2, 12, 23, 35, 69–71, 76, 84–5, 89–90, 94 n.4, 96–7, 102, 110, 116, 139, 167, 208, 275, 284, 291, 298–9, 302
   Ecce Homo 273–4
   Emerson, Ralph Waldo and 12, 23, 85, 102, 110, 118, 172, 273–4, 298
   On the Genealogy of Morality 165–6
   Human, All Too Human 2
   impersonal self-hatred 76
   most musical of all philosophers 187
   as reader of Emerson 110
   "Schopenhauer as Educator" 76, 172, 259 n.23
Non-Fiction (*Doubles vies*, 2018), 299–301, 307, 311–12
North, Michael 130
novels 153–4, 185, 202, 209, 296
novice
   isolation of 77
Now, Voyager (1942) 64, 66, 183–5, 238
Nozick, Robert 79

Observant cloisters 168
O'Connell, Michael 114
O'Connor, David 259 n.24
O'Keefe, Georgia 86
Oneida Community 75, 84
opera 11, 23, 76, 78, 93, 118, 131, 187, 203, 208, 270–1, 305. *See also* jazz; music
ordinary
   attention to the details of the 290–1
   concept of the 65–6, 118
   extraordinary nature of the 226, 252, 280, 290
   philosophy of the 290
   recovery of the 77
   transcendent 291. *See also* everyday
ordinary language
   autobiographical dimension of 104, 306. *See also* autobiography

ordinary language critic, work of ch. 9 (141–60)
ordinary language criticism 3–4, ch. 9 (141–60)
  audience, why it has no 144
ordinary language cynicism 277–8
ordinary language philosophers at Oxford 65–6
ordinary language philosophy 56–7, 221
  anti-philosophy and 225–6
  conception of 100
  philosophical importance of 248–9
  as response to skepticism 80.
  See also commonness; common language; everyday; ordinary
Organization of English Departments (OED) 146–7
originality
  conventionality 17
  discipleship, question of 254–5
  in Emerson and Thoreau 273
  imitation and 18, 30, 301, 310
  influence and 253–4, 258 n.19, 259 n.21
  philosophical, nature of 253–4
  question of 310
  quotation and 285, 301.
  See also anxiety of influence; anxiety of inheritance; Ralph Waldo Emerson: "Quotation and Originality"; inheritance
other minds, 55, 73, 80, 90, 107, 218
"Other Minds" (Austin) 114
  skepticism of, as tragedy 107

Paine, Thomas 285
Partisan Review 53
passionate utterances 7, 93, 115, 117, 134–5, 233
  of praise 115.
  See also J. L. Austin
patriarchy 183, 267, 272
  inheritance from fathers, 272
Pepys, Samuel 271
perfectionism 82–5
  Cavellian 93, 149, 209–10
  democracy and distributive justice, as ground for 93

perfectionism (cont.)
  journey of 57
  marriage and 90
  as model of thought in modernism 226
  as symptom 173.
  See also comedy of remarriage; Emersonian perfectionism; marriage; moral perfectionism
Perkins, V. F. 35, 66
Petrić, Vlada 37
The Philadelphia Story (1940) 89, 167, 306
philistinism 131
  gravitas of 134
philosophers
  as critics of culture 283–4
  going back over something 10
  inheritance by 22
  life as condition for calling 118
  refusal to rest is the condition of being for 151
  who shun the autobiographical 284–5
philosophical
  appeals to ordinary language have autobiographical dimension 104, 306
  attention 298–9
  autobiographical and the ch. 12 (187–98), ch. 16 (231–42), ch. 17 (243–60), ch. 18. (261–8), ch. 19 (269–74), ch. 20 (275–320)
  conversion 51, 55, 100, 105, 122, 118, 237, 251, 301
  convictions, source and nature of 248
  personal and 8–13, 104, 121, 151, 247, 252–3, 264–6, 280–1, 288–9, 296, 306
  writing. *See* Cavell: writing
philosophy
  as abstraction of autobiography 52, 299, 306
  access to 272
  as art 310–11
  autobiographical drive in 231–2

philosophy (cont.)
  autobiography and 6–7, 9–10, 12–14, 25, 29–30, 35–6, 51, 97, 102, 104, ch. 12 (187–98), ch. 16 (231–42), ch. 17 (243–60), ch. 18. (261–8), ch. 19 (269–74), ch. 20 (275–320)
  autobiography
    before Cavell 95
    as calling for romanticism 114
    defining 106
    as dimension of 270–2, 281, 286, 306
    as esoteric 105, 108–9, 201
    as not esoteric 249–50
    internal connection with 237, 264, 273–4, 281–2
  film
    bearing on ch. 11 (181–6)
    as an impulse to 88.
    See also film; movies
  liberating power of 247
  literary criticism, not like 144
  literature and 98, ch. 9 (141–60), ch. 10 (161–78), ch. 19 (269–74), ch. 20 (275–320)
  logic, teaching of in 77
  measures the value of our lives 12, 302, 310
  metaphilosophy and 22, 26, 151, 157, 288, 298–9, 303.
  of movies 87. See also film; movies
  origins in homosocial intimacy 237–8
  personal investment in 252–3
  poetry and 52, 100, 119, ch. 8 (137–40), 153, 208, 235–6, 297
  as practice of reading 246–7
  professors of 69
  redemptive power of 247
  relocating importance, new task for 235
  of science is philosophy enough 284–6, 295
  self-knowledge and 100
  as set of texts not problems 246–7
  state of 271
  therapeutic
    dimension of 251
    possibilities in 173
  as therapy 58, 80

philosophy (cont.)
  the time for 76
  tone. See Cavell: voice: tone
  value in doing 162
  as waste of time 153
  what America offered to 81
  what Cavell made possible for ch. 4 (95–102)
  what one wants of 247–8
  what people call 78
piggybacking 17–20. See also Cavell: horse of thought
pitch
  perfect 52, 118, 122–3, 187, 199–201, 270–1
  of philosophy 13, 29, 113, 201, 236–7, 270–1
  punctuation and 287
Plato 11, 35, 57, 70, 85, 260, 299
  The Academy 75
  cave as allegory of the movies 87
  cave as enacted in Fred Astaire dance routine 56
  philosophy
    poetry and 100
    literature and 152, 154–5
  critique of representation 87
  Phaedrus 16
  Republic 169
Poe, Edgar Allan 56
poetics 7, 27. See also critic; literary criticism; ordinary language criticism
poetry ch. 8 (137–40)
  lyric 153.
  See also philosophy: poetry and
political
  apolitical and 184–5, 298
  awareness of the 185, 209
  psychological and 102
politics, of identity 272, 299, 309
Pope, Alexander 291
pragmatics 233
pragmatism
  transcendentalism and 169
praise
  acknowledgment as 5, 305
  aesthetics of 134
  commitment to a criticism of 130

praise (cont.)
  concept of 9, 11, ch. 6 (113–28), ch. 7 (129–36)
  as consent 134
  the discourse of 118
  dispraise and 132
  experiencing Cavell's 210
  John Cage's work as an aesthetics of 134
  the need for and to 117
  negativity as opposed to 133–5
  practice of 129
  right of 114
  right to be 1
  scolding as opposite of 135.
  See also festschrift; Gedankenschrift
private
  anecdote for the public 275–6, 306
  memory as pertinent to the public 11
  public versus 9, 15–16, 32, 131, 185, 276, 278–9, 286, 288–9, 302, 305, 312
professors
  of philosophy 69–70, 76
  role of 69–70.
  See also philosophers
Proust, Marcel 289, 294–5
psychoanalysis 24, 27, 34, 52, 58
  philosophy and 32, 267
  process of 266
  self-understanding and 172.
  See also Erik Erikson; Sigmund Freud
psychological
  political and 102
psychopharmacology 173
public
  private memory as pertinent to the 11
  private versus 9, 15–16, 32, 131, 185, 276, 278–9, 286, 288–9, 302, 305, 312
  significance of private anecdote for the 275–6, 306
Putnam, Hilary 53, 79, 201

Quine, Willard Van Orman 79, 95, 118–19, 231, 284, 286, 295

Rains, Claude 64, 185
Raritan 243

Rawls, John 79, 96, 138, 299–300, 305
reading
  close 65, 284
  faith in 147
  film 279
  film in autobiographical writing 238
  as listening for a text's sound 200
  lost faith in 145
  memory as text 266
  philosophy as practice of 246–7
  practice of 145
  slow 298–9
  teaching ch. 9 (141–60)
  text, what constitutes a 257 n.5.
  See also Cavell: writing; critic; literary criticism; ordinary language philosophy
realism
  cynicism and 167–9
Reformation 166, ch. 10 (161–78)
reliance
  self- and other 17–20.
  See also self-reliance
remarriage. See comedy of remarriage
Renaissance 96
  in Italy 168, 69
representativeness
  American conditions of 308
  arrogation in the claim to 286
  of Emersonian perfectionist 253–4
  exemplar, exemplarity and 11, 20, 85, 138, 253, 258 n.19, 272, 285–7, 289, 309
  expressed autobiographically 285
  first person perspective and 295
  human capacity for 283–8
  posture and 19
  of a single human life 272
  voice and 282.
  See also arrogation; Cavell: exemplarity of, as exemplar; Cavell: voice
repression
  of desire 170
  of Emerson and Thoreau 24, 27
  of excluded voices 305
  of knowledge 266–7
  psychological 58, 254, 266

restlessness 87, 203–4. *See also* homeless; immigrancy
revenge, inspiration to give up 120
revision, concept of 133
Rhees, Rush 34, 297
Rhu, Lawrence F. 34
Richardson, Joan 199
Rilke, Rainer Maria 85, 126
Rockwell, Norman 86
Rogin, Michael 130
Rohmer, Éric 177 n.11
roman à clef 291, 296, 301
Rorty, Richard
  as American philosophy's Hemingway (Cavell as its Melville) 98
  on the arguments of the epistemologist 55
Rose, Phyllis 92
Roth, Philip 301
Rothko, Mark 86
Rothman, William 31, 116, 277, 279, 306, 313 n.6
Rousseau, Jean-Jacques 70, 97, 187, 253, 271, 289
Russell, Bertrand 79
Ryle, Gilbert 65–6, 78–9, 297

sacraments
  Luther, Martin on 166–8
  Thoreau, Henry David on 177 n.16
Sallybrass, Peter 130
Santayana, George 298
Sartre, Jean-Paul 71, 96–7
Schelling, Friedrich 94 n.4
Schnabel, Arthur 190
Schwartz, Arthur 132
science, hard and soft 295
scientism 97, 284.
  See also logical positivism
Scruton, Roger 90
Sebald, W. G. 289
Sekundenstil 289
self
  call to or communion with a next, unattained but attainable 57–8, 77, 84–5, 90, 293
  future 125–6
  knowing the condition of having a 84

self (cont.)
  marriage as incitement to become a 293
  revolution in the 85
  youth as a dimension of the 172
self-
  improvement 84–5
  knowledge 37, 100, 184, 250
  reliance 57–8
Sellars, Wilfrid 79
Seneca Falls 90–1
separation
  community or 273
  theme of human 271
  threat of (in a marriage) 92, 216
serious
  art 289
  failure of the 221
  intellectual aims 294
  nonserious and 220–1
  philosophy 21, 96
  reading 266
  student of music 101, 265, 304
  thought 38
  uses of language 220
seriously
  inability to take skepticism 97
  permission to take anything 262
  taking Emerson and Thoreau 24, 102
  taking ideas 310
  taking oneself 71, 239–40. *See also* vanity
  take the ordinary 280
seriousness 21, 71, 239–40
  dilettantism versus 261
  humor and 245
  intellectual 21
  one's own 71, 239–40. *See also* vanity
  playfulness and, Cavell as master of 67, 97
  treating Emerson with 101
  about writing 10, 287, 292
Sessions, Roger 187
Shakespeare, William 11, 22–3, 80, 81, 208, 209, 217, 225–6, 299, 205
  comedy 170, 243
  Coriolanus 210
  Descartes and 99
  Emerson and 131, 173

Shakespeare, William (cont.)
  Green World, idea of 170, 176
  Hamlet 34, 273, 293
  Henry VIII 167
  Hollywood movies and 34, 51, 101, 209
  James, Henry and 115, 134
  King Lear 22, 52, 56, 79, 106, 168, 189
  Othello 56, 99, 114–15
  perfectionism in 173
  Rohmer, Éric and 177 n.11
  skepticism and tragedy in 23, 55–6, 80–1, 99
  The Tempest 33
  textual criticism and 130, 132–3
  tragedy 51, 100, 173
  The Winter's Tale 177 n.11
Shifrin, Seymour 53
skepticism
  answer to 80–1
  as business of modern philosophy 55
  Austin's dismissal of 220
  Cartesian 57, 72–3
  Cavell's account of 208–9
  comedy as festive abatement of 115
  as denial of conversation 80
  external world 55, 73, 79, 90, 217–19
  film's image of 37
  gender and 97
  at heart of modern philosophy, mistakenly 99
  Hollywood romantic comedy as allegory of overcoming 215–26
  inexpressiveness and 194, 238–9
  love one's 33
  not merely theoretical 56
  not taking it seriously 97
  ordinary language philosophy as response to 80
  as origin of modernity 224–5
  of other minds as tragedy 107
  overcoming 215, 217–19, 224–5, 227 n.9, 228 n.21
  refutation of 55, 218, 221
  remarriage as allegory of 215
  as self-contradictory, self-defeating, self-refuting 218
  solution is not therapeutic 99

skepticism (cont.)
  threat of 33
  tragedy and 23, 55–6, 80–1, 99
Sklar, Judith 79
slavery, America chattel 84
Slocum, J. David 61–2
snobbery 88, 300
  anti- 300.
  See also elitism
social contract 82–3, 163
Socrates 85, 105, 210, 232, 247, 284, 289
  Freud and 100
  in the *Phaedrus* 16
  seminars on the streets of Athens, 75, 89
  Thoreau and 246
solipsism 73, 139, 292
  realism and 164
  subjectivity is not 97
Sophocles 266, 273
Sorbonne colloquium 106
speak
  about anything and everything that happens to you, philosophically 280–1, 285–6
  right to 2, 22, 73–4, 173, 272–3, 281–2, 285
speech
  acts 70, 93, 115, 129, 233
  music and 192, 194–5.
  See also J. L. Austin
spiritual exercises (*exercises spirituelle*) 12–13
Staël, Germaine de 89–90
Stanwyck, Barbara 210
state of nature 163
Stein, Gertrude 7
Steiner, George 26–8, 261
Stella Dallas (1937) 183, 237–8
Sterne, Lawrence 291
Stewart, Garrett 27–8
Stewart, James 306
St. John's College (Santa Fe) 189
Stoics (ancient Greek and Roman) 12–13, 25, 284, 307
Strawson, P. F. 65, 297
Stroud, Barry 54
Students for a Democratic Society (SDS) 174

subjectivity 262, 267
  critic should include 310–11
  problem of 97
  solipsism is not 97
  women's 237–8
suspicion of cross-disciplinary work 261
Swift, Jonathan 291
symbolic character of things 263–4

A Tale of Winter (*Conte d'hiver*, 1992) 177 n.11. *See also* Shakespeare
teaching students ch. 9 (141–60), ch. 10 (161–78), ch. 13 (199–206), ch. 14 (207–12), ch. 16 (231–42), ch. 17 (243–60). *See also* Cavell: as teacher
temperament
  atemporal 302
  for autophilosophy 307
  as receptive 143
  stance towards the everyday as 291
  tone and 9
  in writing 20
textual criticism
  ch. 7 (129–36)
therapy, therapeutics 81
  conversation as 173
  philosophy as 58, 251
  skepticism and 99
  Wittgenstein and 58, 99
  writing as 5, 80
The Thing from Another World (1951) 245
thinking
  ideal of 280–1
  how we ordinarily proceed in 162
  plagiarism and 285
  as reception 80–1
  thanking and 4–7
Thoreau, Henry David 11–12, 58, 82, 84, 292, 298
  as belated founder of international philosophical culture 25, 272
  on economy 52, 236, 291
  Emerson, Ralph Waldo
    and 21–2, 25, 27, 32, 35, 51, 93, 96–7, 226, 257 n.10, 271, 273
  difference between 156–67

Thoreau, Henry David (cont.)
  inheritance of 24
  John Brown, defense of 97
  language, use of 232–3
  morning/mourning 196 n.7
  moulting season 177 n.17, 196 n.7, 304, 318 n.124
  ordinary, commitment to the 57
  perfectionism in 82–5
  philosophical legitimation of, by Cavell 294
  professors, not philosophers 69
  quiet desperation 56
  as reader of Emerson 110
  recuperation and reception of, by Cavell 307
  resurrection of, by Cavell 101–2, 271
  on settling 118
  skepticism in 55
  Socrates and 246
  Walden 24, 117–18, 177 n.16, 188, 200, 236, 266
  writing as inhabitation 119.
  See also Ralph Waldo Emerson
tragedy
  Greek 22
  Shakespearean 51, 55–6, 99
  skepticism and 23, 55–6, 80–1, 99, 107.
  See also William Shakespeare; skepticism
Transcendentalism (American) 57
  Idealism and 290
  immanent life and 290
  perfectionism and 226
  pragmatism and 169
  as underwriting ordinary language philosophy 57.
  See also Emerson; Thoreau
translation
  feats of absolute 195
  of thoughts into language 31, 289, 297, 309
  untranslatable and 232–3
The Tree of Life (2011), 288–9

university, era of the 69. *See also* academia; academics; humanities, fate of

unsayable
  depictions of the 189–90
  the embarrassing as the 71
  expressible but 191
  music and the 191
  as null set 190
  reality of the 109–10.
  See also musical ineffability
untranslatable 232–3
Utilitarianism 57

vanity 9, 71, 292, 299–301. *See also* seriously, taking oneself; seriousness, one's own
Vega, Lope de 23
Vertigo (1958) 64–5, 67
Vienna Circle 96, 102
Vietnam War 79, 163, 173
virtue
  as wisdom's goal 176

Wagner, Richard 165–6
Wallace, David Foster 289
Walzer, Michael 79
Wayne, John 88
Weil, Simone 24
Weiss, Peter 289
Wheatley, Catherine 27
White, Morton 53, 177 n.21
Wild Strawberries (1957) 163
Williams, Bernard 53
Wilson, George 270
Wittgenstein, Ludwig 29, 36, 202, 243, 270, 298
  analytic tradition and 81
  asceticism of 148–9
  Austin, J. L. and 11, 23, 52, 114, 208, 219, 280, 299, 302, 306
  autobiography as philosophy 281, 283
  Blue Book 114
  bringing words back to their everyday use 148–49
  On Certainty 243–4
  comedies of remarriage and 223–4
  conception of language 194, 197 n.32, 219–20
  criteria, notion of 250–1
  criticism after 144, 148–9, 153–4, 157, 306

Wittgenstein, Ludwig (cont.)
  description, practice of 296
  Drury, Maurice O'Connor 187–8
  early 79, 241
  Emerson and 105, 259 n.24
  emptiness of speech, temptation toward 250–1
  family resemblance, concept of 219–22, 227 n.13
  forms of life 232, 258 n.11
  giving up heterosexual tone in language 237
  grammatical investigations of 250
  on human understanding 194–5, 207, 232
  language games 55
  later 70, 72, 109, 201, 219–25
  obvious and perspicuous 280
  ordinary language, approach to 80, 100, 221, 233–5, 238
  orthodox interpreters of 55
  Philosophical Investigations 2, 80, 182, 193–5, 203–4, 297–8
    as work of instruction 158
  philosophy as therapy 58, 99
  private language argument 209
  as revisionist of his own work 79
  Rhees, Rush and 297
  saying "This is simply what I do" 29, 193
  as teacher 202
  Tractatus Logico-Philosophicus 2, 70
  Übereinsstimmung 270
  Weil, Simone and 24
  words are also deeds 207
  words, bringing them back to everyday use 109, 279
  writing
    of 74, 308
    that seeks to influence its readers 254
Wollheim, Richard 208, 261
Wollstonecraft, Mary 89–90
The Woman in the Window (1944) 63
Wordsworth, William 56, 114, 121, 188, 210

Zarathustra 134

www.ingramcontent.com/pod-product-compliance
Lightning Source LLC
Chambersburg PA
CBHW070806300426
44111CB00014B/2442